"Everybody Was Black Down There"

POLITICS AND CULTURE IN THE TWENTIETH-CENTURY SOUTH
Edited by Bryant Simon and Jane Dailey

The South that could be reasonably termed "the nation's number one economic problem" in 1938 is no more. Today, the South—with its runaway economic and demographic growth, political clout, and influential cultural exports—is arguably the most dynamic region in the United States.

With an eye toward understanding the struggles that have shaped the newest New South, Politics and Culture in the Twentieth-Century South offers interdisciplinary historical studies of the region's social, political, and economic transformation. This series presents the best new research on a range of topics in recent southern history, including the long battle for equal civil rights for all citizens, partisan political realignment, suburbanization and the rise of car culture, changes in gender and sexual cultures, the rise of theocratic politics, industrialization and deindustrialization, immigration, and integration into the global economy of the twenty-first century: fresh scholarship that investigates new areas and reinterprets the familiar.

"Everybody Was Black Down There"

RACE AND INDUSTRIAL CHANGE IN THE ALABAMA COALFIELDS

By Robert H. Woodrum

THE UNIVERSITY OF GEORGIA PRESS

ATHENS AND LONDON

Athens, Georgia 30602
Set in Monotype Janson by Bookcomp, Inc.
Printed and bound by Thomson-Shore
The paper in this book meets the guidelines for
permanence and durability of the Committee on
Production Guidelines for Book Longevity of the
Council on Library Resources.
Printed in the United States of America
10 09 08 07 06 C 5 4 3 2 1
10 09 08 07 06 P 5 4 3 2 1
Library of Congress Cataloging-in-Publication Data
Woodrum, Robert H.
 "Everybody was black down there" : race and industrial
change in the Alabama coalfields / Robert H. Woodrum.
   p. cm. — (Politics and culture in the twentieth-century South)
 Includes bibliographical references and index.
 ISBN-13: 978-0-8203-2739-6 (cloth : alk. paper)
 ISBN-10: 0-8203-2739-5 (cloth : alk. paper)
 ISBN-13: 978-0-8203-2879-9 (pbk. : alk. paper)
 ISBN-10: 0-8203-2879-0 (pbk. : alk. paper)
 1. African American coal miners—Alabama—History.
2. African Americans—Alabama—Social conditions. 3. Alabama—
Race relations—History— 20th century. 4. Coal miners—Labor
unions—Alabama—History—20th century. 5. African American labor
union members—Alabama—History—20th century. 6. United Mine
Workers of America. I. Title. II. Series.
 HD8039.M62A29 2007
331.6'996073076178—dc22   2006014974
British Library Cataloging-in-Publication Data available

For Amanda, My Parents, and Martha Anne

CONTENTS

In the early 1990s, I worked as a labor and business reporter for the *Charleston Gazette*, a daily newspaper in the coal-producing state of West Virginia. In the course of my time in Charleston, I came to know a former editor at the paper, Nelson Sorah. Though he had left the paper years before I arrived, Nelson was active in state politics, an occupation that brought him back to the newsroom on many occasions. My desk happened to be located on the route Nelson sometimes took to the office of the *Gazette*'s investigative reporter, Paul Nyden.

As Nelson passed our desks on his way to Paul's office, he would typically offer words of encouragement to me and the other young reporters. Nelson was an old hand at West Virginia politics, and he always had a few suggestions for stories or some news to share. For someone like me who was not a West Virginia native (I grew up on the other side of the mountains, in Roanoke, Virginia), these brief encounters were invaluable, both because of the perspective I gained from Nelson's observations and from the goodwill he spread through the newsroom.

Years later, I read with a mixture of shock and sadness that his brother, Joseph, and a dozen other men had been killed when a pair of terrible explosions shook a mine in Brookwood, Alabama. Like many West Virginians who found their lives entangled in the coal industry, Joe Sorah left the state to find work when the mines bottomed out in southern West Virginia. In the late 1990s, he ended up in Brookwood at the No. 5 mine, owned by Jim Walter Resources. Interviewed a few days after the tragedy, Nelson told a newspaper reporter that he had always hoped that his brother would leave the mines. "We always live with the dangers of coal mining in West Virginia," an Alabama newspaper quoted Nelson as saying. "We know that some horrendous injury is just around the corner for these guys." In addition to his brother, his mother, and the rest of his extended family, Joe Sorah left behind a wife and a young daughter.[1]

The deaths at Brookwood occurred as I began to write my dissertation, the study that forms the basis for this book. A few months earlier, in July, I had briefly visited the No. 5 mine, riding its elevator deep into the earth for a short tour with a manager. The company put me through a training session before I went underground, but I was not allowed to travel to any of the mine's working sections. I had to be content with a walk around some of the passageways near the elevator. A short time later, my first trip underground was over, and I found myself back on the surface in the blazing heat of the Alabama summer.

As I have worked on this project over the past few years, I suppose that the one thing that has kept me going is the hope that this book will shed some light on the struggles that people such as Joe Sorah and the others who perished in the No. 5 mine have faced. With their labor, coal miners have provided the fuel that has helped build the society in which we live today. And they have not received the full benefits of their efforts. Instead, they have known poor safety conditions and economic uncertainty, while their communities too often have suffered from neglect because they lack the population base that attracts the political system's attention. Nevertheless, miners have made a world, and they and their mining communities survive, though they are very different today than in the past. As much as anything, the outpouring of community support in the wake of the Brookwood disaster illustrates how miners, their communities, and their way of life have persevered despite the enormous changes and challenges that continually beset them. I hope that this book will shed some light on the problems that have plagued the mining industry since its early days in Alabama and the effects of these problems on miners and their communities.

❰ ❰ ❰

Though this book in many ways represents the culmination of a long personal journey, I have been lucky to meet many people who have helped me along the way. This road began at Roanoke College, where I majored in history during the 1980s and was inspired by professors Mark Miller, Dan Richardson, Janice Saunders, and John Selby. Susan Millinger, who was also my academic adviser, is largely responsible for keeping me in college and for encouraging me to think of history in unconventional ways. These professors collectively nurtured the love of history that has carried me through a career as a journalist and through graduate study and remains with me today.

Several friends and colleagues from my days as a newspaper reporter deserve recognition as well. John Waybright, my first editor back in the late 1980s in the small town of Luray, Virginia, taught me about dedication and fighting the good fight. Later, I learned a great deal from friends in Lynchburg, Virginia, among them Valerie Jackson, MacGregor McCance, and Jan Vertefeuille. When I worked in Charleston, West Virginia, I came into the orbit of many talented people, including Linda Blackford, Kate Long, Larry Messina, Jim Noelker, Paul Nyden, Larry Pierce, Dan Radmacher, and Ken Ward. Paul's 1974 dissertation on the reform movement in the United Mine Workers of America provided inspiration throughout the different stages of writing this book. Ken's dedication to workers and the environment and the tenacity with which he has fought to improve conditions in West Virginia are constant sources of motivation for me.

I am grateful to Gary Fink and John Matthews, retired history professors at Georgia State University in Atlanta. In the mid-1990s, they took a chance on me and offered me the opportunity to study labor history at GSU, for which I will always be thankful. This book began in the winter of 1996 as a paper for one of Gary's graduate seminars. He later helped me further develop my ideas when he directed my master's thesis on union reform in the Alabama coalfields. My early efforts on this project benefited tremendously from his intellect, and I have always been grateful for his friendship.

As a student at Georgia State, I was inspired by graduate seminars convened by Mohammad Hassen Ali, Michelle Brattain, Ian Fletcher, Hugh Hudson, Stephen Rapp, Don Reid, Jacqueline Rouse, Charles Steffen, and Wendy Venet. History Department chairs Timothy Crimmins, Hugh Hudson, and Diane Willen supported my graduate study at Georgia State. Ian Fletcher and Anne Brophy read this manuscript in its dissertation stage and offered valuable insights. Cliff Kuhn and Michelle Brattain deserve particular thanks. I worked with Cliff my entire time at Georgia State, and I have always benefited from his wisdom, his friendship, and his vast knowledge of southern history. Michelle directed the dissertation on which this study is based. She has been a tireless advocate and mentor as well as an insightful and sharp critic. Michelle pushed me to explore new directions in my work, and this book reflects those efforts. At Georgia State, my fellow graduate students created a supportive atmosphere where we could explore new ideas. I am grateful to Abou Bamba, Dexter Blackman, Steve Blankenship, Shannon Bontrager, Jennifer Dickey, John Farris, Fakhri Haghani, Barry Lee, Heather Lucas, Chris Lutz, Gnimbin Albert Ouattara, Edie Riehm, Mary Rolinson, Mike Stevens, Aubrey Underwood, Montgomery Wolf, and Larry Youngs, as well as others who offered ideas along the way. Paula Sorrell and Carolyn Whiters always took care of the details, financial and otherwise, helping to create an atmosphere in which graduate students thrived.

I am grateful to the staff at the Historical Collections and Labor Archives at Penn State University, particularly Denise Conklin, Paul Dzyak, and James Quigel, who helped me navigate the records of the United Mine Workers of America, the William Mitch Papers, and the records of the United Steelworkers of America during my frequent travels to State College over the years. My old friend from Alabama, Shyam Sundar Sethuraman, provided friendship, encouragement, a place to stay, and some amazing Indian meals during my visits to PSU.

The staffs of the Department of Archives and Manuscripts and the Tutwiler Collection of Southern History and Literature at the Birmingham Public Library also deserve thanks for the help they provided during my countless visits over the years. In particular, Jim Bagget and Don Veasey helped in almost all of the different aspects of this project. Their support and friendship over the years have simply been invaluable.

I also benefited from assistance provided by the staffs of the Alabama Department of Archives and History in Montgomery, the Special Collection Department at Samford University in Birmingham, and the W. S. Hoole Special Collections Library at the University of Alabama in Tuscaloosa. Bill Tharpe helped me navigate my way around the Alabama Power Company archives in Birmingham, while the staff at the Hollis Burke Frissell Library at Tuskegee University provided access to the valuable microfilm collection housed there. Staff at the Archives of Labor, Urban Affairs, and University Archives at Wayne State University in Detroit made the records of the Miners for Democracy Collection available. Marie Tedesco, a fellow Georgia State alumnus, helped me access important collections on women coal miners at the Archives of Appalachia at East Tennessee State University. Staffs at the Robert Woodruff Library at the Atlanta University Center, the West Virginia and Regional History Collection at West Virginia University, and the Franklin D. Roosevelt Library in New York also provided valuable aid.

I am especially indebted to the archivists and staff at the Southern Labor Archives at Georgia State University. Both during and since my years at GSU, they have provided encouragement and support for this project. Occasionally, they even found me work when times grew thin. I especially want to thank Bob Dinwiddie, Pam Hackbart-Dean, Peter Roberts, Annie Tilden, and Julia Young for all their help over the years.

Finally, I also benefited from the hospitality and wisdom of coal miners and managers in the Birmingham District. In particular, I thank LaMarse Moore, who welcomed me on my visits to Edgewater, shared her personal history, and introduced me to other miners.

This book has benefited from the insight of scholars and activists who offered criticism at various stages, including Eric Arnesen, Ashaki Binta, Heidi Gottfried, George Hopkins, Les Hough, Gretchen Maclachlan, Joseph Reidy, and Robert Zieger. Melvyn Dubofsky, Glenn Feldman, Ron Lewis, and Timothy Minchin provided encouragement and advice along the way. The same is true for Horace Huntley and the staff of the Birmingham Civil Rights Institute, who allowed me to view the institute's collections.

I am grateful to Colin Davis and Ed Brown for including my essay, "Wildcats, Caravans, and Dynamite: Alabama Miners and the 1977–1978 Coal Strike," in their 1999 book, *It Is Union and Liberty: Alabama Coal Miners and the UMW*, which was published by the University of Alabama Press. Colin, in particular, has provided invaluable support over the years. I will always be thankful for the hospitality and kindness he showed me during the summer of 2001, when the bulk of this research was conducted. J. Steven Murray and the staff of the *Alabama Review* deserve thanks as well for publishing my article, "The Rebirth of the UMWA and Racial Anxiety in Alabama, 1933–1942," in the October 2005 edition of their journal.

I also thank my colleagues in the academic community at Miles College, especially those in the Division of Social and Behavioral Sciences, where I taught history from 2003 to 2005. My division chair, Digambar Mishra, provided constant support for my work. Fellow professors Richard Arrington, Melanie Carter, James Feggins, Olivia Green, Beverly Hawk, Fred Hill, Patrick Jarrett, Jason Lindsey, Josna Mishra, John Morgan, Barbara Nunn, Marilyn Peebles, and Eric Tscheschlok also encouraged me at various times. My officemate, Gary Sprayberry, served for several years as an enthusiastic sounding board for my ideas about this book. Robert Cassanello, who lured me to Miles but left before I arrived, has been a great friend and has helped me in countless ways. Frances Pryor kept things in our division running, and she always had kind words of support. I especially would like to thank the students who took my African American experience, African American history, and Alabama history courses at Miles. They provided a constant source of inspiration to me and have influenced this book more than they know. I hope that they will continue the Miles College tradition of pushing for positive change in Birmingham.

My new colleagues at Clark Atlanta University—Karamo Barrow, Claudia Combs, Vicki Crawford, Richard Morton, Barbara Moss, Clarissa Myrick-Harris, David Organ, and Linda Tomlinson—have been especially supportive in the final stages of this book.

Officials at the University of Georgia Press have encouraged me all along. I am grateful to series editors Douglas Flamming and Bryant Simon for all of their efforts on this project. Acquisitions editor Andrew Berzanskis has proved a tireless advocate for this book. Assistant managing editor Jon Davies oversaw the project's final stages, while Ellen D. Goldlust-Gingrich edited the text. Brian Kelly and Judith Stein, the readers for the press, offered invaluable insights that strengthened this manuscript. I am particularly grateful to Brian for all of his encouragement through the years. I first met him in 1997 at the Southern Labor Studies Conference, where we both presented papers. He has been a good friend ever since.

Though the collective efforts of all of these people undoubtedly strengthened this book, they bear no responsibility for any errors of interpretation or fact, which are mine alone.

As I think back, this book has deep roots in the history of my family. Throughout the course of my life, I have benefited tremendously from the support of my sisters, Meredith and Anne, and the wisdom of my parents, Chip and Emily Woodrum. My family collectively instilled in me the belief that positive change is possible, regardless of the circumstances and challenges. In particular I learned a great deal by watching my father over the years. As a Democratic member of the Virginia General Assembly for more than twenty years, he was the rare combination of artful political operative and idealist. In the end, he practiced what he preached, and the state was better off for all of his efforts. I also owe a debt of gratitude to my great-aunt, Martha Anne Woodrum Zillhardt, a pilot and Democratic political activist whose optimism inspired me from an early age. Though she did not live to see this book in print, her spirit fueled my drive to write it.

Finally, words cannot describe the thanks that I owe my wife, Amanda, a native Alabamian. She has always provided strong support, most importantly in her belief that I had the ability to write this book. She has endured long periods of separation from me as I conducted research and taught. She has borne all of these difficulties with patience, understanding, and love, and for this, more than anything, I am most grateful.

"Everybody Was Black Down There"

When he was just nineteen years old, Ernest Walker left behind the life of an impoverished sharecropper. He joined neighbors and family members as they headed out from the small town of Newton, Mississippi, for what they all hoped would be a better life in Walker County, Alabama, at the end of the Great Depression. The people, all of them desperately poor, piled into the back of a large truck owned by Walker's father-in-law. Some of Walker's companions had children with them, while others brought along farm animals—several small pigs and a cow made at least part of the journey. "One truck brought five families from the state of Mississippi to Alabama in 1939," Walker remembered. "I never will forget that part."[1]

After arriving in Alabama, Walker worked for a while in his father-in-law's timber business, then found a job at a large power plant in Gorgas. Walker County was the center of Alabama's coal mining industry, and Ernest Walker eventually felt the pull underground. In 1950 he took a job at Alabama Power Company's Gorgas mine, where he would work until he retired in 1983 on a generous union-negotiated pension.[2]

Walker, a humble and deeply religious man, turned out to be a quiet crusader. In the mid-1950s, when most African Americans lost their jobs in the coal industry, Walker became the first black man to operate a continuous mining machine in the Gorgas mine. He did so over the objections of many of the mine's whites but with the support of his union, the United Mine Workers of America (UMWA). "I was a pioneer," he recalled decades later. "I broke down a barrier between the races in No. 7." Work in the mines and the benefits that UMWA members won from the coal operators in Alabama provided Walker and his family with the financial security to realize many of their dreams.[3]

What follows is the collective narrative of thousands of people like Ernest Walker who spent all or part of their lives laboring to produce the coal that fueled the South's industries. It is, in part, a story of bitter defeats and hardship. But it is also a story about Walker and others who realized a standard of living for themselves and their families that they could never have imagined when they started out in life.

The costs were high, and Walker's story is exceptional in many ways. Most African American miners never saw the benefits for which they had struggled so hard because their numbers declined dramatically in the Alabama coalfields. In 1930, almost 13,000 African Americans worked in the mines around Birmingham, comprising 53 percent of the miners and an estimated 60 percent of the union's members. Six decades later, at the close of the twentieth century, African Americans totaled only about 15 percent of a mining workforce that had shrunk to 12,265.[4]

Why this dramatic decline occurred—and why it happened during the tenure of a strong UMWA presence in the Alabama coalfields—form the central questions examined in this book. Historians have rarely examined the decrease in the number and percentage of African American miners, but the subject remains one of the most important unexplored problems in the history of race relations in the American labor movement. The importance of the UMWA's efforts to bridge the color line should not be underestimated. During the New Deal era, the UMWA played a central role in the establishment of unions that fell under the umbrella of the Congress of Industrial Organizations (CIO). Many of these unions established themselves in industries with large numbers of African Americans and adopted the UMWA's model for organizing and representing blacks and whites in the workplace.[5] How white and black miners dealt with race, therefore, had important implications beyond the coalfields.

This study of race relations in the miners' union has been shaped by an important discussion among labor historians about the extent of white working-class racism and the degree to which labor unions served either to reinforce white supremacy or to provide a forum for interracial cooperation. Herbert Hill ignited the debate when he charged that Herbert Gutman and the "New Labor History" had created a "myth" of interracial solidarity and had failed to "confront the fundamental issue: the historical development of working-class identity as racial identity."[6] More recently, Bruce Nelson, who studied race relations among steelworkers and longshoremen, and Timothy Minchin, who examined

African Americans' efforts to achieve racial equality in the southern paper industry, have shown how unions cooperated in maintaining segregation and worked to limit opportunities for blacks. Nelson, in particular, has explored the issue of "whiteness"—the concept that white workers embraced white supremacy to attain a "public and psychological wage." In an important study of race relations in the Mobile, Alabama, shipyards, he argued that CIO unions made concessions to Jim Crow that left them vulnerable to employers' racial appeals. Nelson noted that the failure to confront white worker racism played a major role in a violent race riot that erupted in the shipyards during World War II and led to dramatic declines in black employment at the facilities after the conflict as the companies either downsized or closed. Nelson placed these ideas into a broader context in his recent book, *Divided We Stand: American Workers and the Struggle for Black Equality*. While Nelson argued that the CIO held much promise for improving relations between white and black dockers and steelworkers, he also found that white workers "demonstrated little or no interest in relinquishing the privileges that positioned them a notch or two above African Americans in the social order."[7]

Other historians, including Michael Honey and Robert Korstad, have argued that despite the racism of many white workers, African Americans used industrial unions as a vehicle to articulate their aspirations on the job and often in society at large. In particular, Korstad has argued that leftist unions that embraced a pronounced civil rights agenda during the 1930s and 1940s reached out aggressively to African American workers in the South and offered hope for transforming the region in ways that benefited both black and white workers. In *Civil Rights Unionism: Tobacco Workers and the Struggle for Democracy in the Mid-Twentieth-Century South*, which chronicled the efforts of the Food, Tobacco, Agricultural, and Allied Workers (FTA) to organize and maintain a presence at R. J. Reynolds Tobacco in North Carolina, Korstad found that the interracial union provided a forum for African American workers to advance a "working class–led, union based, civil rights movement" that realized profound results. This ambitious agenda was ultimately dismantled during the Red Scare and general reaction against unions that swept the country after World War II.[8]

Alan Draper, by contrast, has criticized the "new southern labor history" for overstating the effect of such leftist unions. In a study of the International Union of Mine, Mill, and Smelter Workers in Birmingham, Draper argued that black and white ore miners had success during the New Deal era when they convinced the National Labor Relations Board to intervene on their behalf. More important than Mine Mill's organizing tactics, he wrote, was the decision by the Tennessee Coal, Iron, and Railroad Company (TCI) to recognize the union in the wake of federal intervention.[9]

Indeed, a number of recent studies have focused on race relations in the Birmingham District's mills and mines. Scholars Henry McKiven, who explored race relations in the iron and steel industries in the late 1800s and early 1900s, and Robert J. Norrell, who examined race relations during the industrial union era in steel, generally found that white workers and unions worked to preserve Jim Crow.[10] McKiven argued that mill owners and skilled white workers collaborated to ensure that blacks performed the most common, most physical, and least skilled tasks in Birmingham's iron and steel mills. This cooperation in the subjugation of black labor lessened class divisions between owners and white workers and represented an attempt to ensure labor peace. White workers in the iron and steel industry excluded blacks from their unions and strongly supported the segregation patterns that relegated black workers to substandard housing.[11] Norrell, who focused his examination of race relations in the steel mills from the 1930s through the 1950s, found that Birmingham's industrial unions "gave white workers new power to enforce job discrimination, thus severely curtailing black opportunities." Norrell concluded that because union seniority provisions "froze occupational structures" and left segregation in place in the mills, "unionization made possible by interracial solidarity . . . yielded greater restrictions on black opportunity than existed before the 1930s." The industrial union movement's failure to deal adequately with race, Norrell later wrote, allowed elites to exploit the issue and preserve the "old order" in their industries until the civil rights protests of the early 1960s.[12]

Other scholars, however, have argued that Birmingham's industrial unions created an atmosphere of interracial cooperation that resulted in major advances for both African Americans and whites. Examining much of the same historical period as Norrell, Judith Stein chronicled a high level of black and white cooperation in the iron and steel mills operated by TCI, a subsidiary of U.S. Steel, during the industrial union era. Stein found that after World War II, "Birmingham workers transcended racial and workplace divisions to forge a genuine grassroots presence in the mills and shops of TCI." The results included contracts that encouraged new workplace standards and rights "hitherto unknown" in the region. In his study of the Communist Party in Birmingham, Robin D. G. Kelley found that CIO unions, with their embrace of an "unusually pronounced civil rights agenda," blunted the effect of the region's racially inclusive communists by offering a "better vehicle through which to realize these goals."[13]

More recently, David Montgomery, in an introductory chapter to a larger study that explored the connections between labor and civil rights in Birmingham, argued that unions served as "theaters of conflict and mobilization against racial discrimination" for African Americans, particularly by the 1950s. Blacks joined with white workers to attain fair wages and decent working conditions and to lessen supervisors' workplace power. Montgomery also argued that black unionists supported the basic concept of seniority in the workplace but "fought racist distortions of that principle."[14]

Historians who have examined race relations in the coal mines around Birmingham, while not overlooking white worker racism, have generally found a high level of cooperation between white and black miners. The best recent example of this view is found in the work of Daniel Letwin, who examined the miners' organizing efforts from the 1870s through the UMWA's disastrous 1921 defeat. Letwin's rich and complex study argued that Alabama miners' various organizing efforts "surpassed the racial norms of their time and region." The unions and political groups that coal miners joined—the Greenback Labor Party, the Knights of Labor, and the UMWA—had limits imposed on them by southern white supremacy, Letwin found, but such racial customs were almost always contested within these groups. The color line, he argued, did not define but rather "bisected" the boundaries of the union movement. "Racist thinking bubbled up commonly among white unionists," he wrote, "but in few other groups did it emerge not as the uncontested, dominant theme, but rather as a counterweight to another, more racially inclusive ethos."[15]

While generally agreeing with Letwin's characterization of the miners' organizing efforts, Brian Kelly placed the coal operators at the center of constructing white supremacy in the Birmingham District in his masterful work on coalfield race relations in the early twentieth century. Kelly argued that company officials had a "fundamental and consistent role in maintaining racial divisions" in the region. In Kelly's view, the UMWA's interracialism offered a strong challenge to the operators' hegemony.[16]

In the most comprehensive examination of the rebirth of the UMWA during the New Deal era, Peter Alexander emphasized black and white miners' ability to cross the racial divide even as they made important concessions to Jim Crow. Alexander argued that African Americans' numerical importance within the UMWA allowed them to exert "considerable sway" and that they profoundly shaped the union's racial policies. He emphasized the broader efforts to reestablish the miners' union in the Birmingham District, however, and his study ended in 1941.[17] Many questions remain about the union's commitment to the rights of its black members when it reemerged in Alabama in the 1930s and how the UMWA's compromises on race played out in the decades that followed.

This book argues that the union's accords on race ultimately left its black members vulnerable to the economic and technological changes that transformed the coal industry after World War II. Unlike leftist unions such as the FTA, which embraced "civil rights unionism," the UMWA approached the color line only tentatively.[18] Indeed, this study shows that by the early years of the war, as racial tension rose in Birmingham and the rest of the state and region, the UMWA showed signs of backing away from its commitment to its black members. African Americans no longer constituted the majority of Alabama's miners by 1940, and declining numbers in the decades that followed only exacerbated this problem.[19]

The UMWA did not openly discriminate against its black members, as did craft unions or even most other industrial unions. The interracial cooperation that miners exhibited at times stunned observers and frightened white political and economic elites but was also circumscribed by the wider world of the Birmingham District. The miners' union consequently was slow to respond to black miners' concerns when a massive crisis enveloped the coal industry in the decades after the war. Though a majority of the region's miners lost their jobs during these years, African American miners suffered disproportionately.

A second theme of this study concerns the postwar decline of the Alabama coal industry and its effects on miners, their communities, and race relations. Employment in the state's coal industry dropped from almost twenty thousand miners in 1950 to less than five thousand in 1970. The slump in the Alabama coal industry occurred in the context of the general economic malaise that hit other key parts of the Birmingham District's economy, particularly the iron and steel industries. In many respects, Birmingham stood apart from its Sunbelt neighbors, which boasted high-tech, service-oriented economies that grew in the years after the war. "Southern economic dynamism," Stein has concluded, "reflected Dallas and Atlanta more than Birmingham." In many respects, Birmingham's history in the second half of the twentieth century—with its job losses, economic decline, and urban unrest—had more in common with so-called Rust Belt urban centers such as Detroit than with its southern neighbors.[20]

The economic decline of the Alabama coalfields after World War II devastated the communities that had sustained generations of miners. Throughout the Birmingham District, coal companies abandoned the old towns they had created in the early twentieth century. In many cases, the companies sold the houses to their occupants, but in other cases the towns were completely dismantled. Thousands of miners were forced to leave the coalfields, sometimes abandoning their way of life and traveling to other parts of the country in search of meaningful work. Mechanization in the form of continuous mining machines took hold in the remaining underground mines, and strip mines proliferated. Both of these developments made many miners' jobs unnecessary.

Such economic changes have powerful consequences for race relations, as historian Thomas Sugrue has demonstrated. In *The Origins of the Urban Crisis: Race and Inequality in Postwar Detroit*, Sugrue argued that patterns of segregation in the city's automobile plants left African Americans vulnerable to the industry's postwar structural changes. The resulting black unemployment and decaying urban infrastructure played into white stereotypes about African Americans, their families, and their communities. When African Americans tried to escape the confines of their neighborhoods in Detroit, they met fierce white resistance.[21]

As in Detroit's automobile factories, blacks in the Alabama coalfields suffered a disproportionate share of job losses. Concerns about black miners' future had emerged as early as World War II, during the boom in coal employment. Economist Herbert Northrup, who toured the mining districts of Alabama and West Virginia in the early 1940s, warned about the consequences of the UMWA's failure to obtain equal job opportunities underground for its black members. At the time, coal operators in Alabama and the rest of the country were introducing mechanical loaders, thereby eliminating African American miners' jobs. Managers typically gave jobs operating these machines to whites, and the miners' union rarely contested such arrangements. "These postwar adjustments will put the equalitarian policies of the UMW to their severest tests," he wrote. "If Negroes continue to bear the brunt of technological unemployment, the UMW will no longer be able to claim that it adheres to a policy of racial equality as steadfastly as any other American labor union." The UMWA, in fact, embraced many of the forces—mechanization in particular—that cost African American miners their jobs after the war, historian Ronald Lewis has argued. Lewis concluded that the UMWA practiced "discrimination by omission" when it failed to stand up for the rights of its African American members as technological change and economic decline hit the coalfields.[22]

Of course, the coal operators had a primary role in this process. In many ways they had more power than the UMWA in determining miners' fates. The operators did the hiring, and company officials ultimately determined which work went to which miners by channeling blacks and whites into certain lines of production in the mines. In many cases, this book shows, African American miners received support from UMWA officers and white miners when they attempted to move into machine-operating positions that were considered white jobs. The operators also typically opposed the UMWA's efforts to rectify the racial disparities built into seniority provisions. In this sense, any serious study of race relations in the Birmingham District's coalfields must take into account Kelly's caution about "bringing the employers back" into the debate about race and labor.[23]

The decline of Alabama's coalfields had other effects as well. Desperate white miners searched for answers to their plight, and during the late 1940s and early 1950s, many turned to the Ku Klux Klan, which found both recruits and targets in the coalfields. The economic malaise also threatened the important gains the miners had won from the coal operators in the years that followed the UMWA's return to the Birmingham District. In particular, the union's groundbreaking health and retirement system, funded by royalties from coal production, was plunged into crisis. Many black and white miners consequently never realized the benefits of the system they had helped create.

Finally, this study charts new ground in its examination of how miners and their union confronted the forces of globalization in the final decades of the twentieth century. The brief rebirth of the Alabama coalfields from the late 1960s through the early 1980s was related to increasing domestic demand as well as to the growth of international markets for the region's coal. Once a business limited by both geography and geology, Alabama's coal industry entered the mobile world of international commerce in the 1970s. But for miners as for other workers, global markets carried costs. For decades, workers in the automobile, steel, commercial electronics, garment, and textile industries had found themselves subject to these processes, and in the last three decades of the twentieth century, Alabama miners joined those ranks.[24]

In Alabama, the coalfields benefited in many ways from the growth of international markets in the late 1960s, when companies began to sign contracts to supply customers in Asia, Europe, and Latin America. In general, the growth of these markets resulted in thousands of new jobs as coal companies opened new mines to satisfy the new demand. Women miners claimed some of these jobs by drawing on both traditions of coalfield militancy and new legal avenues opened up by the civil rights movement. The union, however, had long since turned its back on a wider social agenda. So women miners, like black miners in earlier decades, were mostly left to fight these battles on their own, with little help from the UMWA.

Utilities in the region also began to import coal through the docks in Mobile— the same facility that handled Alabama coal for export—from countries such as South Africa and Australia. Jefferson Cowie's observation that "no location has a lock on industrial investment in a free market economy" certainly applied to the Alabama coalfields at the end of the twentieth century. The Birmingham District's biggest coal producer, Drummond Coal, invested in a large Colombian surface mine in the late 1980s. Slightly more than a decade later, as coal flowed into the region from this operation and from huge strip mines in the western United States, Alabama's mining workforce had dwindled to about three thousand people.[25] For miners who remained employed in Alabama, globalization ultimately meant a weakened union, environmental degradation, and a general decline in safety conditions underground.

Returning to the central theme of this book, the UMWA's failure to push aggressively for the rights of its black members loomed large at the end of the twentieth century. As the influence of African Americans within the union declined and its wider agenda fell by the wayside during and after World War II, its focus narrowed. Decades later, as the union's ranks swelled with new members, the UMWA tended to reflect the immediate concerns of protecting jobs and coal production for white men. New fissures opened between working miners and coal communities, and the coalitions the union needed to fight the negative aspects of globalization—imports in particular—proved weak and unsustainable. The failure of the UMWA's campaign to prevent the Southern Company, which owned several regional utilities, from importing millions of tons of South African coal in the mid-1970s dramatically illustrated these problems. Miners in the twenty-first century were left to wrestle with the consequences.

CHAPTER ONE

Race, Class, Gender, and Community before 1941

Jobie Thomas grew up in a segregated mining camp outside of Birmingham, Alabama, in the early decades of the twentieth century. Despite the best efforts of the company that ran the camp, Sloss-Sheffield Steel and Iron, Thomas remembered that racial separation was not complete: on the job, miners of different races "had to pull together" and "go down there and help" each other. Underground, in particular, the color line blurred, with white and black miners working cooperatively to produce coal for the company. "I don't care what color it was, everybody was black down there in all that coal, anyhow," Thomas said.[1]

Thomas voiced a sentiment common among miners of both races when they were asked decades later about relations between whites and blacks. This sentiment perhaps reflects both the complexity of memory and the reality of life in the coal communities around Birmingham. Alessandro Portelli has argued that people often manipulate the facts and sequences of events in their memories. In some cases, such tactics seek to obscure feelings of humiliation or loss of self-esteem, emotions that African Americans who lived through the brutal effects of segregation and racism in the Alabama coalfields would have known intimately. But the complex memories of miners such as Thomas reveal another facet of segregation in the South: complete separation of the races was never achieved. White southerners spent a great deal of time and energy in the late nineteenth and early twentieth centuries attempting to construct separate worlds for themselves and African Americans. While white supremacy may have been the rule in the coal camps of the Birmingham District, African Americans always contested segregation. Thomas's memories, therefore, also likely reflect both the incomplete nature of the segregationist project and the ways that African Americans challenged such arrangements.[2]

In many respects, the Alabama coalfields in the era before World War II serve as a window into the complexity of the color line in the South. Underground, for example, black and white miners depended on each other. They often worked in close quarters under difficult and dangerous working conditions. And they cooperated toward a common goal. Miners of both races also worked away from the racialized public gaze of the outside world. In one sense, everyone was "black," as Thomas and other miners remembered, because the black coal dust that covered them at the end of their shifts sometimes made it difficult to see the color of each miner's skin. Miners in Alabama in the decades before World War II also worked in jobs that were not necessarily the province of one particular race. The large numbers of black coal miners in the Birmingham industrial district—African Americans comprised the majority of the workforce for most of the first half of the twentieth century—allowed African Americans to challenge the white monopoly on skilled work and often made the color line more permeable underground than on the surface.[3]

Above ground, the color line had acquired a more rigid definition. The 1920s had been an especially difficult decade for race relations in Birmingham, the center of the industrial district. The Ku Klux Klan reemerged in the spring of 1918, during a strike by the region's steelworkers, and experienced a period of unparalleled growth in the Magic City. Birmingham's leaders passed a series of laws designed to control black behavior and to force African Americans to live in small, isolated enclaves. By the middle of the decade, according to geographer Bobby M. Wilson, the collection of racist zoning laws passed by municipal officials had translated into "one of the most overt expressions of white supremacy ever put into law in the twentieth century." In the company-run coal camps outside the city, segregation was also the rule. Alabama's coal operators built their towns with distinct white and black sections with separate homes, churches, and schools. The company-owned stores in the towns even featured separate checkout lines for blacks and whites.[4]

The racial situation in Alabama's coal mines differed from that of other southern industries, such as iron, steel, and textiles, however. On the job, the workforce in Birmingham's iron and steel mills, for example, was heavily divided by race, with white workers occupying the most skilled positions and strongly supporting the ideology of white supremacy. In addition, African Americans were virtually absent from the region's textile mills. Any black lucky enough to get a job in a textile mill rarely had the opportunity to operate a machine. In southern textiles, one historian has recently written, "whites relied on race to serve as their entree to politics, jobs, and later, union jobs." Textile historians have demonstrated how white mill hands were willing to defend this privileged position.[5]

In the Birmingham District's coal industry, whites lacked such a complete monopoly on jobs or even on skilled jobs in the early twentieth century. African Americans formed a majority of the mining workforce—almost thirteen thousand of twenty-four thousand miners in 1930—and in many instances used these numbers to challenge the white monopoly on skilled labor. The almost exclusively masculine makeup of the mining workforce, by custom and by statute in Alabama, also set it apart from many of the region's other industries. While women were virtually excluded from the Alabama mines until many decades after World War II, in the textile industry the possibility that black men might work in close proximity to white women provided the justification for whites to limit, sometimes through state law, African American employment. Because that potential encounter was almost nonexistent in Alabama's coal mining industry, however, as historian Daniel Letwin, who chronicled an earlier era in the state's coalfields, has argued, the boundaries of interracial encounter were loosened among male miners underground in ways that were virtually impossible on the surface.[6]

The Alabama coal industry's unique racial and gender mix as well as the solidarity produced by members of both races working together underground served as a backdrop for miners' persistent attempts to reach across the color line to organize unions. Beginning in the late 1800s and continuing through the 1920–21 strike, black and white miners formed biracial organizations and attempted to win contracts with the state's coal operators. Company officials and their supporters often played the race card, claiming that miners' biracial organizing efforts promoted social equality between African Americans and whites despite union activists' efforts to downplay the inflammatory issue. The defeat of the United Mine Workers of America (UMWA) in 1921 in the wake of such charges traumatized the coal communities that ringed Birmingham and vanquished the miners' union from the state's coalfields.[7]

Less than a decade later, the Great Depression swept across the landscape of the Birmingham District. The economic crisis took a toll on the coal towns that surrounded the city, with more than half of the state's mines shutting down and thousands of miners losing their jobs. President Franklin Roosevelt's New Deal programs would provide some relief for ailing mining communities and create the protections that miners needed to bring their union back. The stability of the New Deal and wartime industrial demand briefly revitalized the Alabama coal industry, preserving the mining way of life through the end of the 1940s. But by the late 1930s and early 1940s, the coalfields evidenced signs of change. In his travels through the nation's mining districts, folklorist George Korson chronicled the appearance of consumer goods such as radios, modern refrigerators, and linoleum floors in miners' homes. Better roads and access to automobiles and buses allowed miners to work at mines farther from the coal camps as well as to visit nearby cities on a more regular basis. Still, Korson documented the persistence of the distinct mining culture.[8]

This chapter examines the world in which Alabama coal miners lived from the 1920s through the early 1940s. It briefly explores the coal industry's origins in northern Alabama, describes the nature of the work that coal miners performed, and chronicles the major challenges the coal industry and the miners who worked in it faced during this era. It also attempts to reconstruct, to the extent that doing so is possible, the social world black and white miners and their families inhabited in the early twentieth century. And, finally, this chapter investigates the changes that the depression and New Deal brought to coal communities in the Birmingham District.

Race is central to this analysis. Miners alternately shaped and were shaped by the world around them. Living in the pre–World War II Jim Crow South, black and white miners not only accommodated but also challenged the southern caste system. What emerges from any journey into race relations in Alabama's coalfields is a complex picture where racial boundaries seem to shift dramatically at mine entrances. Race was a contested space, shaped by the daily interactions and struggles between black and white miners and by the outside world.

❰ ❰ ❰

Over millions of years, nature endowed the region around what is now Birmingham, Alabama, with the richest and largest seams of coal in the Deep South. The state of Alabama features four major coalfields, the Warrior Field, the Cahaba Field, the Coosa Field, and the Plateau Region. The Warrior, Cahaba, and Coosa fields, and the cities, towns, and counties that lie within or near these coalfields, make up the region known as the Birmingham District. The Plateau Region consists of several coalfields of lesser importance located mainly in far northeastern Alabama.

Coal mining in Alabama predates the Civil War and the founding of Birmingham. Early mining methods were primitive and produced little coal. The war focused a great deal of attention on efforts to develop the region's mineral districts to meet Confederate demand. With state financing, developers extended a railroad from Montgomery north into Shelby County to exploit the region's coal and ore deposits. Union military raids devastated the region's emerging coal and iron industries and plunged the mineral district into a decadelong economic depression and recession. The area rebounded toward the end of the 1870s, by which time developers had founded Birmingham in Jefferson County and major railroads linked the coalfields to the rest of the region. In the mid-1870s, the coal industry received a major boost when entrepreneurs began to use coke, a by-product of coal, to make pig iron. From this point on, the histories of the coal, iron, and steel industries were closely linked.

An improving economic situation in the 1880s initiated an industrial boom and set in motion the forces that would make the Birmingham District the South's industrial center. Entrepreneurs identified with Birmingham's early development created ironworks, and the railroads laid track. By the end of the decade, the Tennessee Coal, Iron, and Railroad Company (TCI) had arrived, and industrialist Henry DeBardeleben had established himself among the best-known local coal and iron magnates. Coal production would soar from 380,000 tons in 1880 to 16 million tons in 1910. In 1926, Alabama mines would produce 21.5 million tons of coal, the highest amount during the early twentieth century. Mining employment followed the trends in production. At the end of the 1880s, almost eight thousand miners dug coal in the Birmingham District; that number topped twenty-six thousand by 1920.[9]

The region's other heavy industries grew at similar rates. Alabama mills produced 10 percent of the nation's iron by 1920 and 87 percent of the region's supply by the middle of the decade. Steel production had arrived in the late 1890s, but geological and technological problems, combined with discriminatory freight rates, limited the effect of this industry. As a result, Birmingham accounted for only about 3.3 percent of the nation's steel production in 1919. Birmingham nevertheless prospered, with its population soaring to 179,000 by 1920. The region's most impressive skyscrapers dominated the city's landscape, and automobiles crowded its streets.[10]

Like the tall buildings rising in Birmingham, iron and steel companies dominated the region's coalfields. TCI bought sixteen regional coal producers before merging into the U.S. Steel empire in 1907. Other major operators identified with iron and steel had emerged by the early twentieth century, including Sloss-Sheffield Steel and Iron, Republic Iron and Steel, and Woodward Iron. The coal mines that these companies operated typically did not sell their products on the open market but instead produced coal for use in the iron- and steelmaking processes. These operations, called captive coal producers, accounted for more than a third of Alabama's production by the mid-1920s. Other large producers included commercial rail–connected mining companies such as DeBardeleben Coal and Alabama Fuel and Iron (AFICO), both of them run by members of the DeBardeleben family. Such large producers sold their coal on the open market to major consumers including railroads, electric power plants, industries, homes (for heating), and steamships. By the 1930s, smaller truck mines accounted for a growing proportion of Alabama coal production, with hundreds of these marginal operations opening. Statistics from the late 1930s showed that these mines, sometimes run by families, produced more than 5 percent of the state's coal.[11]

Promoters of the Birmingham District never saw the region reach the potential they ardently championed. The area's dependence on iron, steel, and coal left it vulnerable to economic downturns, and it suffered from periodic boom-and-bust cycles throughout its early decades. The region's minerals also never lived up to their billing. Birmingham's iron ore, for example, contained high levels of phosphorous, which made steel production difficult. Industrialists instituted the open-hearth process in the 1890s, thereby allowing the iron companies to make steel. But that production method made the steel expensive, and the region's producers could remain competitive only by keeping production costs low—that is, by paying workers less than their counterparts in the rest of the country. The national corporations that snapped up Birmingham's iron and steel concerns in the 1890s and early 1900s shifted many of the major financial decisions and power within these companies out of the region. Discriminatory freight rates further confined many Alabama industrial products to the region.[12]

Similar problems plagued the district's coal industry. Alabama's landscape contained large quantities of coal, but the presence of impurities in the form of rock, shale, slate, and "bone coal" caused problems for Alabama's coal operators. The size of Alabama's coal seams proved misleading. Most commercial coal companies worked seams that averaged more than three feet in height, but the coal in these seams was often laced with several layers of impurities. Miners could separate some of this material from larger lumps of coal by hand, but removing it from smaller pieces required an expensive washing procedure that drove up production costs. By the mid-1930s, the operators complained that 73 percent of the district's coal had to undergo such a procedure, a larger percentage than any other coal-producing region.[13]

The companies washed the coal two ways. The first method involved mixing crushed coal with water in a large tank called a jig. The pulsating water separated the coal from impurities, with the coal rising to the top of the tank and the heavier impurities sinking to the bottom. The coal could then be scooped off the surface.

Coal could also be mixed with water on a series of large, vibrating tables. The water carried the coal over the tables, and a series of grooves caught the heavier impurities. Alabama companies had constructed more than fifty such washing plants by the mid-1930s.[14]

Another major geologic problem was the prevalence of faults, or breaks in the coal seams, that ranged from a few inches to hundreds of feet in size. In general, faults complicated the mining process and drove up costs. When a fault was encountered, coal companies had to locate the continuation of the coal seam—above, below, or to the side—and then connect the two levels so that miners and their machinery could continue to mine coal. Faults also created unstable geology and made mining more dangerous. While companies often adjusted to the difficulties posed by faults, such conditions at times forced companies to abandon mines altogether. Areas with large faults also tended to feature high levels of explosive methane gas, already present in large quantities in the state's coal seams, which added to safety problems.[15]

Alabama coal operators, because they enjoyed a large supply of low-wage laborers, traditionally had been slow to modernize their mines, but that tendency began to change by the end of the 1930s. Mechanized cutting machines first appeared underground at the end of the nineteenth century. These machines increased production by eliminating the need for miners to undercut coal through the difficult and time-consuming pick-and-shovel method. Before World War I, only 23 percent of Alabama's coal was mined with the help of mechanical cutting machines, compared with a national average of 51 percent. By 1939, however, Alabama operators had caught up with the rest of the country, mining between 70 and 80 percent of their coal using these machines.[16]

Also during the 1930s, Alabama operators began to introduce mechanized coal loaders, which eliminated the need for miners to shovel coal into waiting cars. In Alabama, operators used only a few of these machines in the mid-1930s. By the end of the decade, thirty-three operations used "Joy" and "Jeffrey" loaders to produce more than a quarter of the Birmingham District's coal. The percentage of coal mined with mechanical loaders amounted to only slightly less than the national average of 28 percent, a rate higher than levels in the major coal-producing regions of Kentucky, Pennsylvania, and Virginia.[17]

The introduction of large numbers of these machines displaced many black miners, many of whom had loading jobs. With the UMWA's return to Alabama in the early 1930s and the introduction of federal wage standards, large coal companies began to introduce machines underground to save costs. As a matter of course, coal companies gave white miners the jobs operating the loading and cutting machines, following the historic pattern that viewed this type of labor as "white man's work." "Because the white workers had performed the bulk of the machine jobs before the introduction of mechanical loaders," concluded economist Herbert Northrup, "they often have been in a better position to learn how to operate the mobile loading machines." As a result, thousands of black miners were forced out of the Alabama industry. In 1930, the state's 12,742 black miners made up 53 percent of the coal workforce; a decade later, only 9,566 miners (about 42 percent of the men underground) were African American.[18]

Despite the technological advances making their way into mines, the industry in the 1920s and 1930s operated in much the same fashion as it had since the turn of the century. Mines were developed around a main entry. "Haulageways"—wide tunnels lined with tracks through which miners entered and the coal left—extended out from the entry. Smaller tunnels, known as airways and crosscuts, crisscrossed the mine and channeled air driven by huge fans to miners as they worked.

In the room-and-pillar system, miners worked in rooms branching off from the larger tunnels. Miners left solid pillars of coal between the rooms to help support the roof. Miners did most of their work at the coal face, the part of the room that contained the coal being mined. The size of the seam dictated the dimensions of the working area. A large six-foot seam, for example, might require miners to work in a room that was twenty feet wide and six feet high. As the miners advanced forward, they supported the roof with large pieces of wood known as timbers placed three to six feet apart. In the long-wall system, the working area was much larger—sometimes stretching more than one hundred feet—and the roof was supported only near the area where miners worked. As they mined coal and advanced forward, miners let the roof fall in behind them. In some long-wall mines, companies used hydraulic jacks instead of timbers to prop up the roof where miners worked. Long walls featured more miners working at the face and typically required a more disciplined workforce than the room-and-pillar method.

Workers entered Alabama's mines through a long slope or in an elevator that descended into the earth. In larger operations, man trips (small electrically powered trains) took miners to the section where they worked, sometimes several miles from the entrance. In smaller operations, miners might have to walk or even crawl to their working areas. Miners were not paid for this journey until the UMWA negotiated such a provision during the 1940s.

At the coal face, the day began with officials testing methane gas levels. If the air was safe, miners began loading coal blasted by the previous shift into cars or sometimes onto mechanical conveyors. Through the 1930s, most coal was loaded by men with shovels. After the coal was loaded, miners began undercutting the seam with electric cutting machines. Miners used the machine's cutter bar to carve out a space from four to six inches high and six to nine feet deep into the base of coal face.

After the coal was undercut, miners began placing explosives into the coal face. Many miners bored holes by hand, pressing against a breastplate and turning a steel auger into the coal, although more mechanized operations used power drills. The holes were spaced a few feet apart and ranged from three to seven feet deep. Miners loaded the holes with explosive charges. Fuses or wires were placed in the holes, which were packed with clay or some other nonflammable material. Miners then exploded the charges by lighting the fuse or, in more advanced systems, pressing a detonator. Before blasting, miners often yelled out "Fire in the hole!" or "Fire, fire, fire!" to make sure that no one was in the immediate area.[19]

Though miners tried to be careful, accidents often happened during this process. Ed Stover, a second-generation miner who worked for Alabama By-Products, recalled that his father suffered for the rest of his life after miners, thinking he was out of the area, detonated charges too early and sent coal and electric wire into the man's back. "My dad died when he was sixty-one years old, and [even just before he died,] little old pieces of shooting wire would still work out of his back," Stover recalled. The deafening roar of the blast and the clouds of dust and smoke that billowed through the tunnels after the coal was shot sometimes left new miners disoriented. When Leon Alexander, who worked at Sloss-Sheffield's Lewisburg Mine, heard the explosives go off for the first time, he tried to run out of the mine. "If my daddy hadn't grabbed me, I probably . . . would [have] run into something and killed myself," he said.[20]

In the room-and-pillar system, when miners finished working in an area, they mined the coal from the pillars, a dangerous process known as pulling or robbing the pillars. As the miners retreated from an area, the roof would cave in behind them, sending up a deafening roar. Air pushed out when the roof fell in, stirring up clouds of coal dust. Pillars sometimes collapsed under the weight of the roof during this process, expelling tons of coal and injuring or killing nearby miners.[21]

Explosions underground posed a constant threat to miners. A spark could cause methane gas to explode, igniting coal dust in the air and killing dozens of miners at a time. Alabama's most infamous disaster occurred in 1911 near Birmingham when Pratt Consolidated Coal's Banner Mine exploded, killing 132 men, most of them African American convicts who had been leased to the company. Such large explosions led to periodic efforts at safety reform, but mining remained a very dangerous occupation in Alabama in the 1920s and 1930s, with injury rates outpacing national levels. Each year during the 1920s, an average of 109 men perished underground in Alabama.[22]

Such multiple-fatality events attracted a great deal of attention, but roof falls and random accidents in the dark world underground typically took more miners' lives. "Roof pots" (petrified trees) could suddenly separate from the ceiling rock, crushing the miners below.[23]

Almost all miners had stories of narrow escapes or of friends who perished underground. Many miners found it difficult to return to work after living through a rockfall or explosion, and some left the industry. Others, like Leon Alexander, steeled themselves and went back to work. "Death was a constant companion," Alexander remembered. "You subject to a rock falling on you. You subject to get electrocuted. You subject to be in an explosion. There is just so many ways that you can get killed, but we's never paid too much attention to that. . . . We don't dwell on those kind of negative things." All miners learned methods of testing the roof, and they kept a close watch of the coal face. "I could tell when that coal wouldn't get so easy to cut, that we were getting a rockfall," remembered Ernest Walker. He also knew to be careful when chips of rock "starts to hitting you on your hard hat. Once it's hitting that you know you are getting a rockfall."[24]

Other hazards were less obvious. For years, miners had complained about lung ailments—particularly pneumoconiosis, or black lung—caused by breathing in coal dust and other airborne material underground. Over time, black lung robbed miners of their breath and eventually led to their death. The medical establishment and the mining industry did not recognize the disease until long after World War II, but many years earlier, all signs indicated that the increasing mechanization of the mines and the additional dust mechanical loaders created exposed more miners to this debilitating condition.[25]

Though white and black miners faced many common challenges at work, racial divisions remained a fact of life underground. Since the industry's earliest days in Alabama, the coal operators had hired both white and black miners. In 1880, blacks made up more than 40 percent of Alabama's miners, and by 1910 African Americans totaled 54 percent of the state's 20,778 miners. African Americans continued to comprise the majority of Alabama's miners until 1940, when their share of the workforce declined to 42 percent.[26] Their numbers gave black miners the power to shape the world in which they worked and sometimes to contest white attempts to monopolize skilled work.

During the first half century of mining in the Birmingham District, men arrived from all over the world to work in the mines. Early on, most whites came from neighboring counties in north-central Alabama, but significant numbers traveled to Birmingham from outside the region and from places as far away as Britain and Eastern and Southern Europe. African American miners tended to come from the Black Belt, the plantation-dominated counties south of Birmingham. Others came from the cotton-growing regions of nearby Mississippi and Georgia.[27]

A significant number of Alabama's miners began their careers as prisoners, leased by the state and localities to the coal operators. As many as 90 percent of these "convict miners" were African Americans who had been charged with petty crimes such as vagrancy and theft. Many of those who survived their incarceration stayed in the industry, continuing to work as miners after being released. Historians who have explored the issue cite a variety of different reasons for the growth of the convict lease system in Alabama. Some have argued that trend constituted a response to a growing prison population, while others have emphasized the program's role in helping the coal companies increase their profits and prevent unionization. In the words of historian Alex Lichtenstein, the practice represented "a system of forced labor in an age of emancipation." The state of Alabama leased convicts to the coal operators until 1928, when the system was finally abolished after a public outcry regarding the convicts' brutal treatment.[28]

Though segregation was not consistently applied underground, skin color played an important role in the job opportunities that white and black miners found. At the top of the coal workforce, the operators strictly enforced white supremacy. Almost all managers and supervisors were white. In 1930, according to one estimate, more than 98 percent of the supervisors in Birmingham District mines were white.[29]

In many cases, white managers or foremen most directly and aggressively enforced racial customs underground. In the days before the UMWA returned to the coalfields, mine managers had almost unchecked authority over their miners. Angelo Herndon, a black miner who worked at the TCI operations at Docena during the 1920s, remembered his section foreman as "a rabid Negro hater" who often required miners to work overtime without pay. When Herndon and other black miners eventually rebelled and refused to work without additional compensation, the foreman unleashed a torrent of racial abuse. "What the matter with you fellows?" Herndon remembered the man shouting. "Getting lazy? Trouble with you niggers is that you are getting fat bellies. Too easy life—too much money. . . . I wish I had you Goddamn niggers on my plantation, I'd make you sweat blood all day—Saturday and Sunday, too." Earl Brown, an African American who worked at Woodward Iron's Mulga mine, remembered that managers would retaliate against assertive black miners. Once, when supervisors moved Brown to another shift after he spoke up for other miners, an official informed him, "If you keep your mouth shut, you'll advance. But you got too much mouth."[30]

Among the general mining workforce, skilled work typically remained the domain of whites, while blacks were often relegated to the most physically demanding, lowest paid, and least skilled occupations. Whites were more likely to operate cutting machines and shoot coal. African Americans might help skilled white machine operators but rarely had the opportunity to operate machines or perform skilled work. At Mulga, for example, Brown remembered that management kept blacks out of these higher-paying jobs. Northrup, who traveled the Alabama and West Virginia coalfields during the early 1940s, noted that coal operators almost always assigned machine jobs to whites and unskilled work to African Americans.[31]

Reflecting the centrality of black labor to the mining industry in Alabama, however, racial divisions were shaped by local conditions. Cleatus Burns, a black miner from Walker County, remembered that "black folks loaded coal. And the white folks . . . drilled it down." At the mines where Burns worked, whites operated the "motors," the engines that hauled both coal and miners out of the operation. Burns also remembered that some white miners loaded coal. Burns, however, eventually operated a cutting machine. Alexander, who worked at Sloss-Sheffield's Lewisburg mine, recalled that African Americans occasionally obtained jobs operating cutting machines but speculated that such opportunities had more to do with the demands and risks of the job than with benevolent attitudes on the part of employers or white miners. "It was hard work," he told an interviewer. "Moving under that low top was really a man killer, so they were satisfied for us to have that."[32]

Northrup observed similar underground variations. Loading coal remained the most common job at the time of Northrup's study, with more than half the miners at the operations he visited working in this capacity. He estimated that 77 percent of the African American miners worked as hand loaders, while about 60 percent of whites performed this work. In southern West Virginia, only 2 percent of the black miners operated cutting machines, while about 6 percent of the whites did. Despite the uneven distribution of jobs, Northrup observed a "comparatively high degree of the mixing of the races" underground in both regions. "Segregation either by occupation or by place of work, unlike most factory industries in the South, is conspicuous by its absence in the coal mines," he concluded. "In mines where the two races are employed, they invariably work side by side and at the same occupations."[33]

If working side by side meant that the color line sometimes blurred in the dark world underground, such boundaries were often restored when miners began the journey to the surface in segregated man trips. Whites "were scared to ride in the man trips with us," Walker remembered. "When they would get in the car, if a black was in there, oh, you'd see them get back out of there." When the miners arrived at the surface, they went to segregated bathhouses to change clothes and clean up. From that point on, black and white miners mostly occupied separate worlds. "Sometimes the people that you work with are like two peas in a pod in the mine," black miner Harry Burgess explained. "And there were times where they were with their own group, on the outside, in the street, when they just wouldn't recognize you. You know how that goes. Inside the coal mine you were accepted, you worked side by side, [but] on the street they tried to avoid you as much as possible."[34]

The demarcation between the outside world and the mines was sometimes dramatic, as many of these observations indicate, and white and black miners faced immense pressure from the prevailing standards of racial etiquette. Furthermore, during the first decades of the twentieth century, the demand to conform grew as Birmingham's leaders transformed racial custom into law and created, in the words of one historian, a "spatial manifestation of white supremacy" in the region. City leaders worked to regulate the behavior of blacks and to limit the parts of Birmingham in which they could live. The desired results included an increase in the supply of African Americans available to local industries. The *Birmingham Age-Herald* summarized the effort's goals, proclaiming, "The negro is a good laborer when his labor can be controlled and directed, but he is a very undesirable citizen."[35]

To control African American behavior, leaders passed a series of vagrancy laws beginning in the 1890s that targeted the unemployed, people who appeared drunk in public, gamblers, and others. Though these laws theoretically applied to whites, the city enforced them almost exclusively against blacks. Tighter rules were passed in 1903, 1907, and again during the World War I era. White leaders also worked to limit the social settings in which whites and blacks came together. Some of the most contentious debates of the era involved the attempt to regulate Birmingham's numerous bars and saloons, where blacks and whites sometimes openly defied the color line and mixed freely. Adding to the dismay of city leaders were reports that prostitutes who attracted both white and black customers worked some of these establishments. In 1913 a grand jury discovered "evidence of colored men having visited the white women" in a row of shacks near one such establishment. Though city leaders passed a barrage of ordinances that restricted black entrepreneurs' ability to run saloons, it would take Prohibition, passed by the rural-dominated state legislature in 1915, to dramatically curtail Birmingham's liquor traffic.[36]

A more successful enterprise was the effort to transform the city's racial caste system into law. Birmingham formally segregated its streetcars, cemeteries, and restaurants in the 1900s and 1910s. Few efforts symbolized the movement to codify the racial system in Birmingham as well as the housing ordinances that city officials passed. In the early twentieth century, African Americans lived in scattered enclaves throughout Birmingham, mostly along vacant spaces that whites had not developed—creek beds, railroad lines, and alleys. The quality of the housing stock in these areas was not good—one observer described black homes as "sharecropper cabins"—and city services were largely nonexistent. After the passage of these zoning ordinances, blacks found themselves confined to living in these racial enclaves, typically small, isolated areas within Birmingham's city limits that were separated from each other by larger "white only" areas.[37]

Along with separating whites and blacks came the need to disfranchise African Americans and working-class whites. Whites had long worried about the threat that African Americans, who made up about 39 percent of Birmingham's population in the 1920s, posed to white political control. Beginning in 1888, with the implementation of the city's all-white Democratic Party primary, whites embarked on a systematic attempt to eliminate black voting strength. These efforts finally succeeded in 1901, with the passage of a state constitution that effectively allowed the use of literacy tests, poll taxes, and other means to disfranchise African Americans. The measures also affected poor whites, and the percentage of whites who voted declined from more than 60 percent in 1900 to less than 30 percent in 1906. The rate never again climbed above 38 percent before World War I.[38]

The coal towns that ringed Birmingham were not isolated from these trends. "Following the long established Southern custom," the Alabama Mining Institute euphemistically proclaimed in the mid-1930s, "in the mining villages the portion occupied by the white inhabitants is separated from the living quarters of the Negroes."[39] Such language downplayed the operators' central role in constructing the racial climate in the coal camps. And there were no better examples of such impulses than Charles DeBardeleben's Alabama Fuel and Iron, among the most influential and powerful of the commercial coal-producing companies, and TCI, the region's most important coal, iron, and steel producer.

Alabama Fuel and Iron was founded by Henry DeBardeleben, the state's best-known industrial pioneer, in the early 1900s. But his second son, Charlie, known as the Henry Ford of Alabama, ran the company for most of its existence until his death in the early 1940s. The company had several large mining operations, all of them with AFICO-run towns nearby, at Acmar and Margaret in St. Clair County, as well as a large mine at Overton, in Jefferson County, near the prestigious suburb of Mountain Brook. The company later established another operation at Acton in Shelby County. Charles DeBardeleben traveled to Europe in 1926 and returned to the Birmingham District with new ideas on how to improve his camps. An army of horticulturists and landscapers descended on the settlements, and in the years that followed, the company touted its towns as idyllic villages. DeBardeleben claimed that he was responding to worker concerns about the quality of housing, for which he typically charged $6 a month in rent. The reemergence of the UMWA in the Alabama coalfields in the early 1930s added more urgency to these efforts. In 1934, for example, the company's revenue from its housing declined from $18,208 to $1,697 as AFICO officials made repairs to the homes in the company's mining towns. "I made it a point to rectify any complaint registered against any house, in an effort to keep down any form of dissatisfaction, and am glad to say the houses are now in first class condition, and our income should be restored from this source," DeBardeleben told shareholders.[40]

AFICO general manager F. R. Bell touted the company's "beautification idea," which encouraged miners and their families to grow plants around their homes from cuttings furnished by a company nursery. Women in the towns established garden clubs to help in the effort. AFICO also set up libraries in Acmar and Margaret "for the white people" who lived there. Bell claimed that these efforts helped to create "a keener interest in home life" and—most importantly in the eyes of AFICO's managers—added "to the stability of the employees, being a good investment from many standpoints." The company also operated nine schools for the children of its miners. Thirty teachers, AFICO officials boasted, educated more than one thousand students every year at the company's facilities.[41]

DeBardeleben worked to create a cult of personality at his Birmingham District mining villages. Company officials claimed that "executive offices . . . are always open to the lowest-paid worker in the mines." Stories circulated about DeBardeleben's generosity. He allowed miners in his camps to plow their gardens with company mules, and miners received hogs from DeBardeleben to supplement their diet. "If you wanted a car, he'd buy it for you, whatever you wanted there, he bought it for you," miner Earl Brown remarked sarcastically. "All your money went to Charlie DeBardeleben, you needn't have no need for anything." Company ministers, tightly controlled by DeBardeleben, prayed over miners before they went underground. Walker remembered that during his short stint working for AFICO, a black preacher "would sure enough tell the Lord about us going in there" before each shift. AFICO officials sponsored company picnics designed to reinforce the idea of DeBardeleben's charity. At these events, DeBardeleben would stand before the miners and ask, "Who's the greatest man in the world?" Miners would clap and chant their response: "Uncle Charlie DeBardeleben, Uncle Charlie."[42]

When DeBardeleben's paternalism failed, he quickly resorted to intimidation. At the Margaret camp, for example, company guards restricted who entered and left the town. A searchlight shone on cars as they approached at night. Brown remembered the AFICO operations as "just a regular slave camp." The president of Brown's union local at Mulga came from an AFICO town, and like many miners he had had to sneak away alone and return later for members of his family when he decided to take a job at another mine.[43]

In response to the UMWA's persistent organizing attempts at AFICO's operations, DeBardeleben attempted to construct and enforce an ideology of militant antiunionism that relied heavily on ideas about independence and individuality. AFICO's segregated welfare societies adopted "Ten Commandments" in which the miners pledged to have only "direct dealings" with the company. "I do not believe in putting my affairs in the hands of paid agitators and paying a monthly fee to be told that our company is our worst enemy," read one of the statements. In another, each AFICO miner pledged to "vigorously oppose any and all attempts to handle my affairs with the companies through outside parties."[44]

Even safety was an individual affair at AFICO's operations. The company's mines featured bulletin boards near their entrances. After accidents, company managers posted the names of the miners affected on the boards. "Blame for mishaps is placed squarely on the shoulders of the careless employees involved, innocent ones being exonerated with white lights beside their respective names," a company propagandist boasted. Company officials checked workers heading underground for flammable material such as cigarettes and matches and fined those who violated these safety concerns. The effectiveness of this stress on individuality in preventing accidents is a matter of interpretation. In 1925, for example, AFICO's operations at Overton exploded a couple of weeks before Christmas, killing fifty-three men. In 1934, five miners died in accidents at the company's mines in Acmar and Margaret. In his report to company shareholders, DeBardeleben avoided accepting the type of personal responsibility he required of his workers, instead blaming individual miners and UMWA organizing efforts. "This terrible record is largely accounted for by the fact that we brought in so many new men during the year," he asserted, "and the further fact that our men were more occupied with thinking of their welfare and protection from outside invasion than they were of the dangers they were being subjected to in the mines." In the summer of 1941, with no apparent UMWA organizing drive on, a gas explosion took the lives of eleven miners at Acmar.[45]

Charles DeBardeleben's paternalism extended into the arena of race relations. Like other companies, AFICO enforced strict segregation in its coal camps, but the company claimed that "Negroes receive the same consideration in amusements, housing, rates of pay, hours of work as white employees." In 1934, DeBardeleben boasted that his policies had kept race relations calm at his camps for a quarter of a century.[46]

DeBardeleben strongly enforced white supremacy in his camps, and most of his "progressive" ideas about African Americans rested on racist stereotypes grounded in nineteenth-century paternalism. For example, a feature article on the company's efforts to resist the UMWA that appeared in the pro-industry

Alabama magazine in the spring of 1937 featured a photograph that showed an African American miner with a distorted grin on his face flanked by two serious-looking white miners gazing off into the distance. AFICO and its supporters sought to project the message of white miners and company officials looking after their childlike black coworkers. DeBardeleben worked to increase the ratio of blacks to whites in his operations but justified this effort by drawing on notions of company and white miner paternalism toward African Americans. From 1933 to 1934, the percentage of black miners at AFICO's operations grew from 50.5 percent to 57 percent. During 1934, the number of black workers at Acmar and Margaret grew to more than 70 percent. Far from being racially enlightened, however, DeBardeleben's policies rested on racist notions about the docility and faithfulness of African Americans. "Our past experience has taught us that this is about the right ratio in order to maintain the proper loyalty and cooperative spirit," he claimed.[47]

DeBardeleben and Alabama Fuel and Iron were not alone in their efforts to create private welfare programs to encourage worker loyalty. Indeed, in many ways, TCI, the region's most important coal producer, set the standard. After U.S. Steel absorbed TCI, the parent firm sent George Gordon Crawford to head the new subsidiary. Crawford, a manager rather than an entrepreneur like De-Bardeleben, created and oversaw an elaborate apparatus of welfare services for TCI's employees that included housing, health care, education, and social programs. Collectively, TCI's programs became the region's "most highly developed system of company welfare." By the 1920s, the company had built more than twenty villages across the Birmingham District and operated nine white schools and fourteen African American schools. The company's elaborate Birmingham District operations featured a separate Department of Health and a Department of Social Science.[48]

More than a desire to help its employees, TCI's welfare systems represented an effort to improve the company's bottom line. Sanitation was a major problem in the region's mining communities, and polluted water supplies resulted in periodic typhoid epidemics during the early 1900s. Workers also suffered from a host of other ailments, including hookworm, pellagra, and tuberculosis. Poor sanitation also led to an outbreak of malaria that swept the company's villages in 1912, eventually affecting eight thousand workers.[49]

TCI resisted making improvements for years, but its employees—55 percent of whom were African Americans—forced the company to change simply by walking away from the horrible conditions they endured. For example, the year after the malaria outbreak, turnover and absenteeism soared. The company responded to this pressure from below by improving sanitation and housing and by placing doctors in the company towns. The company later built a modern hospital for its workers and their families in the suburb of Fairfield. In addition to health care and housing, the company implemented extensive educational and recreational programs headed by an army of teachers and social workers.[50]

Like DeBardeleben and the other coal operators, TCI officials enforced strict segregation between blacks and whites. In the village of Docena, for example, blacks outnumbered whites twenty-seven hundred to five hundred in the four hundred homes that the company built at the site. At the town's center, TCI officials constructed a "prado," or central plaza. Whites lived in the area closest to the plaza, while blacks lived in the areas further out. African Americans were discouraged from walking through the white sections of Docena, with company regulations requiring them "to go through their streets."[51]

At TCI's mining village of Edgewater, built in 1910, segregation was also the rule, with blacks living on one side and whites on the other. LaMarse Moore, who grew up in the community, recalled few interactions between people of different races. "I can remember the [black] women going over [to white houses] to work," she said. "Evidently they treated them okay, because they always gave them something to bring home. I don't know about anybody else but my grandmother—they had to treat her right because she wouldn't take it." Sometimes, Moore remembered, whites came over to the African American section to sell "watermelons and vegetables and stuff like that."[52]

To reinforce segregation, the Ku Klux Klan maintained a presence near some TCI villages. Mary Parsons Gray, a white woman whose father was a supervisor at the Docena mine, remembered that the Klan suddenly appeared in her church one Sunday and took up a collection. "I was absolutely terrified, and that is all that I remember about it," she said. "I don't remember any talk about it before or since. You couldn't know who anybody was, but they gave money."[53]

But regulating behavior and enforcing the color line remained mostly the task of company officials in TCI camps. Mine officials had the power to determine who could live in the town. According to one worker, a TCI manager had "the right to ask you to move if you didn't perform or your family didn't behave like he thought they ought to." Workers' leases gave the company the right to evict them with a day's notice. TCI used company police deputized by the Jefferson County Sheriff's Department to keep order. All of the guards were white and heavily armed, and they wore "semi-military uniforms." Christine Cochran, a black woman whose husband worked at Docena, recalled that the company deputies would whip both children and adults. If miners tried to resist these beatings, "he'd just kill you right then."[54]

Interviewed years later, most white residents had fond memories of their years in Docena. But many African Americans took a more jaded view of TCI's programs. While they remembered the schools as better than those in the rest of Jefferson County and appreciated the quality of the housing and the health care programs, many blacks remembered the system as exploitative. Cochran, for example, called the company an "absolute monarchy." Herndon remembered his months in TCI's model town of Docena as a time of "endurance and . . . suffering." Far from enjoying the much-touted fruits of the company's paternalism, Herndon recalled that black miners endured brutal working conditions, "maltreatment, ignorance and a bestial atmosphere contrived to keep them blind as bats to their degradation. Every Saturday when they got their pay they went out on a drunk and awoke to their misery the following day more warped and embittered than ever."[55]

Miners' quality of life in the coal camps varied dramatically. TCI and AFICO spent time and resources developing extensive welfare programs, but the smaller camps, particularly those further away from Birmingham, sometimes featured living conditions that shocked contemporaries. In the Walker County village of Winona, near Gorgas, outbreaks of colitis, tuberculosis, typhoid fever, and malaria were not uncommon in the early 1920s. Observers blamed many of these health problems on the poor conditions of the coal camp, which was jointly operated by Alabama Power and Stith Coal. Officials reported that hogs and cattle roamed freely, refuse littered the settlement, and residents lacked access to running water. One company doctor reported that a patient with a bad case of dermatitis caused by flea bites complained that "ten or fifteen hogs sleep under her house nearly every night, and similar conditions exist all over the Winona camp." Miners and their families used tubs and barrels to collect rainwater for much of their basic household use, another potential health hazard. Physician C. K. Maxwell wrote that "this rain water soon becomes stagnated and is the source of mosquito breeding, in connection with the tin cans and the mud holes, already in the camp."[56]

Like other coal operators, Alabama Power segregated its camps. Though conditions in all parts of Winona left much to be desired, Maxwell reported that in the African American section "sanitary conditions are worse than bad." The company houses had no screens on windows and doors, which allowed flies into the dwellings. Miners kept hogs in pens under some of the houses, and brush and tin cans littered the area. "I have had two or three negroes to tell me that their garbage cans are never carried away and that they have to empty them themselves out on the ground," Maxwell reported to Alabama Power officials. "The open toilets in the negro camp are extremely unsanitary."[57]

Alabama Power officials, worried about the toll the Winona camp might take on their image, eventually attempted to improve conditions. The company ran a water line out to the Winona camp from its Gorgas operations, thereby improving the situation somewhat. However, the camp's lack of sanitary facilities continued to cause health problems. Alabama Power's chief surgeon suggested running a sewer line to the village or providing septic tanks for the houses, arguing that the "open toilets, and pit toilets, as I have stated many times, in and around Gorgas are dangerous due to the character of the soil." Because Alabama Power operated the camp with Stith Coal, however, improvements required the approval of both companies. When informed of the sewer line proposal, Stith Coal officials complained about the potential expense. Further, added company executive A. B. Aldridge, "there is no mining camp in Walker County with such a [sewer] system installed and the records show that the county is among the first of the state as to the general health of its people."[58]

Like the general conditions in the coal camps, the way operators enforced the color line often varied as well. In the Walker County mining settlement of Bankhead, where about one-third of the miners were African American, segregation was the rule, but whites and blacks had a cordial relationship. "They looked at people, they didn't look at race too much, back then," remembered Louise Burns, an African American resident. "I think they were more race conscious in the cities than they were in . . . mining camps." In the settlements around Birmingham, black miners might enjoy more autonomy if they lived in one of the all-black independent camps that dotted the landscape. Earl Brown, who was raised in the black Jefferson County mining community of Booker Heights, remembered that he was "raised here in freedom." "On the mining camp you was subjected to white supremacy, but in this area, we were independent," he explained, "we always thought something of ourselves."[59]

While almost 70 percent of miners lived in company housing, the ties to the old agricultural way of life persisted. Almost all miners either raised livestock and had gardens or farmed part-time. A coal miner "had to raise what he needed to eat," remembered Gene McDaniel, who grew up in Slick Lizard, a mining area in northern Walker County. "He only got to work when they needed some coal, which wasn't very regular. In the wintertime, he could work pretty regular. In the summertime, he didn't get much work, so you had to raise a garden. You had to raise what you eat." Charles Fuller, a white miner who grew up in the coal community of Charlotte, remembered that as a child "we lived on a twenty-acre farm. You moonlighted then, between farming and coal mining. That's how we made our living. And it was rough—I mean, you didn't have very much."[60]

Many of the miners who lived on surrounding farms were white, but many of the black miners also had ties to agriculture and rural life. Many of them had journeyed to the Birmingham District to escape sharecropping or tenant farming.

Ernest Walker, who left Mississippi for the Birmingham District in 1939 to find a way out of the poverty he knew as a cropper, remembered, the "old plantation man, he would get everything. We would have nothing to buy a pair of shoes to go to school. We done share it all with him or her. I won't forget that." Fred Bass Sr., who came from rural Jackson, Alabama, to Jefferson County in 1942, followed his brother, who already worked as a miner. Bass owned a farm, but he "was tired of it. I wasn't making no money. I wanted to try something else."[61]

Moving to north Alabama often meant leaving family members behind. Earl Brown's father left for Birmingham from Georgia after World War I when a combination of debt, pests, and low crop yields forced him to give up his farm. He "had some friends who had migrated here to Birmingham, and they told them there was some work here. And that's why he left his family with his brother [in Georgia] and came to get a job here," Brown remembered. "And then after he began work and made a little money and got a place to stay, then he came back and got us."[62]

Coal operators in Alabama and elsewhere hired agents to enlist labor for the mines from the Black Belt and to lure miners from competitors in the coalfields. Jobie Thomas recalled that these agents cruised public events in the Birmingham District, looking for potential recruits. A labor agent typically "wore overalls and a jumper, [with] large pockets, and if he had six or eight pockets on these overalls, he'd had every one of them filled with tens, twenties, and one hundred dollar bills," he remembered. After beginning a conversation with a potential recruit, the agent would "pull out a handful of twenties" and offer to move family, furniture, and belongings into the coal camp.[63]

Labor agents sometimes enticed miners from Alabama to the northern coalfields. In the early 1920s, a recruiter known as Bowlegged Jones lured William Veasly from Birmingham to Fairmont, West Virginia, with the pledge that he "could make better money than you could in Alabama." Northern coal operators sometimes paid black preachers hundreds of dollars to travel to the Birmingham District in search of experienced miners looking for more money. "He'd have a ticket for you and give you $25 or $30, what they called 'transportation,'" Veasly recalled. "Bowlegged Jones said he was gonna ship them till his legs get straight."[64]

For many miners, the journey into the mines was much shorter. In the rural areas north of Jefferson County, small mines began to crop up in the 1930s, serving local markets such as hospitals or schools. Mostly family-run operations, these mines recruited their workforce from among nearby miners and farmers. Solon Roberts and several of his brothers shifted back and forth among a series of small family-run coal mines located along the border of Marion and Walker Counties north of Birmingham. When the orders were filled, the miners found themselves looking for new jobs. "One operator might get a good market for his coal while other, nearby mines were idle," Roberts recalled. "If a mine that had orders needed more labor, like to expand the mine, to make an additional opening, or to load coal, whatever, there was usually plenty of idle labor around a little mine, located up or down the hollow, or just across the branch."[65]

Family connections could prove important for landing jobs in the mines. Young miners often found work in the mines that employed their fathers. In 1939, James "Bentley" White found outside employment at the Bibb County mine where his father worked. A year later, he went underground with his father, "digging tonnage." He stayed with his dad for a little over a year before finding another job in the mine.[66] William Collins was fifteen years old when his father took him into the mines in the early 1920s. "Back then there wasn't no labor law, and if your parents would sign papers for you to go in, . . . why, you could go," Collins remembered. "I wasn't scared. I went in with my dad, and he guided me through all of that."[67]

For most miners, particularly those who arrived from rural, agricultural regions, the mining communities of the Birmingham District represented a significant material advance over their previous circumstances. Despite the poor conditions at many of the villages, the housing was better overall than in the old plantation belt or on the small farms of north Alabama, and more modern camps had electricity and other amenities. "I came out of the country there. And [the coal town] had lights, electric lights," remembered Louise Burns, who left Starkville, Mississippi, for the Jasper area when she was a child. "We had lamps, kerosene lamps out in the country. If the stars and moon didn't shine at night, you didn't have a light. And I thought I was in a big city." Melba Wilbanks Kizzire, who arrived in Docena as a child when her father took a job in the mines there, recalled the surprise she felt at viewing her new home for the first time. The company house was "papered, we had running water—it was cold, but we had running water. We had electricity, and we had our sanitation provided for, our nice house, our churches, our teachers."[68]

But miners also encountered another facet of company life when they arrived: operators' attempts to control their workers. While miners undoubtedly experienced better living conditions in the camps, they also lost some of the autonomy they had known as sharecroppers and small farmers. Company guards patrolled the streets, keeping union organizers away and making it difficult for miners who found better jobs to leave. Among the most notorious fixtures of the mining camps in Alabama were shack rousters, company guards charged with rounding up miners who missed their shifts. Miner C. D. Patterson, who went to work underground in the early 1900s, remembered that shack rousters rode along on their horses, making handcuffed miners run behind. The enforcement was highly selective. If the foreman or company official did not like a miner, he was more likely to "turn his number over" to the rouster.[69]

Many coal towns featured a company store or commissary where miners could buy food, clothing, appliances, and mining equipment. In the TCI mining community of Edgewater, miners bought fruit, vegetables, meat, clothing, shoes, sewing needs, animal feed, hardware, household goods, and kerosene at the store. The establishment made deliveries to miners' homes. The commissary was a social center at Edgewater, housing a post office and a "dope stand" where miners and their families could purchase soft drinks, candy, cigarettes, and ice cream. Docena's company store also formed the town's social center, with miners and their families congregating there and exchanging the "news of the day, who was sick and who was well, you know, just a village gathering place," remembered Margaret Dorsett. "Everybody went to the store every day."[70]

But like many other features of the Birmingham District's coal communities, commissaries had a coercive side. Most featured segregated checkout lines, which reminded black miners and their families of their second-class status. Many mining companies required miners to trade only with the commissary, paying miners in company scrip, sometimes known in Alabama as "clacker." Companies also delayed paying their miners for several weeks when they initially started work, forcing them to take advances on their first paychecks, which they could use only at the company store.[71]

In some instances, the stores contributed significantly to the company's bottom line. In 1933, for example, Alabama Fuel and Iron posted a profit of more than forty-nine thousand dollars at its commissaries. Although it was the fourth year of the Great Depression, revenues from these operations increased almost ten thousand dollars over the previous year. The company profits at the stores in many of AFICO's camps helped offset the losses the company experienced from decreased demand for coal.[72]

To boost profits, company officials sometimes harassed miners who did not shop at the commissaries. William Collins, who worked at mines in Bibb County, remembered that a mine superintendent threatened to fire Collins's brother-in-law after learning that he had taken his business to a nearby independent store. "I'm telling you now, you traded in the store regardless of the price. You traded in the store, or they'd move you," Collins said. Luther Smith, who lived at Docena, rarely patronized the local commissary, however. He remembered that TCI officials would "want to know why you wasn't trading at the store and if you didn't trade at the store, why you . . . tote the company's money and spend it somewhere's else—not for long."[73]

For the majority of miners, particularly those from rural farming areas, coal company health care represented a vast improvement over what they had previously known. Dorsett voiced a sentiment common among many of her neighbors when she remembered that TCI's hospital in Fairfield had "the best equipment in Birmingham and the nicest hospital. And you were real fortunate to be able to go to the TCI employees' hospital if you needed to be hospitalized."[74]

However, the system presented problems for many miners. Relations between mining families and doctors located in the company towns, for example, were sometimes contentious. The racial attitudes of the middle-class white doctors made visits difficult for many black miners. Isaac Pritchet, a black miner from Edgewater, went to the local TCI physician after having breathing problems as a consequence of inhaling sand underground. The doctor "looked at me and said, 'You damned niggers just don't want to work. That's your trouble—you just don't want to work,'" Pritchet said. Though the doctor presumed that Pritchet was lying about his condition, the miner later won disability payments from the state of Alabama for his breathing problems. The class hostility between doctors and white miners also caused trouble. Interviewed years later, one physician claimed that miners and their families "didn't appreciate [TCI's elaborate health care system]. Hell, no. . . . If people get something for nothing, they just don't appreciate it. And that's the way these miners were."[75]

Other miners remembered health systems as substandard. When Harry Fullman, who worked in Bibb County, sustained a bad injury to his foot underground, company officials brought him to the surface, "dumped" him on the ground, and simply left him alone for several hours. The company eventually placed him on a train bound for Birmingham, but by the time he arrived at the hospital and a doctor examined him, "gangrene had set in, and the doctor had to amputate my foot." The coal company paid Fullman only ninety-six cents a day while he recovered from his injury, and he eventually returned to work underground. Collins remembered that many injured miners just kept working instead of going to the company doctor. "If you got hurt, if you could keep from going to the doctor, it was all right," he recalled. "But if you went to the doctor, you was a fired man."[76]

Churches were among the most important institutions of the Birmingham District's coalfields, and here too the color line was tightly drawn, with blacks and whites attending separate congregations. The largest denominations in both the city and the surrounding coalfields, Methodists and Baptists typically had a presence in the mining camps and coal towns, and the companies often built the churches and paid the ministers. Despite sometimes appearing as a symbol of company power and enforcing strict segregation, churches also provided a place for miners and their families to establish a sense of community. Miner Curtis McAdory described the mining community churches as helping miners learn "how to deal with peoples, how to love people and bring them together."[77]

In some of the coal communities, where the association between the church and company appeared too close, attendance remained low. A regional white Methodist leader, concerned by the general lack of enthusiasm in the camps, recommended that services should be led "as often as possible by a miner in the interest of miners." Over time, many ministers gained independence from the companies. In the camps that were not controlled by the companies, miners had more control over their churches. When Earl Brown started in the mines in the 1930s, for example, "the preachers were paid by the membership, and most of the preachers worked in the mine themselves. So they knew the deprivation that they were getting in there." Herbert South, a miner from Marion County, boasted that he dug coal for two decades "and at the same time preached the gospel of the Holy Man from Galilee" until his lungs gave out in the early 1960s. When the UMWA attempted to organize Alabama's mines in the early 1930s, union leader William Mitch recognized that "churches were always influential institutions among the blacks, perhaps more so than among the white."[78]

In TCI's mining towns, Baptists and Methodists often shared buildings and hosted services on alternating Sundays. "We would all get together and go to church together," remembered LaMarse Moore, who grew up in the black section of the TCI village at Edgewater. "We went for the Baptist . . . we went for the Methodists. We had a good time." Different communities sometimes shared preachers. For example, E. L. McFee ministered to the Methodist denominations in both Edgewater and Docena between 1939 and 1941.[79]

Gospel quartets grew out of the churches and became a regular feature of Birmingham District social and religious life. In Walker County, communities and churches sponsored quartets and glee clubs that traveled throughout the area, serving not only as a point of community pride but also as a vital link between isolated coal camps. "They'd come to Bankhead. . . . Our people there would be going to other places, and that was one way they communicated . . . with one another," Louise Burns said. "Through singing—through church."[80]

The Birmingham District also was the scene of religious revivals that attracted large numbers of miners and their families. In the coal camps, churches tried to recruit the best preachers for these events. Christine Cochran remembered that during these revivals, Docena residents "used to meet church all day. . . . Singing, praying, and just slapping your hands." Such events also provided denominations with the opportunity to recruit new members. "You just meet and sing and pray, and then the pastor would preach, and then take in members if members wanted to join, and they might have come from other churches and they could join," Curtis McAdory recalled. "They may be somebody that has never joined a church. They would take them in."[81]

Though Baptists and Methodists dominated, coal camp communities featured a wide range of other religious denominations. Smaller Protestant groups such as the Church of God and Nazarene established a presence, and the Birmingham District was home to large minorities of Roman Catholics, Orthodox Christians, and Jews. Edgewater's Catholics organized the Sacred Mission Chapel shortly after the village opened and for many years held mass in a company house. The mining town of Brookside, which had a large population from Eastern and Southern Europe, featured both Catholic and Eastern Orthodox denominations. The small group of Orthodox miners initially attended the local Roman Catholic services, remembered Annie Latenosky Patchen, because "they are so similar in the ways that they do in church." When the Orthodox mining families "got a chance to build their own church, they split and went their own way." By the early 1900s, even the small Bibb County community of Blocton featured both a Catholic mission and a Jewish synagogue.[82]

More worldly amusements also attracted the attention of miners and their families in the coal camps. Baseball was among the most important diversions. Most of the major companies sponsored teams, sometimes giving easy jobs to miners who were especially skilled players. After traveling the country with barnstorming Negro League all-star teams, former miner Lorenzo "Piper" Davis returned to Birmingham and took a job that paid $3.36 a day with American Cast Iron Pipe in the late 1930s. The company did not pay him for playing, but team members could leave work early on game days, and there were plenty of fringe benefits. "They'd buy you everything—balls, bats, uniforms," he recalled. "They give you a trip and pay all your traveling; didn't have to worry, insurance and everything was paid for. Baseball players had two lockers, baseball equipment in one locker and work clothes, dress clothes, in the other one. It was a better deal than signing with a traveling club. That's why I stayed."[83]

Archie "Dropo" Young, who worked at Woodward Iron's mines at Mulga and played professional baseball, also decided to keep his job in Birmingham. A Negro League team offered him a position as catcher, but the next day he landed a job at the Mulga mine. Because work in the mines was slow—the mine operated only a few days a week—Young rotated between the two. "I would join the ball team and play with them three or four days, and then when my time was up I would leave and come back," he recalled. "That was the way I played ball in the league. Because, you see, I couldn't afford to give up my job because I had a family. [The professional team] begged me. I was scouted two or three times. . . . I had the chance to leave, but I had a family."[84]

The game attracted an almost fanatical following among both white and black miners. Baseball games, like other public events in the Birmingham District, were segregated events. Most large companies fielded both black and white teams in the industrial leagues, and Birmingham featured professional teams for each race that played their games at Rickwood Field. In many coal communities, however, black and white fans supported each other's teams. "When the white team would play, all the blacks would be right there, rooting for them, and when the . . . black teams would play, the whites would be there rooting for them," Louise Burns recalled.[85]

The companies also sponsored elaborate celebrations in the spring and at Christmas. TCI towns celebrated a May Fete, sometimes held collectively at the company's stadium in Fairfield and other times held in the local camps. Jobie Thomas recalled that the companies brought in ribs, ham, watermelon, and ice cream for their workers. They provided entertainment with games such as tug-of-war and baseball and music. "Everybody'd have a big free-for-all," he said. TCI and other companies also held elaborate Christmas celebrations, complete with visits by Santa Claus. At Edgewater, each child received a paper bag or box full of fruit, nuts, and candy. Miners decorated a large Christmas tree at the local baseball field.[86]

Mining families also enjoyed a rich associational life. The coalfields were home to numerous segregated fraternal organizations, including the Knights of Pythias, the Red Men, Masonic lodges, the Odd Fellows, and the Order of the Eastern Star. These groups provided members with a sense of mutual aid and reciprocity, furnishing economic aid and support during difficult times in an era when such social services were hard to come by in the Birmingham District. Some fraternal groups helped pay for funerals, for example. McAdory remembered that some miners belonged to an organization called Club Seven that helped raise money for sick people and "ones that don't have anything."[87]

Mining families found other outlets for recreation through company-sponsored social programs. Social workers at larger companies such as TCI helped the people in mining communities put on plays that featured local schoolchildren and sometimes adults. Members of mining families also could take classes in speech and grammar, and the companies sometimes sponsored dances and other recreational activities.[88]

Payday was among the most festive events in the coal camps. Miners who loaded coal typically received pay based on the number of tons of coal they shoveled into cars underground. As the companies introduced mechanical coal loaders in the 1930s, however, this type of compensation was replaced by daily wages. Those who performed other tasks, like shooting or cutting coal, received wages. As miners waited in segregated lines to pick up their money, preachers looked for converts, and singers sometimes provided entertainment. Vendors also set up barbecue stands.[89]

But other former miners remembered paydays as a more somber affair. As company guards looked on, bill collectors sought out miners who owed them money. The companies also garnisheed the paychecks of miners who had debts for supplies bought at the company stores. Collins remembered that the guards at TCI's operations in the Bibb County community of Blocton often determined who received a paycheck. "You got in line at the payroll office and you had your statement, and [one of the deputies] would come by and if he knew you he'd punch that statement . . . and the paymaster would give you your money," Collins said. "But if you didn't have that hole in it, you didn't go up there. They wouldn't pay you."[90]

Social life flourished on the weekends, particularly after paydays. In the Walker County town of Carbon Hill, miners sometimes hosted "house brew parties," which featured homemade beer. Each house, remembered miner Harry Burgess, would have entertainment and food such as fried fish and barbecue. In Edgewater, families sometimes would take everything out of a room in their house and hold a dance. "We would clear the room," LaMarse Moore said. "It had nothing in it but that piano. As teenagers, that's what we did. And they would barbecue." Traveling piano players would sometimes pass through the coal towns, performing at house parties or juke joints.[91]

Young miners often took their money and headed to Birmingham, where they could find alcohol and women in abundance. For some, such entertainment existed closer to home. Some miners consumed a kind of alcohol known as Joe Louis whiskey, described by Thomas as "old bad whiskey." Others indulged in gambling, though many companies forbade such activity.[92]

The journey to Birmingham was a routine event for many residents of the surrounding coal towns. Though it was not an especially long distance, the trip could prove difficult for miners and their families, most of whom lacked automobiles. Some found their way to Birmingham by train, taxi, bus, or some combination of these different modes. Miners who could afford cars sometimes ferried people to and from the camps for a small fee.[93]

Nancy Inman, an unmarried woman who lived with her father in Docena, traveled to Ensley by taxi or bus once a week when she had an afternoon off from her job at the town's commissary. Sometimes she would have lunch in Ensley. She often ventured further to Birmingham for window shopping or to see a movie. Patchen remembered that her mother made the trip from the Jefferson County coal town of Brookside to Birmingham once a year to pay the family's property taxes and to "buy a few things." According to Patchen, people from Brookside "went in groups. They would say, 'Well, I'm going to town on the train.' They'd go to pay their property tax and go to the store." Miners and their families also traveled to Birmingham to see films, shop, or socialize with relatives living in the city. Louise Burns remembered that many people in the Walker County coal town where she lived "bought all their clothes in Birmingham." Conversely, some miners who lived in the working-class districts around Birmingham took company trains to their jobs in the coalfields on a daily basis.[94]

The gendered nature of mining—the underground world was male—created separate worlds of work for men and women. While men labored in the mines, women in coal communities performed work around the home or, in the case of many African American women, took on part-time jobs. Women in coal communities woke up early in the morning, before their husbands, to make breakfast and pack lunches. Women were in charge of keeping the house clean, and if the family had a garden, women typically did most of the work in it. In homes without running water, women also performed the difficult task of drawing water from a nearby well or hydrant.[95]

Among the more difficult tasks women faced was that of cleaning miners' work clothes, commonly called muckers. Miners emerged from their underground world caked in coal dust, mud, and salt. Louise Burns remembered that she would put her husband's work clothes "in a pot of sudsy water and boil them. Try and get all that out. And we didn't have washing machines; we had rub boards and tubs." Ila Hendrix spent an entire day every week cleaning her husband's work clothes, boiling them in a large pot, rinsing them, cleaning them on a rub board, and washing them again.[96]

Women also bore responsibility for buying, making, and repairing clothing. If they could afford it, some women purchased clothing from the company store, or from the Sears and Roebuck and Montgomery Ward catalogs. Others recycled sacks that had held animal feed or flour into children's clothes. "My grandmother would take those flour sacks—they had beautiful designs on them—and that's how she would make my dresses," LaMarse Moore remembered. "And I was one of the best-dressed little girls around."[97]

Miners and their families also encountered reminders that they lived close to the margins. Old miners who could no longer stand the physical strain of the job, Christine Cochran remembered, had no choice but to rely on their sons and daughters for help. Those who lacked family ended up destitute. These broken miners "were kind of the pity," she recalled. Some might find some public assistance in Ensley or another nearby city, but in the coal camps at "that time, welfare didn't reach us. . . . They didn't know we were out here." Jefferson County operated a woefully inadequate almshouse for indigent people. In 1928, a grand jury declared the facility "unfit for human beings" and a "monument to the utter indifference of Jefferson County taxpayers and an indictment of every Board of Revenue that has served in the past twenty-five years."[98]

The Great Depression and New Deal would begin the process of transforming the coal towns of the Birmingham District in ways that the coal operators and miners never imagined. Most industries had enjoyed their peak in the mid-1920s and by the time of the stock market crash in the fall of 1929 were already in the midst of a slowdown. By the third year of the crisis, the effects were widespread. In June 1932, twenty-five thousand of the one hundred thousand potential wage and salary earners in Birmingham were unemployed. Officials believed that sixty thousand of those in the city who had jobs worked only part time. One agency estimated that between six thousand and eight thousand people lacked adequate food, fuel, and housing. Three years later, the number of people on relief rolls had risen to one hundred thousand. "Hundreds of people are starving, slowly starving in my district and in many other parts of the country," Congressman George Huddleson of Birmingham told his fellow lawmakers in Washington, D.C. "The situation is desperate."[99]

Birmingham relied mainly on private aid to remedy the effects of the economic crisis. Most of the relief efforts were administered by the Red Cross Family Service and bankrolled by the local Community Chest. By 1931, however, relief officials found that they had less than a quarter of the money needed to help people who had run out of options, and the following year the Red Cross found itself one hundred thousand dollars in debt. The Red Cross, which could meet the needs of 800 families a month, had a caseload of almost 4,000 families and an additional 5,000 applicants for help early in the depression. Four years into the downturn, 23,208 families received some kind of help from the organization. Birmingham officials paid families less in relief money than many other southern cities—only nine dollars per month. Richmond and Dallas, for example, paid recipients fourteen dollars a month.[100]

Homeless camps sprang up throughout the Birmingham District. In the city, the poor gathered in a handful of areas, while Jasper and Carbon Hill also saw large settlements emerge. The Birmingham Salvation Army, which provided some temporary shelter, saw its caseload increase from 7,212 people in 1930 to 19,384 people in 1932. The depression's widespread effects were illustrated by a 1934 federal survey of housing conditions in the Birmingham area. More than half of the nearly eighty-three thousand homes examined needed some kind of repair work, and nearly twenty thousand required serious "structural" improvements.[101]

The Great Depression brought the state's coal industry to its knees, and the effects swept across the mining districts. Few of the state's 23,956 miners enjoyed stable work. Coal production plummeted from more than 21.5 million tons in 1926 to less than 9 million tons in 1933, and the number of large mines in the state dropped from 260 to 108, eliminating an estimated 9,000 jobs. Miners who managed to remain employed worked substantially fewer days: in the 1920s, the typical mine operated more than 232 days a year, but by 1933 that number had dropped to 148.[102]

All of the major markets for Alabama coal—home heating, railroads, steamship fuel, power plants, and coke making—declined by rates approaching 60 percent during the depression years. Birmingham District producers increasingly found their business limited to Alabama, as markets outside the state needed less and less coal. Out-of-state markets took almost a third of the Birmingham District's coal in 1926; nine years later, they consumed less than 14 percent.[103]

Coal communities declined dramatically. So many of Blocton's mines had closed by January 1931 that a local newspaper proclaimed the hamlet a "deserted village." Later that month, in another telling development, the newspaper announced that it was "for lease to [a] reliable local party." In West Blocton, the local bank failed in the fall of 1931. By the mid-1930s, the local chapters of the Knights of Pythias and the Red Men had become inactive. Even West Blocton's Chamber of Commerce, launched with a great deal of fanfare in 1928, ceased to operate.[104]

The crisis forced the commercial giant Alabama Fuel and Iron to suspend its dividends in 1933 when it lost its major railroad customer. As its markets dried up, company president Charles DeBardeleben converted his mining communities into glorified plantations. The company suspended rent payments at its houses and encouraged miners to farm. It advanced employees plows, mules, hogs, jars, and sugar. The amount of acreage under cultivation at the AFICO mining villages grew dramatically from one thousand acres in 1932 to four thousand a year later. The company earned $76,352 from the enterprises, which helped feed the mining villages and lessened the financial losses at some mines where coal production diminished.[105]

As the crisis continued, it deeply affected even the captive mines. By 1932, TCI cut back its Birmingham-area operations by more than 80 percent as its parent company, U.S. Steel, reported losses of $70 million. As the company curtailed coal production, its miners sometimes found themselves working only a few days a year. The payroll for the company's mines at Docena, for example, declined from more than $113,000 annually to under $4,000 by 1933. In 1934, employment at the Docena mining complex had dropped from one thousand to seventy-eight miners. The crisis also forced TCI to begin widespread cutbacks in its prized welfare programs. The company advanced impoverished employees credit that they could use for emergency relief and allowed miners to remain in company-owned housing while they were out of work. But TCI's charity came at a price: the company threatened to evict miners from company housing if they attempted to declare bankruptcy and reorganize their debts.[106]

Miners and their families in most parts of the Birmingham District remembered the early years of the Great Depression as a time of sustained unemployment. Elmer Burton of Gamble in northern Walker County had already labored in the mines for more than twenty years when the company for which he worked shut down in 1929, sending him on an odyssey in search of work. Burton was lucky that he had already purchased a car, and over the next four years he shuttled among three jobs in different parts of Walker and Jefferson Counties. He finally found a regular job at the large operation in Praco in Jefferson County. On some days, his efforts in the mines "wouldn't make a dollar."[107]

Louise Burns recalled that at the height of the Great Depression, miners in Bankhead worked only one day a week. Miners grew food in gardens and often had some livestock, but as the economic crisis continued, they came to depend on food and material assistance from relief officials, supplementing their diets by hunting for rabbits and other game. When they needed fuel for heating, miners and their families combed the surrounding countryside, picking up coal on the side of the road and cutting firewood from nearby forests.[108]

Harry Burgess, a black miner whose father worked in the mines around Fayette and Walker Counties, remembered that many miners went to work for the county, cycling back and forth between the mines—when they operated—and public employment. Like Burns, Burgess recalled relief officials distributing food to help miners who had nothing to eat. Burgess remembered the humiliating ritual of going on public relief: "If you applied for assistance they had to come and see what you had in your house before you got any assistance. It was rough. I was just a kid, but I remember it well."[109]

President Franklin D. Roosevelt's New Deal programs provided some relief to unemployed miners, but even these efforts fell short. In November 1933, the Civil Works Administration began to hire some of Alabama's 129,000 people who would benefit from the agency's programs. Designed to help poor families through the winter of 1933 and 1934, the program extended $15 million in aid to the state before being terminated in the spring of 1934. When the effort ended, however, Birmingham officials faced thousands people who needed help. Furthermore, the program aided only about a third of the city's 46,000 people eligible for assistance.[110]

Other programs lasted longer. The Works Progress Administration (WPA), which provided millions of dollars for public projects, established two large housing developments in the Birmingham District. The Alabama Relief Administration put people to work in small factories and garages. The National Youth Administration began to provide jobs and educational opportunities, while the

Civilian Conservation Corps (CCC) employed 67,000 Alabamians between 1933 and 1942.[111]

For some miners and their families, these programs provided a lifeline as the coal industry lay dormant. Louise Burns found a job at a National Youth Administration nursery school for two days a week when her husband's job evaporated. She remembered federal programs as "the only way they had to survive back then. If it hadn't been for WPA, I don't know what they would have done. That started opening up jobs for people. And helping people to feel sort of independent." Woodie Roberts, who spent his life working the small mines in the northern Birmingham District, entered a CCC camp in the fall of 1940, toward the end of the program's life. He spent seven months in the camp and left when the federal government began to shut the operations down. Though Roberts earned less money in the CCC than he could have in the mines, he hoped to learn valuable skills. To Roberts, the federal program "seemed the thing to do when I did it. A lot of the young fellows I knew there in Marion County were going into the CCC camps."[112]

The depression and New Deal confronted Alabama's mining communities with an unprecedented crisis. Welfare capitalism lost credibility as private and localized efforts largely failed in their attempts to help the Birmingham District's poor. By contrast, New Deal programs helped some miners in the region, but these efforts often emerged as piecemeal programs that provided only limited assistance. To make life better, white and black miners in Alabama would have to take matters into their own hands.

Miners would seek to do so by bringing back their old union, the UMWA, during the early 1930s. The new federal presence provided invaluable assistance for this effort, and the miners used the protections afforded by the New Deal to gain the union a permanent foothold in the Alabama coalfields. Black and white miners drew on their shared culture to confront the color line, the most divisive issue in their communities, the region, and the nation. In so doing, miners extended the complex nature of their relationship in the underground world into the public realm, wrestling with the issues of white supremacy and social equality in a different forum. How they dealt with these issues in large part determined the fate of their union and their place in the Alabama coal industry.

CHAPTER TWO

The UMWA and the Color Line in Alabama, 1933–1942

Black organizer Walter Jones has emerged as a leading figure in the accounts surrounding the reemergence of United Mine Workers of America (UMWA) in Alabama in the early 1930s. Jones was a lifelong activist in the miners' union, joining the organization in 1898 and serving as both a district and international organizer from 1917 to 1919 and 1920 to 1922. After mine operators and state officials vanquished the UMWA from the Birmingham District, he worked in Ohio and Pennsylvania before returning to Alabama in the summer of 1933. He joined the UMWA local at Pratt City and worked as a volunteer with the organizers that the union's president, John L. Lewis, sent to help reestablish the union in the region. The three organizers, district president William Mitch, and international representatives William Dalrymple and William Raney, hailed from other states. All were also white, and when the UMWA appointed Jones as an organizer in the fall of 1933, the action was viewed as a manifestation of the union's commitment to its black members, who comprised a majority of the organization in Alabama.[1]

Jones went on to become perhaps the most revered organizer in the history of District 20, the Alabama branch of the union. His memory has eclipsed even that of Mitch in many older miners' accounts. His oratorical and union-building skills were legendary. Earl Brown, a black

44

miner who much later became a district official for the union, recalled that Jones would rally black miners during organizing meetings and then Mitch would "come in and sign them up." Mitch's son, who knew Jones, remembered him as a "hardshell Baptist" and an "effective orator" who "could speak to his own people." When Jones died in 1937, more than a thousand people attended his funeral. In a tribute to his popularity and his brilliance, the UMWA placed a large headstone at his gravesite.

But the relationship between Walter Jones and the UMWA in Alabama was complicated, illustrating a great deal about the ways that race functioned in the miners' union when it ventured into the southern coalfields. Though Jones was a veteran union organizer, he struggled to find a job with District 20. In particular, Mitch and other UMWA officials worried about how local whites would perceive the presence of a black man in a union leadership position.

Jones's fight for a job began in October 1933, when he wrote to Lewis requesting a paid position with District 20. Though the union had signed up thousands of members and had established locals throughout the Birmingham District, the organization remained on tenuous ground. The region's coal operators had not fully recognized the UMWA, and unrest began to sweep through the region as angry miners walked out in protest. Jones noted that the union officials "will have to stay on the job every minute of the day to combat [coal operators'] efforts" to break the union and told Lewis that organizers would need "local help" to sustain the UMWA in the state. The UMWA president declined the request despite Jones's vast experience as an organizer in District 20. "I appreciate your desire to be of assistance to your organization and would be glad indeed to comply with your request if conditions were such as to permit me to do so," Lewis wrote. "It happens, however, that no additional appointments are contemplated at the present time."[2]

Jones's frustration grew a few weeks later, when he heard that Mitch planned to employ a former UMWA and American Federation of Labor (AFL) official in a paid District 20 position. The former activist, William Harrison, had not played a major role in the 1933 organizing drive. Jones wrote an angry letter to Lewis protesting the proposed appointment, charging that Harrison had "lost his pull with labor in Alabama."[3]

Racial concerns formed the core of Jones's complaint. For the first time since 1898, when the UMWA had emerged in Alabama and when Jones had joined the organization, it employed no African Americans in the state. Jones warned Lewis that District 20's failure to hire blacks could damage the reestablishment efforts. "It is not reason to believe that [African Americans] will continue always to subscribe to the U.M.W. of A. programe, with out some consideration from a representative point of view," Jones warned. "The coal companies and their agents keep it constantly before them, that the U.M.W. of A. is a white man's organization, and the Negro is used only as a tool. We have to fight that propaganda on every side, and it becomes a difficult problem to combat, when there is not a single Negro, that this great host can point to as a legal representative of the U.M.W. of A."[4]

The letter created a major controversy within the UMWA organization in Birmingham. Mitch, placed on the defensive by the criticism, admitted that Jones was a "very good speaker" who had done "splendid work" for the UMWA. But Mitch defended his decision not to put Jones on the payroll "because the operators, bosses, and superintendents give but very little consideration whatever to negroes down here," a situation that would make Jones ineffective in a formal union position. The District 20 president suggested that Jones was "trying to force himself on as a colored representative," adding that "it seems to me that he is going at it backwards."[5]

Jones's protest fed into divisions that had emerged within the District 20 leadership by the fall of 1933. In his letter to Lewis, Jones had informed the union president that Raney and Dalrymple, the other officials in the Alabama district, would back up many of his assertions about Mitch's plans for Harrison. While Jones's letter did not explicitly mention Mitch's management of District 20, the state president clearly was the target of the protest.

The criticism caught the District 20 president by surprise. Mitch voiced concern about Dalrymple and Raney discussing district matters with Jones—an accusation that both men denied—and added "that in some respects I have not received full cooperation down here." In fact, Mitch already had been working behind the scenes to ease Dalrymple out of the Alabama district. Dalrymple's fiery rhetoric resonated with the rank and file but angered coal operators and government officials. Mitch had written to Lewis in October 1933 that the coal operators and government regulators "bitterly oppose dealing with Representative Dalrymple because they contend that he has used profanity and vehemently attacked them and their representatives." Dalrymple had already suggested a transfer, and Mitch urged Lewis to grant the request. Lewis removed Dalrymple from District 20 in December, a development that many Alabama union members protested. Raney would stay, but not before he made a lengthy apology for the Jones episode, praising Mitch's leadership and denying "any breach of friendship, confidence, or cooperation at all between Mr. Mitch and myself."[6]

Mitch and Jones eventually reconciled, and the District 20 president brought the African American activist on as a district representative. Jones later told Lewis that the letter had been "an injustice" and reiterated his support for Mitch. "I have every confidence in Mr. Mitch's ability to handle this district and meant no personal stab at him," Jones wrote to the national president.[7]

However, the difficulties that Jones encountered when he attempted to obtain a paid position with the union illuminated the institutional obstacles to black advancement within the UMWA that existed when it returned to Alabama. Union leaders worried about how the wider world of segregationist Alabama would perceive the organization's racial policies and thus restricted leadership opportunities for African Americans.

An examination of the UMWA's place in the system of race relations in the Birmingham District from the early 1930s through the first year of World War II reveals a complex situation in the union's leadership structure, underground in the mines, and in union halls. The UMWA welcomed both blacks and whites into its ranks, and while the top offices went to whites, avenues to black advancement existed within the union. Most importantly, the UMWA fought for higher wages, better working conditions, and fairer treatment in the mines for all its members, regardless of race. As Jones's example suggests, the miners' union both challenged southern racial norms and accommodated to them. In some ways, the miners' union led a direct assault on the southern racial order—particularly when it fought for the enfranchisement of its black members—but in other ways it left the structural underpinnings of segregation in place.

Despite such compromises, the UMWA occupied a key space in the struggle over the future of race relations in the Birmingham District in the 1930s and early 1940s. After almost a half century of violent suppression by Alabama's coal operators and local and state political leaders, the UMWA established a permanent presence in the coalfields around Birmingham in the early 1930s.[8] The miners' union also played a crucial role in the establishment of the industrial union movement in Alabama in the late 1930s. Under the auspices of the Congress of Industrial Organizations (CIO), unions that included both whites and blacks had established important beachheads in the Birmingham District's iron and steel mills and in its ore mines.

In the Birmingham District, the UMWA was always profoundly shaped by the racial climate, however, and by the first year of World War II racial tensions had reached a boiling point. As white anxiety became more pronounced after the mid-1930s, a complex struggle emerged over the UMWA's racial policies. Industrial and political elites became nearly hysterical in their fears about the demise of the "southern way of life," particularly following summer 1942 hearings in Birmingham by the President's Committee on Fair Employment Practice (FEPC). These elites began sharp attacks on what they perceived as the causes of their anxiety—industrial unionism, assertive African Americans, and the federal government.

Racial fears also divided the Birmingham District's working class, and the UMWA found its policies under attack from elements of the craft-union-dominated AFL after the mid-1930s. In the summer of 1942, following a bitter break between the UMWA and CIO, elements within the miners' union began a racially tinged campaign to represent workers at the region's iron ore mines, who were then members of the leftist International Union of Mine, Mill, and Smelter Workers (commonly known as Mine Mill).

This chapter examines the racial tensions in Birmingham and the region's labor movement during the New Deal era and the early years of World War II. It explores the ways these tensions manifested themselves in Birmingham and within the UMWA and the manner in which the wider world shaped the union's racial policies. The challenges that Walter Jones faced were not uncommon in the UMWA, and the veteran union activist took center stage in some of the early battles over race that occurred both within and outside the union. As racial tension became more pronounced during the late 1930s and early 1940s, the miners' union's commitment to its black members grew increasingly circumscribed.

(((

The Great Depression shattered the illusion of harmony that Birmingham's industrial leaders had sought to construct since the defeat of the UMWA in 1921 and created conditions that allowed miners to reestablish the union. Before the economic crisis, however, the return of the miners' union would have been hard to imagine. The number of UMWA members in Alabama had declined so far after its defeat during the bitter 1920–21 strike that the union had closed its state offices at the end of the decade. But in the early 1930s, the depression had swept across the landscape of the Birmingham District, leading President Roosevelt to label the city the "worst hit town in the country."[9]

The deepening crisis created economic and political conditions that propelled the reestablishment of District 20. As the situation grew more desperate, unrest increased in the mining regions. In July 1932, miners walked out at Republic Steel's Sayreton mine, located just north of Birmingham, to protest poor treatment by supervisors. The strikers had little to lose—at the time, they typically worked one day a week and earned eight dollars a month. Republic officials sent company guards to the scene, but they failed to intimidate the miners, and the strike continued. The miners finally returned to work after the company agreed to discipline the managers in question and to improve working conditions. A few months later, in January 1933, miners walked out in Bankhead to protest a 30 percent wage cut imposed by Cane Creek Coal. These isolated incidents emboldened the UMWA and its president, John L. Lewis, and shortly thereafter, he sent international representative William Dalrymple to lobby the region's political leaders to endorse legislation designed to bring stability to the coal industry. Secondarily, Dalrymple was to survey the district and gauge the chances for a renewed UMWA organizing drive.

Alabama's miners and the UMWA found an important ally in President Roosevelt and the New Deal programs that set about reorganizing American industry in the face of unprecedented crisis. The passage of the National Industrial Recovery Act (NIRA) in the spring of 1933 allowed major industries, including coal, to establish production codes. These codes, though voluntary, regulated everything from wages to production levels. Among the leading coal operators from Alabama who met in Washington, D.C., with officials from around the nation to draft a national code was Henry T. DeBardeleben, president of the militantly antiunion DeBardeleben Coal. DeBardeleben and officials from the Alabama Mining Institute, the major lobbying organization for the state's coal operators, dominated the delegation. The Alabama delegates stressed the difficult geologic conditions faced by the state's operators, which made the region's coal less competitive than that from other areas. Thin seams divided by sections of rock and slate resulted in impurities that had to be removed from the coal and required more labor per ton than coal from competing coalfields, they argued. Hydroelectric power, natural gas, and oil, which the officials called "laborless fuels," also provided a low-cost alternative to Alabama coal.[10]

At the summer 1933 meetings, Alabama operators advocated thirty cents an hour for inside labor and twenty-five cents an hour for outside labor, only a slight increase from the typical maximum wage of $2.00 a day that most miners earned during the depression. The code that bituminous operators and President Roosevelt approved in September included higher wages than Alabama Mining Institute officials had hoped. It allowed operators to pay a daily wage of $3.40 for underground miners and $2.40 for those who worked outside and limited the workday to eight hours. Because the code included regional "differentials," Alabama miners still made less than those in other parts of the country.[11]

In early June, Lewis sent a close UMWA ally, William Mitch, to head up an organizing campaign in Alabama. Mitch, an Ohio native and former Indiana UMWA official, joined Dalrymple and Raney, who was also from Indiana, in the effort. Mitch, a former socialist who had run for both local and federal office, had served as secretary-treasurer of the Indiana district for about fifteen years before miners in District 11 voted him out of office in 1931. Lewis had taken center stage in this election, and Mitch had paid a heavy price for his loyalty to the union president, going down to defeat at the hands of an anti-Lewis candidate. Lewis eventually brought Mitch into the national office as a "special representative," then sent him to Birmingham to head up the organizing drive in the union's southernmost district. In Alabama, Mitch played a central role in the rebirth of the UMWA and the creation of the state's vibrant industrial union movement a few years later. He served as the first president of the state's CIO organization, the Alabama State Industrial Union Council, and as regional director of the CIO-affiliated Steel Workers Organizing Committee (SWOC).[12]

Buoyed by the protections they believed they enjoyed under the NIRA's Section 7(a), which suggested that workers had the right to organize and to bargain collectively with their employers, thousands of Alabama miners flocked into the UMWA fold in the summer and fall of 1933. Carl McKeever, then just a boy, remembered fanning out through the mining communities around Nauvoo in Walker County with his father to sign up union members. In many cases, miners' wives welcomed the effort to reestablish the union although their husbands remained more cautious, remembering the bitter defeat of the early 1920s. McKeever recalled encouraging the women, though they did not work in the mines and were not eligible for union membership, to sign union cards by using their first and middle initials instead of full names. The sight of their wives willingly signing union petitions sometimes shamed men into joining the UMWA. "We'd get two signatures right there," McKeever remembered. "We wound up with about eight or nine hundred members around Nauvoo, and there were about four hundred miners. We had twice as many as we had miners. So it was overwhelming." Both McKeever, who was white, and black miner Harry Burgess, whose fathers enthusiastically joined the UMWA, recalled that miners were driven by a sense of desperation as the depression dragged on. "You didn't have anything to lose," McKeever said. "You had hit rock bottom. If you lost your job, you didn't lose nothing."[13]

Many pro-union miners found themselves unemployed despite the protections that the NIRA supposedly provided. The DeBardeleben family operations—DeBardeleben Coal and Alabama Fuel and Iron (AFICO)—proved among the worst offenders in this respect. A federal investigator, looking into the reports of retaliation against union activists in the summer of 1933, concluded that it would "require more than conciliation to stop them from coercing and interfering with their employees (whom they have in corrals) exercising their rights under the Industrial Recovery Act without interference. In my opinion, if these two companies could be straightened out and could be shown that their idea of rule or ruin would not be tolerated, it would generally clear up the condition in this part of Alabama."[14]

Coal operator opposition to the UMWA presence led to a series of strikes that rolled across Alabama in August and October 1933 as miners attempted to force the companies to recognize the union. Though the October strikes eventually compelled the operators to participate in a local, three-member Coal Labor Board that included Mitch, little was solved. Another series of walkouts would be required before most of the operators settled with the union.[15]

In their efforts to reestablish District 20, Mitch and other union organizers exercised caution when they confronted the color line. The operators had often sought to divide the miners by race during earlier walkouts and organizing drives, with only moderate success. Industrial elites accomplished more when they raised the specter of the union's efforts to promote social equality among black and white miners. In several previous walkouts, most notably a huge 1908 strike, such appeals had provoked the state's political leaders to intervene and break the UMWA. In the 1930s, Mitch was in no mood to take chances. Though the UMWA accepted both white and black miners without hesitation, local meetings were segregated affairs, and miners usually organized racially separate sections of the coal camps. In their attempts to bring blacks into the union, Mitch and other UMWA organizers typically worked through African American leaders who, according to his son, "did their own organizing." Churches proved particularly important in this process. They often provided a focal point for mining communities and played an important role in rallying support for the union. Fraternal organizations such as the Knights of Pythias also helped union organizers spread the word.[16]

Early support for the union may have been strongest among African Americans, who saw the organization as a vehicle through which to fight for their rights both underground and on the surface. In the early 1930s, researchers have estimated, black miners comprised 60 percent of the UMWA's membership in Alabama. Leon Alexander, a black man who worked at Sloss-Sheffield's Lewisburg mine in the early 1930s, remembered that blacks supported the union more in the early organizing efforts "because the news media and other whites just naturally ostracized the whites who would join the union."[17]

The actions of UMWA President John L. Lewis, who voiced a strong commitment to the rights of the union's black members, inspired much of the enthusiasm among black miners. Lewis, Mitch, and other UMWA leaders opposed the poll taxes and literacy tests that kept African Americans as well as many working-class whites from voting in Alabama and the rest of the South. Lewis reiterated his support for political and civil rights for black workers when he addressed the summer 1940 national convention of the National Association for the Advancement of Colored People. At the third National Negro Congress, Lewis proclaimed that he supported "equality of opportunity for the Negro people. I do not try to conceal the fact. I am rather anxious that a great many people find out about our views."

Indeed, some industrialists, seeking to scare white miners away from the UMWA and CIO, claimed that Lewis was "about three quarters Negro himself."[18]

On the local level, the stance by Lewis and other UMWA leaders attracted strong support from black miners. "We as negro in the South have learn who is our frend," Flat Top union official W. L. Bush wrote to Lewis. Bush praised Lewis as "the first one to let us sit in Council with our white works. we know that you were the first one to try to get us the same pay that were pay to all other mens in our class of works." Added Henry Mayfield, a black miner from Pratt City, "The Negro people of the South believe in you and in the principles of the CIO and the UMWA."[19]

Plenty of white miners flocked to the union fold as well, and in the early days the color line seemed to shift in important ways. When state relief officials allocated less money to blacks in northern Jefferson County in the summer of 1934, for example, members of the UMWA local at Kimberly protested and went on strike. "We don't believe that the Congress when Appropriating this Money to feed the Un-Employed meant to Discriminate against the Negro, But it is being done here in Alabama today," they wrote to Lewis. In Dixiana, interracial union activity sparked a resurgence of the Ku Klux Klan, which held a march and burned a cross in front of a union activist's home. "We don't have the slightest intention of [allowing] the Ku Klux Klan or any other kind of a company organization to tear our union up," UMWA members defiantly proclaimed in a statement adopted at a local meeting and forwarded to Lewis.[20]

Persistent reports of armed white and black miners sweeping through the coalfields emerged from the Birmingham District during the early organizing drive. For example, when miners walked out at the mines around Piper and Coleanor in Bibb County in February 1934 to protest the failure of the area's coal companies to deduct union dues from miners' paychecks, officials reported that an "armed mob" of "white and black" miners disarmed a group of fifteen deputy sheriffs sent to break the strike. The miners then guarded the roads to the mines and, according to one observer, searched all vehicles passing by for "strike breakers and deputies."[21]

The appearance of interracial solidarity so disturbed Alabama Governor Benjamin Miller that he sent a battalion of National Guardsmen from Birmingham to Bibb County to prevent the strikes from spreading. Nevertheless, by March, the walkouts had expanded to Walker and Jefferson Counties. Walker County sheriff A. N. Barrentine reported that hundreds of miners armed with "clubs and guns" enforced strikes against companies in an attempt to compel them to deduct union dues from paychecks. At one point, soldiers were sent to the Aldrich mine, where they found "a mob consisting of 540 men, white and black," armed with rifles and shotguns.[22]

By 9 March, a month after the strikes began, the walkouts had spread further, and officials estimated that more than ten thousand miners were on strike. Additional reports of "negroes and white[s]" marching together during the strikes alarmed local and state officials. Miller ordered the head of the Alabama National Guard, General J. C. Persons, to bring the miners and operators together to negotiate. Persons complied, and the strike wave temporarily ended on 16 March when the operators agreed to a dues checkoff. But the Alabama operators refused to comply with the NIRA coal code's wage and hour provisions. By early April, a combination of strikes and lockouts at many commercial operations idled twenty-one thousand miners.[23]

Believing that the public would not support the UMWA's perceived assault on segregation, officials tried to focus attention on the level of cooperation among black and white miners. In one of the largest incidents, 750 miners defied the National Guard and machine guns to close Jefferson County's Porter mine. The company's vice president of operations reported to Governor Miller that "radical labor agitators" and "communists" had "called negroes in this district 'Mister' and 'Brother,' and put their arms around them and fraternized with them in public meeting places." The strike wave had, as a result, moved beyond issues of wages, hours, and working conditions, the official argued, becoming "a question of whether or not mobs composed of illiterate, ignorant blacks, and some illiterate whites, can continue to ignore and defy all of our laws. [Their attitude] is worse than at any time since reconstruction."[24]

Walker County–based DeBardeleben Coal, among the strongest holdouts against the UMWA, protested that mobs of "both whites and blacks, and many of both races" had invaded the company's Coal Valley operations during the walkouts. In an advertisement placed in a local newspaper, the company complained that armed union miners entered "the homes of the workers, threatening and terrorizing their families." DeBardeleben officials noted that the "mob was armed with shotguns and rifles, and consisted of both whites and blacks."[25]

The dramatic reports emanating from the coalfields and the public statements of Mitch and Lewis projected an image of equality. But the reality inside the UMWA in Alabama proved more complex. Though most of the state's miners were black, Mitch and the other top union leaders were white. At the local level, the organization took a gradualist approach to race relations. Its policy, well established by the 1930s, became known as the "UMW formula," where whites represented the union in public and African Americans accepted an auxiliary status in terms of leadership. Regardless of the local union's racial mix, presidents and secretary-treasurers were typically white, while the vice presidents and lower officers were typically black. White and black miners met together in local union halls, sometimes in open defiance of local ordinances that forbade integrated meetings, but often used different entrances and "voluntarily" divided themselves by race. "Neither race shows distaste for being present together in the same hall, but each preserves a plain if unspoken racial distance," an early account of UMWA meetings in Alabama noted. "Almost without exception the two races sit in segregated parts." During these events, according to one early observation, blacks were "never Mister, and are seldom Brother." When Burgess joined the UMWA in the late 1930s, he remembered that the union pledge was altered. "You took an oath that said you wouldn't discriminate against your brother," he said. "They kind of changed that a little bit. Instead of saying 'brother' they said a 'member of the union.'" Mitch outlined his caution in dealing with racial issues in Alabama near the end of the decade to A. D. "Denny" Lewis, the brother of the UMWA national president: Mitch recognized how "delicate the negro question is in Alabama; and knowing that I have always handled it with gloves on . . . and the negroes have cooperated splendidly. And they don't want social relationship or intermingling of negroes and whites."[26]

Still, the UMWA often fought impressively during the early days of the New Deal on behalf of the rights of its African American members. During the early organizing drives, for example, white miners occasionally pressed District 20 officials to establish Jim Crow locals. Organizers stood firm, informing miners "that the labor of both the colored and the white man is on a par industrially." Mitch reported that "the majority seem to readily understand." The union also provided an important arena in which African American miners could make their views known. Though whites typically took the lead during the UMWA's early years in Alabama, for example, observers reported that blacks often rose and spoke. Miners strike a balance "between adherence to and departure from traditional southern ways," one account noted. Where African Americans held the majority in a local, they participated more readily; where they were in the minority, however, they found themselves "Jim-Crowed mightily."[27]

Economist Herbert Northrup, who traveled to the Alabama coalfields in the early 1940s, believed that the UMWA's "gradualism" had resulted in substantial gains for African Americans. Blacks served on mine grievance committees, for example, and challenged arbitrary treatment by white supervisors. African Americans also had substantial influence in their local unions, and cooperation between whites and blacks had led to a general weakening of the color line that divided the two groups. Northrup noted that whites had begun to call blacks "Brother" during meetings and that miners shook hands with those of other races. Black miners also contributed "freely to discussions" in local unions. In general, Northrup noted, relations between whites and blacks were less formalized and more relaxed in the early 1940s than had been the case a decade earlier.[28]

A story told by Alexander illustrated how the color line softened over time. When black and white members of the local at TCI's Edgewater mine, where Alexander later worked, attempted to rent a hall in nearby Wylam to hold meetings, the building's owners demanded that the union enforce strict segregation, requiring that white and black miners use different entrances and sit on separate sides of the hall with a partition dividing the sections. According to Alexander, however, the miners openly defied most of these restrictions, entering the hall together through the African American entrance in the back and refusing to erect the partition. At first, the miners sat in separate white and black sections, but "we soon broke that up. We had some reasonable white men that was in the union that was more concerned about working conditions and living standards than they were about upholding some racial ideology."[29]

In Northrup's eyes, the most important advances for African American miners came in union protections against retribution from supervisors and other company officials. Black miners who "would have risked physical violence had they raised their voices in joint union-management meetings now argue their cases quite freely as their fellow white members." Black miners' involvement in the grievance process resulted in "material, as well as psychological" advancement, Northrup wrote.[30]

But as Northrup noted, UMWA's biracialism failed to confront directly the issue of white supremacy in the mines at a time when technological changes in the coal industry began to eliminate African American jobs. Throughout the 1930s, as unionized miners demanded higher wages, coal operators responded by mechanizing their operations to reduce costs. Black coal miners, who were heavily concentrated in coal loading jobs, increasingly found themselves replaced by loading machines operated by white miners. The UMWA's gradualist approach on race relations left most of the hiring and promoting power in the hands of the coal companies, which considered machine operating jobs "white man's work." The UMWA did not give "technological unemployment" serious consideration and essentially allowed the operators a free hand in replacing hand loaders with machines. Mitch articulated the union's position when he told the FEPC in the summer of 1942 that the UMWA "has nothing to do with the employment" and that the companies "reserve unto themselves under contract the right to employ or discharge" miners. The union's contracts with Alabama's coal producers did not contain specific language on seniority and technological unemployment until the late 1930s, and even then the provisions were vague and deferred to tradition and custom. As a result, Northrup concluded, "white miners may be said to have benefited from unionism to a somewhat greater extent than Negroes."[31]

The wartime demand for labor obscured these losses as African Americans found jobs in other industries or joined the military. But Alabama's coal industry faced underlying problems that posed unsettling questions for the UMWA and its policies toward its black members. Oil and natural gas made major inroads in markets where Alabama's coal companies formerly had enjoyed little competition. Hydroelectric power also ate into Alabama coal markets.

More troubling, perhaps, was the potential loss of the lucrative railroad market. On the eve of World War II, railroads were the largest customers for the commercial coal mines, with about a third of the coal produced in Alabama's mines finding its way to steam locomotives. But by the early 1940s, diesel-electric engines were "gaining by leaps and bounds at the expense of steam locomotives," officials investigating the economic conditions of the Alabama industry found. "This can be interpreted only as a very serious threat to the most important single market enjoyed by the coal industry," they concluded.[32]

Northrup forecast problems for African American miners when the demand for coal dropped after the war. He predicted that mechanization would continue and that the coal industry would also suffer from competition from other fuel sources. Black miners, without support from the UMWA, would suffer disproportionate job losses.[33]

Part of the reason such criticism was ignored stemmed from the UMWA's enormous success in Alabama during the 1930s, which largely obscured these underlying racial problems. The miners had forced 90 percent of the state's operators to sign contracts with the UMWA by the spring of 1934. The miners gained a thirty-five-hour workweek and a forty-cent-a-day raise, allowing underground miners to earn up to $3.80 a day. A year later, Alabama miners joined a national walkout and won a two-year agreement with most major operators that resulted in another round of raises. The 1935 contract instituted a bargaining structure that would continue into the war years, though miners would regularly have to strike to win concessions from the operators.[34]

On the eve of World War II, after a series of difficult walkouts, Alabama miners had increased their wages to $5.90 a day. Despite these gains, the UMWA failed to eliminate the wage differential that allowed the state's operators to pay miners less than companies elsewhere. As a result, Alabama's miners continued to earn less than the $7.00 a day paid to miners in other states before the war.[35]

Two major holdouts against the UMWA were AFICO, a commercial mining operation owned by a branch of the DeBardeleben family, and the Tennessee Coal, Iron, and Railroad Company (TCI), the largest captive mining operation. AFICO never recognized the UMWA and used a combination of violence and intimidation as well as a brand of paternalism to keep the union at bay. TCI first worked to limit the UMWA's influence at its mines by encouraging miners to join an employee association. When that strategy failed, the company made the old association an independent union—it eventually affiliated with the AFL—and worked to drive a wedge between white and black miners.

The legacy of the battles between the UMWA and AFICO remained a subject of bitterness almost fifty years after the company went out of business.[36] While the DeBardeleben family members who ran the separate DeBardeleben Coal opted to settle with the UMWA in 1934, AFICO held out. AFICO steered its miners toward company "welfare societies" in hopes of keeping them from joining an independent union, but this approach often did not keep the UMWA from making inroads. So Charles DeBardeleben also responded by firing union militants and, when that failed, by closing down operations where substantial numbers of miners supported the UMWA. AFICO also converted its mining communities in St. Clair and Jefferson Counties into armed camps. Union organizers who attempted to operate in AFICO camps were attacked and, on at least one occasion, murdered. Race always remained on DeBardeleben's mind, and he sought to construct a paternalistic system of race relations at his operations that would help keep the union at bay.

In 1933, DeBardeleben responded quickly to reports that the UMWA had sent organizers to the Birmingham District. In June, managers held mass meetings with workers at which the miners "elected" to cast their lot with company welfare societies. The workers selected two representatives from each mine to meet with the company and draft a "working contract," which AFICO adopted. DeBardeleben then raised wages by 24–30 percent in August, as the UMWA's first major strike wave swept the region. During the October strikes and in response to new requirements under the NIRA's coal code, AFICO raised wages an additional 8 percent and reduced the typical working day from ten hours to eight hours. In the fall, AFICO officials and the welfare societies quickly signed a contract. DeBardeleben bragged that the agreement contained wages and benefits that matched those enjoyed by miners in other parts of the nation, including the higher-paying "northern field."[37]

DeBardeleben also stepped up his paternalistic practices in an attempt to dissuade his miners from joining the union fold. In this respect, he included both black and white miners in his vision of the AFICO "family." Indeed, during a spring 1937 antiunion rally, black miners sang a rousing version of "I Shall Not Be Moved" as DeBardeleben took the stage to denounce the union. "The house itself seemed to sway as the white [miners] joined in and rocked the rafters with the strains of this theme song," an observer reported. A black minister greeted African American miners as they arrived for the rally, and the crowd divided into black and white sections. During his speech, DeBardeleben referred to black and white miners he recognized in the audience "by their first names" and recalled "crises in which they had stood toe to toe and battled their common enemy." He then denounced union miners as "the slaves of John L. Lewis," conjuring up a powerful image of union miners as dependent and AFICO employees as emancipated.[38]

Paternalism was not Charles DeBardeleben's only weapon against the UMWA. During the union's organizing drives in the early 1930s, AFICO converted its mining towns into fortresses protected by machine guns and electrified fences. The company constructed blockhouses at the entrances to its camps and shined searchlights on automobiles that approached at night. The National Labor Relations Board later determined that during August 1934 the company set an "organizer trap" along the main road that led to its Overton mine near Birmingham, with plans to blow up cars carrying UMWA members.[39]

Even such extreme efforts did not always keep miners from joining the union. In August 1934, after miners at Overton supported the UMWA, DeBardeleben simply closed the operation and began to evict miners—whom DeBardeleben dubbed "undesirables"—from company housing and to remove equipment from the mine. DeBardeleben claimed that the Overton mine had suffered financial losses for several years and that the company had kept it running to keep the miners from going on public assistance. When miners joined the UMWA, however, DeBardeleben "saw no reason for our Company to continue this operation and suffer the loss its continuance would incur." The UMWA contested the evictions in court, but these efforts were dismissed.[40]

The company's public statements on the events at Overton articulated the rage that DeBardeleben and other AFICO officials felt at the miners' rejection of the company's paternalistic system. "Charles DeBardeleben has danced at their weddings and wept at their funerals," read a company statement to the Birmingham press. "He has encouraged and aided them to become self-sustaining. . . . What other answer could we give to such an apparent repudiation of what we had come to cherish as an unwritten law of allegiance, one to the other?" The miners at Overton, by contrast, protested that all they wanted was the "square deal" that President Roosevelt, the federal government, and the NIRA had promised: "That is the right to join an organization of our own choosing and the right of collective bargaining. We are only asking our God-given right to live in decency the same as the coal miners of all other sections are enjoying."[41]

The events at Overton also revealed DeBardeleben's violent opposition to the UMWA. In his addresses before the assembled miners at the camp, the AFICO head pledged that he would "die and go to Hell before he would deal with the union." He and other company officials repeatedly encouraged the Overton miners to take violent action against UMWA organizers. During the spring of 1934, as a strike wave swept across the coalfields, DeBardeleben told his miners that if organizers tried to enter the camp by car, they should "shoot the driver and that would probably wreck the car and in that way we would get them scattered out and could handle them," several Overton miners claimed. Superintendent Hewitt Smith told an Overton night watchman that if he found any UMWA organizers "that it was easier for me to drop him off of that trestle there in the river."[42]

In October 1935, during a national strike that idled the Alabama coalfields, the tensions boiled over. As two carloads of UMWA strikers attempted to drive into AFICO's operations at Acmar in St. Clair County, company officials opened fire with machine guns, killing one miner and wounding six. One witness, the wife of a railroad worker who lived near Acmar, claimed that mine general manager Fred Bell had warned her before the incident that there might be violence and that she should keep her children inside and lie flat on the floor when shooting began. Instead, she watched as the UMWA miners approached and the shooting unfolded. "Two cars of union men came up the road, when John Rich, a company man, went out to the middle of the road, waved at them and they halted." The shooting broke out moments later. None of the UMWA members fired back, and she did not see any of the union miners with firearms.[43]

Upon receiving the news that the murdered UMWA member, Virgil Thomas, had been shot thirty times, Lewis held a press conference outside of his office in Washington, D.C. Pacing back and forth with a coroner's illustration showing where the bullets had struck Thomas, the union president threatened to call a national strike over the incident. "In the name of God look at that," Lewis fumed. "Look at that string of bullet holes about the chest and the few in the legs. The vicious thugs wanted to make sure they got him. Well they did. They got a man who only wanted to work—a man who was asking for nothing but a few pennies more a day so his family could have better food and clothes."[44]

AFICO officials later admitted that they had shot the miners but claimed that the union members had trespassed on company property. Several company leaders—DeBardeleben and Bell among them—were implicated in the incident. Trials held in St. Clair County resulted in no convictions in the shootings. As Mitch bitterly recalled six years later, the trials were a "farce comedy."[45]

Indeed, life for union organizers who ventured into AFICO communities was dangerous. Mitch complained as late as 1942 that union organizers routinely suffered beatings and harassment when they attempted to make inroads into AFICO operations in St. Clair County. In March of that year, for example, UMWA organizer C. A. Chambers was attacked by AFICO henchmen in the community of Springville. Despite some concessions the union and federal officials wrangled from the company during the organizing effort in 1942—the company union was disestablished and fourteen fired union sympathizers were reinstated—the UMWA never organized AFICO operations.[46]

The struggle between the UMWA and TCI was less violent, but the company used racial divisions to weaken the union's presence in Jefferson County. When efforts to encourage miners to join an employee association failed, the company made the old association an independent union—it eventually affiliated with the AFL—and worked to exploit existing divisions between white and black miners at its operations. As late as 1941, this rival union movement attracted support from much of TCI's white mining workforce.[47]

The roots of these problems dated to the early 1930s, when TCI, a subsidiary of U.S. Steel, responded to the union's organizing campaigns by establishing a plan of "employee representation." TCI eventually severed ties with the employee group, and the members of the former company union affiliated with the Brotherhood of Mine Workers of Captive Mines. TCI had recognized the UMWA in 1934. Three years later, however, it also had contracts with the Brotherhood organization at Jefferson County's Hamilton, Wylam, Docena, and Edgewater mines. The former company union also apparently made inroads at TCI's ore mines.[48]

TCI managers had a close relationship with the Brotherhood of Mine Workers organization. The company provided the "union" with meeting places and helped to finance the group. According to Mitch, TCI also gave members "certain treats, such as ice cream, popsicles, etc." The practice of accepting such company assistance earned the Brotherhood the derogatory nickname the "popsicle union," and the men who supported it were known as "popsicles."[49]

Though evidence shows that some black miners joined the Brotherhood, the organization appealed primarily to whites who did not want to join the UMWA. "We have an overwhelming majority of the men in the United Mine Workers," Mitch wrote to Lewis in the spring of 1936. However, in the mining community of Docena, TCI had signed up "practically all the white men . . . in the company union by giving them special consideration." The views of union officials were confirmed by W. B. Turner, who grew up in Docena and remembered that black miners joined the UMWA during the early 1930s while most whites joined the "company union. There was no question about it."[50]

Enticements for members of the captive miners' group included better job assignments and higher wages. District 20 officials suspected that TCI used the better wages included in its contracts with the Brotherhood of Mine Workers as a way to lure miners away from the UMWA. When Mitch entered into talks with some of the leaders of the captive miners' union about joining the UMWA, they claimed that many of the organization's members worried that if they joined, "their wages will be reduced to that set forth in the United Mine Workers agreement." Union officials eventually received assurances from TCI's manager of industrial relations, J. F. Vance, that the company would pay the same wages to members of both organizations.[51]

By the late 1930s, Mitch and other District 20 officials believed that the Brotherhood of Mine Workers was losing members and that the UMWA was gaining converts. TCI began to withdraw its support for the Brotherhood, particularly after members began to explore affiliating with an "international union."[52] However, many of TCI's white miners continued to support the former company union, largely because of the increasing controversy over the UMWA's racial policies.

The Brotherhood of Mine Workers of Captive Mines received a boost in 1939 when the AFL in Alabama granted the organization a charter. The action reflected the hostility at both the national and local levels between industrial and craft-based unionists. By the mid-1930s, the UMWA's Lewis and other industrial unionists on the national level had become frustrated at the AFL's failure to support organizing drives in industries such as steel and automobiles. Lewis and his supporters first formed the CIO as a committee in the AFL. Within a short time, however, the UMWA and several other major unions left to establish the independent CIO.

Before the split, Mitch was elected president of the Alabama State Federation of Labor during a turbulent meeting in Florence in the spring of 1936. With strong support from African American delegates in attendance, Mitch prevailed by a vote of 256 to 126. Many craft unionists disliked the selection of the UMWA's District 20 president, and Mitch complained almost immediately of attempts to undermine his leadership in the state AFL. In particular, the UMWA and other industrial unionists attempted to push the state labor body toward a more progressive position on organizing, which meant including African Americans in unions. This policy put Mitch and other industrial unionists into direct conflict with many of the state's craft unions. As Mitch explained shortly after he was elected, the carpenters' union "will not take a negro in. Neither will they give a charter to the negroes. They work day in and day out as carpenters in and around Birmingham. Also electricians made it clear to me they do not want any more members and won't take any more members into their union. Hence electricians that are not already into their union are compelled to work non union if they work at electrical work." When the split between the CIO and AFL became official in the fall of 1936, the Alabama federation expelled the UMWA and other industrial unions. Mitch became head of the state's CIO organization, the Alabama State Industrial Union Council, and regional director of the affiliated SWOC. The craft-union-dominated AFL, according to historian Judith Stein, consistently attacked industrial unionists as "agents of race mixing and radicalism."[53]

The debate within the Alabama State Federation of Labor and the eventual split between the CIO and craft unions took place against the backdrop of a bitter congressional primary in Birmingham during the spring and early summer of 1936 that pitted longtime incumbent George Huddleston Sr. against Luther Patrick, a young lawyer and ardent New Dealer. Huddleston had supported some early New Deal legislation but had opposed the NIRA, the Social Security Act, and—most importantly from the UMWA's point of view—the Guffey Coal Act, which would have strengthened collective bargaining in the coal industry and regulated wages, hours, prices, and production levels. The miners' union and the CIO strongly supported Patrick, while the craft unionists allied with the region's industrial elites behind Huddleston.

Huddleston and his supporters made race a central issue in the campaign, targeting Mitch and the UMWA for specific criticism. John Altman, a Huddleston ally and former attorney for the state AFL, published numerous newspaper advertisements and pamphlets strongly denouncing Mitch and the UMWA's racial policies and linking both to the attempt to defeat Huddleston. Altman claimed that Mitch "places himself on a basis of equality with the Negro in order to promote his own ambitions and to benefit himself thereby, he is undertaking to drag the membership of Organized Labor down to where he stands." Altman also charged that Mitch "practices what the Communists preach on Negro equality in the ranks of the United Mine Workers of America and in Organized Labor."[54]

Mitch was not the only UMWA target of Altman's attacks. Altman also singled out black organizer Walter Jones. One of Altman's fliers, clearly designed to stir up racial anger, featured a photograph of Jones dressed in a striped coat and white shoes and pants and wearing a white hat. Jones, the flier stated, opposed both Huddleston and the poll tax and had proclaimed that he was "entitled to all the rights and privileges as any other man." Despite the tension that had previously existed between Mitch and Jones, Altman played up the association between the two UMWA officials, noting that Mitch had achieved the presidency of the State Federation of Labor with the help of Jones, who had controlled the convention and swung black support the District 20 president. Altman charged that the UMWA had preached social equality by allowing African Americans to serve as presidents of many local unions—a highly exaggerated claim—and proclaimed that the miners' union's racial policies "will be the ruination of Organized Labor if carried into effect as Mitch and Walter Jones would like for it to be carried."[55]

Patrick easily won the Democratic nomination and thereby the election, taking almost 60 percent of the vote and running strong in all of the city's working-class districts. But Altman's campaign placed the UMWA on the defensive. Responding to his attacks, for example, four white UMWA activists downplayed African American influence in the election of Mitch as state federation president and defended the union's adherence to southern racial custom: "There IS NOT A LOCAL UNION in the State of Alabama which has a Negro as president," they proclaimed, adding that in "all Local Unions, where there are Negroes, they take one side of the hall, and the white men take the other side—JUST LIKE THEY HAVE DONE FOR TWENTY YEARS." The *Union News*, a pro-UMWA Walker County publication, went even further, stating that it opposed "any attempt to place the negro and white upon social equality." As for Jones, the newspaper stated, he "represents the negro side of the organization's activities and as such representative takes up their problems, both with the district office and with employers."[56]

The tensions between the AFL and the UMWA and the growing controversy over the miners' union's racial policies found their way into the difficult battle with the Brotherhood of Mine Workers of Captive Mines at TCI. Rumors of the organization's imminent collapse in 1938 proved premature, and whites remained members, though their numbers declined. When organizers with the Progressive Mine Workers of America, an AFL affiliate, attempted to convince the captive miners to join that union, the TCI miners refused, opting to remain an independent member of the craft federation instead. Mitch reported in early 1941 that the organization's numbers remained small when compared with UMWA support at TCI's operations but added that "most of the white men belong to the A. F. of L. group." The District 20 president worried that the "men here in the A. F. of L. company union are such that we can not handle them, as the bulk of our membership at these mines are negroes." By the spring, federal officials concluded that the Brotherhood had managed to attract almost a third of TCI's coal mine workforce in Jefferson County. The UMWA had about 56 percent of the union members at the company's area mines, while a small number belonged to neither organization.[57]

Other evidence indicated that the Brotherhood was working to expand beyond TCI's operations. The organization, Mitch wrote to UMWA leaders in March, appeared to be making inroads among miners at the Mulga mine operated by Woodward Iron, another major captive coal producer. After a series of walkouts at Mulga, UMWA officials heard rumors about some local leaders attempting "to get an A. F. of L. union." Mitch believed that leaders of the craft federation had "promised some of the so-called local leaders some kind of position if they cause such a division."[58]

The difficulties that the Brotherhood of Mine Workers posed for the UMWA were evident when Alabama miners joined the national walkout in April 1941. Lewis and other union leaders hoped to force operators in Alabama and the rest of the region to eliminate the wage differentials that kept southern miners' pay lower than that of their northern counterparts. In Alabama, twenty-one thousand miners stopped work on 1 April despite operators' attempts to keep the miners working under the terms of their old agreement.

Leaders of the Brotherhood of Mine Workers attempted to undercut the UMWA's position in the walkout by agreeing to return to work under the old contract until negotiators hammered out a new agreement. On 30 March, the day before the contract expired, leaders of the organization met with TCI officials. Organizer C. A. Gaither pledged that "members of the Captive Coal Miners Unions were willing and anxious to continue at work provided proper protection could be given to them in the event any attempt at violence was made as a result of their working." Company officials declined the offer and informed Gaither that unless an agreement was reached between negotiators and the UMWA, the company would cease operations for the duration of the strike.[59]

After the strike's conclusion, Mitch and other UMWA officials focused on eliminating the captive miners' union from TCI's operations. In June, the National Labor Relations Board ruled in favor of a UMWA request and allowed miners collectively to choose between the two organizations at the four mines in Jefferson County. The Brotherhood had pushed for a separate vote at each mine, hoping that they could poll a majority at one of the operations. The organization retained its strongest support at Docena, where it counted about a third of the miners on its rolls, and at Wylam, where an estimated 36 percent belonged. But the National Labor Relations Board rejected this idea, agreeing with the UMWA that the four mines should vote as a single unit. The July election resulted in a resounding victory for Mitch and District 20—the UMWA received 3,554 votes to the Brotherhood's 758, with only 58 votes for "no union."[60]

The Brotherhood of Mine Workers' persistence among whites testified to the resistance the UMWA's racial policies provoked despite the concessions to white supremacy embedded within the miners' formula. The UMWA had attracted opposition not only from industrial and political elites but also from segments of the white working class. This resistance to the UMWA's policies went beyond the AFL craft unions and extended into the mines. As a result, the captive miners' union had continued to exist and showed signs of growth even after TCI withdrew formal support for the organization.

The white miners who had belonged to the Brotherhood now faced a dilemma: they could either join the UMWA or leave their jobs. Leon Alexander remembered that some whites quit working at Edgewater and went to work for De-Bardeleben's AFICO mines to avoid the UMWA. When they lost the election, many of the former captive miners members "just disappeared," remembered William Mitch Jr. Others, he said, "became union people."[61]

Turner remembered that many of the former captive miners' union members felt betrayed by TCI. During one of the early strikes, white miners had watched as a group of black UMWA members descended on a pair of African Americans who had crossed the union's picket lines in Docena. The strikebreakers had been assured that the company would protect them, but when they emerged from the mine, the black miners "whupped them into the ground with all the deputies and everything else and nobody done anything to help them." After this incident, many white miners began to soften their opposition to the UMWA because of the company's failure to live up to its promise. In addition, Turner remembered, white unionists "were told that . . . there would be no strong United Mine Workers. But [TCI officials] lied. And the company just reversed theirselves when [the UMWA] got strong. We were forced to join the other union." Many of these miners subsequently became active in the UMWA at Docena.[62]

TCI's efforts to exploit the racial divisions in its mining communities and the violent opposition the UMWA encountered from Charles DeBardeleben ultimately illustrated the tenuous ground on which the miners' union trod in the late 1930s and early 1940s. Despite its compromises on racial issues, illustrated by the cautious gradualism and the adherence to southern racial norms embedded in the union's biracialism, the most powerful coal operators in the Birmingham District considered the organization a major threat to both the region's economic order and its racial caste system.

Elite whites also came to view the UMWA and the Birmingham District's other industrial unions as part of the New Deal's wider challenge to their political hegemony. Soon after the UMWA reestablished its presence in Alabama, Mitch and other activists began a fight to reform the state's voting laws. When the CIO emerged in the state in the late 1930s, thousands of steelworkers and ore miners joined the effort to expand the franchise. These industrial unionists vehemently opposed the poll tax laws and literacy tests that kept working-class whites and blacks from voting. Alabama's poll tax amounted to $1.50 a year. It was cumulative up to $37.50, an amount well out of reach for most of the Birmingham area's low-income residents of both races. The literacy tests gave registrars wide discretion, easily enabling them to keep members of the working class out of the voting booths.[63]

In the late 1930s, the effect of these disfranchisement mechanisms was staggering. Birmingham, with a population of about three hundred thousand, had only forty thousand registered voters, and between fifteen and twenty-eight thousand voters routinely decided the outcome of the city's elections. In surrounding Jefferson County, which had a population of almost half a million, only sixty thousand people were registered and only forty-five thousand routinely voted.[64]

Election officials had wide latitude in determining voter eligibility, and Birmingham's registration forms were difficult to understand. Registrars helped some prospective white voters fill out applications but did not offer similar assistance to most African Americans. In Birmingham, blacks also needed two whites to vouch for them before they could gain the right to vote. Residents could avoid literacy tests by certifying that they owned at least three hundred dollars worth of property, an amount assumed to be within the reach of white applicants. Prospective voters who did not own enough property had to prove that they had worked for "the greater part of the preceding twelve months." If they overcame this hurdle, they were required to read or write any passage of the U.S. Constitution voting officials deemed appropriate. Officials also found other ways to prevent blacks from voting—for example, by accepting applications but not registering the voters or by interviewing African American applicants about their political affiliations and involvement with organizations such as the National Association for the Advancement of Colored People. Rejected applicants had the right to appeal the registrar's decisions, but winning these appeals was difficult. For blacks and many working-class whites, applying to vote in Alabama proved an exercise in humiliation.[65]

To Mitch and other New Deal liberals in the South, a key step in breaking the reactionary political system lay in expanding the franchise; to do so, unions needed to get both white and black members registered. During the 1930s, the UMWA and the CIO began an effort to increase the number of unionists who could vote. Most dramatically, in 1937, members of a Walker County UMWA local borrowed eleven hundred dollars from the First National Bank of Jasper. Local leaders asked white members to pay their poll taxes and register to vote and then required them to help black members qualify. The effort resulted in the registration of 267 blacks and 218 whites, and the area's CIO unions subsequently repeated this approach.[66]

Not all such programs met with the same success as the Walker County group. In Bibb County, southwest of Birmingham, election officials worked hard to prevent black miners from voting. When about a dozen African Americans attempted to vote, the local probate judge designed especially difficult questions that confounded all but one potential voter. At the end of the 1930s, only about twenty-five African Americans were registered in Bibb County, and, boasted election officials, only eight or nine voted regularly. "We got enough white men in the county to take care of them if they get out of hand," claimed one county election official. "The reason they are fighting so hard—just between you and me and the gatepost—is because them are CIO niggers."[67]

In more urban parts of Jefferson County, blacks also faced a concerted effort to keep them off the voter rolls. Almost all of the two hundred African Americans the UMWA brought to register at Bessemer near the end of the 1930s were turned down. A Democratic county official complained that labor unions were getting too powerful in Birmingham, "especially among the Negroes. . . . [I]t will take eternal vigilance to keep them in check."[68]

As part of the campaign against the poll tax, the UMWA and CIO helped to establish the Southern Conference for Human Welfare (SCHW), which was formed by southern liberals and leftists to address the oppressive conditions outlined in the National Emergency Council's influential *Report on the Economic Conditions of the South.* Birmingham was the site of the first major SCHW conference in November 1938. The participants, about 20 percent of them African American, mixed freely, disregarding segregated seating requirements until Police Commissioner Eugene "Bull" Connor arrived and forced those in attendance to abide by the city's segregated seating laws. In a dramatic moment, Eleanor Roosevelt, who had arrived late for the newly segregated session, sat with the African Americans. Informed by a police officer that she would have to move to the white section of the auditorium, Roosevelt symbolically placed her chair on the line that separated the white and black sides. At the Birmingham meeting and those that followed it, the SCHW adopted policies that advocated a broad range of progressive causes. It endorsed state and federal action to improve economic inequality, supported federal antilynching legislation, and backed equal pay for black and white teachers.[69]

While the UMWA and the CIO actively supported these goals, the reaction that the conference produced in Birmingham clearly concerned Mitch. Shortly after the meeting, opponents of the SCHW organized a mass meeting to "crystallize opposition against 'racial and political agitation' resulting from the last week's welfare congress." The event featured Congressman Joe Starnes of Guntersville, a militant anticommunist, and invited groups included the Alabama Council of Democratic Clubs and the state Sheriffs' and Peace Officers' Association as well as Confederate veterans groups, the American Legion, and the AFL.[70]

Mitch, for his part, confided in national UMWA leaders that he had worked to distance the CIO from direct association with the SCHW meeting in Birmingham. The District 20 president, sometimes listed as a major activist in the group, attended only the conference's final day. He sharply criticized communists in the SCHW who, he claimed, had blundered by attempting to hold an integrated meeting. Mitch concluded "that poor judgment was used in having negroes and whites mixed together in the hall."[71]

Despite the concerns about the reaction to the SCHW, Mitch and Alabama CIO officials remained committed to abolishing the poll tax. He and other industrial union leaders testified before Congress in support of legislation abolishing the tax in the early 1940s. "There has been entirely too much misrepresentation of the poll-tax issue," Mitch said. "The racial issue has been injected from time to time by those who desire to continue the status quo. Labor knows that it is the poor man, whether black or white, that has suffered under this anti-American and undemocratic survival of feudalism." CIO Regional Director Yelverton Cowherd told Congress that large companies such as Republic Steel and AFICO often paid their employees' poll taxes in the hope that they would vote the way the company wanted in elections.[72]

The efforts of Mitch and the CIO activists did not go unnoticed by Alabama's industrial elite and conservative political establishment. At the onset of the UMWA strike in the spring of 1941, Texas Congressman Martin Dies charged the District 20 president and Alabama CIO leader with "UnAmericanism." Dies included Mitch among those "who were either members of the Communist Party or whose records . . . show that they follow the party line in supporting communist front organizations." The attack was directed mostly at Mitch's involvement with the SCHW, but the timing—at the onset of the miners' strike against state and national coal producers—also suggested an attempt to weaken the UMWA's position in Alabama's coalfields. However, the effort failed to tarnish Mitch in the eyes of either the miners or the general public. Perhaps more importantly, it illustrated the dramatic changes under way in the state's political scene. Liberals rallied to Mitch's defense, with New Deal Senators John Bankhead and Lister Hill defending the union leader in public and the press denouncing the attack. Hill called the allegations "absurd and ridiculous and grossly unfair and unjust." Bankhead labeled the attacks "unfair and unfortunate" and lamented "that such a charge against him has been printed in the Congressional Record."[73]

However, the UMWA and CIO had powerful opponents in the conservative wing of the Alabama Democratic Party, and in the early 1940s, rightists rallied around Governor Frank Dixon. By the time of Dixon's election in 1938, FDR's programs had dramatically altered Alabama's political scene, and even conservatives like the new governor had to reach out to labor. Indeed, Dixon had succeeded the liberal Bibb Graves, who had strongly supported the New Deal and helped the labor movement realize some of its greatest gains in Alabama.

Dixon was a more reluctant convert to the New Deal. After spending much of his childhood in Virginia, he graduated from Phillips Exeter Preparatory School and Columbia University and received a law degree from the University of Virginia. Dixon subsequently came to Birmingham and immersed himself in Jefferson County politics. A specialist in corporate law, he became identified with the industrialist-planter alliance, which played an important role in his ascension to the governor's mansion in Montgomery.

Dixon was no friend of the labor movement—he had once called unions "un-American"—and believed that "industrialists, bankers, and other professionals" were best qualified to hold public office. In the words of one historian, the governor was a "technocrat" who was "suspicious of democracy." However, even ideologues such as Dixon realized that the state's labor movement could mobilize a significant number of voters and sought support from this crucial segment of the Democratic Party. Dixon, in fact, won election in 1938 with the backing of organized labor.[74]

As the United States moved toward war, Dixon became an increasingly vocal opponent of expanding the New Deal, and concerns about race relations came to dominate his thinking. Opposed to additional centralization, he feared that the new reach of the federal government might result in additional social reforms and ultimately in an assault on segregation. "Every fanatic social reformer," he argued, "has remained in Washington, greatly increasing his clamor, insisting that his individual crackpot reform is essential to the winning of the war."[75]

Dixon's meddling in a pair of 1941 walkouts by industrial unions illustrated his hardening attitudes toward racial liberalism. The governor intervened early in the UMWA's national strike against major coal operators that idled most Alabama mines in the spring. Dixon appointed a state Board of Mediation to investigate the dispute and followed the coal company line by calling for a return to work "pending the outcome" of national negotiations between Lewis and operator representatives. Mitch and other District 20 officials hoped to eliminate the wage differential in the new contract with the coal operators and viewed Dixon's entrance into the dispute with dismay since he had gone on record in support of the differential. Mitch therefore avoided appearing before the governor's board, even though it included a labor representative. "Knowing the Governor's position is definitely in favor of the operators, we are inclined to believe there would be no chance of getting any favorable consideration from the Commission appointed by him," Mitch informed Lewis.[76]

Mitch's predictions proved accurate. Dixon's board released its report at the end of April, endorsing a continued wage differential. Raising the wages of Alabama miners to bring them in line with those of their counterparts elsewhere in the country would result in massive job losses, the commission concluded, rehearsing the coal industry's old arguments in favor of low wages. Dixon immediately and publicly endorsed the board's report. "Any agreement which ignores local conditions will of necessity mean the closing of nearly all of our Alabama mines and the loss of the livelihood of our workers," the governor said.[77]

A week later, Dixon went a step further. Officials with the state Department of Industrial Relations announced that they would not allow UMWA members to collect unemployment benefits. Members of the white-dominated Brotherhood of Mine Workers of Captive Mines, who had offered to continue working during the UMWA walkout, would receive payments because state law allowed aid to workers not "directly" involved in a labor dispute. State officials based their decision on amendments to the unemployment compensation law as well as court decisions arising from the UMWA's national strike two years earlier. Emboldened by the heightened racial atmosphere of 1941, however, Dixon attempted to use the law to undermine the UMWA's biracialism. The attempt failed, but only because the strike ended before Dixon's efforts could begin to bear fruit.[78]

Dixon took his attack on biracial unionism a step further during a walkout by Birmingham steelworkers in the fall of 1941. The SWOC had made major inroads in organizing the district's steel and iron mills during the 1930s. By the spring of 1937, the SWOC had signed contracts at TCI and most of the region's other major steel and iron producers. The organization, initially headed by the UMWA's Mitch, had thirteen locals operating in the state. The steel companies had used two means to resist the efforts to establish industrial unions: exploiting racial cleavages in their workforce and employing outright violence and intimidation. SWOC locals, like their UMWA counterparts, openly violated segregation ordinances that forbade whites and blacks from meeting in the same buildings. At biracial meetings, reported the SWOC's executive director, Noel Beddow, "each and every man present was subject to arrest and fine on a misdemeanor charge. However, we have ignored the law. . . . [T]oday white men and negro men are meeting in the halls . . . as they meet in the mills of the corporations to do their daily tasks."[79]

However, this cooperation had its limits among steelworkers as among miners. Black mill workers often took the lead in establishing SWOC locals. White steelworkers, who often received higher wages than African Americans for performing the same work, initially hesitated to join the organization, which they saw as a threat to their status. However, large numbers of whites at TCI who had supported company unions began to join the SWOC when the company organizations failed to live up to their promises of achieving job improvements.[80]

Tension rose at TCI's operations as the union made inroads in its mills and attracted white support. In the fall of 1941, a black steelworker was beaten by company guards when he stepped out of a pay line to borrow a pencil. TCI guards arrested the man and fined him eight dollars after administering the beating. The company claimed that the steelworker was drunk, a charge hotly disputed by witnesses. Beddow protested strongly that the steelworkers were "fed up on this thing of having employees beaten up simply because a man happens to have a gun and a badge on him."[81]

In late September, steelworker pickets closed down TCI's operations in Ensley, when union members appeared to conduct a "card inspection" of workers entering the operation. SWOC activists hoped to use the action to protest a range of grievances, the bulk of them stemming from anger that some workers were excluded from the company's incentive plan.[82] Rumors that a crowd of steelworkers—described as "a mob composed of four hundred or more men, partly negroes and partly whites"—planned to conduct a card inspection at Fairfield pushed Dixon over the edge. The governor dispatched National Guardsmen to the company's operations to keep the SWOC unionists at bay. Dixon believed that the unionists would arrive at the Fairfield gates after a union meeting and conduct the card inspection in an attempt "to bring about a closed shop by force and violence if necessary."[83]

Perhaps anticipating Dixon's move, activists called off the inspection. The event turned into a major public relations blunder for the governor. TCI managers and Jefferson County law enforcement officials distanced themselves from Dixon's action, claiming that they had never requested assistance. Federal officials eventually negotiated the removal of the National Guardsmen. The steelworkers had refused to work as long as troops remained outside the Fairfield plant.[84]

While TCI officials and union leaders were puzzled by Dixon's action, many industrialists hailed it. Charles DeBardeleben's son, Prince, who had taken over the day-to-day operation of AFICO by the fall of 1941, praised Dixon's action. "As soon as this organized labor crowd realizes that the public and the public officials are not going to be intim[id]ated the better off we will be and I don't believe we are going to get any relief until this happens," he wrote to Dixon.[85] Dixon's intervention and his attack on the interracial nature of the CIO struck a chord with reactionary industrial leaders such as DeBardeleben, who worried that as the United States was drawn into war, their world might be turned upside down.

White elites felt challenged on several fronts during the early war years. The reestablishment of the UMWA in Alabama and the emergence of the biracial industrial union movement, despite its gradualist approach to race relations, had contested the Birmingham District's white economic and political power structure. The New Deal had aided in this effort, providing protection and emboldening the state's industrial working class. The buildup to the war and the onset of hostilities in December 1941 seemed to promise more changes. White political and economic elites feared the expansion of the federal government that the wartime emergency required. They believed that an assault on white supremacy was in the works as African Americans signed up for the war effort, demanded jobs in wartime industries, and generally appeared more assertive and more willing to violate the bounds of the southern racial system. These fears manifested themselves in the reaction of Dixon and other leaders to the CIO and the perception that African Americans in the Birmingham District planned an assault on segregation. Many whites had come to fear that World War II might herald a racial revolution.

The wartime atmosphere of the early 1940s did indeed spur increased expectations from African Americans across the country, while liberal whites—from Eleanor Roosevelt to Wendell Willkie and Henry Wallace—urged the country to practice what it preached in terms of race relations. The efforts to bring blacks and liberal whites together in groups such as the SCHW, labor unions, and religious organizations heartened blacks in the South, who began to step up their demands for civil rights. Most importantly, African Americans throughout the country began to call for their "fair share" of the jobs that war industries promised.[86]

In response to concerns that African Americans might be shut out of these high-paying jobs, Brotherhood of Sleeping Car Porters founder A. Philip Randolph and other civil rights leaders began to pressure President Roosevelt to take steps to make sure that blacks would benefit from wartime production. When their meetings with Roosevelt and other administration officials failed to produce results, these leaders threatened to organize a massive protest against discrimination. The March on Washington movement mobilized thousands of working-class blacks, and in the early summer of 1941, the president agreed to issue Executive Order 8802 if the activists would cancel the protest. The directive required companies doing business with the federal government to adopt antidiscrimination clauses and essentially prohibited racial discrimination in training programs and defense industries. The order also set up the FEPC, which, though it had no real enforcement power, was charged with investigating complaints of racial discrimination in war-related industries.[87]

Southern elites perceived the federal government as allying itself with African Americans and industrial unions in a concerted effort to overturn segregation, the bedrock of the southern society. To the horror of Dixon and other conservatives, FEPC officials decided to hold hearings in Birmingham in June 1942. As the date for the hearings neared, prominent locals asked committee members to call off the event.[88]

When these requests went unheeded, industrial leaders began a sharp attack on the FEPC. The strongest criticism appeared a week before the hearings in the conservative magazine *Alabama*, whose editors warned that the FEPC would hold "race trials" in Birmingham and labeled the committee "the gravest threat yet to the time-honored right of Southerners to direct the social development of their own region." The magazine called on the region's congressional delegations to advise the administration that such investigations by "Roosevelt racial experts" and "academic theorists" would not be tolerated and urged the South's whites to resist attempts to force change. In fact, the magazine argued, allowing the federal government to examine the region's race relations risked "the disturbance of the delicate relationships of the races" and was "likely to cause the greatest possible amount of harm."[89]

The criticism had a profound effect on many southern liberals, who worried about the reaction that the hearings might provoke. In remarks designed to lessen the tension many southerners perceived regarding the hearings, Louisville newspaper publisher Mark Ethridge, a member of the FEPC, argued that the body had no intention of challenging the southern racial order. In comments reprinted in the *Louisville Courier-Journal*, Ethridge criticized black leaders and newspaper editors who "demand 'all or nothing.'" These leaders, he wrote, "are giving cruel and disillusioning leadership to their people; worse than that, they are playing into the hands of white demagogues who two or three times have piled up tragic consequences by playing upon the emotions of the people." Shortly after the hearings, Ethridge warned Roosevelt administration officials that "the situation in the South is much more serious than people who haven't followed it realize."[90]

The rest of the region's mainstream press shared Ethridge's concerns. Birmingham newspaper coverage of the hearings appeared designed more to calm tensions than to seriously explore the issue of racial discrimination in wartime industries. In typical booster fashion, the *Birmingham News* claimed that "representatives of the committee have found relatively little evidence of discrimination and unfairness here" and concluded that "the aim of this committee is to further this very cause in which this community has shown itself to be a leader."[91]

The hearings seemed designed to produce such coverage. The committee for the most part ignored major Birmingham employers and focused much of its attention on the difficult situations that faced newer war-related industries in Mobile and Nashville. The committee also sharply criticized the racial policies of the region's AFL unions, particularly in Mobile's shipyards.[92]

For his part, Mitch gave relatively mild testimony before the committee, belying the racial tensions that had enveloped the region, its labor movement, and even his union. The District 20 president matter-of-factly told the FEPC that race relations within the miners' union were healthy and that the UMWA had weathered attempts to prevent interracial meetings. Laws passed to prevent such activities, he testified, had "been more or less broken down. [Miners] meet now in meetings, mixed meetings if you please, to consider their common problems."[93]

Despite these efforts to ease the fears surrounding the FEPC, most industrial and political elites and many skilled white workers perceived the hearings as a direct threat to the current state of race relations in the South. The spectacle of black FEPC staff members questioning whites and occupying seats of authority was apparently more than many white observers could stomach. Many white leaders were upset by the instances where black academics testified as experts and where black workers accused white unions and employers of job discrimination. In sharp contrast to the mild reception the hearings received in the mainstream Birmingham press, angry whites flooded the White House with protest letters.[94]

The FEPC hearings in Birmingham dovetailed with white perceptions that African Americans had begun aggressively to challenge the southern racial system. Just how changed southern whites perceived the atmosphere was reflected in the contemporary writings of sociologist Howard Odum, who wrote that the new federal presence and the belief that blacks had grown more assertive led to a host of rumors and stories that "reflected the whole drama of regional and racial crisis." The changes became a "critical point of conflict, upsetting the traditional southern economy of white-Negro work relations and started the flood of talk, stories, rumors and violence."[95]

More recently, historian Bryant Simon has argued that these rumors articulated the "fears and apprehensions" of middle- and upper-class whites during a time of substantial economic, political, and social change. The proliferation of rumors provided a space in which white southerners could discuss their worries as well as "make arguments and advance their views." With white supremacy under assault, such talk helped whites "make rough sense of the incomprehensible."[96]

The reports that Odum explored during the early war years included stories of rebellions by black female domestic workers who either demanded more rights in white homes or refused to work in them. Whites, Odum found, suspected that African American women participated in secret "Eleanor Clubs," named for the First Lady, who whites believed supported increased rights for black women and had given permission to form the organizations. The clubs were essentially "unions in disguise" designed to increase wages, cut hours, and enforce equal treatment. Some rumors were more sinister, involving stories about black men's sexual designs on white women. Many southern whites also feared uprisings by blacks during or after the war.[97]

The reports that Odum received from Alabama articulated many of these concerns. Some of the reports focused on assertive public behavior by African Americans. Others described the existence of the Eleanor Clubs and the perception that African American servants seemed more eager to challenge the terms of their employment. Many of the reports focused on the First Lady herself and reflected middle- and upper-class-white anger at her perceived violations of southern racial norms. Others focused on defiance of segregated seating rules by African American passengers on public transportation. Many of these reports articulated white concerns about black men in uniform. Some gave voice to whites' worries about the potential for sexual encounters between white women and black men. A common thread that emerged in many of these reports was the fear that U.S. involvement in World War II heralded a transformation in race relations in the South. These rumors reflected many whites' belief that the conflict threatened not only to overturn white supremacy but also to usher in an era of "black supremacy" in Alabama.[98]

In such a racially charged atmosphere, it is not surprising that Alabama's political elites took action. Just over a month after the Birmingham FEPC hearings, Dixon refused to sign a contract between Alabama and the federal government to supply cloth produced by state prisoners because it contained a nondiscrimination clause. If he signed the contract, Dixon announced, the FEPC would "descend upon the state with the demand that Negroes be put in positions of responsibility" in prisons.[99] The move, though criticized by moderates, proved a rallying point for conservative whites.

Emboldened by the support, the outgoing governor charged the national Democratic Party with "dynamiting" the southern "social structure" and with "attempting to force crackpot reforms on [southerners] in a time of national crisis." Dixon claimed that southerners might break with Roosevelt and the national Democrats. "Suggestions are rife as to the formation of a Southern Democratic Party, the election of unpledged representatives to the electoral college," he said. "Ways and means are being discussed daily to break our chains." Dixon claimed that the demise of white supremacy was "the one thing we cannot permit, will not permit, whatever the price to ourselves."[100]

Most members of the southern economic elite agreed. At the end of July, shortly after Dixon's challenge to the FEPC, Alabama Mining Institute president I. W. Rouzer sent a letter to right-wing Alabama Congressman Joe Starnes urging an organized fight to preserve white supremacy. Southern members of Congress should "call on the President and tell him in language that can be understood— that the procedure of cramming negro soldiers in southern camps, of so-called committees on unfair employment practices, of demands for this, that and the other 'right' of the negro in a section where he has more rights and freedom, and more downright security than any place on the globe, is a procedure that must be reversed if the negro's lot is to be at all safe." Rouzer also sharply criticized Eleanor Roosevelt for "inspiring a false hope in the breast of the negro race by her stupid determination to break down the wall of social equality. She does not realize, of course, that you can't be on an equality [*sic*] with the negro race—you must either be above or below him."[101]

Perceptions of black assertiveness, along with the FEPC hearings, provoked Horace Wilkinson, a Democratic Party political operative identified with Mitch and the rest of the state's industrial labor movement, to break with his old liberal allies and align himself with racial conservatives. In the summer of 1942, Wilkinson called for the establishment of a League to Maintain White Supremacy and advocated open resistance to the federal government before a meeting of the Birmingham Kiwanis Club. Wilkinson had his speech printed, and copies circulated widely in the Birmingham District.[102]

Dixon administration officials surveyed race relations across the state in the wake of the FEPC hearings, and much of what they found confirmed their fears that African Americans had begun to defy Jim Crow. In early August 1942, for example, Dixon administration officials came into possession of a report on race relations by Major Thomas Vaden, who served with the federal agency responsible for wartime procurement and industrial mobilization. Vaden described the racial situation in the state as "definitely bad," reporting that Tuskegee, Montgomery, Mobile, Tuscaloosa, and Birmingham had experienced racial unrest in recent months. "The law enforcement authorities from the Chief of the Highway Patrol down through the Mayors and Probate Judges and Sheriffs of the counties are seriously alarmed and anticipate trouble," he reported.[103]

The FEPC hearings loomed large in Vaden's report. He claimed that the hearings had "resulted in a crystallization of sentiment throughout the state to a degree which is very unfortunate." As the federal government restricted companies from basing employment on race, tension increased and whites feared that they might be forced to work beside blacks in offices and factories, Vaden reported. "From the adopted policy of the Employment Service and of the Fair Employment Practice Committee, the people of the state seem to fear that the practical effect will be the abolition of segregation," he wrote.[104]

In late August and early September, Dixon dispatched Oliver McDuff to the Birmingham District to investigate rumors of racial unrest. McDuff, an official with the state Department of Public Safety, spent several days interviewing local law enforcement and political leaders, almost all of whom repeated rumors and stories of African Americans acting aggressively toward whites. Others relayed stories they had heard about planned uprisings by blacks. Most of McDuff's informants attributed the rise in racial tension to activity on the part of both the federal government and the CIO.

Birmingham's public safety commissioner, Bull Connor, claimed that city and county courts were filled with cases where blacks had violated segregation laws. Whites found themselves the targets of insults and profanity, particularly at the entrances to department stores and on the city's streetcars. Connor blamed the problems on federal officials, who "seem determined to destroy segregation and bring about amalgamation of the races.... [T]he powers that be insist that negroes work along side whites in industry; labor unions are forced to take in negroes, and the policy of the government seems to be to place negroes at adjoining desks with white people."[105]

Even moderates such as Cooper Green, president of the city commission, believed that the onset of the war had led to an increase in racial incidents. Green focused his discussion on public transportation, where a 34 percent increase in riders during peak hours resulted in tension. Violations of segregation ordinances occurred more frequently as whites and blacks crowded onto buses and streetcars. Green and other city officials sought ways to alleviate the strains that wartime production placed on the local public transit system, including encouraging businesses to stagger shifts, adding buses and streetcars to the system, and placing larger segregation signs and additional personnel on public transit. Though his criticism of the federal government was perhaps less explicit than Connor's, Green told McDuff that the problems facing the city's racial order would have to be solved by local officials, not by "outside interference."[106]

Jefferson County Sheriff Holt A. McDowell reported a host of different rumors to McDuff. Blacks who had just been inducted into the military reportedly had made obscene comments to white women, while black maids had defied their white employers. McDowell also described rumors that African Americans had stockpiled ammunition from three hardware stores in Fairfield. "The proprietor of one of the hardware stores, who was making the report to me, told me then that the sale of the ammunition had been stopped," McDowell said. He blamed all of these incidents on the federal government and "professional agitators who preach social equality"—likely a reference to industrial unionists operating in the area.[107]

Indeed, many of the more inflammatory reports focused on the CIO and the UMWA. W. R. Sims, TCI's chief of police, reported to McDuff that unionized miners at the company's Hamilton mine openly cursed white foremen. On paydays, Sims claimed, CIO officials often arrived at pay offices with loudspeakers and proceeded to "malign the officials of the Company, preach equal rights, and exhort the negroes to exert themselves." The federal government and the National Association for the Advancement of Colored People deserved their fair share of the responsibility for inspiring African Americans to violate racial norms, Sims said, but he placed much of the blame on "the CIO in connection with the Communist Party," which was "taking advantage of the war; injecting racial sentiment to further their organizing." And, Sims believed, "The Jim Crow or Segregation Law not being properly enforced is one of the main reasons for the clashes between the white and negro races."[108]

The visit with Sims left the strongest impression with McDuff. In his report to Dixon, the investigator concluded that the CIO deserved much of the blame for racial unrest in the Birmingham area because its appeals to black workers heightened tensions. "Further investigation reveals that if something is not done to alleviate the situation, serious trouble may arise," McDuff concluded.[109]

The reports suggested the extent to which the industrial union movement and the wartime emergency had emboldened African Americans to challenge the color line. But the reports did not note that the industrial labor unions had become bitterly divided by the summer of 1942. These divisions no longer simply pitted white craft unionists against the CIO. In May, a month before the FEPC hearings in Birmingham, District 20 broke with the state CIO during a heated state meeting. The action reflected the split between John L. Lewis and national CIO leaders, but the rupture between the two labor organizations in Alabama took place against the backdrop of the racial cauldron that Birmingham had become. UMWA officials resorted to red-baiting during the session and in the wake of the meeting attempted to raid a rival CIO union by colluding with white dissidents.

The break between the UMWA and CIO on the national levels was complex and involved a host of different personal and political conflicts. CIO President Philip Murray increasingly supported Franklin Roosevelt's actions as the United States moved toward war in 1940 and 1941, while Lewis publicly opposed the administration. The UMWA's struggle against captive mines in the fall of 1941 had drawn less-than-enthusiastic support from the CIO, which worried about the consequences for industrial production as the U.S. entry into World War II appeared increasingly likely. Murray worked during the early 1940s to bring the CIO out from under the control of the domineering Lewis and his miners' union. For all of these reasons, the relationship between the two leaders and their supporters declined. After the start of the war, Lewis suddenly announced a plan to reunite the AFL and CIO, with the retirement of Murray and AFL President William Green paving the way. Then, in another move that stunned Murray and his supporters, the UMWA presented the CIO with a bill for more than $1.5 million that Lewis claimed his union had spent to establish the industrial organization. Instead of forcing the CIO to pay its debt, Lewis announced that he would withhold UMWA dues from the umbrella group. Murray, Lewis, and their supporters then engaged in months of public arguments and accusations. The UMWA officially endorsed a break with the CIO at its fall 1942 convention.[110]

The rumblings in Alabama began a week before the state industrial union meeting at the District 20 convention in early May, when UMWA officials engaged in a series of red-baiting attacks against their critics within the CIO. In his report to the convention, Mitch, who had been the subject of such attacks since he came to Alabama in 1933, engaged in his own brand of anticommunist rhetoric. The District 20 president claimed that the attacks on Lewis were being "carried on through the recognized official organ of the Communist Party of America, *The Daily Worker*," whose editors "swell up in patriotic fervor while branding the U.M.W. of A. and its leadership."[111]

The tone of the UMWA convention, with its sharp criticism of national CIO leaders and individual unions, concerned many industrial unionists. An observer from Mine Mill, a small, communist-led union that primarily represented African American iron ore miners, reported that the "main theme" of the event was that "Murray had turned the CIO over to the Communists." The coal miners' convention, the observer claimed, served as a "caucus and training ground for the UMW delegates to the CIO convention."[112]

The well-organized miners dominated the state CIO meeting a week later, controlling a majority of the 320 delegates in attendance. The UMWA partisans viewed any support for Murray or Roosevelt as an attack on Lewis and singled out Mine Mill for especially harsh criticism. When Mine Mill's regional director, Alton Lawrence, took the convention floor to reiterate his union's support for Murray and Roosevelt, pro-UMWA delegates perceived his move as a backhanded slap at Lewis. Lawrence was subjected to "several threats . . . by UMWA delegates." Beddow sent a letter to the meeting that denounced the ore miners' union. Mitch and other miner delegates warned Mine Mill members to "stick with the UMWA," one observer reported. "This was taken by nearly everybody at the convention as a clear threat to [Mine Mill's] jurisdiction."[113]

At the convention, Mitch continued his red-baiting attacks, accusing communists of being behind the criticism of Lewis. Other pro-UMWA delegates argued that those who criticized Lewis had opposed Murray and Roosevelt before June 1941, when "Germany attacked their motherland." The District 20 president backed up his claims by reading news clippings from the *Daily Worker* "in great detail." He also claimed that "'New Dealers' were interfering in CIO affairs." When John Brophy, a national CIO official who had previously been a bitter opponent of Lewis within the UMWA, arrived at the Birmingham conference and criticized the miners' union president's failure to cooperate with Murray, many delegates strongly denounced Brophy, hurling "insults . . . during the bitterest of the attack upon him."[114]

Mitch eventually announced that he would no longer serve as president of the Alabama State Industrial Union Council, a position he had held since the organization's inception. Other prominent UMWA supporters, including Cowherd, resigned their posts with the organization in anger over the criticism of Lewis. Delegates ultimately passed resolutions praising both Lewis and Murray and calling on the two leaders to meet and "compose all their differences." Mitch added that the UMWA would cooperate with Alabama industrial unionists but would have to refrain from active involvement in the state organization "until things are straightened out in a national way." The moves signaled an end to the UMWA's membership in the state CIO council, which officially came a short time later.[115]

The red-baiting attacks in many ways reflected the complex manner in which race functioned in the UMWA. At the convention, for example, Mine Mill supporters noted that miners' union officials had reaffirmed their commitment to the rights of Alabama's black workers. "Mitch speaks out clearly in behalf of Negro rights and is able to capitalize as a friend of the Negro workers," one observer noted. CIO officials, by contrast, had failed to take a "clear-cut position on this crucial problem." Outside of Mine Mill, "few if any of the other CIO unions, will carry on a steady fight for the Negro workers." An illustration of the UMWA's influence in this regard appeared in the resolution passed by the state CIO convention. Delegates at the event adopted a resolution that condemned racial discrimination in war or peace and called on federal officials to remove restrictions against blacks serving in the military.[116]

But following the convention, troubling reports reached Mine Mill officials. The UMWA in Alabama began a campaign to bring the ore miners into District 50, a branch of the miners' union that organized workers outside the coal industry. Racial divisions ran deep in Mine Mill, and by the early 1940s, white secessionist movements had begun at some Birmingham District locals. Officials with the mostly black Mine Mill believed that the District 50 organizers worked to attract white separatists in the summer of 1942 in an attempt to bring the iron ore operations into the UMWA fold.[117]

They had good reason for their worries. Virgil Powell, a leading white dissident at Republic Steel's Raimund ore mines, was allegedly "working in behalf" of UMWA's District 50 in Birmingham. Powell had led a protest by a group of nonunion whites who threatened to strike when a black worker received a formerly "white" job. The former president of Mine Mill's Muscoda local, W. C. Gunnin, a white who was defeated when he ran for reelection, became "outspoken against the Negroes" and a "District 50 advocate." White dissidents at Mine Mill locals had threatened union officials and telephoned black local officers "telling them that their white local presidents intend to have them killed," attempting to drive a wedge between white and black officers. At about the same time, Lewis Tarrant, a black vice president at the Raimund local, received death threats from people claiming to be members of the Bessemer Ku Klux Klan, suggesting a relationship between that group, the white dissidents, and by extension District 50. "Unfortunately, District 50 is definitely involved in this anti-Negro group, since they have given them encouragement to fight" Mine Mill, one observer concluded. Further, Mine Mill partisans suspected that Cowherd, a close Mitch ally, had connections with both the dissidents and company officials who exploited the racial divide in the iron ore mines.[118]

District 50's 1942 effort to raid the Mine Mill locals failed. Seven years later, however, the tactics pioneered by the UMWA against the iron ore miners reemerged in a takeover effort by the United Steelworkers of America. The steelworkers used anticommunism and colluded with disgruntled white unionists in their efforts to gain control of many of the Mine Mill locals. The steelworkers' union eventually prevailed over Mine Mill in an election that took place against the backdrop of Klan night riding and violence.[119]

District 50's attempt to take control of the iron ore union locals illustrated how tenuous the UMWA's biracialism had become. The concessions to white supremacy embedded in the "miners' formula" had limited the advancement of African Americans such as Walter Jones in the UMWA structure and ultimately constrained their influence within the organization. Though the union's racial policies remained capable of provoking extreme reactions from many whites, the racial tension of wartime Alabama had caused the UMWA to begin to back off its earlier commitments to its African American members. The ramifications of this trend would emerge a few years after the end of World War II, when a sustained depression swept through the Alabama coal industry. These economic problems, along with a new round of technological changes, caused most miners to lose their jobs. African Americans, however, would suffer a disproportionate share of these job losses. A more immediate struggle loomed for District 20, however. The remaining years of World War II would see the miners in Alabama defy the federal and state governments, coal operators, union leaders, and the wider public in a series of bitter strikes designed to force concessions from the companies despite the atmosphere of crisis.

CHAPTER THREE

The World War II Strikes,
1941–1945

In February 1942, a few months after the beginning of direct American involvement in World War II, leaders of the United Mine Workers of America (UMWA) in Alabama sent out a circular reminding members that the union had adopted "a No Strike policy during the war period." For the duration of the war, the document explained, the policy of the miners' union was "to settle all our differences in the regular orderly way, in line with contract." Further, the circular proclaimed, the union supported the "all-out effort for war production." Echoing the country's popular mood as well as proclamations by the leaders of the UMWA, the Congress of Industrial Organizations (CIO), and the American Federation of Labor (AFL), the directive ordered rank-and-file miners to avoid "participating in a local strike of any character. We feel there are ample provisions in our contract to take care of any and all controversies that arise. Therefore, we urge all our membership, and especially the leaders of all locals, to double their efforts to prevent any cessation of operations."[1]

The circular, events would demonstrate, had little effect in the Birmingham District's mines. Alabama coal miners, like workers in other industries and locations, completely disregarded their leaders' no-strike pledges during the wartime emergency, and wildcat strikes (unauthorized walkouts that often pitted the miners against both their union and the companies) occurred with surprising frequency. In 1944 alone, company officials estimated, wildcat strikes occurred at least two hundred times at mines across the Birmingham District.[2] During 1943 and 1945, national strikes often took on the character of wildcat strikes in the state, with miners acting independently or in open defiance of state and national union leaders.

In a general sense, the wartime strikes in the Birmingham District represent a piece of wartime history that has been hidden as many scholars have emphasized the social unity inspired by the war effort. Particularly in Alabama, the war effort "assumed something of the character of a crusade." However, the state's coalfields were anything but calm and orderly during the wartime era, and the unrest mirrored labor strife on the national level. Robert Zieger, for example, counted fourteen thousand strikes involving seven million workers between 1942 and 1945 in his important study of the CIO.[3]

Scholars believe that these strikes occurred for a host of different reasons. Historian George Lipsitz has argued that the walkouts represented a rebellion against corporate and union efforts to enforce "social harmony" during the war. In this sense, he wrote, workers had to strike to make their grievances known, and such walkouts created a "new workers' public sphere." In some cases, wartime walkouts reflected war-induced disruptions of working-class communities, which found themselves under stress from inflation and the heavy toll the production demands of the war inflicted on workers. In other instances, the strikes illustrated the pressures building on the shop floor as grievances went unresolved. Unauthorized walkouts also erupted when racial tensions boiled over in the workplace and became "hate strikes"—actions where white workers sought to protest the promotion or employment of African Americans.[4]

Both national and local issues inspired these walkouts. The Birmingham District's coal miners of both races entered the wartime emergency from a position of strength. Unionization rates in the Alabama coalfields surpassed 90 percent, and only one major coal producer, Alabama Fuel and Iron (AFICO), had resisted the UMWA. Still, some of the coal operators, particularly Tennessee Coal, Iron, and Railroad (TCI), a captive producer, avoided implementing agreements that state and national UMWA leaders hammered out with the companies. As a result, Alabama miners took matters into their own hands, engaging in wildcat strikes to enforce provisions of national agreements or using national walkouts to force local issues into the agreements that state leaders negotiated.

Though conflict between the coal operators and union inspired many of the wartime walkouts, tensions also emerged between the rank and file and state UMWA leaders. Since the UMWA's return to Alabama in 1933, shadowy opposition movements had existed in the union. Communists initially provided much of the structure that gave voice to the grievances of District 20's rank and file. Although communist influence within the union had declined by the end of the 1930s, such movements continued. Throughout the war years, rank-and-file dissidents encouraged miners to disregard the directives of state and national union leaders. These actions, which union leaders called rump or undercover movements, greatly concerned state union officials, particularly District 20 President William Mitch, who viewed them as a direct challenge to his authority and as a threat to the UMWA.

This chapter examines this unrest, placing it into the context of the economic and social changes that swept through Alabama during the war. The chapter begins with an overview of the transformation that wartime spending brought to the state and the strain that the conflict placed on miners and their communities. It then examines the wildcat strikes that grew as working conditions declined during the conflict. This chapter also places these walkouts in a historical context, tracing the origins of the dissident movements that often drove the wartime protests. Finally, the analysis shifts to the national strikes that swept the nation's coalfields in 1943 and 1945. In these strikes, Alabama miners attempted to force the coal operators, particularly captive coal companies such as TCI, to abide by national agreements. Doing so, however, required miners to defy the operators, the general public, federal and state authorities, and even their union.

❰ ❰ ❰

World War II ushered in an economic transformation of the South. The region experienced massive population shifts as people moved from rural areas into urban centers or areas where defense industries thrived. The change prompted the chair of the War Production Board, Donald M. Nelson, to proclaim that the conflict would bring the "South into the vanguard of world industrial progress." Some spending found its way to the region's older industries, like steel and textiles, while new facilities such as aircraft plants and munitions factories rose along the southern landscape and the region's shipyards and ports found new life. Military dollars also poured in as bases and camps sprouted across the South. More than four billion dollars—36 percent of the total national military spending—made its way to the region during the war years.[5]

Alabama attracted a large share of the region's defense-related business. Huntsville, for example, grew from a sleepy textile town into a major defense center boasting two arsenals and an ordnance depot that attracted thousands of new residents. The number of industrial jobs in the city rose from thirty-five hundred in 1940 to about seventeen thousand in 1944. The old port city of Mobile experienced unparalleled growth as its small shipyards expanded and new ones opened. By the middle of the war, the city found itself overcrowded with tens of thousands of new residents, and the War Manpower Commission labeled it the nation's most congested shipyard center.[6]

Even rural Alabama found itself transformed by the war. An estimated twenty-five thousand workers descended on Talladega County, east of Birmingham, to build Du Pont's Alabama Ordnance Works at Childersburg and the Coosa River Ordnance Plant in Talladega. When completed, the plants provided high-paying jobs for fourteen thousand people. Childersburg's population grew from five hundred in 1940 to nine thousand by the end of the war.[7]

As the South's major center for heavy industry, Birmingham saw its old industrial base of steel and iron expand and attracted a share of the new defense plants. The Magic City's industries eventually accounted for about 75 percent of the munitions, steel, and war-related goods produced in the Southeastern Ordnance District. TCI's mills began operating three eight-hour shifts, and the company expanded its iron ore mining, coal mining, and iron and steel capacity. By 1941, TCI employed an estimated thirty-one thousand workers. New plants also came to Birmingham. Bechtel-McCone Aircraft Modification Company opened a facility that processed and modified half of the B-29 bombers the United States used in the war.[8]

Demand for coal surged with the onset of hostilities. In 1940, Alabama miners had produced 15.2 million tons of coal. Two years later, the level had risen to more than 18 million tons, where it would remain for much of the war. The number of miners increased from 23,513 in 1940 to 26,783 in 1942 and then declined to 21,975 at the end of the war as military recruitment and mechanization took their toll on employment levels.[9]

The wartime emergency and the economic change it produced strained coalfield manpower. By the spring of 1942, the Alabama Mining Institute (AMI), the operators' main lobbying organization, reported an increase in absenteeism as well as high rates of turnover among miners in the Birmingham District. The announcement of the new airplane factory in Birmingham worried AMI officials, who anxiously contacted federal officials to explain the "serious condition existing" with regard to the tightening labor supply, circumstances, the operators feared, that would be worsened by the new plant.[10]

By the following summer, miner absenteeism and turnover had reached crisis levels. Officials estimated that the coal industry faced a shortage of between four thousand and five thousand miners as production demands increased. The labor shortages had caused the mines to operate at about 10 percent below capacity. Testifying before the state's Labor Supply Committee in Montgomery, Mitch blamed the coal companies, which, he contended, refused to pay miners a fair wage for the difficult and dangerous work they performed. Higher wages and better working conditions had lured laborers to defense plants and away from mines, the District 20 president claimed. Absenteeism, Mitch argued, resulted from the physical toll that the difficult work took on an aging workforce. The increased production demands also caused equipment to break down more often, sometimes preventing men from entering the mines. "Coal mining is a peculiar industry," Mitch said. "They go out to their homes not because they don't want to work, but because of the physical condition in the mines."[11]

State officials, union leaders, and managers seemed at a loss about how to resolve these difficulties. AMI officials suggested releasing soldiers from military duty to dig coal. The organization's president, I. W. Rouzer, believed that Utah provided a potential model: there, beginning in the summer of 1943, military leaders allowed an estimated forty-five hundred soldiers to work as metal miners in areas where the labor shortage proved most pronounced. "I predict this same procedure is going to have to be followed in obtaining men to dig coal, if the Selective Service boards continue to draft our coal miners," he wrote. "There is already a shortage of coal, and production is not keeping pace with consumption."[12]

In a report issued in late July, the Labor Supply Committee called on the companies, UMWA, and miners to work together to eliminate the factors that caused turnover and absenteeism. The committee also appealed for "all potential workers" whether "experienced or inexperienced in coal mining" to contact federal employment officials about jobs in the industry. The committee called on Alabama Governor Chauncey Sparks to appeal for increased coal production, stressing that "a man idle for one day reduces the coal output from four to five tons and that this loss of production is an asset to the Axis."[13]

Miners in Alabama faced other problems during the war. Soaring costs ate into their paychecks and nullified the wage increases they had gained over the past decade. Housing and food costs rose rapidly. Nationally, one group of union leaders estimated that prices rose 30 percent between January 1941 and January 1943. Living in small towns and villages outside of urban areas, many of the country's coal miners were particularly hard hit by inflation, as was evidenced by a survey of eighty Pennsylvania mining towns that found that prices had risen almost 125 percent between 1939 and 1943.[14]

In the spring of 1942, miner Lon Thompson of Piper expressed the difficulties that wartime inflation caused for Alabama miners. In a letter to UMWA President John L. Lewis, Thompson claimed that miners in Bibb County saw the rent on a typical three-room company house rise from $6.00 a month to $7.85. Larger homes might cost miners $11.00 a month. Thompson said that miners also were hard pressed by increasing food prices. Since the start of the war, Thompson noted, the cost for a bag of flour had increased from ten cents to forty cents, while a bag of sugar rose from seven cents to twenty cents and lard rose from twenty-seven cents to seventy cents. All of these increases caused major problems for miners, whose paychecks remained stagnant. "The laboring man is hard put to make ends meet," Thompson complained, "and if [prices] continue to rise we can't live in decency."[15]

Many industrial workers found preserving their standard of living more difficult after July 1942, when the National War Labor Board (NWLB) issued its Little Steel Formula. The policy sought to keep wartime inflation under control but did so on the backs of workers, who found themselves limited to wage increases of only 15 percent more than they earned in January 1941. Lewis and other union leaders as well as miners were angered that the federal government appeared to be placing harsher restrictions on workers than on industrialists. Furthermore, many on labor's side opposed the Little Steel Formula because they believed that it kept their wages below those of workers in other war-related industries and left regional wage differentials in place; consequently, much of the miners' resentment was directed at the NWLB. While the board held miners' wages in check, the Office of Price Administration approved a large price increase for coal from western Pennsylvania producers in January 1943. Critics charged that instead of serving as a stabilizing mechanism, the Little Steel Formula amounted to little more than a wage freeze in an era of skyrocketing price increases.[16]

Coal mining wages in Alabama varied between $30 and $45 a week, depending where miners worked and what job they held. Quoting federal officials, Rouzer told Sparks in the summer of 1943 that miners were "among the highest paid workers in the war industries." Rouzer exaggerated the wages available in the Alabama coalfields, which were considerably lower than those in other states because of the regional wage differentials. Miners earned more than textile workers in the South, who took home only about $19.82 a week for much of the war. While the average industrial worker earned $29.23 a week, those who found jobs in Alabama's defense-related industries could earn considerably more. Timekeepers in the Mobile shipyards made $61.20 a week, according to one source, while wages at the Childersburg munitions plant ranged from $35 to $75 a week.[17] Workers' wages in many of the South's older industries, including coal and textiles, remained significantly lower than wages in the newer defense industries. This difference undoubtedly encouraged miners to leave the industry during the war and remained a serious grievance for those who remained underground.

During the war years, a gulf widened between rank-and-file miners and state union officers. This problem manifested itself in a dramatic rise in the number of wildcat strikes. When the United States entered World War II, CIO President Philip Murray had pledged to do everything possible to expand production while keeping labor peace. Shortly after the Japanese attacked Pearl Harbor, major labor leaders, including Lewis, announced that they would not engage in walkouts during the war. "Labor is determined to place itself in the forefront in the battle of achieving maximum production," Murray proclaimed after the attack.[18] All unions would find it difficult to uphold the no-strike pledge, and the problem was particularly acute for the coal miners in light of their declining working conditions.

The dissident rank-and-file movements directly challenged the no-strike pledge. The movements demonstrated a remarkable level of organization, although the names of most of the leaders have been lost. Such dissident movements had a long history in District 20, having begun to take shape shortly after the UMWA returned to Alabama. Throughout the union's first decade in the state, District 20 was beset by rank-and-file movements, secret committees, and internal struggles for control.

From 1933 to 1935, activists associated with the Communist Party provided much of the infrastructure for internal dissent within the miners' union. Organizers infiltrated UMWA locals and developed a strong critique of Mitch's leadership. From its reemergence in 1933 until the early 1970s, when the union experienced a democratic reform movement, Lewis and the national union presidents who followed him appointed all the UMWA's leaders in Alabama. Without elections to exert pressure on district leaders, communists and rank-and-file dissidents organized underground movements and attempted to shape union policies. One of the earliest showdowns between the rank and file and the official union leadership came in October 1933, when state leaders had turned back a strike wave designed to force coal operators to recognize the union and rehire fired militants. Mitch, worried about the UMWA's weakness in the Alabama coalfields, did not feel that the miners would win the strike, so he worked with federal officials to convince the men to return to work.[19]

Communists, who provided much of the structure for these protests, attempted to organize the rank and file into their movement. Tapping into the UMWA militants' anger over Mitch's actions, William Stone attempted to recruit miners for a communist-led meeting in late October to devise a strategy on behalf of the Birmingham District's miners and steelworkers. "Workers themselves must hold the offices created," Stone wrote. "Only actual workers will be admitted to membership." Criticizing Mitch's leadership, Stone claimed that "the miners are being sold out here. Over one thousand have been sent back into the pits without win[n]ing their demands." The meeting failed to produce the desired results. UMWA informants infiltrated the event, and police eventually broke up the meeting and arrested a dozen activists.[20]

Despite the setback, "secret committees" that operated outside of the District 20 leadership's control had emerged in the Birmingham District's mines by December. These committees had been meeting "for the purpose of trying to force action because they contend there has been too much delay and various companies have agitated by discharging men, etc.," Mitch reported. While he agreed with the dissidents about the need for "a little agitation" to force the companies to stop firing union militants and to sign contracts with District 20, the state union president again feared the union's weakness, writing that "the men here cannot strike but a very few days at the most. Hence, I am trying to avoid strikes as far as possible."[21]

The walkouts that swept the Alabama coalfields in the spring of 1934 ultimately resulted in most of the operators recognizing the union, the implementation of a thirty-five-hour workweek, and a wage increase. Though the rolling walkouts essentially had succeeded, UMWA officials had denounced "radical elements" in the miners' union and had cooperated with the operators to limit communist influence in locals. Radicals still maintained some sway in the UMWA, however, and remained sharp critics of Mitch and the District 20 leadership, which they saw as too willing to compromise.[22]

The high-water mark of communist influence came in the spring and fall of 1935, when leftists provided important infrastructure for a series of walkouts. Communists had called for a strike on 1 April, and although that event never materialized, the movement they had established in District 20's mines provided a high level of organization for the longer struggle, which began in September. As early as the winter of 1935, for example, communists began to encourage miners to organize walkouts when their contract expired the following spring. While activists hoped to force concessions from the operators, they also wanted to prevent Mitch and the other District 20 leaders from negotiating a contract without rank-and-file input. Activist G. L. Johnson warned miners that "District officials are issuing orders that the April first agreement will be made by the District officials and that the miners are bound to accept them. In other words Mitch will do his best to shove a false contract down the throats of the miners." The strength of the UMWA organization was its deep presence in coal communities, and leftists worked to make the strike wave a community-based movement, incorporating both unemployed miners and women into auxiliaries that organizers hoped would provide crucial support for the walkout. Highly organized unemployed workers, activists reasoned, could walk picket lines. Unemployed pickets also would be less likely to become strikebreakers. Well-organized women could prove essential to the success of a walkout through their activism and because "the women make good pickets . . . the company gun thugs will not fire on the women folks like they will the men," Johnson wrote.[23]

The issue of whether to organize unemployed miners and women illustrated the divisions between activists and union leaders. While communists generally supported unemployed miners, UMWA officials saw them as a clear threat. The miners' union had reemerged so rapidly in District 20 that union officials sometimes chartered locals that contained large numbers of unemployed miners. The status of these men within the union was unclear, and in some instances, unemployed miners convinced union members to take more militant stands on issues or even to walk out. In the fall of 1934, for example, District 20 officials reported that unemployed miners had provoked a series of strikes at DeBardeleben Coal operations in Coal Valley. Mitch, worrying about the challenge these miners posed to the union leadership, urged Lewis to send an international representative to inform striking miners that "the idle men should not participate in contract affairs that the local should not take action embarrassing" the UMWA. District 20 officials sometimes took the dramatic step of rechartering local unions, an action that weeded out many unemployed miners and made them ineligible to participate in union affairs. Though women constituted crucial members of the coal communities in which the UMWA existed, union officials allowed women no formal role in the union's affairs. Even supporting roles were forbidden for women: at the organization's 1934 international convention, delegates had rejected appeals to allow women to form auxiliaries. Coalfield women who sought involvement in union events had few options.[24]

The organizing work paid off in the fall of 1935, as the strikes pushed the UMWA membership to the brink. Some operators, such as Charles DeBardeleben and AFICO, reacted violently to the walkouts, while federal officials did not make relief to strikers readily available. Alabama Governor Bibb Graves eventually mediated a settlement that included a small wage increase, and the UMWA organization survived.[25]

Rank-and-file activism also figured into divisions that emerged among District 20 leaders in the fall of 1933. Many Alabama miners gravitated toward William Dalrymple, the international representative whom Lewis had first sent into District 20 in the winter of 1933. Dalrymple was a fiery speaker, and as his popularity grew, he and Mitch developed a rivalry in the District 20 office. Though Mitch described the two men as "friends," he quietly worked to have Dalrymple removed from the state in the fall of 1933.[26]

Mitch, who had come to Alabama from Indiana, was acutely conscious of his status as an outsider during his early days in the Birmingham District. His frustration with the situation in Alabama occasionally boiled over. African American organizer Walter Jones reported that he had "heard Mr. Mitch say, that he would welcome a change from this field." As late as 1938, Mitch referred to himself as "a 'carpetbagger' from the North" in communication with other industrial unionists. In the early days of the union's emergence in Alabama, Mitch seemed particularly concerned with the level of rank-and-file activism that Alabama miners displayed. "This place is like a madhouse—numerous committees every day wanting information and making complaints and apparently they are not satisfied until I have met with them and listened and finally told them what to do," he informed Lewis in the fall of 1933. A few months later, Mitch confided in Murray that Alabama "is like a kindergarten . . . because of the men not understanding."[27]

Though Dalrymple had come to Alabama from outside the state as well, his connection with average miners may have provoked Mitch to perceive him as a rival. At some point—the exact moment, cause, and extent of the rupture remain unclear—a division emerged between the two officials. The dispute clearly existed during the November 1933 row over whether to give Walter Jones a paid position on the UMWA staff. Mitch suspected that Dalrymple and William Raney, another District 20 official, had discussed hiring the African American activist. Mitch perceived this as an act of disloyalty and complained to Lewis "that in some respects I have not received full cooperation down here."[28]

In his efforts to have Dalrymple removed from District 20, Mitch focused on the opposition Dalrymple's fiery rhetoric had aroused among government officials and coal operators. "I feel sure that it is not what has been said by Representative Dalrymple as much as it is the way he says it," Mitch told Lewis. "Of course, the workers generally like to hear attacks on the operators or their managers and are liberal with their applause and while we know that attacks could be justified in every respect, yet this does not get us together as we should be at least moving in that direction." Government and operator representatives refused to meet with Dalrymple, which meant that Mitch and Raney had to perform extra work.[29]

Walker County Sheriff A. N. Barrentine described the contrast in styles to Lewis in an October 1933 letter. According to Barrentine, Dalrymple "is doing more harm than good." While Mitch and Raney urged miners to "go ahead and work and co-operate with the coal operators," Dalrymple had encouraged the miners to take a hard line. "It is my information that [Dalrymple] curses the operators and it seems to be his purpose to stir the men up rather than give them sound advice."[30]

Lewis took Mitch's advice, transferring Dalrymple out of Alabama at the end of 1933. Letters protesting the decision streamed into the union's national office in early 1934. Herbert Weaver, an activist at AFICO's operations at Acmar, begged

Lewis to reconsider his decision "as the miners down here responds to [Dalrymple's] presence at the mass meetings all over the state, [more] than any of the other Representatives, Mr. Mitch or Raney." The officers of the UMWA local at Aldrich agreed, informing Lewis that "William Dalrymple is needed more in the State of Alabama now than ever. We hope you will again assign him for Alabama, as he already knows these conditions and would be of great help to our other Officials as well as the miners."[31] The UMWA president stood firm on his decision, and Dalrymple eventually settled in Seattle, Washington.

The move did not bring an end to the friction between Mitch and Dalrymple. Dalrymple maintained contact with Alabama activists and occasionally wrote a column for the local labor newspaper, the *Labor Advocate*. In one issue, Dalrymple criticized the industry policy of deducting a fee from miners' paychecks for washing coal, charging that the practice was "the biggest dam steal that could be made against the coal miners by the coal companies; why it has been permitted to continue is beyond my powers of reasoning." Mitch perceived the column as a criticism of his leadership and convinced other state UMWA officials to sign a letter to Lewis accusing Dalrymple of "meddling in affairs he knows nothing about." District officials asked Lewis to prevent Dalrymple from authoring future columns in the publication, claiming that the articles "will create a feeling of unrest and play right into the hands of the Communists, who are active to quite a degree in this section." Lewis heeded this advice, wiring Dalrymple to stop "all communications" with Alabama newspapers.[32]

Though dissident movements faded after 1935, they would reemerge during a fall 1941 national walkout when Lewis attempted to use a series of carefully orchestrated strikes to force U.S. Steel and other captive coal companies to end their commitment to the open shop. On 15 September, fifty-three thousand miners walked out across the country for two days before Lewis and the captive operators reached a temporary agreement. On 28 October, miners again walked out for two days before Lewis called them back to work with a mid-November deadline set for the captive operators to grant the union shop. When federal officials ruled against the UMWA's demand, union members walked out on 17 November, and miners did not return until the federal government imposed the union shop on 7 December, the same day the Japanese attacked Pearl Harbor.

But early in the strikes, Alabama miners openly defied Lewis and other UMWA leaders. District 20 miners began to stop work in early September, weeks before the walkouts began in other coalfields. By 5 September, all of the state's major union coal mines stood idle. Lewis and other UMWA officials blamed the coal companies for the walkout, noting that the Alabama operators had failed "to accept and apply" the terms of the major regional settlement reached the preceding spring. Furthermore, the companies had delayed adding forty cents a day to miners' paychecks, a concession granted after a national walkout in the spring. This amount would have raised Alabama miners' basic wage to $5.90 a day, still less than the $7.00 a day guaranteed miners in other parts of the South.[33]

The strike that hit the Alabama coalfields in the fall of 1941 appears to have been a highly coordinated attempt by local miners to force the captive coal operators to pay money owned as a result of the spring agreement. The state UMWA had failed to convince the companies to comply with this provision, so miners initiated a walkout outside the control of local union leaders. Early in the strike wave, Mitch publicly labeled the actions "unauthorized" and appealed to the miners to return to work "immediately." The independent nature of the strike movement greatly disturbed Mitch, who complained to Lewis that an "outlaw bunch is working with ulterior motive trying to keep mines from going to work." Most miners heeded an appeal from Lewis and returned to work after a few days on strike. But three thousand TCI miners refused to end their walkouts. Militant unionists set up pickets and examined union cards, a process that idled several of the company's operations. The miners returned only after the National Defense Mediation Board requested that production remain constant while it debated the miners' demands.[34]

Still, rank-and-file militants agitated for a showdown with the state's coal operators. District officials headed off a wildcat movement in late September, convincing a mass meeting of miners in Wylam to vote to continue work. The "unanimous" vote of the five hundred miners at the meeting masked the dissent building in the state. International representative John A. Hanratty confirmed union officials' tenuous hold on the state's miners when he described the vote as "a killing blow to an 'undercover movement to set September 20 as a deadline' for the negotiation of a permanent settlement of the mine dispute in Alabama."[35] By late September 1941, then, a highly organized effort, operating independently of the UMWA leadership, had emerged in Alabama. This movement played an important role in the coalfield strikes that erupted two years later.

Most walkouts during the war years, however, involved only a single mine or a small number of operations. These wildcat strikes grew from a host of different sources. Some of these problems were related to situations in the mines—typically, conflicts between managers and miners. UMWA contracts contained grievance procedures, but many disputes often fell outside such mechanisms; moreover, District 20 officials often sided with the companies in disputes that were covered by the contractual language. In other instances, miners took matters into their own hands when companies refused to abide by measures they had signed.

Many of these disputes were local in nature and confined to a single mine or company. In these cases, UMWA members sometimes walked out to protest poor treatment underground or sudden changes in their work assignments. In some cases, however, local disputes resonated with miners at nearby operations, and walkouts that began at a single mine would spread, threatening to develop into a much larger, better coordinated wave of wildcat strikes.

An August 1945 change in job classification and pay rates at DeBardeleben Coal's Sipsey mine sparked one such strike.[36] The adjustments lowered the pay of three miners, required the men to perform more work, and exposed them to more dust underground. When the company refused to listen to their complaints, the three men went on strike, idling the entire Sipsey operation. After several days, the miners at Sipsey convinced UMWA members at a neighboring DeBardeleben operation to honor their pickets. "It seems to be a spreading proposition," lamented Mitch.[37]

District 20 officials sided with the company, supporting the new pay rates and job changes. The union told the miners to return to work, but the strikers refused, even after Lewis repeatedly appealed to them to do so. After one such request, local unionists called a meeting to vote on whether to return to work, but only a handful of members showed up, and the event was adjourned "without action." At a regularly scheduled local meeting a few days later, secretary Arthur Short reported "much discussion on the dispute" but no "change in the attitude of the men. . . . [T]he mine is still idle today."[38]

Company violations of seniority also provoked wildcat strikes, as rank-and-file miners walked when contract language prevented them from using grievance procedures. In the case of a fall 1944 walkout at the Sipsey mine, DeBardeleben Coal abided by the rules of its agreement with the UMWA, but the miners walked out anyway, openly violating their contract. The company had brought in a section foreman from another mine to fill the position of haulage boss, causing the Sipsey miners to argue that "the oldest motorman at the . . . mine should have had that job" and to go on strike. As in many other disputes, the UMWA sided with the company but reported "considerable trouble getting [the Sipsey miners] to agree with us and go back to work."[39]

The always tense relations between managers and miners deteriorated further during the wartime emergency. As a result, miners often struck when supervisors attempted to discipline union members. A wildcat strike idled Brookside-Pratt's Blossburg mine for more than a week in the spring of 1943 when a foreman refused to let a union official work underground. The miners demanded that the "mine foreman be laid off" until the dispute was settled. Miners struck TCI's Wylam operation when supervisors attempted to fire a trip rider for absenteeism and for showing up to work intoxicated. Several strikes that hit Sloss-Sheffield Steel and Iron's Flat Top mine in Jefferson County erupted in the winter of 1944 after supervisors became "abusive with the men."[40]

A strike at DeBardeleben Coal's Empire mine demonstrated the difficulties the UMWA faced in trying to mediate such disputes, particularly when miners perceived the union as siding with the companies. In October 1944, miners at the Empire operation walked out and demanded the removal of a mine foreman whom they disliked. District 20 officials made two attempts to schedule a meeting with union militants, but "the men did not want one." When UMWA officials attempted to mediate the walkout, miners at Empire rejected the overtures. "Our representatives are utterly unable to get them to state what complaint they had against the boss, or state reasons for the stoppage of work," Mitch complained to Lewis.[41] Miners used these walkouts to challenge the authority of the bosses underground and to shape working conditions, in the process demonstrating a willingness, as the Empire case illustrated, to defy union leaders to achieve these goals.

Nothing illustrated the divided mind of the UMWA leaders better than disputes over safety. The war emergency led managers to place an increased premium on production, resulting in an often-deadly decline in working conditions. The number of miners injured nationally at work skyrocketed from sixty-four thousand in 1941 to seventy-five thousand in 1942 to one hundred thousand in 1943.[42] A pair of horrific 1943 Alabama mine disasters illustrated how dangerous mining had become and showed the breadth of the gap between working miners and District 20 officials.

The first explosion, which occurred in May 1943 at the Praco mine owned by Alabama By-Products, killed ten miners and injured five others. Officials blamed the explosion on a spark from a coal-cutting machine that ignited a pocket of methane gas. More than twenty men worked in the section where the blast occurred, more than a mile from the mine entrance. Many of the miners, investigators believed, had died after the initial explosion. "The opinion was voiced that the miners had been suffocated after having been trapped in a section of the slope beyond that from which their companions escaped," a news report concluded.[43]

UMWA President Lewis, in the midst of heated talks with company officials and the federal government, used the disaster to bolster the union's position in the negotiations. "Your international officers and members of the National Policy Committee believe that mine disasters are preventable, and that they occur because of carelessness, stupidity or greed on the part of mine management," he wrote. "We believe that the mine workers of the nation should be accorded justice commensurate with the hazards and the exhaustive work of the industry, and we will continue our fight toward this end." But Lewis and the UMWA did little else, and no record of a major investigation into the accident survives in the union's papers. Lewis and other national union officers pledged only to send "a contribution . . . to be used in behalf of the bereaved families of the victims, and we hope that it will serve to alleviate some of the material distress which surrounds them."[44]

The second mine disaster called into serious question the union's commitment to the safety of its members. In August, two blasts rocked Republic Steel Company's Sayreton mine, killing twenty-five people and injuring nineteen others. During the two years leading up to the explosion, miners at the operation had walked out at least seven times to protest grievances. Mitch had harshly criticized the local's members, and union officials consistently urged the miners to end their protests. Federal investigators had issued warnings about unsafe conditions at the mine only a few months before the tragedy, but both the company and the UMWA failed to heed the warnings.

In their responses to wildcats by miners at Sayreton, District 20 officials often blamed the local. After the miners struck in July 1941, for example, Mitch lectured the local's president, Huey Sewell, that the miners were in violation of their contract with the company: Republic officials knew "nothing about the cause of the strike" and were at a "loss to understand this line of procedure." Mitch then complained to Lewis about the Sayreton local's "obnoxious practice of striking when the management has not been apprized of any complaint."[45]

A year later, Sayreton local officials appealed to Lewis for help following another wildcat strike. Foremen at the Sayreton mine harassed miners "which in a manner is cruelty," new local president Howard Nail and recording secretary R. H. Walker claimed. The company crowded too many men, many of them new hires, into working places underground, creating dangerous conditions. The local unionists also believed that the company hoped "to wreck or weaken the united fortification which we have strive[d] to build up in working conditions for the past seven or more years" and sharply criticized District 20 officials who had been unable to help remedy these problems. "We sometimes wonder if the District Officers are performing their full duty by taking up our grievances whole-heartedly," the miners complained.[46]

A report by federal investigators issued in February 1943, six months before the fatal explosions, warned about the unsafe conditions at the Sayreton mine. The report found that the mine—rated "gassy" by state authorities—contained dangerous levels of "standing gas during the inspection." Investigators determined that the mine lacked adequate ventilation to remove the pockets of methane and noted that miners operated in dangerous areas with "non-permissible" electrical equipment. The inspectors reported that Republic operated the mine with trolley locomotives, mining machines, coal drills, pump motors, air compressors, and rock-dust motors that posed a danger to the miners. "Should large quantities of methane be suddenly liberated in this mine, an ignition or explosion would probably occur because non-permissible equipment and bare power wires are used," they warned. The coal dust detected at the mine also concerned the federal officials. It had a ratio of "volatile to total combustible matter" of almost three times the level authorities considered dangerous. The inspectors concluded that "the coal dust in the mine is highly explosive."[47]

Their report proved prophetic. On the night of 28 August, two blasts rocked the Sayreton mine. The first explosion occurred at 10:20 p.m. and the second about two hours later. Officials believed that sixteen miners died in the first incident, while the second blast killed nine miners, managers, and state officials attempting to rescue injured miners and investigate the causes of the initial explosion. The first blast occurred after methane gas was pushed into a working part of the mine from an abandoned section and sparks from a nonpermissible electric motor ignited the gas. The second explosion took place after a door that had been blown open by the first blast was closed, causing the mine's ventilation system to carry gas back into the area of the initial blast, where it exploded when it came in contact with fires still burning in the wake of the first incident.[48]

The explosions exacted a terrifying toll on those underground. When rescuer Andy King entered the mine after the first blast, he found six bodies "stretched along the track, one behind the other, as if they had been running when they died. One fellow further down—a great big fellow . . . was huddled on his hands and knees. He must've died on his knees." The second explosion hit as King carried another rescuer, who had suddenly collapsed as methane flooded into the area, back to the surface. The blast hurled the two men thirty feet. Some of the bodies, the UMWA reported, were "so scorched and blackened that they were hardly recognizable." When UMWA investigator Harrison Combs ventured into the mine following the second explosion, he saw, to his horror, "the complete skin together with the nails of both hands of a miner who had attempted to crawl out after the explosion. This skin like a pair of gloves was still laying in the middle of the tracks."[49]

Officials concluded that Republic Steel had disregarded the earlier warnings about the dangers miners faced at the Sayreton operation. During their inquiry, Combs and his team found cutting and loading machines, drills, and haulage motors that violated accepted safety standards. Cables and electrical circuits also appeared in a poor state. The investigators concluded that "it would be possible at any time for gas to be ignited by sparks from this machinery."[50]

Federal and union inspectors proposed a number of improvements to the Sayreton operation following investigations of the August explosions. Republic officials agreed to upgrade ventilation but claimed that the "non-permissible" equipment would have to remain until they could purchase new machinery. Furthermore, Republic officials antagonized rather than cooperated with local union representatives. When members of the Sayreton local attempted to help with the investigation following the blasts, the company had state police remove the miners. Managers also refused the Sayreton unionists' demand for publication of a third-party investigation on the explosions. Combs reported that the miners "were in a very disturbed condition and unwilling to return to work" until their demands were met.[51]

The tension between the miners and company continued during the months that followed. In January 1944 miners walked out in protest. An attempt to reorganize work regulations and the company's disregard for seniority rules sparked the miners' protests. Mitch noted that the "physical condition of the mine is bad," a fact that undoubtedly played a major role in provoking the walkout. After repeated appeals from Mitch and Lewis, the Sayreton miners went back to work.[52]

Republic's problems between managers and miners continued, and the UMWA failed to resolve these tensions and persuade the company to improve Sayreton's conditions. A dozen miners walked out in early October, claiming that a manager was "dogging" them, and a week later the rest of the operation's miners joined the wildcat strike. UMWA officials attempted to mediate, and after hearing the miners' contention "that the boss had violated certain safety rules," the union filed a formal complaint with state regulators, convincing the UMWA members to return to work on 20 October. Three days later, the miners again quit work for two days. Mitch dismissed the miners' concerns, arguing that "the only thing they contended was that the boss had technically violated some of the company's safety rules."[53]

The division between the miners and union officials at Sayreton was repeated countless times across District 20 during the war. Mitch complained that in most cases, the walkouts occurred "in violation of the contract and the matter could be settled better while the mine is in operation." Alabama union officials considered removing the charters of problem locals but decided that "it would be better that the International wire on stubborn cases that we have."[54]

Such action probably would have provoked even more dissension within the union. A policy of fining locals whose members engaged in wildcats, for example, provoked more strikes. In the spring of 1943, miners at DeBardeleben Coal and Galloway Coal stopped work and forced the companies to refund fines paid by their local unions. Shortly after these operations reopened, miners at Southern

Cotton Oil's mine at Sumiton walked out over a series of fines imposed on their union. Mitch wrote to Lewis of fearing the "possibility of a progressive spread of these local strikes."[55] In the tense atmosphere underground, strong actions on the part of union officers likely would have backfired and inspired more unrest.

Though state union officials typically sided with the companies in wildcat strikes, the union's presence and the protections it provided against employer retribution undoubtedly played a role in emboldening the miners to take such dramatic actions. Furthermore, the UMWA leadership defended the miners in many instances, particularly when Mitch and other leaders felt that the operators had provoked walkouts, as illustrated by a situation that emerged at De-Bardeleben Coal's Hull mine in the spring of 1944. Believing that the company was attempting to weed out militant unionists, miners struck the operation in June after DeBardeleben officials refused to ask for deferments for the local union president and another member of the mine committee. The action was unusual because both men had good work records and because both were over thirty years old and had families. "The men feel that the company's failure to ask for deferment . . . is eliminating these men as employees because it is contended by the company that they are contentious and hard to get along with," Mitch complained to military officials. "I understand that there has been no question as to their being good workers. The management did make complaint that they felt one of these men, at least, caused a previous stoppage of work." The District 20 president believed that at least two other coal companies had taken similar actions against militant unionists. "We do not want coal companies to use the process of having men inducted into the service because of their activities in union affairs," Mitch protested.[56]

District 20 officials also suspected that many of the disturbances might be part of a coordinated effort on the part of the operators. Under this scenario, companies provoked the miners into wildcat strikes, which the coal operators used to portray the UMWA in a bad light. Mitch also suspected, as the dispute at the Hull mine suggested, that the operators sometimes worked in concert with federal officials in this effort. The operators "have gone to the extreme in getting the FBI interested in all these work stoppages, and numerous investigations have been made and [are] continuing to be made," he wrote.[57]

Racial tension remained a feature of life in the Alabama coalfields during the war, though divisions between white and black miners became less explicit. Still, investigators for the President's Committee on Fair Employment Practice (FEPC) compiled statistics during the war showing that racial hostilities manifested themselves more often at larger mines in the Birmingham District. Black miners sometimes used the labor shortage and the demands for high production to challenge white miners and white supervisors and to demand access to skilled jobs and better treatment. Hate strikes, where white miners walked out to protest the promotion of African Americans into formerly white jobs, often occurred in the Birmingham District's mines.[58]

TCI's operations, the scene of the racial tension between the Brotherhood of Mine Workers of Captive Mines and the UMWA in the 1930s, remained some of the region's most racially divided mines. According to federal statistics, Docena, site of the largest prewar gulf between white and black miners, saw the most problems from hate strikes. In the spring of 1944 alone, such walkouts cost the operation more than two thousand man-days.[59]

Racial tensions frequently boiled over at TCI's large Edgewater mine as African Americans fought back against racial harassment by managers. In one instance, miners at Edgewater walked out in the fall of 1944 when a foreman suspended a miner for five days for calling the supervisor by his first name. Though the correspondence between local and national UMWA officials makes no reference to the miner's race, he was very likely African American, since a white miner who called a supervisor by his first name likely would have received only a minor sanction, if any. The action by the company was "brutish unfair to prison much lest free labor," one local official argued. "We protest this kind of treatments to the fullest degree of Americanism. We were right in our action."[60]

In other ways, the wildcat strikes represented miners' attempts to respond to problems facing their communities. Throughout the war years, pressure built as miners' wages did not keep pace with inflation, in part because of federal rulings embodied in the Little Steel Formula. Many of the Birmingham District's miners believed that they played a crucial role in the war effort and deeply resented industry and government leaders' failure to acknowledge the miners' sacrifices to produce the coal that was so essential to defense industries.

The major showdown between miners, coal operators, and federal officials came in a pair of national strikes in 1943 and 1945. The earlier struggle emerged as a fight to help remedy the problems that miners faced under the Little Steel Formula. Lewis and the UMWA rallied rank-and-file miners around the issue of portal-to-portal pay, which they hoped might offset some of the restrictions the NWLB had imposed on the miners. Miners had long hoped to compel the operators to pay workers for the time they spent traveling to and from the working coal face, a journey that in some cases covered more than a mile. Union leaders hoped the two dollars a day more they might gain from the portal-to-portal proposal would help alleviate the financial difficulties that the Little Steel Formula's wage controls imposed on miners.[61]

The proposal had strong support among Alabama coal miners, but local issues played more important roles in the 1943 strikes. Many miners aimed their discontent at TCI and other major producers, which had not established a six-day workweek at the state's mines. On the national level, U.S. Steel had adopted the longer workweek, but the company allowed its TCI subsidiary to hold out. Mitch and other District 20 union leaders hoped to compel Alabama operators to implement the longer workweek and thereby boost miners' wages with overtime pay. Mitch told federal officials that the proposal "would give [miners] relief in a measure for the poor earnings they now receive, as a whole." Under pressure from TCI, however, only a few of the state's commercial operators had experimented with the extended week. Alabama miners urged Lewis and other leaders to force TCI to end the practice, which they described as "laying off men during the week to work Saturday and Sunday." "Our men are tired of this treatment and wish to be treated like other miners of the outlying districts," wrote Henry Dickerson, president of the local at TCI's Edgewater mine.[62]

In March 1943, as the expiration of the union's national contract with major operators neared, negotiations between District 20 officers and AMI officials bogged down. Many Alabama operators disliked both the six-day workweek and the portal-to-portal proposal, and at a December 1942 meeting of AMI leaders, several officials claimed that the six-day week would add twenty cents for every ton of coal mined. TCI manager C. E. Abbott boasted of defying the UMWA's overtime proposals, bragging that his company used swing shifts that limited coal miners to thirty-five hours a week. Under this plan, TCI also accumulated a "reservoir of men" that helped offset absenteeism and kept wages low.[63]

With pressure building on union leaders from below and the operators showing little interest in compromise, Mitch held out an olive branch. He offered to keep miners working after the contract expired "on a retroactive basis of what is agreed to in either the Northern or Southern Appalachian area." Company negotiators told union officials that they did not believe that other operators would agree to these terms. "Right at the moment," Mitch lamented, "we are not making any progress with the coal operators of Alabama."[64]

Though Lewis and other union leaders agreed to temporary contract extensions that stretched the pact through the end of April, Alabama's miners began sporadic strikes in the middle of the month. Miners at Sloss-Sheffield Steel and Iron's large Flat Top mine stopped work on 15 April, and miners at TCI's operations followed. Two days later, more than five thousand Alabama miners were on strike. They subsequently returned to work, but sporadic walkouts continued, and observers noted that the strikes reflected "growing unrest because of failure to negotiate a new contract and apply the six-day week in this district."[65]

A full-blown strike began in Alabama during the final week of April, before

Lewis had scheduled the national walkout. Thousands of miners had walked out in the Birmingham District by 27 April. Operators reported the following day that miners had idled more than 60 percent of the state's coal production, or thirty-seven of the fifty largest mines. In all, more than sixteen thousand miners were on strike in Alabama. By the start of the national strike on 1 May, almost all of the state's union miners had already walked out.[66]

The first strike wave was brief. The national walkout forced President Franklin Roosevelt to intervene, and he instructed Secretary of the Interior Harold L. Ickes to seize the nation's coal mines and operate them for the federal government. UMWA officials in Alabama told miners to return to work following this executive action and pledged to make "every effort" to see that the mines could reopen in the Birmingham District by the afternoon and evening shifts on 3 May. "We want to impress upon the mine workers this fact: that under this arrangement the coal miners of this country are returning to work for the government of the United States," District 20 international representative John Hanratty optimistically proclaimed. "Get into the mines, boys, roll out the coal. You are working for Uncle Sam now. And he is the best boss in the world."[67] Hanratty and other union officials hoped that the federal government might use the wartime emergency to impose a longer workweek and remedy the union's other complaints.

Coal companies began to fly the American flag on their property and placed notices at mine entrances signaling that the federal government was in charge. Underground, however, major changes were in the works. Federal officials quickly took action to remedy the miners' major grievances in Alabama. They required the operators, including the captive mining companies, to implement the six-day workweek with overtime pay. Dr. C. J. Potter, Ickes's representative in Birmingham, pledged to investigate the miners' complaints and "explore all possibilities" for improving conditions.[68]

Coming in the middle of the war, however, the walkout aroused a great deal of public opposition. The *Birmingham News*, an influential voice among the region's elites, editorialized that the strike was "intolerable in a time of national peril; its continuance was unthinkable." The newspaper leveled sharp criticism at Lewis. "Overshadowing all of these matters, important as they are, is the simple one of whether John L. Lewis is to continue to defy the United States government," the newspaper wrote. "Now is the time for men to stifle personal attitudes and feelings for the common cause of victory. Now is the time to submerge private desires to the national good. Lewis is not doing these things."[69] Like most of the public, the editors at the *News* missed the point of the walkout. By focusing on Lewis and the UMWA leadership, newspaper officials overlooked the key roles played by the intransigence of Alabama operators and militancy of rank-and-file miners, factors that would become more obvious as time went on.

The miners further inflamed public opinion when they walked out in early June after negotiations failed and the national contract extension expired. In Alabama, twenty-four thousand union miners joined the five hundred thousand nationwide on strike. While miners in most other fields returned to work after less than a week on the picket lines following the resumption of national negotiations, Alabama miners remained out for a month, until 4 July. The strike took on the tone of an open insurrection against the coal companies, state and federal officials, and even national and local union leaders.[70]

Early in the walkout, Governor Sparks publicly called on Mitch to convince the miners to go back to work, then ordered that miners on strike would lose their occupational draft deferments. The action provoked a bitter response from Mitch and many rank-and-file miners, who deeply resented having Sparks question their patriotism. The miners saw their efforts underground, in a dangerous work environment, as a patriotic duty that mirrored the sacrifices of American soldiers on the battlefield. Miners and their leaders protested that Sparks's statement constituted "a reflection upon them" and strongly denied that they had "shirked military duty." Unionists in Bibb County informed the governor that their local had contributed seventy-five members to the armed forces. Miners in the local never protested their draft classifications and actively bought war bonds. "We also wish you to know we are just as patriotic a group as there is in America," they wrote.[71]

While Sparks's action in some ways indicated that he correctly recognized the key role that rank-and-file miners had played in the unrest, most elites focused their anger on Lewis. The Alabama legislature adopted resolutions denouncing the UMWA president for "openly rebelling against the government of this nation in wartime." The resolution, approved "amid cheers" in the lower house, called Lewis's actions "tyrannical, high handed and treasonable." The state's major newspapers joined the legislators. The miners had legitimate grievances, the *Birmingham Age-Herald* wrote, but "that fact, however, does not do anything with the strong probability that the general attitude of Lewis in defiance of the government has infected the miners with a similar disrespect of authority. The miners have caught from Lewis the feeling that they can disregard the government and the nation's need."[72]

Communist Party officials in Alabama echoed their national leaders and engaged in a round of Lewis bashing. The Communists urged miners to honor their union's no-strike pledge and accused the UMWA president of setting himself ahead of the best interests of the labor movement and the government. The miners had to choose between the good of their country and their union president, Communist leaders argued. "Nothing can be allowed to sabotage victory in war. This is labor's war. The no-strike policy is labor's policy," Communists proclaimed. "The whole working class and its trade union movement will uphold the Commander-in-Chief in whatever steps may be necessary to insure uninterrupted production and orderly labor relations."[73] The attack on Lewis and the UMWA, though predictable, given the Communist leaders' stance, also indicated their declining influence in the coalfields. The rank-and-file movements of 1943 took little notice of Communist proclamations.

On the national level, the reaction against the miners was swift and far reaching. In June, Congress passed the War Labor Disputes Act, commonly known as the Smith-Connally Act, over Roosevelt's veto. The legislation gave the NWLB more power—it could subpoena witnesses—and banned direct union contributions to political candidates. Most importantly in the context of the UMWA's struggles against the Little Steel Formula that summer, the Smith-Connally Act required written notices of the intent to strike, mandated secret strike votes supervised by the National Labor Relations Board, and provided for a thirty-day cooling off period. It endorsed federal seizure of strikebound facilities and provided penalties—including fines and jail time—for people who encouraged workers to walk out.[74]

At the end of June, Alabama legislators met in a special session and approved the Bradford Act, a state version of the Smith-Connally Act. The measure ended the closed shop in Alabama, allowing workers "to join or to refrain from joining a labor organization." The legislation resurrected the state Department of Labor and provided for the establishment of government-appointed mediation boards to settle strikes. It also required unions to reveal detailed information, including the names and addresses of officers, their financial compensation, and the union's property and investments. Penalties for violating the act ranged from five hundred to one thousand dollars.[75]

The Bradford Act was not the only antilabor measure enacted during the Alabama Legislature's 1943 special session. Antiunion legislators placed additional restrictions on unemployment payments and defeated measures to expand worker's compensation benefits. The legislature also limited employees' ability to sue companies. In his report on the session, the AMI's secretary-treasurer, H. E. Mills, noted that an "important factor which contributed to our success was the public sentiment against strikes and it will be recalled that we were in the [midst] of our most serious work stoppage in the coal mines while the Legislature was in session."[76]

The Alabama coal operators also worked to shape press coverage of the walk-outs and to limit the effect of government control. AMI officials set up a public relations committee designed to stir up local press support for the companies' position in the strike. The coal operators eventually hired an advertising agency to help promote their side in the dispute, spending five thousand dollars on public relations through the end of July. The coal operators' power and influence had deep roots in the local media establishment, and the wartime emergency allowed the two groups to forge a close alliance. At the end of June, for example, officials from the *Birmingham News* and the *Birmingham Post* attended an AMI meeting and "joined in the discussion on publicity and the handling of news concerning the strike situation and Government control of the mines." A few weeks later, members of the public relations committee held a "long conference" with newspaper editors that featured a "full and frank discussion of cooperation between the operators, or Institute, and the papers."[77]

The operators succeeded in their efforts to arouse concern about the toll the strike wave took on war production in the Birmingham District. Press reports surfaced in June that area steel producers had begun to cut back their production. In the walkout's third week, officials announced that some war industries were shutting down and that steel companies had only enough coal for ten days of production. Iron production also reportedly reached wartime-era lows as coal stockpiles dwindled.[78]

UMWA officials in Alabama grew increasingly concerned and began to appeal for the miners to return to work. On one level, these calls appeared as part of a coordinated effort by the UMWA to avoid being blamed for the walkouts and held legally responsible for them under the Smith-Connally Act. For example, after Roosevelt issued a back-to-work order in early June, Hanratty ambiguously stated that the decision on whether to resume work "will be up to the individual miner."[79] By issuing such vague responses, UMWA officials attempted to avoid both legal liability and public accountability for encouraging miners to remain on strike.

But by the end of the month, rank-and-file dissidents began to play an increasingly important role in shaping the strike, a fact that greatly concerned UMWA leaders, who believed they were losing control of the coalfields. Militants called an unauthorized meeting in Wylam on 24 June, encouraging locals to send delegates. When District 20 officials learned of the movement, they descended on the meeting and convinced those present to endorse an end to the walkouts. Several days later, Mitch denounced such unauthorized conferences and urged the miners to return to work. The District 20 president condemned the events as "rump mass meetings" and declared them "illegal and contrary to the policy of the United Mine Workers of America." Unionists organizing and participating in these meetings were damaging the UMWA, Mitch complained, and he urged local union officers to rein in their men.[80]

The meetings, however, brought the concerns of dissidents and many average miners onto the public stage for the first time during the 1943 walkouts. The press subsequently began to report that state and national UMWA officials did not completely control events in the Alabama coalfields. One miner told a reporter that Mitch and Lewis still had the support of local unionists, "but if they can't get us a raise, then we'll see if we can't do something about it ourselves."[81]

The state's UMWA members did not universally approve of the Wylam miners' actions. The underground dissidents demonstrated their highest levels of organization in the coal towns closest to Birmingham and dominated by the larger captive mining interests such as Sloss-Sheffield, Republic, and particularly TCI. Outside of Jefferson County, support for the militants was weaker. Local unions in the northern Walker County communities of Carbon Hill and Nauvoo illustrated this point when they supported the union's call to return to work and condemned the unauthorized meetings sweeping through Jefferson County. In early July, the miners heeded the back-to-work calls.[82]

Miners also demonstrated a sophisticated understanding of the role the federal government played by seizing control of the coal industry. Many Alabama miners, in fact, wanted a larger federal presence in their mines. "I just want to say our men will not work until we receive checks from the government," said Ed Smith of Republic. Many miners wanted Ickes and the Department of the Interior, perceived as supporters of the miners and their union, to take charge of that expanded presence, although support for the federal government was not universal. For example, Alabama miners sharply criticized the NWLB, the architect of the Little Steel Formula. "The miners have started out to blot out the War Labor Board," claimed Bob Cunningham, a black miner from Dolomite. "If Mr. Roosevelt will remove the [NWLB,] every miner will march down the mines in the morning."[83]

Though the miners returned to work, Alabama's coal companies and union failed to resolve their issues during the following months. When the federal government began to return the mines to private hands in mid-October, Alabama miners walked out again, protesting the action as well as the fact that the UMWA had never reached a formal agreement with the state's coal companies. Predictably, the strikes began at TCI, Sloss-Sheffield, Republic Steel, and other captive companies, where miners' grievances remained strongest. The walkouts soon spread to commercial operations. Lewis publicly told the miners to go back to work but signaled his approval of their action when he claimed that the miners were "righteously outraged" over their treatment by the operators and federal officials. "You are denied a wage that will provide adequate food for your families, while the coal operators are making the greatest profits in history," Lewis announced.[84]

With Lewis's support, the strikes began to spread. By 16 October, almost all of the union mines in District 20 were out. For the rest of the month, Alabama miners found themselves at the forefront of the growing national walkout with an estimated nineteen thousand miners on strike in the state, more than in any other state. Only after 29 October did the strike begin to spread deep into other coalfields. By 1 November, more than five hundred thousand miners nationwide had walked out.[85]

While Lewis had seemed to endorse the strike's early stages, District 20 officials had taken a hard line against the spread of walkouts, mainly because they appeared to be operating outside of the union's control. In mid-October, Mitch returned to Alabama from negotiations in Washington, D.C., and attempted to persuade the miners to return to work. "There is no question in my mind that they will go back to work," he said. "We are urging them to return to the mines and we have men in the field meeting with various locals." The appeals made some initial headway with rank-and-file miners, and more than three thousand returned to their jobs after Mitch's request. But most stayed away, and a few days later reports abounded that the back-to-work movement had faltered.[86]

The depth of concern that the independent movements spurred in the minds of state UMWA officials manifested itself in the increasingly threatening language they used in their attempts to rein in the dissidents. At the end of October, International Executive Board member James Terry had warned that those responsible for the walkouts in Alabama could be prosecuted under the much-despised Bradford Act. Terry blamed the Alabama strikes on "a small group of agitators—self appointed leaders moving from mine to mine urging a continuance of the walkout." Attempts to track down these militants failed. Alabama miners, Terry claimed, simply refused to reveal the instigators' identities to local officials.[87]

The press and public, however, believed that Lewis, Mitch, and other UMWA officials were pulling the strings in an intricate and complex game designed to compel the federal government to seize the mines and force the operators to reach an agreement. Under this scenario, Mitch's actions constituted mere window dressing in an attempt to avoid criminal prosecution under terms of the Smith-Connally Act. In this way, editorial writers and pundits speculated, "if the rank-and-file acts without instructions, there has been no breach of law." The Birmingham press borrowed this idea from the *New York Times*, which had theorized on 23 October that Lewis directed the strikes but obscured his actions with language that allowed him to avoid indictment under Smith-Connolly. "This is precisely the result that we do have in the Alabama coal mines today," the newspaper concluded.[88] While this idea contained an element of truth—Lewis at times endorsed the walkouts—this view also missed the sharp divisions within the UMWA. Lewis, Mitch, and other UMWA leaders did not always control events on the ground in Alabama in the fall of 1943; in many ways, these officials were merely reacting to pressure from below.

The NWLB eventually acknowledged this fact. When Alabama's miners continued to refuse to return to work, the body ordered Mitch and Lewis to appear before it on 23 October. Though Lewis never testified—UMWA officials claimed that he was ill—Mitch told board members that restlessness in the Alabama mines sprung from many different sources. Miners received less pay than workers in other defense-related industries, he told the board, and the coal operators had yet to sign a contract with the union. Another major issue was the toll the war effort had taken on miners, a problem exacerbated by "a general shortage of men down there." Board Chair William H. Davis, no friend to the UMWA or rank-and-file miners, indicated that he believed that the UMWA "cooperated with the War Labor Board in a sincere endeavor to end the local stoppages, but without success."[89]

Birmingham's industrial elite began to rally public opinion against the miners. At the end of October, reports surfaced that the lack of coal meant that machinery that pumped natural gas would not function. As a result, homes might go without heat and office buildings might have to close. Most importantly, the developing coal shortage threatened to idle TCI's massive operations at Ensley. The company claimed that the mill would have to close by early November, which could cut the Birmingham District's steel and iron production by 50 percent.[90] By late October, officials said, the strikes had idled a third of the region's iron and steel production as TCI closed blast furnaces and open hearths because of the lack of coal.[91]

These reports further rallied public opinion against the miners. While expressing appreciation for Mitch's attempts to resolve the dispute, Governor Sparks appealed to the miners to return to work "to relieve the suffering now entailed and also to continue support of the war effort and await orderly adjustment of their grievances through constituted channels."[92]

Other leaders were not as forgiving. "Intolerable!" screamed an editorial in the *Birmingham News*, which denounced the strikers as "misguided" and demanded "an end to the present situation—and it must come promptly!" Readers found an even more strident tone in the pages of the *Birmingham Age-Herald*, which wrote that unless the strikes ended, "drastic measures will become inevitable" and suggested that the government might have to force the miners back underground.

The editors noted that such a policy would prove difficult to enforce. "So far it has been hoped that such action could be avoided," the paper argued. "But such patience and inaction will not continue if this grave and appalling state of affairs persists."[93] Such declarations, however absurd, indicated the growing level of public anger at the miners and the UMWA.

Even other unions became vocal critics of Lewis and the UMWA. The *Labor Advocate*, the conservative voice of Birmingham's AFL, attacked the UMWA throughout the walkouts of 1943, labeling Lewis and the miners traitors. "The notorious barbarian Japs only stabbed America once in the back at Pearl Harbor, while John L and the 200 'contemptibles' of his Policies Committee stabbed their own country four times in the back—every strike was a deadly stab," the union newspaper claimed. "Neither the Japs nor the miners have yet apologized for the back stabs."[94]

The walkouts ended in early November, after Roosevelt announced that the mines would return to government hands. Alabama's miners remained out until federal officials imposed a settlement on the companies and the UMWA that provided a $1.50-per-day raise and included provisions that paid miners for their travel time to work. "It is the duty of all members of our union to respond to this call back to work and put the mines in operations immediately, this afternoon if that is at all possible," said Hanratty. The mines would remain in government hands throughout much of 1944, reverting back to private control in a "piecemeal fashion as the year progressed."[95]

In many respects, the miners appeared to have won their fight. They had a new wage agreement, though southern producers would delay and draw out formal signing of the deal that Lewis and Ickes had reached. But the miners' gains also were limited. The new wages, even with the new portal-to-portal pay system in place, amounted to less than three dollars a week more than the 1941 contract provided. The Little Steel Formula remained intact, as did the UMWA's archnemesis on the national level, the NWLB. Perhaps most importantly, Lewis and the miners' union found themselves reviled throughout American society.[96]

The union had difficulty convincing the state's largest coal operators to honor, much less sign, the contract. TCI and other captive operators delayed paying miners for their travel time. The UMWA in Alabama followed the tedious strategy of attempting to convince federal agencies and courts to impose the measure on the companies. A few months after the miners returned to work, the rank and file took matters into their own hands. Roving pickets began to fan out through the district's coal communities in the spring of 1944, pulling out miners in an attempt to compel the operators to live up to the agreement. The origins of this action remain obscure—even UMWA leaders seemed mystified—but the goals were quite clear. The miners hoped to force the Birmingham District's major captive coal companies—Sloss-Sheffield, Republic, Woodward, and, most importantly, TCI—to pay the compensation they owed under terms of the 1943 contract.

As it had throughout the war, the emergence of the independent movement worried the UMWA officials. By the spring of 1944, with the federal government in control of the region's mines, the independent strike movement showed signs of picking up momentum. Mitch urged the miners to be patient as the travel time issue wound its way through the federal system. "I sometimes feel the operators, themselves, in many instances, are doing everything they can to help embarras[s] the situation, so DON'T FALL INTO ANY SUCH TRAP BY TAKING ACTION THAT WOULD BE DETRIMENTAL TO THE COURSE PURSUED BY YOUR UNION IN HANDLING THIS MATTER," Mitch wrote to local officials.[97]

Mitch's effort seems to have headed off the major walkout at the captive operators, but when the government returned the mines to private hands a few months later, hundreds of miners stopped work. By early June, their numbers had swelled to almost two thousand. Militants claimed that the union essentially had "no contract" with the captive operators because they had not honored the portal-to-portal provisions. The wildcat strike movement idled Republic's Sayreton mine, three mines owned by Sloss-Sheffield Steel and Iron, Alabama By-Products' Labuco mine, the Blue Creek mine of Black Diamond Mining Company, and miners in the coal community of Powhatan. More than twenty-three hundred Jefferson County miners ultimately joined the walkouts, and the unionists went back only after Lewis personally appealed to them, writing, "It is your duty, and the duty of each member of your local union, to put the mines back in operation at once, in accordance with the provisions of the contract."[98]

The militants demonstrated a high level of organization. Bewildered local leaders in Powhatan, for example, claimed that the wildcats were caused by "mens from other mines that comes into our mining village with propganda such as why are you working without a contract, and if you will stop the production of coal we can make the operators pay, the portal to portal pay in a lump sum." Coalfield militants proved highly effective at shutting down operations as angry miners honored picket lines. Powhatan union leaders complained that miners walked out "before the officers of the local knows what is happening."[99]

With little resolved, miners agitated for a showdown with the Alabama coal operators when the contract expired in the spring of 1945. Lewis began marshaling the miners for another confrontation in late March, when he took a vote of UMWA members across the country—as the Smith-Connally Act required—to gauge support for a walkout. The miners endorsed a strike by a six-to-one ratio nationwide and more than twice that in Alabama, where 9,333 yes votes and only 723 no votes were recorded.[100]

As part of his goals for the new contract, Lewis sought a ten-cent-per-ton royalty on coal mined by unionists that would be placed in a welfare trust fund. Believing the union in a weak position, Lewis backed off many of the demands and reached a settlement with the major bituminous operators on 11 April. The miners won a wage increase of just over six dollars a week under terms worked out among the union, operators, and the Department of Labor.[101]

In the context of the overall negotiations, therefore, what happened in Alabama can only be described as a massive wildcat strike. While Lewis agreed to contract extensions on the national level, Alabama miners walked out by the thousands to protest the fact that the union did not have a new agreement. They had little reason to believe that the Alabama operators would live up to the terms of the extension of the old contract, which the companies had already failed for more than a year to honor. Only a relatively small number of Pennsylvania and West Virginia miners joined Alabama's miners in striking. By 4 April, miners had idled most of Alabama's operations, with only sixteen mines and a few thousand miners working. Production dropped to only 5 percent of normal levels, according to AMI officials. The strike caught District 20 leaders completely off guard, with Mitch claiming that the walkouts would "only hurt the negotiations that are now being carried on in Washington" and begging the strikers to begin "returning to work at once."[102]

UMWA officials initiated a back-to-work movement that initially appeared to gain support but collapsed by 8 April, when the militants had won out: 90 percent of the miners stayed away from work. Reports of violence surfaced as miners who attempted to return to work claimed that militants shot at them. The militants restricted coal output, strangling Birmingham's iron and steel production. TCI and Republic announced plans to idle their furnaces, prompting federal authorities to seize more than fifty strikebound mines. Not even Lewis's appeal to local officers to "give me a lift" and convince their members to go back had a significant effect. By 19 April, the union and major operators had signed new agreements and miners in other fields had returned to work, "leaving Alabama the lone holdout."[103]

State and federal officials were at a loss to explain the strike in Alabama. Sparks blamed federal officials, sending an angry telegram to Ickes to appeal for "prompt, vigorous and immediate" action to end the walkouts. Federal officials, for their part, seemed baffled. Department of the Interior officials admitted that "the situation in Alabama has been more serious than in the other producing fields" but had no idea why the miners remained out. The press believed that the miners were simply misguided and failed to understand the full implications of their actions. "The whole situation in Alabama is strange, depressing and dangerous," the *Birmingham News* editorialized. "The action of the idle miners calls for the most forthright condemnation. But at the same time it must be that these miners cannot be fully aware of the consequences of what they are doing."[104]

Though the expiration of the national agreement initially provoked the wild-cat strike, resentment over the problems that miners had experienced during the war years played an important role in keeping the protest alive. Journalist Robert Kincey traveled into the coalfields in the midst of the walkouts and found the miners among the state's most patriotic and community-oriented citizens. They were "liberal" buyers of War Bonds. They supported charities including the Community Chest, the Crippled Children's Clinic, and the Red Cross. Most, he wrote, had someone—a son, nephew, or other relative—fighting in the war. "The miners as a class," Kincey concluded, "are inherently imbued with the conviction that their lot over the years has been a sorry one economically, that while there has consistently been raised a hue and cry as to the essential nature of their occupation in times of war, they have not been paid wages comparable with industries classified as less essential, and that they have been able to get where they are today only through the liberal use of the only weapon they know—the strike."[105]

District 20 leaders finally convinced the miners to return to work with a desperate appeal at a mass meeting in Wylam. Mitch admonished the miners to disregard the rumors spreading through the coalfields and not to "make further fools of ourselves." He attacked "certain disgruntled groups" that fueled such rumors in an attempt to confuse the situation and hold out for more gains. When the District 20 president asked if anyone opposed returning to work on Monday, 23 April, only one miner was brave enough to raise his hand. The large Edgewater and Docena locals subsequently announced plans to hold meetings to vote on whether to return to the mines. The miners slowly returned. By Monday, TCI reported 60 percent of its miners back, while Sloss-Sheffield and Republic reported 56 and 75 percent back, respectively. Other captive and commercial producers had returned to normal production.[106]

The walkout had taken a heavy toll. "This strike has been the most costly, from the standpoint of lost production (coal, iron, and steel), that Alabama has ever had," the AMI's Rouzer concluded. "The cost to the war effort is incalculable." The miners, battered, would continue sporadic wildcats for the remaining months of the war, but the actions would not approach their former levels. A fall 1945 national strike by foremen seeking to join the UMWA's District 50 idled thousands of miners in major coalfields across the country but had little or no effect in Alabama.[107]

The spring 1945 strike had represented rank-and-file miners' attempt to improve their social and economic situation and to exert some control over their lives. The level of unrest after the 1943 walkouts— an estimated two hundred wildcats in 1944—demonstrated how little had been resolved by those difficult strikes.[108] Opposed by the operators and the union in many of these disputes, miners found themselves forced to take matters into their own hands, and the spring 1945 walkout gave them the opportunity to do so on a massive scale.

With the war nearing an end in Europe and victory in sight in the Pacific, Alabama miners also must have worried about whether their industry could sustain such production and employment levels when demand slackened. For years, Alabama's operators had warned about future problems in the business, and while some of these predictions represented an effort to keep wages low and the UMWA weak, they also reflected very legitimate concerns on the part of both operators and miners. Though the wartime crisis produced an increase in coal production, the underlying problems that had plagued the Alabama coal industry since the late 1920s remained in place. A state commission that investigated the industry's health in the spring of 1941 had concluded that alternative energy sources including oil, natural gas, and hydroelectric power posed serious future challenges to the coal industry. Ominously, the largest single market for the commercial mines—railroads—had begun during the 1930s to convert engines from steam power to diesel-electric, a trend that the war did not reverse. The commission concluded that the state's coal industry was "in a precarious condition."[109]

Other concerns existed as well. The coal operators had introduced machine loaders and further mechanized their mines during the war, thereby eliminating many miners' jobs. Finding jobs during a time of nearly full employment was relatively easy. But what would the postwar order offer miners who had lost their jobs to machines? This type of displacement posed especially troubling questions for black miners, who lost a disproportionate share of jobs to mechanization underground.

The burden of answering these difficult questions would fall to African American miners such as Harry Burgess, who returned home from service in World War II and went back underground. The war had shown Burgess a side of the world he had never known before. Burgess spent most of the war in a segregated service battalion in Europe, loading and unloading equipment. After the invasion at Normandy, he moved across the English Channel to France. When the German army broke though Allied lines at the Battle of the Bulge in late 1944, Burgess remembered officers asking African Americans in service battalions to volunteer for the infantry to help repel the attack. He declined the offer. "I didn't feel like dying for nobody," he recalled.[110]

Despite the segregation he experienced in the military, Burgess remembered

France as "a liberal country, different from America, in that people accepted you . . . as a person. Not as a black or not as a white." It was, for the most part, a new experience for Burgess, who had known segregation in Alabama and with the American military in France. Yet Burgess had worked in the mines and been a UMWA member before the war, and he had seen whites and blacks take tentative steps across the racial divide. "I knew how things were in Alabama," he recalled. "When I came out of the service, I came back and went back into the coal mines. You had a certain liberalism because we were all accepted as union—not accepted as union brothers but as union members."[111]

That liberalism was challenged after the war as the problems that faced the Alabama coal industry became more acute. As economist Herbert Northrup had predicted, the UMWA's racial policies would face their most difficult test as the coal industry collapsed and mechanization swept through the coalfields in the years after World War II.[112] The tenuous biracialism of the miners' union faltered, and African Americans virtually disappeared from the Birmingham District's mines.

Coal miner John Sutton and his large family crowded into this four-room house with no electric lights and an outdoor toilet owned by Sloss-Sheffield Steel and Iron in Flat Top, ca. World War II. United Mine Workers of America Photograph Collection, Historical Collections and Labor Archives, The Pennsylvania State University, University Park, Pa.

Huge machines at work at Drummond Coal's Cedrum Mine in Walker County, ca. 1970. Strip mines like this one proliferated in Alabama during the 1960s and 1970s. Library of Congress, HAER ALA, 64-TOWN, 3A-6.

An interior view of a Birmingham District coal mine, probably during the 1920s. Department of Archives and Manuscripts, Photographs—Miners Folder 24.34, Birmingham Public Library, Birmingham, Ala.

TCI coal miners pose on a coal tipple, ca. 1939. White miners appear in the front, while African Americans are relegated to the rear. Department of Archives and Manuscripts, Photographs—Miners Folder 24.43, Birmingham Public Library, Birmingham, Ala.

A black miner drives an "electric mule," one of the skilled mining jobs typically open to African Americans in the Birmingham District, ca. 1930. Department of Archives and Manuscripts, Photographs—Miners Folder 24.40, Birmingham Public Library, Birmingham, Ala.

A white miner operates a drag line in an Alabama coal mine, ca. 1930. The African American miner was probably his helper. Department of Archives and Manuscripts, Photographs—Miners Folder 24.39, Birmingham Public Library, Birmingham, Ala.

Coal miners aboard a man trip, which took them in and out of the coal mine, ca. 1930. African American miners are segregated in the cars at the front. Department of Archives and Manuscripts, Photographs—Miners Folder 24.36, Birmingham Public Library, Birmingham, Ala.

Miners and activists protest the Southern Company's 1974 decision to
purchase millions of tons of coal from South Africa. Department of Archives
and Manuscripts, Birmingham Police Department Surveillance Files, 1947–80,
Folder 1125.10.15d, Birmingham Public Library, Birmingham, Ala.

Veteran coal miners of both races and a young activist during the
Birmingham demonstrations against South African coal, 1974. Department
of Archives and Manuscripts, Birmingham Police Department Surveillance Files,
1947–80, Folder 1125.10.15a, Birmingham Public Library, Birmingham, Ala.

Miners leave the Sloss-Sheffield Steel and Iron Company's Bessie Mine at the end of
their shift in this undated photograph. Department of Archives and Manuscripts,
Photographs—Miners Folder 47.53, Birmingham Public Library, Birmingham, Ala.

CHAPTER FOUR

Race, Economic Decline, and the Fight for the Welfare and Retirement Fund, 1946–1950

In many ways, Marshlar's Café in the mining community of Brookside served as a window on race relations in the Alabama coalfields after World War II. Miners of both races frequented the tavern, located a few miles north of Birmingham. To conform with the requirements of segregation, however, blacks and whites used separate entrances, and the establishment featured a large, six-foot partition that divided it into sections reserved for each race.[1]

Nevertheless, the color line sometimes blurred in the café, as it often did in the United Mine Workers of America (UMWA) in Alabama. To get to the bathrooms, for example, white miners had to cross into the section of the tavern reserved for African Americans. "Some of them would stop and say a word or two," remembered Fred Bass Sr., a black miner who sometimes went to the establishment. To further complicate matters, Steve Marshlar, a well-known Catholic businessman whose brother served on Brookside's city council, owned the tavern. The town had a substantial population of both Catholics and Orthodox Christians, many of them descended from Eastern European immigrants who had come to the region to dig coal at the turn of the century.[2] The café's patrons and owners, therefore, crossed the boundaries of race and ethnicity in the Birmingham District in a variety of ways.

In the spring and summer of 1949, as the Ku Klux Klan sought to reinforce the color line, Marshlar's Café quickly attracted attention. On the evening of 10 June, a crowd of hooded Klansmen entered the café and demanded to see the manager. Steve Marshlar spoke up and was asked to come outside with the Klansmen. "We're tired of you damned Catholics running this town," one of the leaders told Marshlar. "We know what's going on here. Furthermore, you're going to clean up these niggers here, cussing and raising hell inside and outside of the place." The Klansmen then brought the African American customers out of the restaurant and forced them to watch a cross burning. "You niggers see that? That's your warning," one of the hooded men said. The Klansmen eventually left the scene. Far from being intimidated, however, the black miners simply went back inside the tavern and finished their beers.[3]

The Klan actions at Marshlar's Café reflected the different levels of racial anxiety running through Brookside and the rest of the Birmingham District. The town had seen a rise in Klan activity prior to the incident at the tavern. Klan caravans, some of them escorted by local police, had driven through the area on several weekends, and debates over "morality"—"Decency" or "Indecency," as Klan fliers described the goings-on at Marshlar's Café—had taken place at recent city council meetings.[4]

Other coal communities had experienced similar activities. The Klan saw itself as enforcing the state's moral standards, including segregation and white supremacy. As part of this project, the Klan also sought to impose its interpretation of the ideals of manhood and womanhood on people who it believed lived outside the mainstream. And, as in its earlier incarnations, the hooded order used violence and intimidation to force people to conform to conventional social and sexual norms. E. P. Pruitt, an Alabama physician and Klan leader, claimed that he opposed "mob violence" but added, "If I saw a mad dog or snake, I would shoot it. And some people are like mad dogs and snakes."[5]

Throughout the late 1940s, the revived Klan again rode in Alabama. In Birmingham, the Klan concentrated much of its activism on preserving segregation and on targeting African American activists for violence. In the coalfields and industrial towns and neighborhoods that ringed the city, the KKK focused much of its energy on upholding conventional morality, targeting moral nonconformists for intimidation and violence. Far from being opposed to industrial unions, the Klan often sought to infiltrate and influence them. This approach posed difficult questions for the miners' union and its Alabama leaders, who sought to prevent white union members from joining the Klan and participating in its violent activities.[6] Many white miners disregarded the union's prohibition on membership in the organization.

But the Klan was not the only political force operating in the Alabama coalfields. As the Klan found recruits among whites in coal towns, even more miners and industrial workers joined the liberal political coalition that helped elect racial moderate James E. "Big Jim" Folsom as governor in 1946. "They can't stop us by trying to divide race and race, class and class, or religion and religion," Folsom had told supporters on his way to the governor's mansion. "We've just finished fighting a war against hatred and violence."[7]

Folsom was not the only liberal to enjoy electoral success in Alabama. Two years later, coal miners and other unionists played an important role in the election to the U.S. Congress of a little-known lawyer, Carl Elliott, who represented a district north of Birmingham that included the heart of the Alabama coalfields. Together with U.S. Senators Lister Hill and John Sparkman, liberals such as Elliott made the Alabama congressional delegation among the region's most progressive. A group of historians recently concluded that "no state congressional delegation did more to expand federal powers to assist the nation's weakest and most vulnerable people" than the one that Alabama voters sent to Washington after World War II.[8] Coal miners constituted a key part of this coalition, delivering their votes to Alabama's liberals at the same time that the Klan began its night riding in their communities.

Coal communities faced a host of different challenges after World War II. The UMWA began a series of bitter fights for the establishment of the union's health and pension system that again pushed its Alabama members to their limit. After a final round of walkouts in the spring of 1950, the coal companies agreed to the permanent establishment of the jointly administered UMWA Welfare and Retirement Fund, which was financed through a tax on coal produced in union mines. During the years that followed, however, most Alabama coal miners—indeed, most miners across the nation—lost their jobs as coal production plummeted and mechanization took a heavy toll on the positions that remained. Nationally, the amount of coal produced in the United States declined between 1950 and 1960 from more than 516 million tons to 415.5 million tons. The number of coal miners dropped by almost half over that period, from more than 480,818 to 253,799. The effect on black miners was even more dramatic: their numbers shrunk from more than 30,000 to slightly more than 10,000—a drop of more than 65 percent.[9]

In Alabama, the dire predictions about coal losing markets to natural gas, oil, and diesel fuel finally came true in the late 1940s. Wartime demand for the state's coal evaporated, and commercial coal mines closed across the district. Alabama miners suffered even higher rates of job loss during this era than did miners in the rest of the country. More than 60 percent of the state's coal miners lost their jobs between 1950 and 1960, with the number of workers dropping from 20,084 to 7,798. The number of black coal miners dropped by more than 70 percent during the 1950s, from 6,756 to less than 2,000. Between 1945 and 1960, the state's annual coal production declined from 18.3 million tons to 13.1 million tons.[10]

This chapter begins with an examination of the economic decline of the post–World War II Alabama coal industry and its effects on the Birmingham District. The chapter examines the political changes under way in the state after the war that propelled the rise of liberal politicians such as Folsom and Elliott and then explores the rebirth of the Klan. Finally, it chronicles the struggles between the UMWA and the coal operators over the creation of a health and pension system. In this context, the chapter probes the complex relationships among strikes, political change, economic decline, and Klan night riding.

(((

The Birmingham District coal industry's post–World War II problems had their roots in the 1930s, when railroads began to convert from steam to diesel locomotives and homeowners began to switch to natural gas or other "laborless fuels" for heating. In the mid-1930s, railroads had consumed a third of the coal produced by Alabama mines, while more than 10 percent of the coal mined in the state went to domestic uses such as home heating. World War II created an artificial demand for Alabama coal that temporarily offset some of the declines in these crucial markets, but the downturn resumed when the conflict ended. Railroads replaced their steam-powered locomotives with diesel engines on a large scale, and homeowners eagerly converted to cleaner-burning fuels or switched to electric heaters.[11]

The Birmingham District's coalfields had benefited for eighty years from their proximity to iron and steel production. But in the late 1940s, location mattered less and in some instances even constituted a drawback. Despite its possession of huge coal reserves, for example, the Tennessee Coal, Iron, and Railroad Company (TCI) decided to replace its thirty-three steam locomotives with newer, more efficient diesel engines. Birmingham's proximity to gas and oil fields along the Gulf Coast, by contrast, allowed officials to extend pipelines that could deliver natural gas to homeowners and businesses. Birmingham's natural gas utility extended lines out to the new high-end suburban housing developments. Demand for the fuel proved so strong that the gas company had a backlog of six thousand applications for connections in the fall of 1946. To coal executives, it seemed that people everywhere wanted natural gas heating systems. "Atlanta newspapers of a few days ago carried full page ads from the Gas Company urging householders not to purchase gas equipment until they ascertained whether the Gas Company could make connections and serve them," complained Alabama Mining Institute (AMI) President I. W. Rouzer in 1946. "The inroads of natural gas is limited only by the capacity of the gas lines, and this capacity is constantly being increased."[12]

Miners and coal operators needed no better illustration of this problem than Jasper officials' decision to extend city-financed gas lines to the municipality in the summer of 1949, as the coal industry that sustained the region went into steep decline. "Nearly all of the people depend on coal in one way or another," the *Union News*, a pro-UMWA newspaper in Walker County, explained as it attempted to argue against the project. "The coal miner for his wages. The businessman for the business of the miner. The wholesaler for the business of the businessman who depends on the wages. The land owner for the coal mined on his property. The mine operator for the sale of the coal. Insurance men, bankers, lawyers, doctors, automobile dealers—everyone is affected when the coal industry is affected." District 20 President William Mitch vowed to make sure "that the miners don't vote for a city commission that will bring in a commodity to put them out of work." Supporters, however, equated natural gas with economic diversity, and some hoped that providing the fuel to Jasper could help lure new businesses to the region. Others argued that natural gas would have only a minimal impact on coal production. F. A. Brotherton, the chair of the city commission and a pipeline supporter, informed his opponents, "You can't stop progress no matter how hard you try." Following Brotherton's lead, Jasper city officials endorsed the plan in June 1949.[13]

The coal operators proved powerless either to stop these changes or to adapt to the new market realities. The amount of coal consumed by the railroads dropped from 22 percent of the country's annual coal production in 1945 to 13 percent by 1950. Residential consumption dropped less quickly over the same period, from about 21 percent to 19 percent. By the early 1960s, however, these markets had almost completely vanished for Alabama producers.[14]

The loss of these markets devastated the Alabama coal industry. In 1945, 21,975 miners had produced 18.3 million tons of coal in the Birmingham District's mines; by 1950, the number of miners had dropped to 17,780, and only 12.1 million tons of coal were produced. For the rest of the decade, production remained relatively stagnant, at between 12 and 13 million tons, while the number of miners declined to under 8,000.[15]

Alabama's coal operators argued that the UMWA, with the high wages and safety improvements it demanded, bore primary responsibility for the coal industry's troubles. Rouzer and other AMI officials complained loudly that national agreements negotiated by the union president, John L. Lewis, and the federal officials who periodically took control of the nation's coal industry priced Alabama coal out of regional markets. Alabama's industry officials also claimed that the strikes that swept the coal industry every year after the war encouraged customers to switch to other fuels. "Our customers are being deprived of coal, are being driven to the use of other fuels, and your men are being deprived of needed employment," Rouzer complained to Mitch in the fall of 1949. "It isn't a matter of the lost business being accumulative and recouped at some later date. At least a substantial part of the commercial tonnage will be lost forever to the Alabama mines."[16]

Rouzer's associate, D. A. Thomas, employed similar arguments when he announced major cutbacks at Boothton Coal Mining in the fall of 1950. Boothton closed four mines, idling 430 miners and affecting a total of 2,500 people. Thomas claimed he had warned union officials "about what was going to ultimately happen to the Alabama operators and miners if the parade of high wages continued to be forced on the industry in this state."[17]

While the high wages and safety requirements that the union demanded undoubtedly drove up production costs, the loss of crucial markets constituted a much greater problem for the commercial coal industry. Coalfield unrest at worst merely provided incentives for the railroads and homeowners to convert to new, more efficient fuels. Congressman Elliott, who represented Alabama's worst-hit areas, recognized the complexities involved in this process and refused to blame the UMWA. "The troubles of our coal industry in Walker County are much more basic than the mere matter of a labor-management dispute," he wrote to federal officials in the fall of 1949.[18] The union's acceptance of low wages and poor safety or refraining from strikes would only have delayed the inevitable as markets vanished.

The 1950 demise of Alabama Fuel and Iron (AFICO) drove home this point. The company's downfall ended a brutal era in labor relations and essentially nullified the argument that the Alabama industry's woes resulted solely from the UMWA's wage and safety demands. AFICO had never recognized the union and was not directly subject to its contracts. The erosion of crucial railroad and home heating markets, however, deeply affected the company and prompted officials to cease operations.

When Charles DeBardeleben died in the fall of 1941, the Alabama coal operators passed the torch of militant antiunionism to his son, Prince, who became AFICO's president. Though Charles DeBardeleben's carefully crafted personality cult did not survive him, AFICO remained a bastion of antiunionism. The UMWA's extensive postwar attempts to organize AFICO's operations at Acmar and Margaret failed. In the summer of 1945, for example, John O'Leary, the

UMWA national vice president, gave District 20 officials his personal approval to begin another organizing drive at AFICO's mines and funneled twenty-five hundred dollars to the Alabama district to support the effort.[19]

But AFICO fought the UMWA's organizing efforts in the courts. A year earlier, perhaps expecting another attempt to organize their operations, company officials filed a $28.5 million lawsuit in a St. Clair County court against union organizers, the UMWA, and the state Congress of Industrial Organizations (CIO), charging them with "libel and conspiracy" in connection with statements published in the *Alabama News Digest*. The plaintiffs, among them Prince DeBardeleben, were represented by a legal team that included Horace Wilkinson, a well-known Birmingham District political activist associated with the Klan and the conservative wing of the state's labor movement who had broken with Mitch and industrial unionists during the war. The UMWA and other defendants eventually settled the matter for $25,000 and court costs in February 1946.[20]

But the legal action, filed in a DeBardeleben-controlled local court, had a chilling effect on UMWA. Organizer James H. Terry complained that union leaders would not let anyone named as a defendant in the suit participate in the drive, and many of the defendants were the organizers with the most knowledge about AFICO and its company towns. As a result, Terry made little headway in St. Clair County, and this effort, like others, ultimately failed.[21]

Though AFICO kept the UMWA out of the company's mines, it fell victim to the same market conditions that decimated the rest of Alabama's commercial coal industry. In 1948, Prince DeBardeleben warned the company's stockholders of "mining difficulties existing at present such as reduced requirements on Railroad Contracts, a general falling off in demand for coal, and the reduced out put of our mines resulting in abnormal high cost." Over the next year, AFICO began leasing and selling many of its coal properties to other companies in an effort to improve its bottom line, but the company continued to suffer from a general decrease in coal orders.[22]

AFICO's end came quickly. In June 1950, Prince DeBardeleben outlined the bleak economic future facing Alabama's coal industry. DeBardeleben recommended and the directors unanimously approved measures that authorized "drastic reductions in both personnel and operating expenses." Two months later, the company sold all of its coal property in Walker County to Alabama Power for $1.2 million, and in September it sold its Acmar and old Overton company towns to West Virginia developer Marc Levine for $175,000. Finally, less than two weeks before Christmas, DeBardeleben recommended that the company "completely cease its business of mining and selling coal" and unload its remaining assets.[23]

In the wake of the decision to close down the company, Prince DeBardeleben's advice to his employees must have seemed like a cruel joke. Their pension fund depleted, DeBardeleben told the employees "they might get a helping hand from the union." AFICO's miners took the hint and voted to join the UMWA in a desperate attempt to salvage some kind of future. Union officials, realizing what had prompted such a sudden change of heart among AFICO's miners, "didn't take them," remembered William Mitch Jr., son of the District 20 president.[24]

Observers who visited AFICO's towns after the company's decision became known saw a bleak landscape. One journalist reported that the "once thriving villages with their churches, schools, commissaries, water works and electric light systems" now appeared "rather forlorn and forsaken looking. The hustle and bustle is gone. Community affairs are neglected. School functions have ceased, and church socials are few and far between." Levine offered to sell homes to their residents where possible, and Prince DeBardeleben told the miners that they could farm on AFICO property until they found new work. The company temporarily continued to pay part of the salaries of the teachers at the three white and two black schools in Acmar and Margaret. The miners who remained in the villages spent their time looking for new work and expressing their "bitterness about it all."[25]

Indeed, finding a job in one of Alabama's mines in the fall of 1950 appeared a daunting task. Walker County, the heart of Alabama's coalfields, felt the economic and social costs of the coal industry's collapse most acutely. By the winter of 1949, commercial operators of mines of all sizes began to lay off miners. "Right here in Walker County unemployment has reached a degree which in the least is distressing," reported newspaper columnist and union leader Lester F. Lawrence.[26]

A. W. Vogtle, who headed DeBardeleben Coal's sales operations, proclaimed a dire future for the region's industry. Southern Railway, which had once consumed more than a million tons of Alabama coal a year, ceased buying coal in July 1949. Georgia Power also planned to reduce its coal purchases. At the same time, Vogtle told an audience at the Jasper Rotary Club, out-of-state coal companies were making inroads into Alabama markets. By the fall of 1949, federal officials had placed Walker County on a list of areas with critically high rates of unemployment. A year later, federal officials estimated the county's unemployment rate at 12 percent. Throughout the 1950s, Jasper, the county's largest town, appeared on lists of the nation's economically distressed areas, the only southern municipality so designated.[27]

Congressman Elliott and other officials privately expressed their belief that Walker County's employment situation was much worse than federal statistics revealed. The congressman estimated that by 1950, nearly forty-five hundred of the county's six thousand miners had lost their jobs and that the county's true unemployment rate had reached about 26 percent. Other critical areas in Elliott's congressional district included Marion, Blount, and Winston Counties. Federal officials eventually imported surplus farm commodities into many of these areas to feed the unemployed miners and their families.[28]

The economic transformation of the Birmingham District's coalfields took place during a time of political change that directly involved thousands of coal miners. Union miners were part of the coalition that had helped propel Folsom into the governor's office. Backed by the traditional outsiders in Alabama politics—industrial workers, small farmers, women, educators, and the few African Americans who could vote—Folsom triumphed over the entrenched industrialist and planter alliance, seeming to herald a major shift in favor of the liberal wing of the state's Democratic Party. Folsom's tendency to downplay issues of race and his willingness to blur the color line also suggested a movement toward a mild form of biracialism or gradualism that in many respects mirrored the UMWA's racial policies.

In his 1946 campaign, Folsom built on the grassroots style he had used in an unsuccessful gubernatorial bid four years earlier. He traveled the state's farming and industrial communities with a string band, the Strawberry Pickers, that occasionally included Hank Williams Sr. Perennially short of money, Folsom passed around a bucket for donations. At these folksy events, Folsom often wielded a symbolic corn shuck mop and pledged to sweep Montgomery clean.[29]

Folsom's platform included a mix of ideas that appealed to poor and lower-middle-class voters. He campaigned for free textbooks in the public schools and a nine-month school term, better pay for teachers, and more schools. He supported increased payments to disabled workers from the state's worker's compensation program as well as higher unemployment payments. In an even more direct appeal to industrial workers, Folsom called for compensation for occupational diseases, including the dreaded black lung. Issues that appealed specifically to rural farmers included Folsom's support for paving more rural farm-to-market roads and a minimum state pension of fifty dollars a month for residents over age sixty-five.[30]

Folsom's campaign also touched on issues of race and class in ways that issued an important challenge to white elites. He supported the reapportionment of the state legislature so that it did not as heavily favor the planters and industrialists, advocated the repeal of the state's poll tax, and openly favored enfranchising blacks and poor whites. African Americans began to appear in the large crowds that gathered to hear Folsom speak, even when he ventured into the Black Belt, the plantation region that cut a swath through the southern part of the state. The candidate frequently shook hands with the black workers and farmers who attended his rallies, and observers commented on how Folsom emerged from his automobile before a rally and immediately moved to "shake hands first with black laborers watching on the fringes of the crowd."[31]

Folsom finished first in the May 1946 primary, garnering more than 28 percent of the vote. He carried most of the state's important mining districts, beating his nearest competitor, Lieutenant Governor Handy Ellis, by a two-to-one margin in Walker County. In Jefferson County, Folsom finished a close second to Ellis, 14,764 to 13,597.[32]

The biracialism of the UMWA and CIO, however mild, became a major issue in the runoff between Ellis and Folsom. When the CIO endorsed Folsom, Ellis tried to rally support by attacking the organization's biracialism. The lieutenant governor warned that if the industrial union body "seizes the sole power, it will wreck all other unions in our state, destroy our traditions, and disrupt our fine and wholesome race relations by breaking down segregation laws." As the runoff date approached, Ellis grew more desperate. A Folsom victory, Ellis warned, threatened "the complete destruction of our segregation laws—laws which are best for the white man and the colored man—laws under which our white folks and colored folks here in Alabama and the South have lived in peace and harmony and friendly understanding." All of these tactics failed. When the results of the runoff were tabulated on the evening of 4 June, Folsom had defeated Ellis, 195,000 to 140,000. Folsom carried Jefferson County 26,377 to 23,407 and Walker County by an even larger ratio, 7,594 to 2,285.[33]

Miners played an even more direct role in Elliott's election to Congress two years later. Elliott, a more traditional liberal than Folsom, also came from a humble background. A Jasper lawyer and city judge, Elliott decided to run in part because he was moved by the plight of the poor people whose fates he determined. "Depression or not, war or no war, times continued to be tough for these people, awfully tough," Elliott wrote later. "A fellow couldn't help but feel that, and I was feeling it mighty strongly by then. I was chomping at the bit to get the chance to start doing something about this politically."[34]

In the race to represent the nine-county Seventh Congressional District, Elliott faced off against a well-entrenched incumbent, Carter Manasco, who had held the seat for seven years. Unlike Manasco, Elliott worked hard during the election, traveling the rural district's mud roads and promising to get them paved. Elliott also stressed education, "telling those miners and farmers that there was no reason on earth their children shouldn't have schooling of the same quality as that of children who live in large cities."[35]

Miners and other unionists flocked to Elliott's campaign, donating what they could. Lawrence, the president of a UMWA local in Parrish, believed that Manasco was a "tool" of the industrialists in Walker County and was among labor's "enemies." Elliott, by contrast, was an "outstanding young lawyer" who had "satisfied our leaders . . . that he will go along with Labor." The members of Lawrence's local had hoped to make voluntary contributions each payday, but those plans were shelved after a national strike idled the Birmingham District's mines. "Mr. Elliott has the misfortune of being a poor man," Lawrence wrote to UMWA President Lewis, "with only such financial backing as the working class can provide for him." That proved to be enough, however, and Elliott defeated Manasco by about nine thousand votes in the May primary.[36]

But Folsom's victory and the election of liberals to Congress masked Alabama's remaining tensions. Conservative Democrats, including former Governor Frank Dixon, remained important players in the state's politics. They had not cooled in their opposition to expanding federal authority, and they remained committed to white supremacy. Dixon and his ally, state party chair Gessner McCorvey, retained control over the Democratic Party's machinery and led the regional rebellion that became known as the States' Rights Democratic Party, or simply the Dixiecrats, after the national Democratic Party added relatively mild civil rights planks to its 1948 platform.[37]

Though victories by Folsom, Elliott, and Senators Hill and Sparkman pointed elsewhere, race remained a central theme in Alabama politics. Nothing illustrated the divided minds of Alabama's postwar voters better than the passage of the Boswell Amendment, a measure created by Wilkinson, outgoing Governor Chauncey Sparks, Dixon, and McCorvey, all of whom were conservative Democrats. The amendment allowed registrars wide latitude in registering voters by requiring them to read, write, or interpret parts of the U.S. Constitution. The measure, drafted in response to the U.S. Supreme Court's abolition of the all-white primary in 1944, was aimed primarily at keeping black voters disfranchised but also prevented some poor whites from registering. McCorvey urged white voters to support the amendment "to preserve white supremacy in our State."[38]

To become part of the Alabama constitution, the measure required approval in a statewide vote. Folsom, Hill, Sparkman, and other progressives joined with labor groups and the state's major newspapers in opposing the measure. District 20 President Mitch and many other state labor leaders joined a Citizens' Committee against Amendment No. 4, as the Boswell Amendment appeared on the ballot. Voters in Alabama ratified the amendment in November, 89,163 to 76,843, just a few months after electing Folsom governor. The results illustrated citizens' divided views on racial issues. The amendment fared best in the counties with the highest proportions of African Americans and where potential black voting posed more of a direct political threat. The amendment also passed in Birmingham, where, in the words of one political observer, "swanky residential districts" voted heavily in favor. In all other large cities, voters rejected the measure.[39] On the one hand, voters gave Folsom a large victory over Ellis, suggesting that a majority endorsed the new governor's gradualist approach to race relations. On the other hand, voters approved of measures designed to ensure that most blacks remained disfranchised.

The leaders of Alabama's Dixiecrat revolt—most of the same people who crafted the Boswell Amendment—sought to tap into the citizenry's racial anxieties. Angered by civil rights planks adopted at the Democratic Party's 1948 national convention in Philadelphia, much of the Alabama delegation walked out of the convention hall, taking with them delegates from other parts of the South. Dixon had threatened such action since the early 1940s and had helped carefully orchestrate the show at the national convention. The dissidents formed the States' Rights Democratic Party and held a convention in Birmingham in July. They nominated South Carolina Governor Strom Thurmond for president and began a national campaign. Elites in the Alabama Democratic Party kept President Harry Truman's name off the ballot in the fall election. The Dixiecrats failed to attract the support they had hoped for but nevertheless won Alabama, Louisiana, South Carolina, and Mississippi.[40]

The leaders of the conservative wing of the Alabama Democratic Party did not have a monopoly on the issue of race in the Alabama coalfields during the late 1940s. The Dixiecrats found an ally in the Klan. Scandals had derailed the organization in Alabama in the 1920s, but beginning in the late 1930s, the group began to make a comeback as whites began to feel threatened by the growth of the federal government and by challenges to the racial status quo. For much of World War II, the Alabama Klan had only four chapters and a thousand members, but less than a year after the end of hostilities, the Klan had reemerged as a major force.

In late March 1946, ceremonies commemorating the rebirth of the Klan took place in Atlanta, and crosses burned across the Birmingham District. Investigators remarked that the events heralded the "revival" of the Klan in Birmingham. That summer, an organization called the Federated Ku Klux Klans filed incorporation papers in Jefferson County; listed among the group's officers were William Hugh Morris, a roofing contractor; E. P. Pruitt, a physician; and Robert S. Gullege Sr., a "real estate developer and fraternal organizer." Klan leaders soon claimed that thirty thousand people statewide had paid dues, seven thousand of them in Birmingham. Although probably inflated, these numbers indicate a high level of support for the organization.[41]

Early in its rebirth, the Klan reflected anxiety that the color line in the Birmingham District had blurred since the Great Depression with the rise of biracial unions such as the UMWA. World War II had seemed further to threaten white supremacy, as African Americans became more assertive and challenged segregation ordinances. The increasing federal presence—particularly the Birmingham President's Committee on Fair Employment Practice hearings—had led many whites to feel that the South as they knew it had come under assault. The Klan dedicated itself to stopping the drift. Gullege, for example, claimed that the group hoped "to save the Negro from his own folly." At a rally in the late 1940s, the leader of the Georgia Klan expanded on these ideals, linking the softening of the color line with the increasing presence of the federal government since the New Deal. "God segregated the races," Samuel Green told a rally of two thousand supporters in Tarrant City, north of Birmingham. "There is no law that can be passed by Harry Truman, or Congress, or by the legislature of your state that can supersede the law of the Lord. If He had wanted all to be white—or if He had wanted all to be black—it would have been that way."[42]

Gendered concerns about the proper place of white men and women in the South also occupied much of the Klan's thinking. World War II had encouraged women to enter the industrial workplace in greater numbers than ever before, threatening to place them both outside the home and in close proximity to black men. To the Klan and other white conservatives, the proper role of white women—a key pillar of white supremacy—seemed under assault. The Klan had listed the "protection of the chastity of white womanhood" high among its objectives in its incorporation papers. But the organization also saw the status of white women as linked to the supremacy of white men. Green struck a chord with Birmingham supporters when he thundered, "White men, being the supreme race, intend to keep it that way."[43]

The Klan articulated its views in the language of morality. Racial concerns remained key to the Klan's ideas about morality, as did people who existed outside traditional notions of morality. The coalfields around Birmingham, where the UMWA had negotiated the difficult terrain of race for more than a decade, seemed a natural place for the group to focus much of its energy. To root out moral and racial transgressors, Morris claimed, the organization had hundreds of members traveling throughout Jefferson and Walker Counties looking for "honky-tonk operators, common brier patch prostitutes, and people of that type." The coalfields around Birmingham consequently became contested spaces where night riders sought to restore the South's moral and racial boundaries. Miners, their families, and those who lived in coal communities found themselves on both sides of the Klan activities. Historian Glenn Feldman has argued that many miners undoubtedly joined the Klan and participated in its violent escapades. But some also found themselves the targets of the organization's terror.[44]

Perhaps fearing members' involvement with the reborn Klan, many union leaders remained silent. When the Klan raided an African American Girl Scout camp near Bessemer in early June 1948, local and national organizations denounced the action. But major union groups said little. In response, the Birmingham chapter of the National Association for the Advancement of Colored People urged state and local labor leaders, including Mitch, to condemn the upsurge in Klan activity. "We call this to your attention not because you have listed among your membership thousands of Negro workers, but because the trade union movement has always stood in the forefront of these forces fighting Ku Klux Klan outfits," the association argued. "We believe that many of your Negro members along with us are disturbed over the fact that labor's leadership has not as yet lifted its hand or raised its voice against this outrage in disturbing contrast to that of the clergy, newspapers and civic organizations that have. Naturally, labor's silence leaves the public as well as Negro dues payers of your union in doubt as to where you stand on the question of Klan terrorism and violence."[45]

Labor leaders' concerns about where unionists stood on the Klan issue likely encouraged the silence. About six months after the raid on the Girl Scout camp, for example, investigator Stetson Kennedy warned of a Klan push to take control of labor unions. KKK leaders printed leaflets urging members of the organization to vote as a solid bloc to elect members to every office in their locals. "Everything will be O.K. after the K.K.K., moves in and takes over," claimed J. B. Stoner, a Tennessee Klan leader.[46] The Federated Klan, though led by physicians and roofing contractors, hoped to attract members in the coalfields and the industrial districts around Birmingham using such methods as night riding, cross burnings, and mass rallies.

In April 1949, the Klan intervened in a bitter and violent jurisdictional rivalry between the International Union of Mine, Mill, and Smelter Workers (known as Mine Mill) and the United Steelworkers of America. The dispute was rife with anticommunist rhetoric, reminiscent of the tactics used by the UMWA's District 50 a few years earlier. In the late 1940s, with the Red Scare sweeping the country, the charges carried extra weight. Mine Mill, which had represented iron ore miners in the Birmingham District since the late 1930s, had been expelled from the CIO for alleged connections to the Communist Party. Race also played a central role in the dispute. Mine Mill fully practiced the biracialism pioneered by the UMWA, reserving local offices for African Americans. The steelworkers and CIO in Birmingham took advantage of Mine Mill's vulnerability after the war to challenge for control of the ore miners who worked at TCI and other major iron and steel producers. As District 50 had in the early 1940s, the steelworkers' union colluded with white secessionists, effectively exploiting the heightened racial tensions in the Birmingham District. Mine Mill was vulnerable in this respect because it had traditionally appealed to black ore miners and had for years fought off white secessionists and company-backed unions.

But after World War II, the demographic balance within the Birmingham District's ore mines had changed, with whites becoming a majority in the industry. Mine Mill's biracialism became harder to maintain. Many newly hired white miners provided a strong base from which the steelworkers could contest Mine Mill's jurisdiction, and in the spring of 1949, the CIO, backed by the steelworkers' union, issued such a challenge at TCI's ore mines.

As the date for a vote to determine which union would represent the iron ore miners drew near, clashes erupted between Mine Mill and steelworker activists. The Klan intervened, taking the side of local steelworkers who were not "tainted" by charges of communism or racial egalitarianism. About one hundred Klansmen rode past the Mine Mill district office in Bessemer shortly before the election vote, dressed in full robed regalia and blowing their car horns. In the May election, the United Steelworkers defeated Mine Mill by a vote of 2,996 to 2,233. The KKK's intervention showed that the organization no longer opposed the idea of industrial unionism and might even support the limited biracialism implemented by the steelworkers' union as long as whites maintained control. By the late 1940s, as Kennedy had warned, the Klan sought to shape the nature of the Birmingham District's industrial unions to ensure white control.[47]

The United Steelworkers' campaign against Mine Mill took place against the backdrop of a violent wave of night riding across the state initiated by the Federated Ku Klux Klan. While the Klan targeted African American activists and those who attempted to break Birmingham's segregation barriers, its targets in the surrounding coalfields included many whites—typically those who violated traditional ideas of morality or, as in the case of Marshlar's Café, who were accused of violating segregation norms. Coal towns and mining neighborhoods became scenes of dramatic conflicts as the Klan sought to impose its racial and gendered moral order through terror.[48]

William Hamilton, a white mechanic who lived in the Jefferson County mining community of Coalburg, was among the first to experience the Klan's efforts. In April 1949, a group of robed and hooded Klansmen visited Hamilton's home and warned him to "straighten up." The men then burned a cross in front of his house. A month later, two robed men entered Hamilton's home while he was sleeping and hauled him out of bed and into a waiting automobile. The Klansmen drove

Hamilton and William Rochester, a disabled white miner kidnapped and brought along to serve as a witness, to an isolated area and marched them away from the road. The mob ordered Hamilton to disrobe. "Before I could finish," he told investigators, "one of the Klansmen tore my underwear off and threw me down on the ground, face down." The hooded men then beat Hamilton about twenty times with a leather strap. After they finished, the Klansmen threatened Rochester. "You see that?" one of them asked. "That's just a sample of what you'll get."[49]

Why had the Klan singled out Hamilton and Rochester? Investigators suspected that Hamilton's personal behavior—he drank and was not working regularly—provoked the incident and that the Klansmen believed that Rochester was not supporting his family. When Rochester, who had recently been fitted for a back brace as a result of his mining injuries, protested that he "was unable to work and was under the doctors' care," the Klansmen vowed to check with his physicians. The action had the desired effect on Hamilton—he stopped drinking—but caused Rochester to live "in fear of his life," according to state investigators.[50]

The attacks on Hamilton and Rochester inaugurated a wave of night riding by Klansmen in the Birmingham District. Edna McDanal, a forty-two-year-old grandmother, became a target of the Klan's efforts make good on its promise to protect the "chastity of white womanhood." Armed Klansmen forced their way into McDanal's Birmingham home while her husband, a truck driver, was at work on the evening of 10 June. McDanal, a strong woman, retreated to the rear of the house and found her husband's shotgun. Klansmen reached her as she attempted to load the weapon and disarmed her by striking her head with a blackjack. McDanal continued to resist the men and managed to lift at least one of the Klansmen's masks. "We could kill you for that," the man told her.[51]

The hooded and robed men dragged McDanal outside and forced her to watch a cross burn in her front yard. McDanal, in her nightgown, asked the men to allow her to get some clothes, but she was told she "did not need them because she was not going to live long." One man in the crowd told McDanal that the Klansmen planned to "string you up." Another proclaimed, "We are going to burn you and string you to the cross." Terror, however, not torture, was their main goal, and they eventually released McDanal and left, heading away from her home with a police car from nearby Graysville leading the way.[52]

The attack on McDanal illustrated much about the anxiety racing through the Birmingham District about the proper place of women in postwar Alabama. Acting on rumors fomented by neighbors, the Klansmen had chosen McDanal because, as one man told her, "You run a whore house and sell whiskey." But the roots of the attack ran much deeper. McDanal, who was raised in a small Walker County coal mining community, had been a heavy drinker. Her father had been shot and killed by a sheriff's deputy several years earlier, and she and her husband had lived in Irondale for several years, earning "a bad reputation for morality." The real reason for the McDanal incident, however, may have been the fact that their next-door neighbor, J. E. Woods, had designs on their home and that they had asked for too much money when he offered to buy it. When investigators visited Woods a few days after the Klan incident, he repeated the rumors about Edna McDanal's personal life and called the cross burning outside her home "the prettiest sight I ever saw."[53]

Four days after the incident at the McDanal residence, Klansmen abducted U.S. Navy veteran Billy Stovall from his home in Birmingham, drove him several miles to an isolated area, and beat him. Klansmen accused Stovall, who worked two jobs and took business classes at night, of forcing his wife to "work and neglecting his children." Stovall's wife, Roxie, worked at the Spotlight Café and was "brought home at nite . . . by men who had cars," an investigator concluded. "This seems to be [the] fact that instigated the attact [sic] on subject." As in the McDanal case, investigators suspected that a neighbor, J. Thurman Kimbrough, "possibly a religious fanatic in some respects," had either organized or helped with the incident.[54] Roxie Stovall's status as a wage earner clearly played a role in provoking some of her neighbors and the Klan, with its concerns regarding the status of women, into action.

In April and May, a band of Klansmen from Adamsville singled out roughly a dozen people near the Jefferson County mining community of Praco. In most of the incidents, groups of more than a hundred hooded Klansmen abducted the victims. In early June, a group of about a hundred masked people took Jack Alexander and Mary Henderson from a home at gunpoint and drove them to an isolated area known as Pumpkin Center. The Klan also abducted a third person, William Stevens, who lived about a mile from Alexander. The mob was led by a minister who "prayed for us," Alexander reported. "He said he hoped God would teach us what was right."[55]

The Klansmen then beat Alexander, Henderson, and Stevens. They meted out especially rough treatment to Henderson. The Klansmen lashed her five times and then tied a rope around her neck and dragged her along the ground. Alexander said he believed that the hooded men were "from the Adamsville Ku Klux Klan. . . . I know one of them. He came to see me last Tuesday while I was down on the creek fishing, and said that if I didn't go to work, the Klan would come and get me again."[56]

Alexander claimed at the time that he did not know why the three were singled out by the mob, but Henderson told officials that the Klansmen had threatened to kill her "if she didn't stop seeing Jack Alexander." He had not held a regular job since 1939, when he came down with tuberculosis. Alexander had subsequently spent two periods in a tuberculosis sanitarium and had been rejected when he tried to enlist in the armed services. At the time of the attack, Alexander lived in his mother's home with his thirteen-year-old son and worked odd jobs; as he recalled years later, he "was drinking and running around with women at the time."[57] Alexander's personal behavior and his status as a part-time wage earner clearly violated the Klan's ideas of proper behavior and likely attracted the organization's attention.

Like many of the other night-riding events in the spring and early summer of 1949, the incident at Marshlar's Café reflected the Klan's concerns about proper behavior and the color line. But rivalries within the Brookside community may have played a more prominent role. In particular, Steve Marshlar and his brother, Johnny, who served on the city council, had become bitter foes of Elmer Brock, the city's police chief. Johnny Marshlar told investigators that he believed that the Klan raid had resulted from "personal grievances and grudges" and that Brock had something to do with the incident. "I've lived here for almost 40 years and I never saw friction like this before Brock became Chief of Police," John Marshlar said months later. Brock, a member of the painters' union, had a troubling record on race relations. One of his former officers, Fred Caneker, told state investigators that he had resigned from the city's police force in protest over the "whipping" of a black prisoner.[58]

The police chief's actions the evening of the Klan raid raised many questions. Brock had arrived at the café while the Klansmen were still there and had refused to stop them. After initially telling state investigators that he had never had any complaints about conduct at Marshlar's Café, Brock suddenly began a profanity-laden diatribe against the brothers. He told investigators that the Marshlars were "contrary," that black patrons "had gotten to where they wanted to hang out there all the time, ganged up at the back," and that the police had received "numerous complaints about their conduct." Law enforcement officials did not buy Brock's professions of innocence in the matter, and in July 1949 a Jefferson County grand jury indicted the police chief for "neglect of duty" and intimidating a witness in connection with the incident.[59]

In Brookside, the night riding opened deep rifts in the community that carried over into the fall. After Brock's indictment, John Marshlar clashed verbally and physically with his opponents on the city council. At a meeting in October, Brock's advocates on the council, led by Floyd Shaffer, Brock's assistant on the police force, passed a resolution of support for the beleaguered chief. The action was even more infuriating to the Marshlars because Shaffer was also under indictment in connection with the incident at their café. When Johnny Marshlar heard about the measure, he confronted Brookside's mayor, John Bensko, and the resulting argument ended with Bensko punching Marshlar.[60]

The Klan's night riding did not go unnoticed by state officials. The poor and marginal targets of Klan violence in the coalfields had a sympathetic occupant at the head of state government, and Governor Folsom soon intervened in the Birmingham District and moved to stop the night riding. In mid-May, he ordered the state police to crack down on the incidents and instructed investigators to find out who was behind the terrorism. The governor later denounced KKK members on statewide radio as "would-be Hitlers" who "have prowled the streets at night, burning their crosses of hate and frightening innocent women and children and beating up veterans and workers." The "stamp of dishonor is upon them. . . . [T]here is no rhyme or reason for their existence," Folsom declared. "They won't be tolerated as long as I am governor."[61]

The governor asked the state's attorney general, Albert Carmichael, to study means of revoking the Klan's corporate charter and threw his political weight behind a legislative effort, initiated by State Senator Henry Mize of Tuscaloosa County, that prohibited adults from donning masks in public unless they were observing a legal holiday. The bill became law on 28 June, providing penalties of five hundred dollars and up to a year in jail.[62]

Elements of the labor movement and its allies also took stands against the Klan, particularly in the mining center of Walker County. The pro-UMWA *Union News* issued a series of strong denunciations of the hooded order's activities. Editor Paul Trawick went on a local radio station and denounced "the recent rise in mob rule and violence which has been prevalent in Walker County during recent weeks." When an unidentified telephone caller subsequently threatened Trawick, he refused to be intimidated, denouncing the Klan in the next edition of the newspaper as a "terrorist" organization. Trawick also testified before a congressional committee holding hearings on the night riding but was less bold, urging the legislators to "shelve and forget any intended legislation which would in any way impair the sovereignty of the individual states."[63]

Labor's Non-Partisan League, a political lobbying group closely linked to the UMWA, took a vocal stand against the Klan activities. At the end of June, the league's Walker County branch scheduled speakers who called for labor unions to oppose the Klan. In mid-July, Labor's Non-Partisan League denounced the KKK as "an un-American organization" and condemned the organization as an agent of "masked mob rule."[64] These actions suggested that many miners in the UMWA stronghold opposed the Klan's actions and were willing to take a strong, vocal stand against the violence.

Occasional links, however, emerged between the miners and the Klan's campaign, and a few UMWA members' names surfaced as reports flowed out of the coalfields in the summer and fall of 1949. For example, Boyd Killingsworth, a member of the UMWA local at Labuco, was later indicted in connection with the McDanal attack. The local's leaders told Killingsworth to get out of the Klan, and he apparently complied. By the fall of 1949, however, two other members of the local, Pete Howton and J. D. McLemore, had their names linked publicly with Klan night riding. Like Killingsworth, Howton confessed his membership to union officials, but McLemore denied belonging to the Klan. The revelations left local leaders in a bind. Under the UMWA's constitution, none of the men could continue to belong to the union. The leaders, probably fearing Klan retribution, appealed to Mitch for assistance. "All of these men are our neighbors and no one man of us desires to file charges against them," they wrote to the district president.[65]

Mitch offered little help, referring the matter back to local officials and noting that the "local union has full jurisdiction." Instead of taking a tough stand on the issue, he suggested that requiring the men to file affidavits that they were no longer members of the organization might "materially help in handling this situation."[66]

One of the main Klan activists operating in the Birmingham District's coalfields was not a union miner but a former mine owner. C. A. "Brownie" Lollar, who had operated a small mine in the Praco area at one time, became a major force in the Klan organization in Adamsville during the summer of 1949. State police investigators encountered Lollar on 17 June 1949 as he led a team of sentries in an effort to cover the license plates of automobiles parked outside a KKK meeting. Lollar also had a commission as a "special" deputy with the Jefferson County Sheriff's Department, so he expressed surprise when the state investigators informed him that he was breaking the law by covering the license plates. He also was shocked when the investigators emerged from their cars heavily armed. Lollar told the state officers that "most of these boys worked for me. I'm kind of a leader here and they do whatever I say. I told them to cover up the tags on the cars because this is a Klan parking place." Lollar was forced to give up his deputy's commission, and a grand jury later indicted him in connection with the night riding.[67]

In June, Mitch began a public campaign to distance the UMWA from the Klan's actions. He reminded miners that the UMWA's constitution prohibited members from belonging to the KKK. A month later, Mitch issued a stronger statement, warning miners "to get out of the Klan or get out of the union." The state UMWA leader also joined a fifteen-person committee made up of Jefferson County leaders formed to combat the Klan's activities in the region.[68]

The Jefferson County grand jury that convened in the summer of 1949 eventually indicted more than a dozen people in connection with the night ridings and floggings that had swept the Birmingham District. Lollar, Brock, and a lesser-known activist, Robert "Dynamite Bob" Chambliss, were among those who faced criminal charges in connection with the Klan's terrorism. In general, however, the prosecutions failed dismally. Two years later, after juries returned a rash of not-guilty verdicts, officials dropped the remaining cases.[69]

The Klan's violent moral crusade in the Alabama coalfields in the spring and summer of 1949 reflected concerns about the fluctuating color line in an era of biracial unionism as well as a perception that the ideals of manhood and woman-hood were in crisis. Almost all of the targets of hooded violence in the coalfields of Walker and Jefferson Counties lived on the margins of southern society in an era of industrial decline, which added urgency to the Klan's actions. While political leaders such as Folsom took strong action, Mitch and other union leaders proved more cautious and avoided a direct fight with the Klan, which had infiltrated the unions' ranks. In many ways, the cautious approach of Mitch and other leaders stood in contrast to the actions of the UMWA's allies, who sometimes spoke out strongly against the night riding despite the great risks of doing so. Instead of tak-ing a lead role and rallying the miners against the KKK, Mitch and the UMWA tried as much as possible to avoid the issue.

Against this backdrop, the UMWA engaged in a series of fights over the creation of a health care and pension system for union miners. UMWA President John L. Lewis had first broached the idea of a fund based on a production tax during negotiations late in the war. But Lewis and the union found themselves in a poor bargaining position in the spring of 1945, and the UMWA president withdrew the proposal when it met with opposition from both the coal operators and federal negotiators.[70]

The UMWA and its president recognized better than the operators and the federal government that high social costs of coal mining demanded action. By the late 1940s, the nation had an estimated fifty thousand permanently disabled coal miners, a constant reminder to Lewis and union activists of mining's toll. The future also weighed heavily on the minds of union miners and their families. In 1944, the average miner was forty-five years old, and almost 60 percent of Alabama's coal miners were over thirty-five. "We need the health and welfare fund," argued J. V. Comer, whose husband worked in the mines of the Birmingham District, "for when our men go into the mines we don't know whether they will come out or not, and they have nothing to look to in sickness and accidents."[71]

In the spring of 1946, Lewis began to push hard for the creation of a mechanism to help aging and injured union members. He notified the nation's coal operators that he wanted to reopen national negotiations. When talks began in March, Lewis fought to have a health and retirement fund included in the new agreement, along with a wage increase and improvements in working and living conditions. The operators refused seriously to negotiate the health and retirement provision, and the talks went nowhere. On 1 April, more than three hundred thousand union miners across the country walked out.[72]

The more than twenty thousand Alabama miners who stopped work thought that the walkout would prove a short one. Mitch initially characterized the strike as a "much needed" vacation from the long workweeks of the war years, and the UMWA at first kept pickets away from the mines. "Coal mining is probably the most strenuous work in the world, and the operators know it is to their economic advantage for the miners to get a lull in their work after a long stretch at 54 hours a week," Mitch said.[73]

Serious issues were at stake, however, and the UMWA underestimated the operators' intransigence. Lewis asked the miners to return to work in early May, after the federal government again stepped in and took control of the mines. Secretary of the Interior Julius A. Krug and Lewis then negotiated an agreement that essentially forced the operators to agree to a welfare and pension fund bankrolled by a tax of five cents on every ton of coal produced in union mines. The agreement also included assurances that federal officials would create a national mine safety code.

Alabama operators opposed the new agreement. As a result, thousands of the state's miners walked out when the federal government used the War Labor Disputes Act to take control of the mines on 22 May, idling most of the Birmingham District's captive operations and about half of its commercial mines. The miners' defiance of Lewis mystified Mitch, who complained that the reasons for the walkout were "a complete mystery to me, I had hoped and expected the miners would continue on the job until the end of this week."[74]

The miners returned to work in early June, but the coal operators' opposition to the Krug-Lewis agreement ensured more turmoil. The Alabama operators did not sign the contract because it was negotiated between Lewis and the federal government. AMI President Rouzer predictably complained that the agreement "is most unfavorable to the country as a whole and particularly Alabama which is one of the so-called marginal fields. It will prove expensive to the public, a great boon to the oil and gas industries and if continued beyond the present period of acute coal shortages will sound the death knell for a large part of the Alabama commercial coal industry."[75]

The Krug-Lewis agreement remained in effect through the summer of 1946. In the fall, the secretary of the interior began the process of returning the mines to private hands by convening national negotiations between the companies and the UMWA. The opposition of many operators to the agreement's pension fund and safety provisions virtually ensured another national walkout that fall. When Lewis initiated a strike in the middle of November, President Harry Truman retaliated by obtaining an injunction forbidding the UMWA and its leaders from striking. The miners stopped work anyway, in open defiance of the courts and the Truman administration, and a federal judge levied huge fines against the UMWA and Lewis before the strike ended on 7 December.

Most of the issues that divided the union and operators remained unresolved. The operators resisted and delayed the creation of the UMWA Welfare and Retirement Fund, and the country's mines remained unsafe places for the people who worked in them. A massive March 1947 explosion that killed 111 men in Centralia, Illinois, pushed mine safety back into the national consciousness. In the months leading up to this horrific disaster, federal inspectors had twice visited the mine and found the coal company in violation of the new federal safety code. Although they cited the mine for inadequate rock dusting and poor ventilation, the inspectors did not close the operation. Lewis harshly criticized federal authorities for these failures, and during congressional testimony on the Centralia disaster, he noted that of the thousands of mines visited by regulators in 1946, only two completely passed inspection.[76]

Pressure forced Krug to close more than five hundred coal mines, including thirty-five in Alabama. Five of the six large mines operated by Alabama By-Products were closed. Large captive producers Woodward Iron and Republic Steel also had mines shut down by federal authorities. In closing the operations, the U.S. Bureau of Mines complained that "few coal mines in Alabama are completely and adequately rock-dusted in all respects." Rock dust, made up of lime, was spread along exposed underground pillars of coal, cutting down on the coal dust in the air and making the dust less volatile in the event of an explosion. Lewis called a national memorial period—essentially a strike—in late March and early April to call attention to safety problems in the nation's mines.[77]

The miners' support for Folsom's election a year earlier began to pay off, and they used the memorial period to push for an overhaul of the state's mining laws, which were clearly outdated. The last revisions had taken place in the mid-1930s, before mechanization dramatically changed the industry and increased the potential hazards underground. The proliferation of small wagon and truck mines, most of which were "extremely dangerous," also presented regulators with daunting problems.[78]

Another major difficulty concerned the close relationship between state mine inspectors and the coal companies. The problem was dramatically illustrated in the case of Lee Grant Cleveland, a miner from Dolomite who was fired when he refused to work a cutting machine in ten inches of water. In the late 1930s, Cleveland had seen a man killed while operating a coal cutting machine in a wet part of the mine. "The place was wet and the machine had a de[a]d ground on it and it killed the man," Cleveland wrote. When a foreman told Cleveland to operate a cutting machine in water in 1946, he refused "because the machine cable had several splices in it and it was lying across the face in the water and I was afraid to get in that water." The company fired him, but Cleveland and the union challenged the action. District 20 officials were shocked when the state's chief inspector testified during an arbitration hearing that mining equipment could be operated safely in standing water. As a result of this testimony, the company's action was upheld, and Cleveland did not get his job back. The incident, according to Mitch, "shows how far the [chief inspector] is willing to go in taking chances with the life and limbs of the men."[79]

The close relationship between inspectors and the operators was also illustrated by the treatment that safety committee members received when they attempted to investigate accidents. When committee members sought to help inspect the site of a fatality at Black Diamond Coal's Blue Creek mine, company officials and a state inspector stonewalled them. The inspector eventually permitted the union miners on the committee to attend the inspection, but they were not allowed to make any comments or ask questions. After completing his investigation of the accident scene, the inspector met behind closed doors with Black Diamond officials. Members of the safety committee were not allowed to attend.[80]

Mitch and the miners used public events during the Centralia memorial period to rally public support for a reexamination of Alabama's mining codes. At a UMWA rally in Wylam Park, Mitch called the disaster "nothing short of mass murder. . . . Where we know reports show that things are wrong in the mine, we must demand protection." International representative John Hanratty told the miners gathered for the ceremony that he had "no faith literally in the state mine inspector's department at this time." At a rally in Jasper the following day, Mitch warned the operators that the miners in Alabama had "tolerated conditions in the past that we are not going to tolerate in the future."[81]

The AMI, realizing that the miners had a sympathetic ear in the governor's mansion, also went on the offensive with a public relations campaign designed, in its words, to counteract the "widespread impression that Alabama coal mines were unduly dangerous for the miners." The effort failed, unintentionally reinforcing the UMWA's arguments. AMI officials, for example, boasted that the six federal inspectors and eight state inspectors assigned to the Alabama coalfields had not "rendered a single report that classifies any mine in Alabama as unsafe or dangerous. They have not recommended the closing of a single Alabama mine for lack of safety or for any other reason."[82] The significance or lack of concern evidenced by this statement was not lost on the miners, the union, the public, or the new governor.

The Alabama legislature began to make moves to improve the enforcement of safety in the state's coalfields. In early April, lawmakers voted to increase the budget of the Department of Industrial Relations. Led by a young lawmaker from Barbour County, George Wallace, the legislature voted to add ten thousand dollars to the agency's funding over the next two years.[83]

Folsom then appointed a seventeen-member committee that included operators and union officials to study the state's coal mining laws. AMI officials agreed to participate in the effort. The committee included numerous company officials as well as Mitch, Hanratty, and Thomas Crawford, a district representative with the UMWA. The body met for more than two years before making a list of recommendations that the legislature approved and Folsom signed into law in the summer of 1949. Mitch praised the changes as "a great improvement for safety in the coal mines."[84]

The Centralia memorial period ended on 8 April 1947, and the miners, operators, and federal authorities began a new round of contract talks. The miners struck briefly in late June after Congress overrode President Truman's veto of the Taft-Hartley Act, but the negotiations between Lewis and national negotiators were notable for their civility. By mid-July, the operators and Lewis had produced a new two-year agreement that included a substantial raise—up to three dollars a day—and reduction of the workday from nine to eight hours. Most importantly, the new contract institutionalized the Welfare and Retirement Fund that Krug and Lewis had negotiated a year earlier. The Alabama operators grumbled that they might attempt to negotiate a separate agreement with the UMWA when they met to discuss the contract but in the end voted overwhelmingly to support the national agreement.[85]

The 1947 agreement, however, did not bring peace to the coalfields of Alabama or of the rest of the nation. The issue that divided the UMWA and the operators was no longer the establishment of the Welfare and Retirement Fund but who should control it and how it should function. Lewis and the coal operators fought for almost three years over these issues before resolving them in 1950. Lewis clashed often with operator representative Ezra Van Horn on the three-member board that oversaw the fund. As a result of the infighting, the fund did not begin operations in 1947 as planned. In frustration over the deadlock, the neutral trustee resigned in January 1948, throwing the entire process into confusion and triggering a rash of wildcat strikes across the country.

Lewis issued a circular to union officials in early March 1948, charging that the operators "have dishonored the 1947 Wage Agreement and defaulted under its provisions affecting the Welfare Fund." The action provoked walkouts by miners across the nation and set up another confrontation between the UMWA and the federal government, this time under the Taft-Hartley Act. In Alabama, walkouts began in force on 15 March, when most of the state's captive miners walked out. The strike soon idled most of the state's mines, curtailing more than 90 percent of the Birmingham District's coal production and throwing the iron and steel industries into a panic as coal shortages mounted.[86]

The Truman administration moved to seek a Taft-Hartley back-to-work order against Lewis and the UMWA. Courts issued injunctions to force the miners to return to the pits, and the threat of massive fines again hung over Lewis and the union. Lewis and negotiators for the major operators reached a compromise over the Welfare and Retirement Fund by resolving an acrimonious dispute over pensions. The agreement allocated a twelve-hundred-dollar annual pension to UMWA members who were sixty-two years old and had at least twenty years in the mines as of 29 May 1946. Lewis ordered the miners back to work in the wake of the compromise. In late June, the UMWA and major operators reached a new agreement that included a raise of a dollar per day and increased the royalty to the fund to twenty cents a ton.[87]

The agreement would prove only a temporary truce between the union and operators. The treatment that Lewis and the UMWA received in Washington hardened the resolve of miners in Alabama and the rest of the country. When the fund compromise appeared in the works in April, Mitch began frantic efforts to convince Alabama's miners to return to work. "The question at issue has been settled," he proclaimed. The miners, angry over Lewis's treatment at the hands of federal officials and not convinced that the battle was over, slowly went back to work. An uneasy truce held for a year.[88]

In the spring of 1949, as Alabama's coal industry went into its steep decline, Lewis and the coal operators began a prolonged battle that did not end until March 1950. The strikes and job actions of 1949–50 would be the last major walkouts in the Alabama coalfields for a generation. Miners knew better than anyone that they worked in an industry that had entered a major depression from which it might not emerge. In this context, the effort to shore up pensions and health benefits resonated with the aging miners. Union miners were literally fighting for their future, and as coal mines closed for good when markets dried up, the battle to keep the fund alive took on an added significance.

The long struggle began when the Southern Coal Producers' Association, the main negotiating group for companies in southern West Virginia, Kentucky, and

Tennessee, reopened negotiations with the UMWA. As the coal depression began to take a toll on production, the southern group demanded major concessions from Lewis and the union. At the same time, the UMWA opened separate negotiations with the main northern operators' group and representatives for the captive mine companies. The chaotic negotiating framework predictably led to stalemate, and the miners walked out during another "memorial period" in June as the expiration date for the 1947 contract grew near. Instead of taking the miners out on strike when the old national agreement expired on 30 June, however, Lewis declared an extension. But the union leader also imposed a three-day workweek in an attempt to draw down coal stockpiles and improve the UMWA's bargaining position. The three-day week dragged on throughout the summer and into the fall. The southern operators retaliated and refused to pay production royalties into the fund, throwing the system into financial distress. On 19 September, the fund stopped pension and health care payments, and thousands of angry miners walked out in protest across the nation.[89]

By the start of the strike, the Alabama coal industry had started its descent. U.S. Secretary of Commerce Charles Sawyer traveled through the Alabama coalfields and announced that the counties of Walker, Winston, Marion, and Blount faced a desperate crisis as small coal operators went out of business. Sawyer declared the economic effects of the decline of the industry in these counties "the worst problem" he had seen in his travels through the Southeast.[90] The months of only three days a week of work, the economic crisis, and the initiation of a national strike in mid-September took a harsh toll on Alabama's union miners. For almost a decade, they had engaged in a continuous warfare with the state's operators, and by 1949 they began to grow desperate.

Letters flooded into the UMWA's national headquarters begging for help. Walker County miner Luther Barrett penned a desperate plea to Lewis, informing the union president that UMWA members were "being persecuted by the operators by every means in the world that they can possible think of." The few commercial operators in the Alabama coalfields who remained financially viable began "hollowing [sic] 'there is no reason why you should not be ready to go to work, rather than starve and have your families starve to death.'" Barrett warned Lewis that the situation in Walker County was becoming "more and more acute by the [hour]. The statement has been made that Walker County is a test tube for the Nation, that if Organized Labor can be broken Down in Walker County it can be broken all over the Nation. We have already had bloodshed here and stand a very good chance of having still more if there is not something done and now."[91]

A month after the strike started in the fall of 1949, miner James Lackey found himself in "such bad shape I don't know what to do." Lackey had worked at a small Cordova mine that employed only eleven men. The three-day week that summer depleted his savings, a situation that grew worse when the mine shut down for repairs. To make ends meet, the miner took out a mortgage on his home. By the fall, however, the money had run out and stores refused Lackey credit. "I haven't got any groceries in my house and my kid hasn't even got any shoes and now its turning off [sic] cold and no money for coal and I guess my electricity will be cut off, because I can't pay my bill, and I can't get on the relief, because Walker County can't take any more on," he wrote. "I'm just at my rope's end."[92]

The economic crisis overwhelmed coal communities in the Birmingham District. Many unionists reported that company stores refused cash-strapped miners credit when the strike began. The miners and their local leaders turned to nearby independent merchants, who were rooted in coal communities in ways that the company-controlled commissaries were not and who agreed to extend credit in an attempt to avert a humanitarian crisis. But the scale of the problem simply overwhelmed most of these small business operators. Searcy Sullivan, secretary of Local 5863 in Tuscaloosa County, warned national leaders that the members of his union were "in a bad condition for something to eat as the company store closed its doors when the mines shut down and the [independent] merchants have carried them as far as they can without getting help from the international as we do not have anything in treasure in the local." James Harbin, of Brilliant in Marion County, told officials that his local's members were "up against it for support of their families. The grocery men around here have been liberal in helping the miners [and] have gone their limit. Please rush us some aid at once."[93]

The local unions became centers of relief efforts. Union officials often negotiated with area grocers and guaranteed that the merchants would be repaid. Other times, the officials bought groceries with their limited union funds, thereby amassing huge debts. Officers of a local in Birmingham, for example, found their organization six thousand dollars in debt after months of three-day workweeks and a few weeks on strike. District 20 officials pledged $852 in mid-October to help the members of the local, but more was needed. "That will amount to about one and onehalf dollars to the man. That will be for only one week. Which isnt nearly enough to begin with," they complained. "To prevent more suffering in our local we would appreciate any and all the aid that you feel that you can afford at this time."[94]

The social and economic crisis also overwhelmed District 20 officials. When the district treasury dipped to just seventeen thousand dollars, Mitch requested help from the national office. Lewis and Mitch discussed the bleak situation in

Alabama over the telephone in late October, and the national president sent the district a twenty-thousand-dollar check "for essential purposes of relief."[95]

For the first time, members of Alabama mining families wrote letters criticizing Lewis to the union's headquarters in Washington, D.C. A letter from Mrs. Louis Hill, a miner's wife from Carbon Hill in northern Walker County, reflected the frustration that many miners felt as months of the three-day weeks bled into a full-blown strike. "Mr. Lewis you don't know how the minor has to suffer or how the family suffers when they are on strike," she wrote in October. "The mines here has been slack for over a year and we could bareley get by when they were at work one or two days a week." After five weeks on strike, the members of her husband's local received only $1.50 in relief from the UMWA. The company store agreed to let the men have $10 a week worth of credit, then immediately raised prices 10–15 cents on every item. The miners were not allowed to buy clothes at the store, and the amount of credit was not enough to feed the typical miner's family, Hill wrote. "The weather is cold turning colder and our children have no shoes and coats to put on when they start to school," she informed Lewis. "We all want our family to believe in union and our minor husbands to stick to the union. But what we go through is enough to make anyone loose faith in the Union, In America, and the man who is their leader, meaning you Mr. Lewis."[96]

But this type of letter was the exception. Though the miners' letters to Lewis and other union officials described bleak scenarios, many of the writers also included professions of loyalty and statements that they believed the fight for the Welfare and Retirement Fund was just. Officials from a Birmingham local, for example, told Lewis that "every union member in this district will be pulling for you to get the best contract yet, and we are sure you will." Officers from the Sayre local told Lewis that despite their desperate situation, "We are Behind You One Hundred Percent."[97] The creation of a viable health and retirement plan controlled by the union promised these miners a future, even in an era of massive economic decline.

The small truck and push mines also contributed to the chaotic situation Alabama's union miners faced. The UMWA had trouble keeping these marginal operations, which had proliferated since the late 1930s, under contract, particularly after the creation of the royalty-based Welfare and Retirement Fund. Many of the small mines openly violated their union contracts, and in 1949 some of them operated at normal levels during the three-day week and attempted to remain open after Lewis called the national strike in September. With their backs to the wall and their families suffering, union miners took matters into their own hands. On several occasions, armed bands of UMWA miners descended on truck mines, attempting to compel them to honor their contracts with the union and adhere to the limited workweek and strike.

Such a scenario evolved into a violent confrontation at a Shelby County truck mine in June. Owner William Hinz had angered UMWA miners when he decided to operate his small pit on a nonunion basis in the spring. When the mine did not close for the memorial period in June, a biracial crowd estimated at two hundred whites and one hundred African Americans descended on the operation. Armed with guns, clubs, and blackjacks, the union crowd beat Hinz and other company officials. They forced Hinz and his miners to stop work and told the mine owner to "straighten out the welfare fund." Shortly after the strike ended in November, a blast rocked another small mine in Shelby County. Though the mine, owned by Ben Williams, was represented by the UMWA, it had continued to operate during the strike. The blast destroyed a hoist engine and damaged a structure and coal tipple. Police arrested the miner in charge of blasting powder in connection with the incident.[98]

In late September, after the walkout had begun in earnest, shooting broke out between union supporters and nonunion miners at a truck mine in Walker County. Union miner Hershell Davis of Jasper was killed, and several other UMWA members were hurt in the incident. Those injured were part of a large group of union miners who descended on the strip mine, operated by members of the Preskitt family, in an attempt to shut it down during the strike. Though the mine owners apparently did most of the shooting, they filed a five-hundred-thousand-dollar lawsuit against the UMWA in Birmingham federal court over the matter. Supporters of the Preskitts also appealed to the governor's office to intervene in the dispute. The sheriff of Walker County told members of the family to remain at home for the duration of the strike because their lives were in danger and he could not guarantee their safety, Juanita Milam, who supported the Preskitts, complained to Folsom. "Other states are giving state aid to non-union mines," she wrote, "why not Alabama?"[99]

The coalfield violence continued, though the Walker County miners appeared to change tactics. Instead of marching on mines in large numbers, union miners attempted to disable the large trucks that hauled coal from operations that continued to work during the strike. An independent truck owner who had continued to haul coal had his vehicle dynamited in Carbon Hill in late October. A few days later, miners fired on a truck hauling coal from Walker County to Cullman County. The driver and his assistant estimated that six miners were involved in the early morning attack. As the two men drove into Cullman County, a miner appeared on the side of the road and shot out the vehicle's lights with a shotgun. The driver pulled the truck over, and both men fled into nearby woods. From behind the trees, they watched as a group of union miners surrounded the vehicle and shot out its tires. The two men eventually took a bus into Cullman, where they reported the incident. Finally, in early November, UMWA members poured seventeen bullets into a truck in which a union miner was hauling coal.[100]

Lewis and the operators continued bargaining throughout much of the strike, but negotiations went nowhere. The UMWA pulled the miners off the picket lines on 9 November after federal mediators demanded that the UMWA and operators resume supervised talks. Though serious negotiating did not resume, miners in Alabama and the rest of the country began to return to work on the three-day workweek.[101]

Though the walkout had ended, negotiators made little headway, and during the early winter the Truman administration moved to seize the nation's coal mines and operate them under government control. Miners in Alabama joined sixty thousand across the country in a wildcat strike that began on 11 January 1950 after the operators attempted to obtain a National Labor Relations Board injunction against the UMWA for unfair labor practices. The strikes in Alabama involved about six thousand miners and were focused on the larger, captive mining companies. Walkouts completely idled TCI's operations, while Sloss-Sheffield Steel and Iron and Republic Steel also saw their operations partially shut down. Alabama's miners returned to work five days later. National negotiations briefly resumed in early February, and when they broke down a national strike again idled the nation's mines.[102]

Journalists who filed into the Alabama coalfields to cover the 1950 strike reported a desperate situation. After almost a year of continuous strife, most locals had emptied their treasuries and could not help their members. Credit had long since been exhausted with local grocers, whose resources were depleted. In the mining communities around Birmingham, reporters described critical food shortages. Miners and their families were ineligible for most relief from county and state agencies because they were on strike.[103]

A journalist who visited the small mining community of Porter, about twenty miles northwest of Birmingham, discovered that teachers had transformed their local grammar school into a relief agency for many of the area's white children. The largest mine near Porter closed in the fall of 1948, forcing many residents to leave. About 250 people stayed in the community, some finding work at nearby mines. After the memorial periods and three-day week over the summer and the two-month strike in the fall of 1949, however, most families in the community simply had no food. The teachers at the small school realized the dire nature of the situation in September, when small groups of children would remain at the school during their lunch recess and "watch the teachers eat their lunch." So the teachers began a community effort to get food for the children. The teachers found a source for surplus federal food—mainly powdered milk, dried eggs, and apples. The students brought in whatever food they could to supplement the commodities. The teachers cooked meals on an old hot plate and boiled water on a potbellied stove in the rear of the school. Similar programs existed at many schools in the Birmingham District.[104]

Conditions in Porter's black community were even bleaker. Most of the community's African American residents had been out of work since the mine closed in the fall of 1948 and were eking out an existence on twenty dollars a week in social security. Children were bused to a black school, where they often ate their only meal of the day. Parents complained that the driver sometimes failed to stop and pick up the children, causing them to miss their meal. Asked how they managed to survive, one resident replied, "You don't keep anything. You just get it if you can, and eat it right then. You don't know when the next time to eat will be or where you will get something to eat."[105]

Where possible, local unions continued to work with independent grocers to extend credit to UMWA members. In some cases, locals ran up tens of thousands of dollars worth of debt during the strike and worked for years to repay the money. The local at Praco, for example, found itself saddled with eighty-three hundred dollars in debt to one store. The local paid down almost half the debt after the end of the 1950 walkout, and District 20 officials contributed thirty-three hundred dollars toward the debt, leaving more than a thousand dollars outstanding in the fall of 1951. One independent grocer threatened to sue a large TCI local that he claimed still owed him twenty-five thousand dollars in the spring of 1952, two years after the 1950 strike was resolved.[106]

The walkout would end for miners in Alabama and the rest of the nation when the operators and Lewis, prodded again by the threat of federal intervention, reached a new agreement on 5 March 1950. The contract institutionalized the Welfare and Retirement Fund and enabled Lewis to bring his ally, Josephine Roche, onto the fund's three-member board of trustees as the neutral representative. Roche's presence ensured that the UMWA president had ultimate control over the fund. The new contract also increased the royalty to thirty cents a ton.[107]

Curtis Seltzer has called the 1950 national agreement "the single most important change in the coal industry since the New Deal." Indeed, the UMWA had won its long battle to formally establish and then control the Welfare and Retirement Fund. In the wake of the agreement, the major coal operators formed the Bituminous Coal Operators' Association, which brought together the major northern coal producers and the captive mining operations. Because association members produced more than half the nation's coal, the organization could bring stability to the industry in its dealings with the UMWA.

But Lewis had made important compromises that changed the face of both the industry and his union. In return for the fund concession, Lewis gave the operators a free hand to mechanize their operations. The union president had long believed that mechanization would benefit the larger, financially sound operators and tame the chaotic situation. At the time of the agreement, mechanization seemed to herald in an era of prosperity. It also would increase production, which would benefit the Welfare and Retirement Fund by bringing in more royalty money.[108] The future would prove otherwise.

Miners had weathered much in Alabama in the five years since the end of World War II. They had engaged in almost constant conflict with the operators and then realized their most important goals—the extension of health care benefits and pensions. They had participated in important political rebellions and had played a crucial role in the election of genuine progressives, including Governor James E. Folsom and Congressman Carl Elliott. But they had also seen the appearance of the Klan in their communities, and while some miners joined the organization, others found themselves the targets of its violence. The UMWA's tepid response to the growth of the Klan cast more doubt on the union's commitment to the rights of its black members. When pressed on the matter, the miners' union opted not to directly confront the racists in its ranks and took a safer route that ensured institutional preservation.

Finally, almost overnight, half of the Alabama coal industry disappeared, throwing thousands of miners out of work. While both white and black miners would suffer from the effects of this catastrophe, African Americans would bear the brunt of the job losses caused by the decline of the Alabama industry and the 1950 contract. For them and for union members, claiming the promised health benefits and pensions proved more difficult than they had imagined.

CHAPTER FIVE

Industrial Transformation and the Struggle over Health Care, 1950–1961

On a January morning in 1961, hundreds of union miners descended on a strip mine in eastern Tuscaloosa County. The miners cut down trees and blocked the main entrance to the mine. When coal trucks approached, the miners forced them to stop and broke their windows. At least one worker at the Abston Construction strip mine was injured when a union miner beat him with a wrench. Miners also blocked railroad tracks that led to the mine "with massed pickets" and threatened to blow up both coal cars and tracks. At one point, before sheriff's department officials arrived and restored some semblance of order, miners claimed that they would hang one of the owners of the mine, C. L. Abston, if he attempted to produce coal. "The whole thing is just over contracts," H. A. Swanger, a local union official, told a reporter who asked what had sparked the violence.[1]

In many ways, Swanger's statement seemed to diminish the significance of the protest at Abston Construction, but in other respects he cut right to the heart of the matter. Abston Construction's owners had for years violated contracts with the United Mine Workers of America (UMWA) by failing to make payments to the union's Welfare and Retirement Fund, which miners had fought bitterly to establish during the late 1940s. When the union went to federal court to collect the money the company owed, District 20 officials discovered that Abston's owners had played a complex corporate shell game, creating subsidiaries that were not subject to union contracts. Federal officials ruled that the Abston-related company that had signed a contract with the union was not subject to UMWA national agreements after 1955.[2]

When the company refused to grant the miners at its operation near Brookwood a contract in the wake of the revelations, twenty of them went on strike in the fall of 1960. The strike dragged on for months. Abston Construction easily recruited unemployed miners to cross union pickets. In an unusual move, the UMWA sent thousands of dollars into District 20 to help the miners on strike hold out until union officials convinced the company to recognize the union. When these efforts failed, hundreds of rank-and-file miners from across the Birmingham District attempted to force the company to recognize the union by storming the strip mine. All of these tactics failed to bring the company under contract. Abston officials retaliated against the violence of the winter of 1961 by making complaints to the National Labor Relations Board and filing a federal lawsuit against the UMWA. Though the charges were eventually dismissed, the Abston operation remained nonunion.[3]

The violence at Abston Construction grew from tensions that had simmered in the Birmingham District's coalfields since the end of World War II. Miners had become desperate after more than a decade of depression in the Alabama coal industry that saw both production and employment drop dramatically. Abston and other small strip mines ignored their union contracts or avoided paying into the UMWA's health and pension system through other means. The companies' failure to pay into the fund contributed to the financial chaos that enveloped the health and retirement system. The financial crisis, in turn, required fund administrators to cut back service and inspired them to tighten pension-eligibility requirements. By the early 1960s, the UMWA had exhausted its legal means of compelling operators such as Abston to honor their obligations, so union miners responded with violence.

Though all miners, regardless of race, felt the effects of the forces that aroused so much anger at Abston, black miners were most dramatically affected. Opposed by such industry leaders as the Tennessee Coal, Iron, and Railroad Company (TCI), the UMWA failed in negotiating a companywide seniority system in Alabama until the late 1950s. Miners laid off when their old mines declined and closed thus had no official standing when they applied for jobs at new operations opened by the same companies, enabling operators to whiten their workforces by hiring white miners for new, highly mechanized underground mines. At mines where operators introduced machinery, the UMWA deferred to custom in the industry, a practice that typically allowed the companies to hire and promote white miners into these positions. Strip mining, which grew dramatically in the decades after World War II, constituted another technological and market change that impacted black miners. The owners of these operations, which essentially had as much in common with road-building operations as with traditional underground mining, hired mainly white miners.

The cumulative effect of these changes proved staggering. Almost five thousand black miners—more than 70 percent of the total—lost their jobs in Alabama during the course of the 1950s. In 1960, African Americans represented just 25 percent of Alabama's miners, down from 34 percent a decade earlier and from more than half in 1930.[4]

This chapter examines the economic transformation that swept through the Alabama coalfields in the 1950s and the challenges it posed to miners and coal communities. The chapter chronicles the effect of these changes on black miners and describes the tactics they developed to remain employed underground. It also examines the difficulties miners experienced with the small strip mines that proliferated in the region. The problems that beset the UMWA's Welfare and Retirement Fund in the 1950s occupy a central focus in this chapter because they sprang from the economic changes that the coal industry experienced. Health care, in particular, pitted miners against the companies as well as against the administrators who ran the fund. The declining royalties paid into the system required administrators to make cutbacks, inaugurating a wave of protest and a bitter struggle for control of the fund. Miners lost that fight, and when the UMWA failed in its attempt to force small strip mining companies to honor their union contracts and pay the fund the money they owed, mobs of union miners attempted to remedy the situation on their own. In many respects, this chapter will show, the violent clashes at Abston Construction were propelled by the setbacks the miners suffered in the Birmingham District after World War II.

❰ ❰ ❰

The southern economy emerged from World War II as a "more integral part of the Union and of the world than ever before," according to historian George Tindall. More southerners worked in factories and fewer labored on farms at the end of the conflict. The number of factories in the South rose from 26,516 to 42,739 between 1939 and 1947. People moved from farms to the new shipyards, war plants, and military training camps that dotted the region to take advantage of higher wages. Atlanta, Houston, and Dallas grew to more than two million residents, while many of the region's governors traveled the country offering lucrative incentives and tax breaks in an effort to lure high-tech industry and skilled jobs.

Federal spending and highway development also played important roles in southern economic development. Commentators eventually coined the term *Sunbelt* to describe the economic phenomenon.

But the benefits of the region's economic transformation spread unevenly across the southern landscape, helping middle-class whites more than African Americans and working-class whites. Only 8 percent of the wartime spending went to older enterprises such as iron and steel plants. Less than 5 percent went to the electronics industry, machine shops, and the region's automotive plants. As a result, many of the region's traditional manufacturing industries declined after the war, much like their northern counterparts.

Historian Bruce Schulman and others have concluded that instead of producing widespread prosperity, the economic transformation manifested itself as a series of wealthy oases surrounded by a region of poverty. Racial and class inequalities were deeply embedded in the growth of the Sunbelt South. Poor whites and blacks found themselves left out of the high-paying jobs. African Americans bore the brunt of the dislocation caused by the declines in agriculture and traditional industries. In the midst of economic prosperity, many southerners found themselves stranded—"high, dry, and unemployed," in Schulman's words.[5]

Alabama's economy reflected these wider economic trends. Huntsville, for example, attracted large amounts of federal investment and emerged as one of the region's economic success stories. In 1960, the National Aeronautics and Space Administration established the $100 million Marshall Space Flight Center in the city. The center attracted additional investment from nationally known firms such as Boeing, Chrysler, and General Electric. Brown Engineering and other home-grown companies took advantage of the high-tech boom to establish a national presence. Started in the early 1950s, Brown employed three thousand people and had branches in Houston and Florida by the early 1960s. Huntsville's growth sprang from other sources as well. The Redstone Arsenal employed ten thousand workers. These industries and the high wages they paid propelled Huntsville's population from about sixteen thousand in 1950 to more than seventy-two thousand a decade later.[6]

While Huntsville and Atlanta enjoyed an unprecedented boom, Birmingham's economy remained stagnant. The city's population declined from 326,000 in 1950 to 301,000 two decades later. Birmingham added only seven thousand manufacturing jobs between 1950 and 1960.[7]

Indeed, Birmingham in many respects had more in common with a Rust Belt center such as Detroit than with its Sunbelt neighbors. A dramatic corporate restructuring was under way in the early 1950s in the Magic City. The city's largest employer, TCI, began to curtail production at its area plants. In 1964, TCI's corporate parent, U.S. Steel, relocated most of its important regional offices to Pittsburgh. Employment at the company's operations in Birmingham dropped from seventeen thousand in 1953 to ten thousand in the mid-1960s. The proportion of the region's steel produced in Birmingham reflected these declines, shrinking from about half in the 1950s to 20 percent in the next decade. Perhaps most tellingly, Birmingham ranked last among more than a dozen major urban areas in the South in the percentage and number of manufacturing jobs created between 1950 and 1960.[8]

The economic stagnation had its greatest impact on Birmingham's black workers. By the middle of the 1950s, 42 percent of Birmingham's black families earned less than $2,000, while only 8.4 percent of white families earned so little. In 1960, the median income for black workers was only $1,287, just over half of the $3,456 median for whites, and about a third of black adults earned less than $1,000 a year. Perhaps most shocking, Jefferson County officials found that nearly seventy thousand residents, most of them African American, were malnourished. At the same time, Birmingham's aggressive "slum clearance" programs eliminated entire black working-class neighborhoods, only partially replacing them with public housing. And when African Americans attempted to move into traditionally white neighborhoods, aggressive and often violent opposition from white residents and local authorities resulted. Between 1947 and 1965, white terrorists exploded some fifty bombs in an attempt both to prevent African Americans from moving into formerly all-white neighborhoods and to slow the civil rights movement.[9]

In the coalfields around the city, a coal depression enveloped the mining communities. The closing of mines and the loss of jobs took a massive toll on the Birmingham District's coal towns, and many residents had to choose between remaining and living in dire poverty or leaving the region altogether. While UMWA members who remained underground enjoyed high wages and benefits, miners who lost jobs were transformed into a coalfield underclass.[10] Living primarily in rural areas in the counties of north-central Alabama, most unemployed miners who remained had little chance of finding new jobs.

Speaking before a group of mine inspectors in 1953, Milton Fies, a mining official with Alabama Power, claimed that the coal industry was "suffering in a measure not exceeded, as far as Alabama is concerned, by even the period of 1930 to '35." The following year, Alabama Mining Institute (AMI) President I. W. Rouzer outlined the "sad picture": Only fifteen of the thirty Alabama companies that had mined coal for commercial markets in 1945 remained in operation. More than half of the sixty-three large commercial mines had closed when markets dried up. "The shut down mines now abandoned are unlikely ever to reopen as they have liquidated—sold equipment and cancelled mineral leases," Rouzer wrote.[11]

By the mid-1950s, thousands of people who were physically able simply gave up and left the region. The postwar migration had its roots in the 1930s, when African Americans from the Birmingham District's coalfields joined the masses of blacks streaming out of the region. This wave represented a response to both the decline of the coal industry during the depression and the mechanization that New Deal programs and unionization encouraged. Although Birmingham's steel and iron industry and Mobile's booming shipyards attracted thousands of migrants, most of the people who moved to Alabama from surrounding states were white. African Americans who left Alabama moved to areas both in and outside the region. The wartime centers of Charleston, South Carolina, and New Orleans attracted many new residents, according to federal researchers. Others headed north to Pennsylvania, New York, Ohio, Indiana, Nebraska, Illinois, and Michigan.[12]

After the war, African Americans continued to leave Alabama and the rest of the South in large numbers. The proportion of the nation's African American population living in the South declined from about 80 percent in 1940 to about 50 percent in 1970. While statistics on the migration patterns for coal miners are not available, many likely followed traditional paths. As in earlier years, these migrants typically headed north to the industrial centers of Ohio, Michigan, Illinois, New York, and Pennsylvania.[13]

Whites too left Alabama after the war but were more likely than African Americans to stay in the region, moving in large numbers to the Sunbelt boom areas of Florida, Georgia, and Texas. A few found their way to Louisiana, Tennessee, and Mississippi. Whites who left the region typically ended up in California, Illinois, Michigan, and Ohio.[14]

The migration from Alabama's coalfields had its strongest impact on Walker County, the former center of the commercial industry. Between 1949 and 1955, an estimated thirty-six hundred former miners moved from Walker County to other areas. Federal officials believed that significant numbers relocated to Wyoming, Colorado, Detroit, and Chicago, where numerous jobs were available. Many of these migrants remained permanently in their new locations. Others cycled back periodically between Walker County and their new homes. Some Walker County miners found work at larger mines close to Birmingham, while others found positions at manufacturing plants such as Hayes Aircraft, which federal officials reported had a significant number of employees from Walker County. Despite the Magic City's stagnant economy, the roads between Birmingham and Jasper were often crowded with commuters in the morning and evening.[15]

For the most part, coal miners had few skills attractive to the region's newer industries. With their bodies worn out from the dangerous, physical work underground, they had little chance of participating in the Sunbelt's high-tech boom. The tradition of labor activism in the Birmingham District's coalfields also worked against the former miners. Most hung on to their mining jobs as long as possible. Former miner Cecil Morgan, who helped establish the UMWA local at Sloss-Sheffield's Lewisburg mine near Birmingham, reported that "no one seems to want to hire men who have spent their best days in the Mines, employers seem to be biased against ex-miners, other industries do not want coal miners."[16]

Morgan's story would have sounded familiar to thousands of miners in the Birmingham District. He had served on the safety committee at the Lewisburg mine, a respected position among rank-and-file unionists, and lost his job when he was injured in the late summer of 1949. Sloss-Sheffield refused to rehire him, ostensibly because his injuries prevented him from passing a physical examination; however, he believed that the real reason was that his service on the mine safety committee identified him as a militant. The UMWA's efforts to appeal Sloss-Sheffield's decision not to rehire Morgan failed. "Operators seem to take pleasure at throwing Union men out of work," Morgan told UMWA President John L. Lewis. "This threat of being cut-off hanging over a man's head is weak[en]ing the Union, due to the fact that the fear of being cut-off prevents many from standing up for their contract rights." Losing his job meant that Morgan could no longer pay rent on his company-owned house. Sloss-Sheffield landlords attempted to evict the ex-miner; when that effort failed, the company "sued me in Court for possession of the house and the full amount I owed them for rent."[17]

Increasingly in the late 1940s and 1950s, the operators began to withdraw from their old coal towns. In some cases, the companies followed the pattern established by Alabama Fuel and Iron, which closed in 1950, selling the homes to developers, who then remodeled and resold the homes, typically giving resident mining families the first option to buy their houses. In some instances, the mining communities remained, but in others they vanished altogether. Many of the coal companies around Nauvoo in northwestern Walker County, for example, offered homes to residents for three hundred dollars each, but the miners had to move the homes off company property. Miner Gene McDaniel remembered that the decline of mining around Nauvoo "closed this country down. It was awful." In the early 1950s, McDaniel's father left Walker County for Tennessee, where the coal business was slightly better. After graduating from high school in 1954, McDaniel followed his father north, leaving behind a community that already "was just nothing."[18]

Though the mining industry remained more viable around Gorgas to the south, officials nevertheless dismantled the mining village of Short Creek. As in Nauvoo, the company that owned the homes sold them to miners, who then moved the structures off company property. Former resident James Custred remembered that the company "just got out all at once. It wasn't no such thing as just gradually moving out of it. They just all of the sudden said, 'We are going to quit.'"[19]

Closer to Birmingham, many of the villages remained intact. TCI, which sold its towns in the early 1950s, allowed the new homeowners to remain in their old communities. The decision to sell off the former model towns came at the end of a long process during which the company gradually shed its social programs. The company sold its commissaries to Union Supply, a private firm, in 1944. Jefferson County purchased many of TCI's company schools in 1946, and the company began to phase out its highly touted welfare capitalism. TCI began running large deficits in its housing division after the war, and by 1949 the losses approached three hundred thousand dollars per year. Four years later, Ohio developer John W. Galbreath bought TCI's eight villages for just over five million dollars.[20]

Galbreath made major improvements, repairing the aging housing stock, replacing outhouses with bathrooms, installing hot water heaters and septic tanks, and paving the streets. Decades later, residents remembered that most people in the communities had purchased their homes. Though the miners and their families undoubtedly appreciated the improvements, residents of TCI towns such as Edgewater and Docena also realized that the mines that sustained the communities were nearing the end of their productivity. Reflecting this anxiety, Docena resident Melba Wilbanks Kizzire remembered the improvements as just some of the "many, many changes [that] came to our small village" in the early 1950s.[21]

The mechanization processes that had dramatically altered the mining process since the 1930s continued. Mechanized loaders, for example, eliminated most of the remaining jobs hand loading coal at the state's larger mines, and by the late 1960s, 97.2 percent of Alabama's underground coal was mechanically loaded.[22]

The appearance of continuous miners, machines that sheared and loaded coal in a single process, thereby eliminating the need to undercut, drill, blast, and load coal, heralded even greater changes for the industry. TCI officials had unveiled their continuous miners in December 1948 in Pittsburgh and subsequently installed one of the machines at the company's Concord mine, but information about the machine's performance remained a guarded secret. Alabama Power soon purchased a machine for its Gorgas operation, and the equipment favorably impressed managers. Perhaps most importantly for managers, continuous miners increased the production level per man nearly threefold.[23]

Alabama Power's Fies boasted to national officials in 1953 that the company's Gorgas operation had purchased six continuous miners, "a greater number than employed in any other mine in the United States." The technological sophistication of the Gorgas and Concord mines was reflected in their astounding production statistics. TCI's mine routinely produced more than a million tons per year, and the Gorgas operation also surpassed that level during the mid-1950s. These mines displaced TCI's aging Edgewater and Docena operations, mines with heavily black workforces, as the state's most productive mines.[24]

Officials with Alabama By-Products and the Southern Company, the corporate parent of Alabama Power, opened another productive mine in the early 1950s. The Maxine mine, a highly mechanized operation that featured continuous miners underground, was largely Fies's creation. When managers announced the mine's opening in the summer of 1954, they conservatively estimated that it might produce six hundred thousand tons of coal a year. The miners at Maxine astounded even the most optimistic managers by producing well over a million tons of coal annually and leading the state by the end of the 1950s.[25]

The concentration of production into large mechanized mines reflected the growth of electric utilities as coal consumers. Alabama Power and other utilities began to build more coal-fired generating plants. While the Birmingham District's coal production remained steady at between twelve and thirteen million tons a year in the 1950s, large, highly mechanized mines increasingly came to dominate underground production. These mines sent more and more of their coal to electric power plants.[26]

The Southern Company, which owned utilities in Alabama, Georgia, Mississippi, and northern Florida, used coal to produce 63 percent of its electricity in the late 1950s. Company officials expected that level to grow to more than 80 percent by the mid-1970s. Alabama Power's Gorgas Steam Plant in Walker County used 1.6 million tons of coal a year. Another plant being built by the Southern Company on the Coosa River was expected to consume 3 million tons annually.[27]

The 1950s also saw strip mining, another highly mechanized form of coal production, take hold across the Birmingham District. In the summer of 1944, these operations produced hundreds of thousands of tons of coal, and officials expected that level soon to surpass a million tons. The proportion of coal produced by Alabama's surface mines increased to 13 percent in 1950 and to nearly 25 percent by the end of the decade. Strip pits accounted for 2.6 million tons of coal mined in Alabama by 1960.[28]

Strip mining represented a dramatic change in the method of producing coal. Coal seams in these operations were typically located closer to the surface than those found in large underground mines. Miners on the surface cleared the land and then drilled deep holes and used explosives to fracture the ground above the coal seam. Huge cranes with shovels, known as drag lines, scooped away the "overburden," as the dirt, rock, and other material above the coal was known. Miners then used more explosives to fracture the coal, which was taken to preparation plants for washing.[29] Instead of working underground, miners at strip operations worked outside.

If Alabama Power, Alabama By-Products, and TCI saw their future in mechanization of underground mines, what remained of the old DeBardeleben Coal concern found brief salvation in huge strip operations. The company unveiled the largest strip-mining machine in Alabama—156 feet across and 90 feet high—at its Empire mine in 1953. The huge "walking drag line" used its enormous shovel to scoop up six hundred cubic yards of overburden every hour. Three years later, DeBardeleben officials opened a large strip operation a few hundred yards from the Black Warrior River in southeastern Walker County. Company officials used barges to float the coal produced there to Mobile, where it was used to power an International Paper plant. By 1958, the Waterside operation produced 150,000 tons a year.[30]

The increase in strip mining and the mechanization of underground mines had profound consequences for the Birmingham District's African American miners. The miners' union left hiring decisions up to the coal operators, confining its activities to relations in the workplace. Testifying during the summer of 1942 before the President's Commission on Fair Employment Practice, District 20 President William Mitch had emphatically stated that the UMWA "has nothing to do with the employment." Contracts during the war years typically made no reference to companywide seniority. "The management of the mine, the direction of the working force, and the right to hire and discharge are vested exclusively in the Company, and this right shall not be abridged," a 1942 contract between TCI and District 20 read. The agreement did not alter seniority "in principle and practice" as it was "recognized by the Company." Miners who lost jobs because of mechanization or cutbacks in employment levels would constitute a panel from which managers at the mine would hire new workers. The contract clearly implied that laid-off miners were eligible for jobs only at the mine where they had formerly been employed.[31]

Throughout most of the 1940s, the contracts the UMWA and the Alabama operators reached endorsed a practice known as "classification" seniority. Under this custom, length of time on a particular job was more important than overall time at the mine. As a result, miners who lost jobs to mechanization often had difficulty moving into different positions in the mines. Though the UMWA pushed during the 1950s to change this practice, the union did not formally negotiate a system of companywide seniority in Alabama until the end of the decade. Miners who lost jobs at one mine, therefore, had no seniority rights at other mines owned by the same company or even at newly opened mines.[32] This situation caused massive problems for black miners in particular.

African American Archie Young remembered that as a result of classification seniority, the Mulga mine where he worked became increasingly white. "The company was . . . smart enough, that they would go and hire a young white fellow and bring him in the mine," Young remembered. "But they would put him on a classified job like mechanic unit man, and if he stayed on that job two days, and some man been in the mine twenty years, well, he had what they called job classification." The system at Mulga protected white miners in skilled, secure lines at the expense of black miners, whose jobs were more likely to be mechanized. "That's the system [the company] had to keep men that they wanted in the mines," Young remembered.[33]

The failure to include companywide seniority "made it possible for a company to hire whites from outside in preference to Negroes who had worked at another of the company's mines," economist Darold Barnum concluded. District 20 officials negotiated companywide seniority provisions into their contracts by the end of the 1950s, but by then the racist hiring practices of the coal operators had taken a terrible toll on African American miners.

African Americans found few employment opportunities at the region's strip mines, particularly the larger, more productive operations. The companies often hired construction workers to operate drag lines, bulldozers, and dump trucks. Experienced workers stood first in line for jobs, and since many construction companies and craft unions restricted African American opportunities or refused to hire blacks, they found themselves at a distinct disadvantage. Moreover, during the mining depression of the 1950s, managers found plenty of white applicants for these jobs and had little incentive to hire African Americans.[34]

William Young was among the first black miners to experience post–World War II seniority problems when he was laid off from his job at TCI's Edgewater mine in 1946. When he tried to get a job at one of the company's other mines, managers informed Young that they did not have to hire him. Young suggested that laid-off miners should have preference for jobs at the company's other operations and complained that the current system gave all of the power to TCI officials and consequently resulted in the weeding out of militant unionists. But District 20 officials gave Young's idea no support. Mitch initially failed to recognize the difficulties that these policies posed for miners who lost jobs at older mines. "I do not see how men, when they are laid off at one mine, can force employment at another," he wrote to Young.[35]

The views of the District 20 president and the union changed after the onset of the coalfield depression of the 1950s. The miners' union had come to recognize the advantages of companywide seniority but ran into strong opposition from industry leader TCI, which refused to discuss the measure. Furthermore, the state's most important coal producer sought to roll back or limit the effectiveness of existing seniority provisions. TCI negotiators refused to acknowledge "bumping rights," which allowed miners with enough seniority to move down to positions occupied by miners with less seniority, and pushed to eliminate panel rights for miners who had been laid off for two years. The problems at TCI were especially significant, union negotiator Thomas Crawford wrote, because the company held "the whiphand over the other operators, making them reluctant to write out interpretations of the seniority provisions until we can reach a decision with this company." [36] By the early 1950s, then, when the UMWA began to push to protect the jobs of its African American members, it met with opposition from TCI and other operators, which delayed these efforts and resulted in large numbers of black miners losing their jobs.

The UMWA also encountered opposition from white miners when it attempted to break down the traditional barriers to black employment in skilled jobs. At mines where African Americans held a large proportion of the jobs, racial friction occurred less frequently. But the opposition of whites at mines with only a small number of black employees often created problems when African American miners and UMWA officials attempted to break down the color line underground. At one Jefferson County mining concern, white miners announced that they "would no longer work with Negroes." The white miners persuaded the company to stop hiring African Americans at one of its mines and to limit employment of blacks at its other operation. "At present, the company's policy is not to hire Negroes in any circumstance which might lead to friction," a researcher concluded. The UMWA's failure to confront this issue earlier, white miners' determination to oppose the promotion of African Americans, and most of all the company's racist hiring policies resulted in a dramatic decline in the number of black employees from about 22 percent of the workforce in 1939 to 4 percent in 1951. [37]

Mechanization of underground mines also restricted the options for black miners at captive companies. Since many of the mines that remained open were captive operations and did not produce coal for commercial markets, efficiency was slightly less important. Captive operators, therefore, tended not to upgrade their older mines. African Americans, who were concentrated at these older operations, had few opportunities to gain experience on modern mining equipment. When old captive mines closed and the companies opened new mines, whites thus typically had an advantage in getting jobs at the mechanized mines, an advantage further strengthened by the companies' racial hiring practices. By the

1950s, moreover, mine jobs paid an average of $14.25 a day, and the better wages attracted more whites.[38]

Attempting to break into the most skilled, most stable jobs underground, African American miners appealed to the UMWA's egalitarian rhetoric from its early days in Alabama, and the union frequently stuck up for the rights of its black members. Sympathetic white miners also at times helped out longtime African American coworkers. Mostly, however, black miners were left on their own, and they developed a multitude of strategies for preserving their jobs.

Ernest Walker, a black veteran miner at Alabama Power's Gorgas mine, attempted to break into segregated production lines underground in the 1950s when he bid on a job as a continuous miner operator. Walker had enough seniority for the job, but white miners had monopolized such positions at Gorgas. Adding to Walker's difficulties was the fact that at least one white miner also wanted the job, so going after the job opened Walker up to reprisals from white miners and the company. "The white man didn't want me to operate the machine," Walker remembered decades later. "Because I was black, I wasn't supposed to have that good-paying job. [Continuous mining machine operator] was the highest-paying job they had. They didn't want the black man to have that. The white man was supposed to have the highest-paying job." Most of the miners he knew, even his fellow African Americans, warned Walker about the potential risks. "The black men said, 'You're black, you don't go down there,'" Walker remembered. "Some of my own black people told me this, not only the white men, some of the blacks."[39]

But Walker knew his rights. His many years as a union member had instilled in him a sense of entitlement, and he knew that despite the union's cautious approach, its constitution forbade racial discrimination. The UMWA ultimately backed up its racial rhetoric and stood behind Walker, and, though some white miners grumbled, he got the job, becoming the first black man to operate a continuous miner at the Gorgas mine.[40]

Other black miners often proved themselves crucial allies. At Woodward Iron's Mulga mine in Jefferson County, for example, when an African American miner attempted to bid on a job as an electrician's helper, a skilled occupation previously reserved for whites, the company quickly announced that it had cut out all of the helper positions. Earl Brown, a black union activist, believed that the company had eliminated the helper job "to keep the blacks from it" and found a sympathetic white miner willing to testify against the company. Brown then confronted a foreman about the issue. "I'm bringing it to you to keep it in the family," Brown told the supervisor. "If you don't do anything about it, I'm going to the big office. If the big office don't do anything about it, then I'll have to do what I have to do." Woodward management backed down, kept the helper positions in place, and gave the black miner one of them.[41]

Brown later challenged the color line himself and "saw one of the hardest times that you've ever seen." After more than two decades underground, Brown put in a bid for a job in the Mulga mine's lamp house, another position that had previously been closed to African Americans. The job, which required keeping the equipment in working order, was racially sensitive because the lamp house man also kept the segregated bathhouses clean. The white incumbent in the position encouraged Brown to apply. "I know you've been talking about these jobs being integrated, how the company's been keeping you off because you had to come up through the ranks," the white miner said. "So why don't you break the line? You're about the only one can do it." The lamp house job paid less than Brown's current position as a motorman, operating the vehicles that pulled coal cars to and from the surface, but Brown remembered that he wanted "to get out in the air."[42]

When Brown inquired about the lamp house job, the mine manager "about jumped out of his skin" and refused to discuss the position. Brown later learned that Woodward officials had panicked over the request. A team of company lawyers and other officials reviewed his career in the mines and checked to see if he was a member of the National Association for the Advancement of Colored People or "any kind of insurrectionists or whatnot." The president of the UMWA local at Mulga pulled Brown aside after he applied for the job and asked point-blank, "You aren't going to go down there and integrate the bathhouse or anything?" When Brown replied that he was not, he was put on the "owl shift," working in the early morning hours in the lamp house.[43]

A combination of factors began to break down the rigid segregation in the Mulga mine. Woodward officials transferred the manager of the company's Dolomite mine, which had more black miners and less rigid segregation, to the Mulga facility with the express purpose of integrating the mine, Young remembered. The new manager began to allow African Americans into traditionally white occupations such as operating coal-cutting machines and promoted blacks to jobs as helpers in lines of production traditionally dominated by whites. White miners occasionally refused to work and sometimes struck to protest the changes. "It happened several times," Young recalled. "The only thing [black miners] could do was go down there and shovel coal in the shuttle cars or something like that."[44]

The UMWA local at Mulga intervened in the chaotic situation. The older Dolomite mine began to lay off miners, many of them African Americans, creating a large pool of people with the experience needed to operate skilled equipment at Mulga. The local president, Young remembered, warned the angry whites, "This mine's not going to shut down if the company's got men to do the work." The hate strikes happened less frequently, and blacks began to move into skilled jobs. Brown remembered that when whites stopped striking, it "began integration in that whole mine."[45]

But not all African American miners were bold enough to challenge segregation. Retaliation by companies and white miners intimidated many blacks from even considering such actions. Fred Bass Sr., an African American who worked at Sloss-Sheffield's Flat Top mine near Brookside, remembered the harassment that white miners and managers meted out to a black miner who claimed a position on a cutting machine: "I don't know how he stood up to it." But UMWA officials backed up the African American miner "100 percent," Bass recalled, so "he won out" and kept the job. But Bass declined to take similar risks. He retired from the Flat Top mine in the early 1970s as a motorman, a traditionally African American job at that operation. "I just tried to live with what I had, to any little advance or whatnot," Bass recalled. "I never had no problem with that. But I know guys that did have problems with that."[46]

Indeed, Bass and other black miners faced formidable odds in maintaining jobs underground. Their union was generally slow to respond to the problems caused by mechanization and seniority issues. By the 1950s, when the UMWA in Alabama began to address these concerns, most African American miners in the Birmingham District had already lost their jobs. "If present trends continue," warned Barnum in 1970, after two decades of economic decline in the nation's coalfields, "the black man will vanish from the coal mines during the next three decades." Barnum's predictions proved prophetic, though the union's commitment to companywide seniority slowed the slide. By 1970, the number of black miners had shrunk to fewer than two thousand, less than 20 percent of the total.[47]

The desperate situation in the mines made the problems confronting the Welfare and Retirement Fund even more urgent for the Birmingham District's coal miners. At the end of 1948, the fund made Birmingham one of its regional centers. Officials named Allen F. Koplin, a former administrative officer for the U.S. Public Health Service, to head the office.[48]

The fund confronted deep racial disparities in health care when it attempted to establish a presence in the Birmingham District. In a study of the situation in the Birmingham area in the early 1950s, the Jefferson County Coordinating Council of Social Forces, a progressive biracial group, noted that segregation was a central feature of the region's health care system. Hospitals, for example, reserved 72 percent of their beds for whites although they comprised only 63 percent of the area's population. The group also noted a dramatic shortage of qualified black doctors and nurses. Activists had formed the Negro Hospital Association in 1943 in an effort to alleviate the strain. Though the efforts bore some fruit a decade later, when the 162-bed Holy Family Hospital opened for African Americans, racial inequalities remained a problem.[49]

UMWA's Welfare and Retirement Fund investigators who came to Birmingham in 1956 concluded that health care for area miners was "unsatisfactory," mainly because of the system's racial disparities. About 45 percent of those receiving help from the union's system were African Americans, and the officials estimated that the number of beds for African Americans would have to nearly double—from 703 to 1,303—to satisfy the ratio of beds to people recommended by the U.S. Public Health Service.[50]

Among the researchers' more shocking revelations was the fact that racialized health care disparities were even greater at UMWA-affiliated hospitals than in the Birmingham area as a whole. Black miners and their families had access to only about 20 percent of the beds in hospitals that participated in the UMWA's system. Many district hospitals used by the fund had no beds at all for African American patients, while others placed blacks in crowded and substandard wards. The administrators concluded that "little progress has been recorded in Birmingham" since the fund began its operations.[51]

The UMWA system's decision not to use a pair of hospitals that had large numbers of beds for African Americans and high-quality care contributed to the problems faced by black miners. Lloyd Noland Hospital in Fairfield ranked among the region's best, but a dispute with TCI, which ran the hospital through 1951, kept it off the fund's list of acceptable facilities. The hospital had 273 beds, half of them reserved for African Americans. TCI's parent, U.S. Steel, initially refused to bill or accept payments from the UMWA's Welfare and Retirement Fund. Patients had to pay up front and be reimbursed by the fund. The payment arrangements proved unpopular with district officials and miners. The facility also had an association as a company-run hospital "in which the diagnosis and treatment of occupational illnesses and injuries has always been suspect." For all of these reasons, miners and their leaders elected to use other hospitals.[52]

The fund also had no arrangement with Jefferson-Hillman Hospital, a facility with 660 beds, more than 40 percent of which were reserved for African Americans. The hospital had suffered from poor administration, overcrowding, and substandard service, particularly for African Americans, and the fund consequently severed its relationship with the facility in 1953.[53] While that decision was understandable in light of the facility's problems, declining to use the hospital also deprived African American miners of much-needed options.

The fund also proved problematic for white miners. Proving eligibility for pensions was among the more difficult prospects for all miners, regardless of race. The union initially granted retirement benefits of one hundred dollars per month to members who had twenty years in the industry and who retired at age sixty-two or older. Eligibility was limited to those miners who were working in 1946, when the UMWA and the federal government signed the agreement setting up the fund. Miners' work records often were difficult to find, as was evidence that they had kept up with their union dues. Many Alabama miners migrated among coalfields. A. L. Pickens, for example, worked in Illinois for seven years, labored for a short time in Kentucky, and then spent twenty-seven years in West Virginia's mines. Near the end of his career, he found a job at a small operation in Alabama. Pickens claimed that he led the tiny operation's eight men into the UMWA. "I feel that I done some good," he wrote to Lewis, "so I am sending all of the papers to you and asking you to send them to the proper places for me."[54] Similar letters flooded the District 20 offices and national headquarters in the late 1940s and early 1950s.

Women were another group who experienced ambiguity under the terms of the Welfare and Retirement Fund. Fund administrators viewed coalfield women solely through the status of their husbands. Married women initially were eligible for part of their husband's pension. Loss of husbands or fathers in the mines left coalfield women in desperate circumstances, and the fund offices, the UMWA's national headquarters, and the Birmingham District office received scores of letters describing such women's plight in the late 1940s and early 1950s. For example, Lucy Brasfield, a sixty-eight-year-old widow, had lost all of her husband's work records. The advocate who drafted a letter on her behalf to union officials warned that she was in dire need of a widow's pension: "She has an income of only $20 a month (this is a relief check), and out of this small amount she must not only feed and clothe herself but also pay house rent and a medical bill. At the moment, she is in very poor health and is under a doctor's care. She needs immediate help."[55]

Almost from the start, financial problems beset the Welfare and Retirement Fund, a result of declining production and employment. By the mid-1950s, District 20 had lost thirteen thousand dues-paying members, and officials could foresee no change "in the near future." The Alabama union began to lose money, and by the middle of the decade the District 20 office ran a deficit of twelve hundred dollars a month.[56]

The poor economic conditions were not limited to Alabama, and declining royalties forced fund officials to begin tightening eligibility requirements. In 1953, the health and retirement system required miners and dependents to prove that the twenty years of union membership and work in the mines had occurred within thirty years of the application for benefits. The following year, the fund's trustees cut partial pensions paid to widows and disabled miners who were too young to qualify for full benefits, casting at least thirty thousand disabled miners and twenty-four thousand widows and children—the most vulnerable people in the coalfields—out of the fund's social safety net. Like many others, Viola Hill of Cottondale found herself with "no income at all" after she lost her widow's benefits. She angrily told fund officials that she believed that the fund had been established "to help widows as well as miners."[57]

Koplin, the fund's regional administrator, began to eliminate local services. Officials required miners to obtain referrals from general practitioners before they could visit medical specialists. Many of the general physicians lived in or near coal communities and had current or past affiliations with the companies, and the miners suspected that the operators controlled the doctors. Koplin's decision thus "made miners more dependent on camp physicians or company physicians for referral slips."[58]

Though Koplin's efforts to cut costs in many ways reflected nationwide problems with the fund's operations, Alabama miners blamed him for many of their difficulties. The large TCI locals, which had previously enjoyed the most advanced health care programs under the old company-run systems, became the center of dissent. The TCI locals, for example, showed their independence early on by requesting permission to charge their members an additional $2.50 so that they could choose their own doctors rather than select from the limited field offered by fund administrators.[59] TCI unionists formed the core of a widespread movement across the Birmingham District that rose in opposition to Koplin's efforts to centralize control over fund operations.

In the early 1950s, many TCI locals began to protest the quality of the health care provided by the UMWA system. In 1952, at least three TCI locals pushed for the fund to enlist more centrally located hospitals that provided better service. A common complaint, in addition to the time it took to travel to fund-approved hospitals, was that miners and their family members often had to wait several days before they were allowed to enter these facilities. In addition, many miners, H. B. Odom wrote, believed that participating doctors failed to provide fair diagnoses. J. B. Benson of the Edgewater local complained that the hospitals treated miners poorly, placing fund recipients "in the charity section" and treating them like "charity patients."[60]

Many TCI locals still had large numbers of black members, and their poor treatment at fund hospitals emerged as a prominent complaint. Black miners, wrote Glenn Terry and Lou Mutry, "get a bad deal because they [*sic*] rooms are a limited number for them and their dependents and they sometimes have to wait a long time to get a bed, and then it is in the basement." Black members of the large Edgewater local at TCI were "treated worse than the white members because there are a very limited number of available rooms for them and their dependents," complained Benson. Even unionists at TCI's newer, highly mechanized Concord mine complained that African American unionists "get worse treatment than the white."[61]

Miners increasingly singled out Koplin for criticism. Officials with the Edgewater local, for example, complained in the spring and summer of 1954 that the shrinking number of fund-approved hospitals treated the miners "like dogs or charity patients." While the local's officers realized that the fund was experiencing financial difficulty and that some cutbacks were unavoidable, they also believed that the regional medical officer was "not doing everything for the coal miners interest." Koplin either ignored or admonished miners who complained. George Glover of the TCI local at Short Creek reported that union officers found themselves deluged by protests about Koplin's "seemingly uncooperative attitude toward just complaints."[62]

Furthermore, Koplin's changes had not remedied the problems with poor care and in some cases had led to even greater difficulties. Miners complained that when they obtained referrals to see specialists, they shared diagnoses and treatment recommendations with the referring physicians. Many miners suspected that the local doctors passed this information along to the coal companies, which then fired miners with occupational ailments in an attempt to avoid responsibility for the conditions. "The company requires the doctor to report patients with chest conditions that might be associated with work in the mines," the miners complained. "Men thus reported are discharged at the earliest opportunity for any reason that can be devised. Men showing no disability have been discharged because the specialist told the Company doctor what the nature of the illness was." As a result, miners complained, the Welfare and Retirement Fund "which was designed to benefit the miners is really causing them to lose their jobs."[63]

The miners believed that Koplin's changes in part represented an effort to wrest control of the system from the workers. And the administrator's decision to remove the Friedman Clinic, an operation run by a crusading doctor perceived as an ally of miners, from the list of approved institutions seemed to confirm the worst suspicions. The miners' loyalty to Louis Friedman had grown from his efforts to help them win benefits for coal workers' pneumoconiosis, or black lung disease.

Observers, including Mitch, the union's District 20 president, had long noted that many miners suffered from a debilitating condition related to their work underground.[64] The symptoms included difficulty breathing and chest pains, which slowly worsened. Miners often developed a violent cough, and the coal dust in their lungs turned their saliva black. Over time, the condition caused severe respiratory and cardiac problems, eventually depriving miners of their lives in what one authoritative source called a "slow, strangling torture." "At work you are covered with dust," physician Lorin Kerr explained to miners in terms they recognized at a national convention in the late 1960s. "You suck so much of it into your lungs that until you die you never stop spitting up coal dust. Some of you cough so hard that you wonder if you have a lung left. Slowly you notice you are getting short of breath when you walk up a hill. On the job you stop more often to catch your breath. Finally, just walking across the room at home is an effort." One Alabama miner's wife whose husband suffered from the condition reported that he could "walk but just a few steps now without using the spray he can't breathe and has coughing and choking spells."[65]

In Alabama, company doctors diagnosed the condition as tuberculosis or bronchitis, effectively denying that black lung even existed. In the mid-1940s, Friedman, a professor at the University of Alabama Medical College in Birmingham and a pulmonary specialist, began to raise the issue with state UMWA leaders. By 1946, Friedman was an internationally recognized authority on work-related lung ailments. The young doctor called the condition he observed in the miners of the Birmingham District "pneumoconiosis in soft coal workers" and developed a method for detecting the ailment with X-rays. The process proved expensive, and the UMWA Welfare and Retirement Fund helped to pay for Friedman's tests.[66]

Because the condition was not included under the state worker's compensation provisions, miners and the union sued the coal companies in court. The legal department of District 20 filed the damage suits, and Friedman served as an expert witness in the trials. The plight of the miners generated sympathy from the local judges and juries.[67]

Though state laws made such legal actions difficult, the miners and the UMWA won many of the lawsuits, and the courts required the companies to pay damages. The strategy forced the operators to act, and they agreed to work with union lawyers William Mitch Jr., the District 20 president's son, and Jerome "Buddy" Cooper on an amendment to the state compensation program. The state legislature enacted the reforms in 1951.[68]

Friedman's efforts endeared the physician to both rank-and-file miners and union officers. Friedman also represented a potent challenge to the prestige and power of the medical establishment in the Birmingham District. In the mid-1940s, about the time he began his black lung crusade, Friedman drew the attention of the Jefferson County chapter of the American Medical Association for his involvement with a Birmingham clinic that catered to poor patients. The facility, partially state funded, was managed by Dr. Thomas Spies and stressed the importance of nutrition and preventative medicine. The local medical association chapter lobbied the legislature not to provide state funding for the clinic but made the mistake of doing so during Governor James E. "Big Jim" Folsom's first term. Friedman and Spies had little trouble convincing Folsom, a strong advocate for Alabama's poor and downtrodden, to support the clinic. After a visit to the Birmingham facility, the governor used his connections to convince Alabama Power and local banks to back the clinic, scuttling the local American Medical Association's plans.[69]

The association between Friedman and Folsom grew after the governor was elected to a second term in 1954. Folsom's opponents in the press often referred to Friedman as the "court physician" and the governor's "constant fishing companion." Friedman briefly and controversially coordinated the distribution of the Salk polio vaccine in Alabama. He also served short stints on the state Alcohol Beverage Control Board and as director of the state docks, blatantly political appointments by Folsom that did little to improve the doctor's standing in the eyes of the medical establishment and of professionals such as Koplin.[70]

Miners, however, held a different view. They saw Friedman as a crusader who had fought with them in the struggle for black lung benefits when the medical establishment had turned a blind eye to the condition or had argued against its existence. Fiercely loyal to the doctor, miners and union leaders were shocked when Koplin removed the Friedman Clinic from the union's medical system in Alabama in early 1956. Officers at TCI's Docena local, for example, complained that the "clinic gave the best service to miners in Alabama." The members of the local asked national fund officials to provide "a fair and impartial investigation" of the decision to remove Friedman from the system. The Edgewater local's Benson wrote to officials that Koplin "cut one of the best doctors off the list last month (Feb. 1), the only doctor who stood by the miners in court and in other ways."[71]

When complaints reached fund officials in Washington, D.C.—miners usually sent their letters to Lewis, who forwarded them to medical officials—the miners received little sympathy. Fund officials remained loyal to Koplin and tended to dismiss the complaints arriving from the Birmingham District as frivolous. Warren Draper, the system's executive medical officer, believed that the "matter is solely one of medical practices and medical costs" and that the regional officer was "doing everything possible to work it out satisfactorily."[72]

In the fall of 1955, prior to the removal of the Friedman Clinic, many of the state's largest locals demanded a meeting with Welfare and Retirement Fund leaders in Washington, D.C. When the national officials agreed to the request, ten men representing locals that controlled a "large portion of the coal producing area in Alabama" traveled to the organization's headquarters and met with Draper, fund trustee and director Josephine Roche, and other leading staff. The session did little to satisfy the miners or to remedy the problems they experienced with health care in the Birmingham District, however. Fund officials promised to investigate the complaints, but months after the meeting, many union leaders complained that nothing had been done. Roche, an Edgewater unionist said, merely sent a letter to the local "informing [union leaders] that Dr. Koplin is in complete charge and he is the boss."[73]

Roche and other fund officials in Washington believed that the problems in the Birmingham District resulted purely from Koplin's cost-cutting measures, not from his management style. Rather than taking the concerns of the miners at face value or giving them serious consideration, Draper dismissed them as "either not substantiated or due to lack of understanding."[74]

Koplin, for his part, responded to the meeting by undertaking a series of moves designed to shore up his position with national officials. He informed Draper that a dozen hospitals—more than double the number that miners believed they could use—remained affiliated with the fund. Koplin also claimed that only eighteen of the ninety-six doctors who referred fund cases to specialists had been affiliated with coal companies and assured Draper that he would prevent doctors from misusing professional information and turning diagnoses and treatment recommendations over to the companies.[75]

Koplin dismissed outright African American miners' complaints. Basements were used in some hospitals because "they are the only places . . . where wards and semi-private rooms exist. Fund beneficiaries and others alike must use these accommodations." Although he noted that the accommodations "for colored people are admittedly inferior" to those for whites, he told Draper that the situation was "characteristic of the area and beyond the ability of the Fund to remedy all at once."[76]

District 20 officials, with a few exceptions, generally attempted to remain outside the fray. Mitch was an old hand at the rough-and-tumble world of the UMWA's internal politics, and he knew that to cross Lewis meant ruin. By intervening in the dispute between rank-and-file miners and Koplin, he risked angering Roche, one of Lewis's closest allies. The District 20 president consequently avoided direct involvement in the dispute.

Despite Mitch's efforts, however, some fund officials suspected that he silently supported the dissident miners. Instead of urging Koplin to better communicate with miners about his decisions, for example, Draper recommended that Roche pressure Mitch to rein in the miners.[77] She issued a backhanded rebuke to Mitch in December 1955, claiming that the miners' complaints "were either entirely unsubstantiated, or were misunderstandings" and should have been handled in Birmingham by UMWA and fund officials. Roche reminded Mitch that final authority for all fund operations rested with the medical staff in "every professional matter" and that Koplin had "full jurisdiction" in Birmingham. "Both Mr. Lewis and the Undersigned are fully aware of all Doctor Koplin has achieved, and of all the obstacles which he has had to meet and overcome in developing the Hospital and Medical Care Program for beneficiaries in his area," she told Mitch. "Doctor Koplin has the complete confidence and backing of the Trustees of the Fund." Realizing the implications of Lewis's support for Koplin and the local fund staff, Mitch quickly informed Roche that the complaints about the administrator were not "general in the District." He also told Roche that he doubted that the dispute would escalate into a wildcat strike.[78]

Aware that the national officers stood behind him, Koplin consolidated his control over the Welfare and Retirement Fund's operations in Birmingham and pushed for a confrontation with dissident miners. At a February 1956 meeting called to discuss problems with the changes in the fund, Koplin dismissed the miners' concerns. When the angry miners asked if Mitch had approved of the changes, Koplin replied that the District 20 president "neither approved nor disapproved." One of the miners shot back, "Well, is he boss of this district or are you? I'm beginning to think you are boss." Koplin's answer revealed that power over the fund indeed rested firmly in his hands: "He's boss of the miners in this district," the administrator said. "I'm boss of the medical program."[79]

Complaints about Koplin's management continued to flow into the fund's offices, but the fight was over. In the spring of 1956, fund officials sent two staff members, Lorin Kerr and Paul Streit, to the Birmingham District to investigate the complaints about the health and retirement system. Their interviews with District 20 officials revealed much about the evolution of the dispute between Koplin and the locals. The investigators found Mitch "dispassionate and objective" about the administrator's changes. In an effort to distance himself from both the concerns of rank-and-file miners and his failure to rein in Birmingham District militants, Mitch downplayed black miners' problems with the region's health care, implying "that some locals have made an issue of the pattern of segregation observed in all hospitals in an effort to discredit the Area Medical Office. There have been no complaints made by Negro beneficiaries about this matter to either the District or Area Office," the investigators concluded.[80]

Kerr and Streit found that the quality of health care for miners in the Birmingham District needed improvement and suggested adding several of the region's better hospitals to the list of acceptable institutions.[81] Yet they included no recommendations for improving Koplin's management, effectively sanctioning the shift of power from miners and their supporters to medical professionals and administrators. By the end of the decade, Koplin had won.

By then, however, miners and the union faced even more critical problems in the Birmingham District. The union had difficulty keeping the small truck and wagon mines under contract and making sure that they paid royalties to the fund. Small strip operators proliferated in Alabama, Tennessee, and Kentucky during the 1950s, selling coal on the spot market to satisfy sudden demands from electric utilities and relying on low wages to remain competitive. The Tennessee Valley Authority, the nation's largest consumer of coal by the middle of the decade, purchased much of the low-priced coal for its electric plants. By the end of the 1950s, small, nonunion operations produced almost one-fifth of the coal in the United States. Many of these companies violated their UMWA contracts or resisted organizing efforts.[82]

In Alabama, small mines had long been a problem for the UMWA. As early as 1935, union officials estimated that the state had hundreds of such operations, whose owners often resisted paying union wages and adhering to union-approved working conditions. After World War II, however, the problems became acute. In the fall of 1946, just months after Lewis and U.S. Secretary of the Interior Julius Krug had negotiated the first agreement that established the fund, Mitch described a chaotic situation. Many of the small coal companies sent their royalties to the Welfare and Retirement Fund directly to the District 20 office in the form of money orders, checks, or even cash. In other instances, the larger companies, which often processed coal from small mines, collected the royalties for the union. District 20 officials found it almost impossible to establish any uniform practice for collecting such royalties because the small mines seemed to open and close overnight. Many signed contracts with the union but then failed to collect union dues from miners or pay royalties to the fund.[83]

UMWA officials put the onus on local unions to police the agreements between the union and the companies. If locals failed in this effort, Mitch warned, members might lose their pension and health care benefits. "We have entirely too much hedging on the part of irresponsible individuals attempting to operate truck mines by subterfuge," the state leader told union miners at a statewide convention. "Some truck mine operators sign a contract, then lease or sublease to an irresponsible individual who takes advantage of state laws protecting their irresponsibility. They fail to make payments due under contract; they often cease operating and default pay due for wages and vacation claims. Workers assume a risk of loss when they work for such operators."[84]

Local miners tried to enforce such agreements, often resorting to the wildcat strike, the old tactic that had served them so well during World War II. In early

1953, for example, miners at a Republic Steel strip pit went on strike to protest the company's refusal to grant union recognition to between fifteen and seventeen truck drivers who worked at the operation. Republic Steel operated the mine but claimed that the truckers were employees of another company, known simply as Blackwell. The union miners, supported by Mitch, believed that Republic merely leased the trucks to the other company and that the drivers should be covered by the UMWA's agreement with Republic.[85]

A year later, another problem emerged involving Republic Steel's complicated arrangement with a small truck mine. The W. M. Franklin mine operated on land leased from Republic near Adamsville and sold its coal to the steel producer. Operating on a shoestring, Franklin soon fell behind in its payments to the Welfare and Retirement Fund and failed to forward miners' dues to the District 20 office. The company also refused to adhere to the union's seniority provisions. When the mine closed in January 1954, the company refused to pay its miners for their final two weeks of work. Thomas Crawford, Mitch's assistant, reported that the mine owner "told his foremen employees that when and if [the union] decided to let him hire the men that he wanted to at that mine, he would again resume operation."[86]

Republic Steel apparently provided the operator with the opportunity to do so a short while later. The steel producer closed one of its mines near Sayreton, then leased land adjacent to the old mine to Franklin so that it could avoid rehiring its old miners. The new Franklin mine operated in much the same fashion as the old—the coal was sent to Republic, which washed it. The UMWA believed that the relationship to Republic obligated Franklin to sign a contract with the union, but Franklin managers refused. Mitch believed that the situation allowed Republic managers to avoid "their moral obligation to their employees who are now on the waiting list from the Sayreton No. 2 mine."[87]

To counter the growth of such practices, the Bituminous Coal Operators' Association, an industry group, and the UMWA had included "protection" clauses in their national agreement that forbade the companies that signed from processing coal mined from nonunion operations. Small operators across the country began to challenge these agreements in court, arguing that they violated antitrust statutes. By the end of the decade, District 20 had become a target for such lawsuits. In January 1959, small operator Claude Kelley filed a class-action lawsuit in Birmingham federal court charging that the operators' association contract represented an agreement to restrain trade. Kelley, who had previously recognized the union at his operation in Walker County, demanded one hundred thousand dollars in damages for his company and "triple damages for him and all other coal operators in the same 'class.' "[88]

The Alabama UMWA countered with legalistic methods of its own against the small operators. The mixed results illustrated the difficulties that the strip pits posed for the union. The Welfare and Retirement Fund filed suits against small operators beginning in the late 1950s in a desperate attempt to recover money owed. By the early 1960s, the organization had sued for more than $544,000 from nineteen small mines in the state. When District 20 took these actions, however, some of the operators simply closed down their mines, subsequently reopening with new names in other parts of the Birmingham District's coalfields. One company, Mitch reported, even forced employees to sign yellow-dog contracts pledging not to join the union.[89]

As the decade drew to a close, miners began to call for district officials to organize the small strip operations. District 20's strategy of leaving the policing of contracts to local unionists had failed, and its legalistic strategies also did not bear fruit. Many rank-and-file miners consequently began to criticize Mitch and other officials for their failure to keep small mines under contract. Miners in Alabama had their confidence shaken in 1960 when John L. Lewis retired as president of the UMWA. Most of them had never known another president of the national union, and the aging leaders of District 20 seemed increasingly remote and their policies ineffective.[90]

Rank-and-file miners decided to remedy the situation themselves, as they had so often since the union had reemerged in Alabama. First, they protested loudly about the District 20 situation to Lewis's successors. Members of a Brookwood local wrote to the UMWA's new president, Thomas Kennedy, condemning district officials' failure to resolve problems in the coalfields of eastern Tuscaloosa County. Small strip mining companies in the area were going out of business and reopening without the union. Those operators that continued to recognize the union threatened to do the same unless they won concessions from the area's locals. James T. Hatcher, a union miner for most of his life, angrily informed Kennedy that men in his local might have to scab to make a living. "What do you do when a company tell us they can do what they want to?" Hatcher asked. "They know as well as we do that the District won't do anything about it."[91]

By the summer of 1960, members of the local at Alabama Power's Gorgas mine reported that utilities in the area were buying large amounts of nonunion coal from small operators, some of whom simply voided their union contracts. District officials seemed at a loss to advise the members at Gorgas, one of the largest locals in the state, about how to deal with the problem. "We feel if something isn't done at this time, that our union is in grave danger also our jobs and welfare fund," wrote Berry Tatum, the local's president, and Charles Fuller, its financial secretary. "This is getting to be a grave situation we think."[92]

When they failed to get a response, the Gorgas miners acted. Many of them descended on the District 20 offices in downtown Birmingham and told Mitch that they planned to picket Alabama Power's main offices to bring attention to the problem. Mitch persuaded the men not to stage their protest but conceded that the miners had a point. He believed that the unrest was caused in part by "the policy of Alabama Power Company of buying non-union coal on a bid price that is such that these operators could not live up to the contract and operate."[93] Still, Mitch and other UMWA officials did nothing to remedy the situation.

Tensions came to a head in the spring of 1961 at an Abston Construction strip mine in eastern Tuscaloosa County. In many ways, the events at this mine reflected the different currents racing through the Birmingham District's coalfields. The mine's operator had long opposed the UMWA.[94] In 1947, for example, miners refused to work at an Abston operation when the company, in the words of black miner Oscar Hill, "would not sign the contract and we would not go back to work and scab for nothing." Hill told Lewis that he and nine other African Americans who attempted to apply for unemployment when they lost their jobs could not get it. "They dont treat us Colored miners right at all," Hill complained. "We done sign up several times."[95] The problems at Abston, therefore, symbolized both the racial and the economic difficulties that consumed the UMWA just after World War II.

The complexity of the Abston situation also confounded the UMWA, illustrating another problem with keeping small operators under union contract: coal operators increasingly engaged in complicated corporate shell games that made it difficult for the union to enforce its agreements. Three Abston-related companies operated in the Alabama coalfields by the early 1960s. UMWA officials believed that Abston Construction and two related companies, G. Abston Coal and Abston Coal, owed more than $150,000 in back royalties to the fund.[96] The union sued the companies and won, forcing the entities to pay $52,000 in back royalties. In the course of the lawsuits, however, company officials revealed that they had misled the union into thinking that they had signed a union contract. In fact, only employees of Abston Construction were members of the UMWA and had received benefits from the fund. Furthermore, in the course of ruling in the fund's favor, the court found that Abston Construction was not subject to the UMWA's national agreements after 1955.[97] Even when the union could prove it was right, it appeared, the courts rewarded the strip mining companies for their corporate shenanigans.

Abston Construction officials simply told their miners that the company could not afford to live up to the union's wage standards and royalty payments. To force Abston's hand, the company's twenty UMWA miners went on strike in November

1960. Several weeks later, the UMWA's national office sent thousands of dollars to help the miners.[98] The union made little headway, however, and the company simply continued to refuse to adhere to the union contract.

With the legal and mediation tactics stalled, hundreds of rank-and-file miners descended on the company's strip pit near Brookwood in January 1961. The actions merely resulted in a protracted legal battle between the UMWA and Abston Construction, which found much more sympathy in the federal courts than the union had encountered when it tried to collect its royalties. The coal company and the Louisville and Nashville Railroad sued the union in federal court for $250,000 and protested to the National Labor Relations Board. The lawsuit was dismissed, but the UMWA failed to bring the company under contract. Abston's miners were no longer eligible for Welfare and Retirement Fund benefits.[99]

The difficult situation at the Abston operations dramatically illustrated the problems the UMWA faced when confronted with the growth of small strip mines. The union's legalistic strategies met with little success. Mitch and other District 20 leaders could not police the union's contracts when operators refused to abide by them. Perhaps most importantly, even rank-and-file militancy failed the miners when they confronted small operations that could draw on a large number of unemployed miners.

During the 1950s, Alabama miners found themselves pressed on many fronts. The UMWA's biracialism was no longer underpinned by black miners, who were increasingly being replaced by machines. Strip mines, which would produce more and more of Alabama's coal through the 1960s, rarely hired African Americans. The union's attempts to remedy these problems by negotiating new seniority agreements came too late for most African Americans. Moreover, the proliferation of strip mines and small mining operations weakened the union's power, and the miners lost their battle with Koplin for control of the Welfare and Retirement Fund. The old UMWA leadership seemed powerless to adapt to the new realities.

Subsequent decades would bring new challenges to the UMWA in Alabama as coal production and employment would rise dramatically. Would the union and the rank-and-file miners have the strength to meet these challenges?

CHAPTER SIX

Globalization, Race, and Gender, 1961–1980

Thousands of miners walked off the job in a massive wildcat strike that idled most of the Alabama coalfields on 22 May 1974. The miners called the strike to protest planned imports of South African coal announced by a utility holding company. After the strike shut down production at most large mines, hundreds of members of the United Mine Workers of America (UMWA) and their activist allies descended on downtown Birmingham's Kahler Plaza Hotel, where the Southern Company, which sought to import the coal, was holding its annual shareholders' meeting.

Rallying outside of the hotel, the miners and their supporters denounced Southern's plan. Much of the criticism reflected the belief that company leaders valued the company's bottom line over the Birmingham District's well-being. "They say that they're concerned about Alabama coal because they live here too," said Andy Himes, an activist with the Selma Project, a civil rights organization. "Well, that's a damn lie. Look at the top ten stockholders of the Southern Company, they're all New York City banks and all they care about is more profit."[1]

Miners and activists opposed to the imports gained admission to Southern's annual meeting, peppering company officials with tough questions about the South African coal purchases. Southern President Alvin Vogtle, a veteran of the Alabama coal industry, attempted to turn the tables on the protesters by characterizing the activist groups involved as communists and outsiders. When Roger Friedman of the Georgia Power Project questioned Vogtle about the South African coal, for example, he launched into a red-baiting attack on the organization. "There is communistic influence in [the Georgia Power Project] and we are going to maintain private enterprise and keep ourselves out of the government's hands," Vogtle proclaimed. He went on to charge that the demonstration had been "stirred up by outsiders" and that his company had "no willingness to go along with socialists and communists."[2]

Tom Youngblood, a Birmingham District miner and union activist, summed up the views of many of the region's coal miners when he addressed Southern officials: "You say your true allegiance is to America. Well, we're the people. We need the jobs, we want the jobs. We want to work for our families, and make a decent living. You're out to protect your dollars. We're out to protect our jobs. This is our livelihood, we want to work here. We want a decent wage. Let us keep our jobs. Does that sound fair and honest? What kind of a company can we have if you can't be fair and godly?"[3]

The revelation that the Southern Company planned to import millions of tons of South African coal shocked Alabama's miners and their union and symbolized the difficulties faced by an industry subject to global markets. On the one hand, miners benefited from the internationalization of their industry. The coal Birmingham District miners produced, once primarily limited to markets in Alabama, now found its way to outlets in Japan, Latin America, and Europe. On its way to these destinations, the coal passed through Mobile's port facilities. The rise in exports of Alabama coal, a phenomenon that began in the late 1960s, helped fuel a boom in employment that briefly revived the coalfields after decades of depressed economic conditions.

On the other hand, miners discovered that conglomerates such as the Southern Company could now draw on international markets—and coal mined in places such as South Africa and Australia—to fuel power plants in the southern United States. In Southern's case, the company brought the imports through the same facilities at the Alabama State Docks in Mobile through which Birmingham District coal passed on its way to foreign consumers. In the early 1970s, Alabama miners discovered that coal could be imported as easily as almost any commodity. Living and working in Alabama, in close proximity to the power plants and steel mills that consumed coal, no longer insulated miners from global pressures.[4]

In the 1970s, even the face of the Alabama coal industry looked different. Many of the old producers had left the business during the coal depression. Tennessee Coal, Iron and Railroad Company (TCI), historically the region's most important coal company, had been completely absorbed by its parent, U.S. Steel, while new companies became dominant in the state. Some, including Drummond Coal, were homegrown entities with connections to old operators. Others, such as Florida-based manufactured-home builder Jim Walter Homes, were huge conglomerates with little or no prior mining experience and had entered the industry as an investment designed to diversify corporate holdings.[5]

The changes in Alabama mirrored the transformation of the national coal industry. The old coal companies that had dominated the Bituminous Coal Operators' Association became less important during the 1970s. Leading global energy companies "carved coal into distinct spheres of influence" and pushed for rollbacks in the wages and benefits for which union miners had struggled mightily.[6] A series of long and difficult national wildcats and contract strikes culminated in the 1977–78 strike, the longest and most acrimonious national walkout by the UMWA since World War II.

Alabama miners in the 1970s faced a different world than their predecessors. The benefits of the resurgence of the Birmingham District's coal industry largely bypassed the coal communities that had suffered through the coalfield depression. Miners who found jobs at the new mines often drove many miles to their jobs. Much of this new production came from surface mines, which proved a mixed blessing for aging coal towns. Many coalfield residents now owned homes and property, often placing them in direct conflict with nearby surface mines. The strip mining process sometimes damaged neighboring property and ruined the wells that provided residents' water.

African American miners, who comprised only about 20 percent of the coal workforce in 1970, found themselves excluded from most of the benefits of the revival of the Alabama coal industry. During the 1970s, although the number of blacks employed in District 20 increased slightly, the percentage of African Americans continued to drop, and by 1980 a mere 11 percent of Alabama's more than 13,500 coal miners were black.[7]

The UMWA's focus in Alabama narrowed as well, and the union typically sided with the coal companies on major issues such as strip mine regulation, pitting the locals against coal communities, progressive state leaders, and even the national union leadership. Miners' union leaders also forged strong connections with reactionary politicians such as George Wallace. As in earlier decades, however, rank-and-file miners were not above defying their leaders, both those appointed by UMWA presidents and those elected after the union instituted democratic reforms in the early 1970s. Miners expressed their anger at their state presidents through wildcat strikes and by rejecting appeals to return to work. In the mid-1970s, such unauthorized walkouts sometimes played a role in dislodging unpopular leaders in favor of moderate district officials.

Women became a new force in the mines after the mid-1970s, when a combination of grassroots activism and lawsuits enabled them to claim a small share of the industry's jobs. Largely neglected by the UMWA, which had traditionally fought to preserve the male world underground, these women, like African American men in earlier decades, had to develop tactics that would enable them to carve out a place for themselves in the mines. They formed rank-and-file organizations and used direct action to pressure Alabama coal companies. When that strategy met with only mixed success in obtaining jobs for women, they took legal action against the coal operators. Such organizing and legal maneuvers ultimately paid off, and the coal industry began to hire more women.[8] Crossing through the portals in District 20 after 1975, women entered a male-dominated world in which they encountered prejudice from both managers and fellow miners, who did all they could to keep the numbers of women low.

This chapter examines the world in which Birmingham District coal miners lived and worked in the late 1960s and 1970s. It begins with an overview of the political and social turmoil of the civil rights movement, the white reaction that followed, and the impact of these developments on the coalfields. The growth of international coal markets and the expansion of strip mining also are explored, as is the UMWA's attempt to prevent the Southern Company from importing South African coal. The failure of this movement had profound consequences for miners, particularly after the coal industry began another period of economic decline early in the 1980s.

Finally, this chapter chronicles women's efforts to find and keep mining jobs. Women who found employment in the coal industry in the 1970s drew on both coalfield traditions of labor militancy and the activist spirit inspired by the black freedom movement that swept through the South in the late 1950s and 1960s. Female miners in many ways represented the embodiment of the social agenda for which coalfield activists had hoped when they reestablished the miners' union four decades earlier, though, as this chapter shows, the UMWA did little to help women enter the mines.

❰ ❰ ❰

In the Birmingham District, the central drama of this era began in the streets, as hundreds of African American schoolchildren braved fire hoses, police dogs, and incarceration to demand racial equality and black freedom in the spring of 1963. Their demonstrations riveted the nation, forming some of the most enduring images of Birmingham in the American mind. The protest movement, led by the Alabama Christian Movement for Human Rights and the Southern Christian Leadership Conference and staffed by young students, culminated in the accords of May, in which city business leaders agreed to desegregate their stores and restaurants and pledged to begin hiring African Americans. Four months later, the brutal murder of four African American schoolgirls—Denise McNair, Carole Robertson, Addie Mae Collins, and Cynthia Wesley—by white terrorists in the infamous Sixteenth Street Baptist Church bombing stamped another image of Birmingham on the nation's consciousness. The civil rights protests and the violent response to them transformed the city. They also "nationalized the faltering civil rights movement and galvanized public opinion behind federal legislation to abolish segregation," journalist Diane McWhorter has recently written.[9] In the wake of the events in Birmingham, Congress passed and President Lyndon Johnson signed into law the Civil Rights Act of 1964, which outlawed discrimination based on, among other things, race, sex, ethnicity, national origin, or religion.

In the decade before the climax of the civil rights movement in Birmingham, racial issues drove deep fractures into the biracial liberalism that held together both James E. "Big Jim" Folsom's political coalition and the industrial union movement. In the spring of 1954, as voters elected the racially progressive Folsom to his second term as governor, the U.S. Supreme Court struck down the doctrine of separate but equal in public education when it issued its decision in the *Brown* case. The decision spurred massive anger among whites in Alabama and the rest of the South, and its ramifications dominated Folsom's second term. The governor's soft stance on segregation, his personal antics, and persistent charges of corruption in his administration made Folsom a pariah among white voters. The liberal coalition that had sustained him lay in tatters by the end of his second term in 1958.

Civil rights agitation grew in the wake of the *Brown* ruling as blacks sought to claim the full citizenship they had long been denied. In the winter of 1955 and 1956, the Montgomery Improvement Association coordinated a massive bus boycott by African Americans in the wake of Rosa Parks's arrest for refusing to vacate her seat on a city bus for a white passenger. By the end of 1956, the boycott had prevailed, and the Supreme Court had ruled Montgomery's segregated public transportation unconstitutional. That same year, Autherine Lucy, an African American woman, attempted to enroll at the University of Alabama in Tuscaloosa. The effort ended in disaster, with violent mobs of whites descending on campus and the university's board of trustees expelling Lucy "for her protection and for the protection of other students and staff members."[10]

The movement had spread to the Birmingham District by the end of the 1950s. The Alabama Christian Movement for Human Rights, led by the dynamic Reverend Fred Shuttlesworth, began to challenge the city's segregated transportation and school systems. Vigilantes responded to civil rights activism after World

War II with a wave of bombings that targeted black leaders, churches, and homes in or near white neighborhoods. The violence became almost an accepted fact of life in Birmingham during these years. When freedom riders arrived at the Birmingham Trailways station, for example, Klansmen and other whites savagely attacked the activists.[11] The violence earned the city distinction as a brutal and lawless haven of terrorism and illustrated how polarized the Birmingham District had grown since the mid-1950s.

The civil rights movement unleashed a strong reaction from Birmingham's white working class as well. Attempts by the United Steelworkers of America to desegregate its Birmingham District union halls failed. When national labor leaders adopted pro–civil rights positions, hundreds of union members protested, threatening to withhold their dues or to secede from their unions. These protests represented the hardening of racial lines in the Birmingham District, as white workers sought to protect their privileged position in the region's mills. Many of them flocked into the ranks of the Citizens' Councils and Klan groups that grew in the racially polarized atmosphere of the 1950s. Officials estimated that union-ists comprised 90 percent of the members of one Birmingham Citizens' Council chapter.[12]

The tide of white racial anxiety came to a head in the political rebirth of George Wallace, a former Folsom ally who had turned on his mentor when racial moderation became unpopular. Attorney General John Patterson defeated Wal-lace, a circuit court judge, in the racially charged 1958 gubernatorial election. Patterson ran hard on the race issue and gained the support of the state's largest Klan group, while Wallace campaigned as a relative racial moderate, emphasizing economic and educational issues while defending segregation. Patterson easily defeated Wallace by about a hundred thousand votes. Wallace rebounded to win election four years later, outdistancing his closest opponents, including Folsom and a young progressive, Ryan deGraffenried, behind a pledge to defend segre-gation.

As governor, Wallace took racial demagoguery to new heights in Alabama poli-tics. He symbolically attempted—unsuccessfully—to prevent two African Amer-ican students from integrating the University of Alabama with his "stand in the schoolhouse door" in June 1963. Two years later, Wallace's state police units par-ticipated in a brutal attack on civil rights marchers in Selma. The governor's racially tinged 1964 and 1968 presidential campaigns made him a national fig-ure and began the process of pulling the North's white workers away from the coalition that had sustained the national Democratic Party.[13]

In Alabama, Wallace worked hard for the votes of working-class whites and tai-lored his racial appeals specifically to them. His record of opposing right-to-work legislation and his support for higher corporate taxes made him popular with many local unionists. The Alabama American Federation of Labor–Congress of Industrial Organizations, which endorsed Wallace and his two closest competitors in the 1962 election (no candidate had enough backing to gain the endorsement outright, though Wallace had the most support in the organization), proved less enthusiastic after he became governor. The state body did not endorse Wallace in his first presidential bid two years later, despite strong lobbying efforts by his supporters both in and out of the labor movement. Wallace's forces promptly froze the state labor federation out of their administration, then colluded with dissident unions that threatened to disaffiliate with the state and national union body over civil rights.[14]

The UMWA, though it no longer enjoyed the central position in the state's labor movement it had occupied during the New Deal era, was not above the fray of the Wallace years. In the fall of 1963, after Wallace shepherded an increase in worker's compensation payments through the state legislature, new District 20 President Thomas Crawford praised the governor: "This came through as you had predicted and we again say, in behalf of those we represent, that we are very grateful." Wallace later assured District 20 leaders that he would seek additional improvements to the unemployment compensation law. "Again, let me say that it was good to hear from you," Wallace wrote to Crawford, "and please convey my kind regards to our friends in the United Mine Workers' office." Crawford's membership on a state Unemployment Compensation Committee during Wallace's first administration, in the wake of his first unsuccessful presidential race, further testified to the close relationship between union leaders and the segregationist governor.[15]

A coal strike in the last year of Wallace's first term—voters essentially reelected him by sending his wife, Lurleen, to the governor's office in 1966—provided the UMWA leaders with an opportunity to test their friendship with the governor. In the spring of 1966, as the UMWA's national president, W. A. "Tony" Boyle, attempted to negotiate a new agreement with large national operators, strikes swept the nation's coalfields. In Alabama, more than six thousand miners stopped work on 11 April, and the strike dragged on for weeks. District 20 leaders, like Boyle and other national leaders, attempted to convince miners to end their walkout but met with little success.

Continuing a tactic they had used since World War II, rank-and-file miners remained on strike in another attempt to bring small, independent coal operations under UMWA contract. Some of these operations had signed contracts with the Southern Labor Union (SLU), a company-dominated union that had made inroads into the Tennessee and Kentucky coalfields during the 1960s. In Alabama, the organization remained small, but its presence clearly concerned UMWA miners and their leaders. District 20 officials had conducted a "vigorous" campaign to defeat SLU organizing efforts in the Birmingham District in the early 1960s, but the association persisted at a few strip operations.[16]

During the walkout, UMWA members fanned out across the Birmingham District and shut down nonunion and SLU-affiliated operations. Letters with reports of UMWA actions streamed into Wallace's office from small operators and their supporters. Miners from K and S Coal and Clay Mining complained of violence and threats from UMWA picketers in early May. Donald Peters of Peters Coal told the governor that the situation approached anarchy in Walker County as thousands of miners picketed small operations and warned them not to produce coal.[17]

The Wallace administration remained out of the dispute, essentially signaling its support for or at least tolerance of the UMWA members' actions. The responses from state Labor Secretary Arlis Fant to the operator complaints that flooded into state offices revealed the administration's position. After reminding Peters that federal officials had jurisdiction over the strike, for example, Fant told the operators that administration officials "regret that the relationship between some of the coal companies and the two labor organizations has broken down and will assist in any way possible in cementing the relationship to its former status." The responses indicated what union miners already knew: the administration would permit local law enforcement to control the situation. Unlike their predecessors in the early part of the century, many police and sheriff's department officials in the 1960s supported the UMWA and did little to rein in the miners.

Wallace administration officials briefly investigated the reports of violence in Walker County but determined that the local sheriff was "keeping a check on the situation and picketing is going on without any violence or law violation. There has been no destruction of property in any way." If miners had any doubts about the governor's stance on the strike, they likely were laid to rest after an early May meeting between Wallace and a delegation of Walker County UMWA supporters. According to a state legislator present at the meeting, Wallace pledged the "full cooperation of his office and the office of the labor department in making a determination of the facts and to seek a peaceful and speedy solution of the dispute."[18] The administration maintained its hands-off policy, to the benefit of the UMWA.

The close relationship between the union bureaucracy and Wallace came during a period of major change in the leadership in Alabama. After serving for thirty years as District 20 president, William Mitch resigned in 1963, and Boyle appointed Crawford as the new head of Alabama's miners. Mitch, no longer involved in the union's daily operations, continued on the union's International Executive Board (IEB) until the fall of 1967. When Crawford, a longtime Mitch associate who had been a working miner in District 20, became seriously ill after the 1966 strike, Boyle relieved him of his official duties.

Boyle solidified his control of District 20 by appointing E. E. Holleyfield to replace Crawford. Holleyfield had less of a connection to the union's rank and file and depended on Boyle for support. When Mitch resigned from the IEB in 1967, the autocratic union president appointed District 19 secretary-treasurer Albert Pass as his successor. Alabama's miners chafed under Holleyfield's heavy-handed tactics. When the president was severely injured in a 1970 automobile accident, Boyle replaced Holleyfield with C. E. Beane, a career UMWA organizer who had worked in Alabama in the 1940s and who would serve as District 20's president until 1973.[19]

Mitch's successors headed up a different union. The UMWA in Alabama was a majority white organization, so balancing Wallace's racism against his support for unionized workers was relatively easy. The UMWA leadership demonstrated little sensitivity to the concerns of the few remaining African American miners. In his first major address to the Alabama Mining Institute, in 1963, for example, Crawford stated that there "was at one time a rule of thumb among the coal operators of Alabama that the only way to mine coal, when the railroads controlled the coal markets, was 'with a pine pole tipple, a three-wheel car, a one-eyed drunk and a one-legged nigger.'" Much of his speech went on to praise the policies that had led to the decline of African Americans in the Alabama coalfields. The union, Crawford told the operators, had forced the industry to mechanize. The UMWA also compelled the companies to "provide a higher standard of living for the men who work in the mines."[20] But it had done so at the expense of African Americans, as the industry became increasingly white in the Birmingham District. The cozy relationship between Wallace and the UMWA in many ways reflected these changes.

Alabama's remaining miners enjoyed the union's protection and the high wages its contracts brought. By the mid-1960s, the state's mining jobs paid an average of $126 a week, only slightly less than the national average of $135. Despite concerns about the SLU's presence, the UMWA had more than 90 percent of Alabama's mines under contract, surpassing the rates in most other major coal-producing areas as well as the national average of 81 percent.[21]

Miners had reason to worry about the future, however. The Birmingham District's economy, with its reliance on heavy industry, continued to lag behind such Sunbelt powerhouses as Atlanta. Many people gave up and left the region, most of them in search of better opportunities than declining heavy industries offered. Between 1950 and 1960, Birmingham lost more than 25,000 people, while the counties that ringed the city lost almost 111,000 residents. Researchers attributed much of the decline to problems in mining and in agricultural employment. The population drain continued in the decade that followed, when the region lost more than 52,000 additional people, most of them African Americans.[22]

The reliance on manufacturing industries meant that the Birmingham District's economy remained vulnerable to fluctuations in international markets. U.S. Steel and other producers found themselves hard-hit by imports from Japan and Germany as well as by the growth of the aluminum industry. The region's industrial base meant that national recessions often lasted longer. The downturn of the late 1950s, for example, hit the Birmingham District especially hard. By the end of the decade, when the rest of the country had begun to recover, the Magic City lagged behind, with economic problems lingering through the mid-1960s. U.S. Steel experienced the most noticeable declines, as employment plummeted from seventeen thousand in the early 1950s to ten thousand in 1966. According to one estimate, the industrial district lost twenty-five thousand jobs in steel and related industries between 1950 and 1970. New enterprises such as health care, symbolized by the University of Alabama at Birmingham Medical Center, and telecommunications, which received a boost when South Central Bell moved its headquarters to the city, only partially offset these losses.

The civil rights movement could hope to address only a small part of the problems that African Americans faced in Birmingham, and the decline of the region's manufacturing base hit black residents particularly hard. The economy's construction, services, and financial sectors that showed growth in the 1960s had traditionally hired few African Americans. Moreover, many development projects—the medical center, interstate highways, and efforts at urban renewal—displaced thousands of African Americans, increasing Birmingham's segregation despite the civil rights protests' success. African Americans continued to reside in substandard and overcrowded housing in the most polluted parts of the city, to earn less than whites, and to have fewer educational opportunities.[23]

The coal communities around Birmingham faced many of the same problems. During the coalfield depression, many families had simply packed up and moved to search for new opportunities. Residents of the old coal towns complained that young people had no reason to stay, and many of them left the region when they finished high school. Miners lucky enough to have jobs typically drove long distances to their mine sites. In the early 1970s, for example, residents of Mulga described young people leaving "because there just aren't any jobs." The town's mayor, V. A. Hogan, claimed that when he arrived in Mulga in the early 1920s, "there were close to 1,500 miners and their families living in the area. Now I'd say there are only 500–600 miners left, and the mines have been moved almost ten miles away from town."[24]

Coal communities suffered infrastructure problems as well. As mines closed and residents left, water and sewer systems often declined—that is, when they existed at all. Many residents continued to rely on wells and septic tanks. In Cardiff, north of Birmingham, residents depended "upon wells, and when we have a long dry spell people suffer," Mayor Charlie Country complained in 1962. "Most of the wells go dry until it rains." The mayor hoped to convince some nearby small towns to extend water to his community's two hundred residents.[25]

Cardiff was not alone. As late as the 1970s, water and sewer difficulties proved a problem for many coal communities. Residents of Jefferson County besieged local planning meetings with complaints and accounts of dire circumstances. Nancy Lee Hughes, who lived near Adamsville, reported that in her community, people carried water to their homes "in rusty pails." The contents, she complained, were "often too muddy to drink." Concerns about water quality even intruded into union meetings. Members of a steelworkers local protested to the Jefferson County Commission that they were "very much surprised to find people literally begging for water, with a water supply just a few feet away." The unionists wrote that they could not "understand why in this year of 1977 this type of situation exists."[26]

After decades of decline, coal communities unquestionably lacked the resources to expand or modernize their infrastructure. The rise of strip mining compounded the problem, disturbing the geology and often contaminating wells. In the mid-1970s, Porter resident Jerry Williams complained that nearby strip mines "had sunk the water," causing his well to run dry. He periodically had to haul a two-ton tank from his home to a water source. A resident of the town of Warrior claimed that strip mines had fouled much of the water in his area with iron and other minerals, resulting in low ratings for the water from the county health department.[27]

Drummond Coal, an Alabama conglomerate that grew into one of the nation's largest operators, became a focal point for citizen discontent. Residents of Beltona, a small northern Jefferson County coal community, complained that blasting at a nearby Drummond strip mine often sent rocks and large boulders tumbling onto their property. Explosions and other activity at the mine cracked the foundations of nearby homes and caused wells to run dry or become contaminated. Residents near other Drummond operations voiced similar concerns. The concussion from an explosion at a mine near Warrior shattered a plate-glass window at a car dealership and cracked a wall at a medical supply firm.[28]

Such problems increased as surface operations grew dramatically. Strip mining accounted for about a third of the fifteen million tons of coal produced in Alabama in 1965. Five years later, surface mines produced almost nine million tons of coal, about half of the state's production, and by the mid-1970s, strip operations produced almost two-thirds of Alabama's coal.[29]

The increasing reliance on strip mines brought operators into conflict with both coalfield residents and environmentalists, who feared the practice's toll on the land. In the late 1960s, when concerns about strip mining began to parallel its growth, Alabama still had no laws to regulate the procedure. Some companies simply abandoned the land when they finished mining, leaving the property owners who had leased out the land to clean up the mess. Since most of these landowners lacked the financial means to restore the land, many old surface mines remained as silent testimonials to the problems of strip mining. Early journalistic accounts communicated shock at seeing the "mounds of earth and gaping pits, many of them filled with deep, brackish water," that characterized such moonscapes.[30]

The environmental effects of strip operations were not limited to mine sites. Runoff polluted creeks and rivers with silt and acid mine drainage, which killed fish and aquatic plants. The mines affected water storage, river navigation, and flood control. Former strip pits could sustain little in the way of vegetation, and the sixty- to eighty-foot-high walls left standing were hazardous.

Many critics of the practice warned about its future economic and social impact. The cost of abandoned strip mines and even poorly reclaimed operations would be "paid by innocent parties in the mined areas," wrote University of Alabama Professor Earl Bailey. He and others worried about the long-term viability of strip mining: the state had only 157 million tons of coal close enough to the surface to be mined economically in this fashion, a sharp contrast to nearly 1.8 billion tons of deep reserves. Bailey predicted that at current production levels, accessible coal reserves near the surface would be depleted by the mid-1990s. "The industry may run its course before effectively regulated or before we gain the knowledge through research that is necessary to effectively regulate or to justify a phase-out of surface mining," he wrote. Bailey encouraged officials to pursue policies that replaced strip mining with underground mining, because deep mines, which required more miners, provided more economic benefits to coal communities and had less impact on the environment. Edward Passerini, also a University of Alabama professor, suggested phasing out strip mining through a system of tax credits to help open up more deep mines. These operations would replace surface mines and "would provide many more jobs per ton than strip-coal and, since we have hundreds of years of deep mineable coal, a long-term economic boom." Such a switch, Passerini argued, would provide jobs for "three times as many workers as are presently employed in strip-mining."[31]

The coal industry easily co-opted Alabama's mid-1970s' attempts to control strip mining. Attorney General Bill Baxley, a liberal with a prolabor record, labeled state regulatory efforts a "farce." Even the *Birmingham News* sharply criticized Alabama's lackluster attempts to rein in the industry's excesses. The normally staid newspaper denounced the 1975 law that created the Alabama Surface Mining Reclamation Commission as a "travesty" that had resulted from "industry-approved legislation" and described the commission as "staffed with industry-approved appointees." The new legislation provided little solace for coalfield residents, the newspaper complained. These people faced damage to their homes, difficulty with home loans, and contaminated water supplies. Under such lackluster regulations, lawsuits proved their only option. The situation was particularly troublesome, according to the *News*, because most of the people who live near strip mines "derive no income from strip mining."[32]

In this respect, surface operations sometimes placed miners and coal communities in conflict with each other. During the early 1970s, the UMWA's Alabama leaders typically opposed regulations that residents of coal communities supported. District 20 officers protested the Udall-Mink bill, federal strip mining legislation that came before the U.S. House of Representatives in the summer of 1974. The measure called for a thirty-cent tax on every ton of coal to help reclaim land at strip mines. District 20 President Sam Littlefield claimed that the bill would result in the closure of forty-five mines and the loss of twelve hundred jobs. Hundreds of Drummond Coal miners went on "strike"—with company support—to protest the bill.[33]

When Baxley attempted to file injunctions against surface mines with poor environmental records, the UMWA strongly opposed him. In 1974, Littlefield even appealed to Wallace, getting ready to run for reelection as governor, to intervene: "I know personally for the many years that I have been associated with you that you also will cooperate and use your influence in every way possible regarding the above problem that threatens hundreds of jobs of the mine workers."[34] Littlefield's actions illustrated how distant the UMWA had grown from the coal communities. The debate over strip mining showed that the union represented merely the interests of its members rather than those of the people who lived in the Birmingham District's coalfields.

At least some of the increasing reliance on surface mining related to the growth of export markets for Alabama coal. This development, along with the oil crisis of the early 1970s, propelled the rise of local operators such as Drummond Coal. The potential profits in the energy industry also prompted Jim Walter Homes and other conglomerates to buy their way into the Birmingham District's coal industry.[35]

Drummond Coal had a long history in Alabama. The company's founder, Heman Drummond, had worked for DeBardeleben Coal before starting his own small operation in the late 1930s. The company primarily sold coal for home heating, and employment in the early days ranged from four to forty miners, depending on the volume of orders. The work was generally seasonal, reaching its peak during the cold months and then slowing in the summer. Though the company expanded during World War II, it remained a small firm when Drummond died in 1956 and passed it on to his children. Drummond's sons expanded operations in the 1960s, and at the end of the decade Gary Neil Drummond signed an export deal with a Japanese steel producer that transformed the company. The ten-year agreement was valued at one hundred million dollars, and Drummond suddenly became the second-largest exporter of American coal to Japan.[36]

Drummond did not thrive by exports alone. The company shrewdly acquired coal leases in the 1960s and by the time of the Japanese deal employed hundreds of miners and had about eight million dollars in sales each year. At the end of the 1970s and in the early 1980s, much of Drummond's coal went to domestic customers such as Alabama Power. The company's strip mines dotted the Birmingham District's landscape, bringing Drummond into conflict with neighboring property owners.[37]

Drummond also attracted attention from state and federal regulators. The state Ethics Commission, for example, criticized Drummond's close relationship with the Alabama Surface Mining Reclamation Commission. The commission leased its offices from a company partly owned by Drummond interests, and the commission's chair had to resign after regulators discovered that company officials had given him free tickets and an airplane ride to watch a college football game. Several Drummond officials, including Gary Neil Drummond, stood trial in 1980 on charges that the company had bribed state officials in return for political influence and inside information on Alabama Power Company. After an eleven-week trial, however, a federal judge tossed out the case for insufficient evidence.[38]

Drummond's acquisition of Alabama By-Products at the end of the 1970s gave Drummond control of six underground mines and made it a leader in this type of mining as well. Drummond Coal paid $75.3 million to buy 65 percent of the company's voting stock, and Gary Drummond became chair and his brother vice chair. Alabama By-Products, a mining company with strong ties to First National Bank and Alabama Power, resisted the efforts to combine its operations with Drummond. When Drummond officials filed a plan to merge Alabama By-Products into their company, other Alabama By-Products stockholders challenged the deal in federal court. Drummond eventually backed off its plans, though it retained control of Alabama By-Products.[39]

The purchase of Alabama By-Products gave Drummond officials ownership of one of the state's last company towns, Praco, near the border of Jefferson and Walker Counties. At its founding in the 1930s, Praco housed more than fifteen hundred miners in its six hundred homes, but by 1981, only about eighty homes remained, and most of their residents were elderly and had low incomes. The commissary had lingered on until the summer of 1980, when it closed. In December 1981, company officials announced plans to evict the community's remaining residents, giving them one month to leave. "It's got people, sure enough, in a pickle," said Gurley Vines, a mechanic who lived in the town. "Especially it being so close to Christmas. . . . And it is going to be real hard on those people who are living in these hills on fixed incomes from Social Security and retirement." After a series of protests, officials gave Praco residents an additional six months to pack up and go.[40]

Because Drummond specialized in surface mining, its complete acquisition of Alabama By-Products unsettled many underground miners. Their concerns were borne out when the company promptly closed two Alabama By-Products mines, idling nine hundred miners. "I'd been in that mine 16 years, and I thought I had a future in this industry in this mine," said Lynsse Blackston, among those who lost his job. "We were told by Alabama By-Products that we could all retire at that mine, that the coal was there. [Drummond] claimed that the coal was 'depleted.' Well if depleted means what I think it does, it means the coal was about gone. But coal was there. I was down there, I saw it." The company announced that its strip mines would fill the orders of the two underground operations it closed.[41]

Jim Walter Homes found its way into the Alabama industry in 1969 when it purchased U.S. Pipe and Foundry, which had two aging coal mines and large reserves on the Blue Creek seam considered too deep to mine economically. Six years later, Jim Walter Resources, as the coal mining division of the company was known, inked a two-billion-dollar deal to export coal to six Japanese steel companies. Jim Walter announced plans to develop mines on the Blue Creek seam that would produce ten million tons of coal per year.[42]

By the end of the 1970s, Drummond and Jim Walter dominated Alabama's coal industry. They were not, however, the originators of the idea of exporting Alabama coal. U.S. Congressman Carl Elliott, who represented part of north Alabama from the late 1940s until the early 1960s, explored such opportunities in an attempt to improve the dismal economic conditions in Walker County and other parts of his district. He was attracted to the concept by Milton Fies, a veteran of Alabama Power and DeBardeleben Coal, who began to examine the coal seams in northeastern Alabama along the Plateau Field in the late 1940s and early 1950s. Fies believed that the coal mined from operations in this region could be sold to Tennessee Valley Authority power plants and that at least some of it eventually could be floated down the Tennessee-Tombigbee waterway to the port at Mobile, making it available for export. The coal from Alabama could reach Asian markets—in particular, Japan—through the Panama Canal, Fies hoped. The coal also might find consumers in Brazil and other parts of South America as well as Central America and the Caribbean. Fies eventually purchased the mineral rights to the Fabius mine, located in Jackson County. By the mid-1960s the Fabius strip mine employed about fifty-five miners and sent much of its coal to a Tennessee Valley Authority plant at Widow's Creek along the Tennessee River.[43]

Many of the Alabama operators sent coal to Japan as the markets expanded in the early 1970s. The Mead Corporation had purchased the old Mulga mine from Woodward Iron by the end of the decade and subsequently sent eight hundred thousand tons a year from the operation to Japan.[44] Republic Steel began to develop the North River mine in Fayette County, north of Tuscaloosa, in the early 1970s to supply Japanese demand. The company hoped that the mine would eventually employ four hundred miners and send about two million tons of coal a year to Asian markets. Alabama coal also found its way to other destinations. Belgium, Spain, West Germany, and Latin American countries imported coal produced in the Birmingham District.[45]

The exported coal went through the Alabama State Docks in Mobile. In the early 1970s, the state financed massive improvements to the port's coal loading facilities. The companies chipped in five hundred thousand dollars to improve the docks, while the state issued fifteen million dollars in bonds to help build a high-speed loading operation. Exports of Alabama coal rose from about 600 tons in 1969 (before Drummond's huge deal) to 379,000 tons the following year. The facilities in Mobile exported about 3 million tons of coal per year by the mid-1970s.[46]

Alabama operators attributed the increased Japanese demand to a number of factors. Gary Drummond claimed that his company had reached its first deal after it learned of a shortage of metallurgical coal, used to make steel, in Japan: "They were running out and were mining way down under the sea to get at thin seams at a high cost, so there was an opening for us." The Japanese stockpiled at least some of Drummond's coal, placing it in lakes or gullies as a hedge against inflation and future energy problems. Other coal industry officials attributed the new markets to stricter Japanese environmental laws. Alabama's relatively low-sulfur coal produced less pollution, industry officials claimed.[47]

Many of these explanations tended to obscure the end result of the coal exports.

Coal from producers in Alabama and the rest of the United States, Canada, and Australia helped turn the Japanese steel industry into a global power. Much of Japan's success came in the form of exports, which accounted for 40 percent of its growth from the late 1950s through the mid-1970s. More than half of Japan's steel production headed for the United States by the end of the 1960s, according to historian Judith Stein.[48] Some of this Japanese steel likely accounted for the decline of U.S. Steel's operations in the Birmingham District.

The growth in coal employment in the late 1960s and early 1970s overshadowed these potential problems. As coal producers found new markets abroad, consumption began to increase at home and the energy crisis of the early 1970s drove up the price of coal. The average cost per ton, for example, doubled between 1971 and 1974, reaching $15.75. Nationally, production surged in the 1970s to satisfy the increasing demand. In 1970, American mines produced almost 603 million tons of coal, a number that grew to almost 824 million tons a decade later. Employment in coal mining rose from 144,000 at the start of the decade to 241,000 in 1978. As in Alabama, companies not traditionally involved in coal production made major investments in the national industry. Large energy conglomerates, many of them oil companies, controlled a third of the U.S. coal production by the end of the decade.[49]

With improved conditions, Alabama's post–World War II coalfield depression began to vanish. In 1970, fewer than 5,000 miners produced 18.1 million tons of coal; ten years later, 12,735 miners produced almost 26 million tons of coal in the state's mines. Strip mining accounted for 49 percent of the state's production in 1970 and 64 percent in 1980. Surface mines produced 8.9 million tons of coal at the start of the decade and 16.8 million tons at its end.[50]

Thousands of miners found jobs in the revived coal industry. The new miners and the industry's structural changes fueled a transformation of the UMWA at the national level. In particular, a grassroots movement centered on the issues of union democracy, problems with the UMWA Welfare and Retirement Fund, and coal workers' pneumoconiosis (black lung) challenged the UMWA's entrenched national leadership. Tony Boyle, who had assumed the union's presidency in 1963 after Thomas Kennedy's death, never had the rank-and-file support that his predecessors enjoyed. Many of the dissidents coalesced around the candidacy of Joseph A. "Jock" Yablonski, a Pennsylvania UMWA leader and one-time Boyle supporter, who ran against the UMWA president in 1969. In an election rampant with fraud and intimidation, Boyle triumphed by a vote of 80,577 to 46,073. Yablonski challenged the election with the U.S. Department of Labor, but assassins murdered him, along with his wife and a daughter, before he could see the case to a conclusion. Boyle and several UMWA officials loyal to him eventually were convicted of arranging the murders.[51]

Boyle would continue as UMWA president for three years after the killings, however. A reform movement, known as Miners for Democracy, rose from the ashes of Yablonski's defeat and murder. In 1972, federal officials overturned the 1969 election and ordered a new vote. A Miners for Democracy slate featuring Arnold Miller, a former local union official and black lung activist from West Virginia, defeated the besieged union president that fall.[52]

Only a small number of democracy activists were active in District 20 in the late 1960s and early 1970s, however, and Birmingham District miners gave Boyle strong victories—4,651 to 391 over Yablonski and 4,170 to 1,144 over Miller. After the reformers took power at the national level, they largely ignored District 20. Miller appointed Frank Clements, an activist with Miners for Democracy, as Alabama's representative on the union's IEB but left other Boyle appointees in place.[53]

As a result, reformers made few gains in district elections in the fall of 1973. Clements defeated former District 20 president C. E. Beane in the race to represent Alabama's miners on the IEB, but Boyle loyalists were elected to most other important positions. Sam Littlefield was chosen president, while Lloyd Baker held onto the office of secretary-treasurer despite the fact that he had never worked in a coal mine.[54] Union reformers' failure to make headway in Alabama accounted for the posture the UMWA adopted in the mid-1970s. Littlefield, Baker, and other leaders had difficulty forging the alliances and developing strategies the union needed to fight the importation of South African coal.

The struggle over the coal imports began in the spring of 1974 when the UMWA discovered that the Southern Company intended to import 2.4 million tons of South African coal over the next three years. The company claimed that it needed the coal to comply with environmental regulations at two of its coal-burning plants in Florida. Southern's agreement with Coal Exports of South Africa and Mannessman Pipe and Steel called for the importation of 500,000 tons of coal in 1974, 920,000 tons in 1975 and just over 1,000,000 tons in 1976. Southern planned to bring the coal through the Alabama State Docks—the same facility that processed coal exports—and use it at plants in Pensacola and Panama City, Florida.[55]

Southern could afford to import coal from nine thousand miles away rather than to buying low-sulfur coal mined just a few hundred miles away because South African coal companies paid their miners low wages. Black miners, who produced most of the coal in South Africa, labored under poor safety conditions and had few rights. They could join unions, but labor organizations with black members could not conduct official negotiations with companies. South African miners, according to the UMWA, faced among the worst working conditions of any in the world. UMWA officials and activists linked the coal from South Africa to the economic situation faced by Alabama miners, noting that the imported coal represented enough production to account for the jobs of more than 375 Alabama miners.[56]

The national union connected the exports directly to the oppression of black South African miners. Miller accused the Southern Company of "subsidizing South African conscript labor at the expense of American miners, who will lose jobs to blacks in South Africa working under slave labor conditions." The union also forged important links with regional activists. The Georgia Power Project, a consumer rights organization that was a constant thorn in Southern's side, proved among the most helpful. The different groups coalesced into an organization called the Committee to Stop South African Coal, which coordinated local and regional efforts and carried on an intense corporate accountability campaign that lasted several years. The protest at Southern's spring 1974 shareholder meeting in Birmingham represented the organization's first major event.

District 20 officials had little troubling linking the importation of South African coal to the potential loss of jobs in Alabama. Many miners believed that the coal shipments from South Africa represented only the beginning of a wave of low-cost imports. In this respect, the plight of the Birmingham District's iron ore miners loomed large. Concerns such as U.S. Steel had begun to import inexpensive ore from South America in the 1960s, a move that cost hundreds of red-ore miners their jobs. "When they shut down the ore mines and started bringing the ore in from South America, I was out in the cold," remembered Cliff Pierson. Like many other ore miners, however, Pierson soon found employment in the booming coal industry.[57]

Littlefield, District 20's president, told national UMWA officials that miners worried that the South African coal imports would have the same results as the previous decade's iron ore imports from South America. "These red ore miners were advised that the brown ore from South America was being brought in a small amount to blend with the red ore and their jobs would not be affected," Littlefield wrote to Joseph A. Yablonski Jr., the UMWA's general counsel as well as the son of the murdered reformer. "With a short period of time, all red ore mines were closed due to the importation of the ore from South America and today there is not the first red ore miner working. Hundreds of these men were forced out of work in their late forties and early fifties, and have not been employed since."[58]

The miners argued that Southern had access to billions of tons of low-sulfur coal in Alabama and other domestic coalfields. The U.S. Bureau of Mines indicated that Alabama contained 2 billion tons of deep, low-sulfur coal and an additional 33 million tons that could be strip mined. Coalfields in the eastern United States had almost 16 billion tons of deep, low-sulfur coal and about 724 million tons of low-sulfur coal suitable for strip mines.

The miners also criticized the Southern Company for its failure to install scrubbers on its Crist Steam Plant Unit 7, one of the plants designated to receive the South African coal. The UMWA charged that scrubbers and other modern pollution technology would have allowed the company to burn medium-sulfur coal and remain in compliance with Florida emissions requirements. When the company claimed that such advanced equipment did not exist, the UMWA pointed out that utilities in other parts of the country had installed similar technology.[59]

Like their national leaders, Alabama UMWA members criticized Southern for the coal purchase on the grounds that the South African miners worked in slave-like conditions under the country's apartheid system. "Slavery in the South went out a long time ago. We don't believe in slavery," said Howard Tedford, a miner from Adger. "Slave labor in Africa is real cheap and it's my information that this coal is produced under slave labor conditions. We no longer have this any more and we are strictly against slavery. We don't want any coal coming in to this country that's got blood on it. The information we got is that the safety conditions in South Africa for the miners is real bad. If it's worked under slave labor, then you know it's as bad as you can get." Added Joe Cruce of Brookwood, "The miners in South Africa work under slave conditions for $3 a day. They are black miners. No blacks are allowed to hold supervisory positions. Of course South Africa has laws on which makes it impossible for a black man in South Africa to hold any high position."[60]

Meanwhile, Vogtle and other Southern Company officials publicly maintained that they undertook South African imports only to comply with sulfur emission regulations. Privately, however, company officials suggested another motive: reining in militant miners in the wake of the reformers' victory. Alabama coal mines, like those across the nation, had seen wildcat strikes in the 1960s and early 1970s. Despite their lack of support for union reform, Alabama miners often used unauthorized walkouts to contest violations of national contracts or to protest unsafe conditions. Southern officials had this in mind when they claimed that production in Alabama had "been insufficient to meet the company's needs. The company had to go out-of-state to buy coal to make up the difference." The company stated that the "best way to ensure that Alabama Power will not find it necessary in the future to buy foreign coal is to maintain high production in American mines, especially those in Alabama. When Alabama miners do not work, production losses inevitably occur. The only way Alabama Power can make up the difference is to buy coal in areas where miners are working."[61] The newly globalized industry provided Alabama coal producers and utilities with the means to enforce labor discipline in their mining workforce by threatening to import coal.

The campaign against the South African coal continued in the wake of the shareholder protest and the May wildcat strike. District 20 leaders lobbied Alabama officials, including Governor George Wallace, to help in stopping the imports from coming through the state docks in Mobile. About a month earlier, the Alabama UMWA had endorsed Wallace in his reelection campaign, so District 20 leaders likely believed that they had the governor's sympathies. Wallace, however, avoided direct involvement in the dispute.

Other political leaders proved more accommodating. Attorney General Baxley, whose environmental policies Littlefield had sharply criticized, became a valuable ally to the miners' cause. During the summer of 1974, Baxley announced that he had dedicated several members of his staff to investigate the import issue. These investigators were vaguely charged with determining "the legal steps necessary" to keep the Southern Company from breaking the law.[62]

National UMWA leaders also appealed to federal officials for help. Miller asked the U.S. commissioner of customs to issue an administrative order preventing the unloading of the imported coal until an investigation determined the legality of the transaction. The UMWA argued that the coal imports violated an old federal statute that prohibited companies from bringing in materials produced by "indentured labor under penal sanction." The Lawyers' Committee for Civil Rights under Law joined the UMWA in a formal complaint to federal officials. Baxley also signed on to the customs commissioner protest, providing a boost to the UMWA. The Alabama attorney general said that the importation of South African coal was "clearly the kind of situation which is covered by the statute. Only because of this cheap forced labor was South Africa able to sell the coal at a price low enough to enable it to be shipped 9,000 miles to the United States and offered competitively with domestic coal, including that mined in Alabama."[63]

The coal boycott gained national attention. In New York City, protesters from the Center for United Labor Action set up pickets at the Southern Company's offices on Wall Street. The demonstrators included machinists, transport workers, telephone operators, waitresses, and cab drivers. Picketers held banners and signs, some of them reading "SOUTHERN CO.—WALL ST. BANKS—HANDS OFF

U.S. & S. AFRICAN MINERS!" and "ALABAMA & SOUTH AFRICAN MIN-
ERS UNITED AGAINST COAL COMPANIES!"[64]

Because Southern planned to bring the coal through the Alabama State Docks,
District 20 officials also began a campaign to enlist the support of Mobile's longshoremen. The UMWA initially appealed to the dock workers' notions of union
solidarity. "The longshoremen's union will not unload anything in the docks of
Mobile that has a legitimate boycott against it," said Leon Alexander, a miner from
Bessemer. "They have been fined for refusing to unload things. We know that if
we boycott that coal, the longshoremen will back us." Added Earl Askew, "I've got
no doubt at all that the longshoremen are good union men. They'll support us all
the way."[65]

But union solidarity went only so far in the global economy. Members of the
International Longshoremen's Association (ILA) in Mobile were not interested in
a purely protectionist protest, because they spent much of their time loading coal
from Alabama onto ships for export to Japan and other countries. The reaction to
the unexpected arrival of a cargo of coal from Australia seemed to confirm these
reservations. The UMWA learned of the shipment shortly before it arrived on
16 August. Southern Company executives hoped to send the Australian coal to
an Alabama Power plant near Mobile. Between fifteen and twenty-four demonstrators arrived to picket the unloading of the Australian coal, but longshoremen
ignored the protest and took the cargo off the ship. The shipment caught the
UMWA members by surprise. District 20 officials had known about the South
African coal, but Baker later admitted that the Australian shipment "caught us
with our pants down. We did a hell of a lot of research on the South African
coal—how it is mined and so forth—but we don't really know anything about
the Australian coal."[66]

The Australian protests alienated the longshoremen, who remained suspicious
of the miners' true motivations. Many longshoremen doubted white miners' level
of genuine concern for the exploitation of black South Africans. At least some
Mobile ILA members believed that the District 20 miners used the issue to enlist
the longshoremen in a purely protectionist protest, a perception confirmed with
the demonstrations over the arrival of the Australian coal. The longshoremen
had plenty of reason to question the overall impact of the Australian coal imports
on the jobs of Alabama miners. As District 20 members protested the Australian
coal, an estimated six ships waited in the harbor to take Alabama coal for export
to other countries, mainly Japan.[67]

Littlefield's actions could not have created much support among longshoremen. The District 20 president publicly criticized Mobile ILA President Isom
Clemon for allowing dockworkers to cross UMWA pickets. If Clemon were a true

union leader, "he would have told those men not to cross miners' picket lines," Littlefield told demonstrators in Birmingham about a week after the Australian shipment arrived.[68]

Littlefield traveled to Mobile on 22 August and announced to the local press that he wanted to meet with Clemon. When the ILA local president ignored the offer, Littlefield publicly criticized him. "All of the citizens and civic groups, including law enforcement groups, have been very nice to us in Mobile," Littlefield said at a press conference. "Only the longshoremen have been uncooperative so far."[69]

The South African coal imports presented the ILA with a difficult dilemma. The union was contractually bound to unload the coal, and if it failed to honor its agreement, the shipping companies could give the business to nonunion workers or divert the shipments to another port. This situation likely accounted for the silence with which ILA officials greeted Littlefield's attempts to bully them into honoring UMWA pickets. Either way, Clemon avoided commenting publicly on the issue and declined Littlefield's invitations for meetings.

In addition, because the Alabama UMWA had become overwhelmingly white, the attack on Clemon and the ILA carried racial overtones that weakened support for the miners' cause. Clemon, an African American, was a highly respected union leader who had played an important role in Mobile during the civil rights era. One observer noted that the longshoremen suspected that Littlefield and the other white UMWA leaders were not committed to raising the issue of the oppression of black people "even within their union."[70] The UMWA's support for reactionary politicians such as Wallace, the decline of African Americans in the coalfields, and Littlefield's actions in Mobile only confirmed this impression.

Rank-and-file ILA members also had mixed reactions to the boycott issue because the UMWA relied so heavily on protectionist rhetoric. A key development, according to one account, in rallying support among the longshoremen came in early August, when they heard a plea for support from a member of the Zimbabwe African National Union, which was engaged in a war against the white minority government in Rhodesia. The group's North American representative, Tapson Mawere, spoke to more than two hundred longshoremen at the local hall and apparently convinced his audience of the coal industry's role in supporting the racist governments of South Africa and Rhodesia. The economic and racial connection resonated with the mainly African American dockworkers. After hearing Mawere speak, the ILA's Mobile members pledged to support a boycott of shipments of coal from either Rhodesia or South Africa.[71]

A few days later, Mawere spoke to UMWA leaders and members in Sumiton, a small Walker County community. Rank-and-file miners greeted the activist warmly when he conveyed the African liberation movements' appreciation for the solidarity displayed by Alabama miners. Their leaders, however, reportedly gave Mawere a "cool and unfriendly" welcome, despite his crucial efforts to convince the Mobile longshoremen to honor UMWA pickets. Indeed, the UMWA leaders went out of their way to distance themselves from Mawere and other activists. In Mobile, for example, Littlefield told the press that the miners' union had not "brought in outsiders to fight our battle. We've been accused of being affiliated with the left wing, but no member can belong to the Communist Party or he would be kicked out of the UMW."[72]

Despite the problems, the shaky coalition between miners and longshoremen held when the first cargo of South African coal arrived on 25 August. The shipment of between twenty-five and thirty thousand tons arrived at 5:00 p.m., and unloading started. A small number of UMWA pickets appeared at the main gates to the state docks soon after. The next shift of about seventy-five union dockworkers, who arrived an hour later, refused to work. The miners' pickets partially shut down the docks, and work stopped on most ships in the port. ILA leaders urged dock officials to allow the miners to picket at one end of the facility to allow longshoremen to resume work on the other ships. The following day, UMWA and dock officials reached such an agreement. Dock officials permitted two pickets to travel inside the port facility to the coal unloading area. The agreement allowed ILA members to unload the cargoes of other ships but kept the longshoremen away from the South African coal shipment.[73]

While union solidarity held in Mobile, the coalition between District 20 leaders and community activists showed signs of unraveling. Alabama UMWA officials reportedly engaged in "red baiting attacks" on members of the Coalition to Stop South African Coal, the umbrella group activists had formed to work with miners on the effort. A year later, Alabama UMWA official Frank Clements claimed that "communists" had tried to join the UMWA pickets in Mobile, but "I had them chased off."[74]

District 20 officials and the ILA then suffered a series of legal setbacks that crippled their involvement in the protest effort. The Southern Company found a potent ally in the National Labor Relations Board. The board's regional director, Walter Phillips, urged a federal judge to force the miners to stop further wildcat strikes against the South African coal imports. But he went further, asking the judge to ban the UMWA from picketing and protesting the shipments, arguing that the pickets violated federal labor law and constituted a "secondary" boycott. Judge J. Foy Guin Jr. agreed, and he ruled on 28 August that the UMWA had to remove its pickets and end its protests against the imports.[75]

The Mobile Steamship Association took the ILA to court in an attempt to force the dockworkers to unload the coal. A federal judge in Mobile sided with the industry group on 26 August and ordered ILA officials to put the longshoremen back to work. Judge W. B. Hand warned union leaders that they could face costly penalties if they did not convince their members to unload the South African coal. With few options left, ILA work gangs began to unload the coal.[76] With union solidarity collapsing under enormous pressure and federal officials ordering miners to end their protests, District 20 officials removed the last pickets.

The roadblocks from federal officials continued. The Commerce Department announced at the end of August that it had sided with the Southern Company. The agency said it believed that the South African imports represented a "stop-gap" measure and that the Southern Company planned to end them after domestic coal operators developed more low-sulfur coal mines. Months later, the UMWA and Baxley lost their legal appeal with the U.S. Customs Service. In siding with Southern, the customs agency ruled in February 1975 that low-sulfur coal "is not mined in sufficient quantities in the United States at the present time to meet the total present consumptive demands of the United States." Neither of these agencies seriously considered the conditions under which the coal was produced, preferring instead to support Southern's actions because they concluded—erroneously—that not enough low-sulfur coal was produced in the United States for the utility to supply its Florida power plants in a timely manner.[77]

Law enforcement agencies also helped the Southern Company defeat the boycott. The Birmingham Police Department, worried about the involvement of leftist groups in the protests, photographed demonstrators and infiltrated their protests. As the first coal shipment was about to arrive, Birmingham Police, Alabama Power security officials, and representatives from the Federal Bureau of Investigation met in early August to discuss the upcoming protests. "While there," Sergeant T. W. McDonald of the Birmingham police reported, "there was an exchange of information and identification of participants in recent demonstrations." The officials compiled a list of thirty people that included Georgia Power Project members and at least one former UMWA reform activist.[78]

Alabama UMWA members spent most of their energy later that fall in an industry-wide strike against the Bituminous Coal Operators' Association. The strike began on 12 November and ended on 5 December, when miners approved a new three-year agreement with the association. In the middle of national negotiations, a bandit shot and killed Littlefield when he walked in on a Washington, D.C., hotel robbery. Baker assumed the presidency of District 20. Restricted by federal courts and with sharp internal divisions, the miners played only a small role in the effort to stop South African coal imports after August 1974.[79]

With little direct UMWA involvement, the protest limped along with activists and community groups shouldering the burden. Protests would continue at Southern Company shareholder meetings throughout the remainder of the decade and into the 1980s. Southern received its final shipment from Mannessman sometime in 1976 and then announced that it had signed an even longer contract to import more coal from South African producers.[80]

The protest against the Southern Company's imports from South Africa revealed much about the UMWA's difficulties as the coal industry globalized. Reformers' failure to gain much support and the decline of African American miners left the union controlled by leaders narrowly focused on keeping the number of jobs high. Though the coal industry expanded and thousands of miners found jobs, the rise of strip mining often placed miners and their union in opposition to coal communities in the Birmingham District. At the same time, the growth in exports helped to fuel the increase in coal employment but left District 20 miners vulnerable to imports. Federal government agencies and law enforcement sided squarely with the Southern Company and global capital against the UMWA, and the union-activist coalition remained relatively weak because District 20's leaders could not forge the connections necessary to confront such power.

For the next few years, Alabama miners engaged in internal disputes that divided the union's leaders and rank-and-file militants. A series of wildcat strikes during the summers of 1975, 1976, and 1977 played a significant role in dislodging Baker from the district presidency. The strikes constituted demonstrations of solidarity between Birmingham District miners and union members in other parts of the nation, harkening back to the New Deal and World War II years. Most of these strikes began in West Virginia, where coal companies attempted to use federal injunctions to compel local unions to end wildcat strikes, and spread to other coalfields. These disputes illustrated problems with the 1974 national contract, which allowed companies to delay processing grievances. The difficulties with the grievance procedure had wide resonance with working miners across the country. Miners believed the attempts by coal companies to use federal courts to force them back in the mines constituted an attack on their right to strike over working conditions and unfair company policies.

These massive wildcat strikes, therefore, drew on miners' powerful notions of solidarity. Ernest Walker of Jasper remembered years later that such disputes arose when the company wanted "to fire that one man off his job. He ain't violating no rule or no law or anything like that. The company, they just don't like him. They don't like the way he looks or they don't like his color or something, and the company will be discriminating. . . . Then the whole mine will strike for that one man. There ain't but one man involved. But that whole mine will strike, and they will call a nationwide strike off of one [man]. It would spread, keep on spreading, then spread nationwide."[81] The significance of these protests was lost on national UMWA leaders, union staff members, and particularly on District 20 leaders.

The first of these unauthorized strikes occurred in August 1975, when almost seven thousand Alabama miners went on strike in support of their West Virginia brethren. District 20 officials quickly denounced the walkout, while the coal companies went to federal court to obtain injunctions to force the miners back to work. Clements, District 20's IEB representative, formerly an ally of the reform movement, illustrated the growing gulf between rank-and-file miners and union leaders when he blamed the strikes on "left-leaning" agitators and claimed that the Birmingham District's miners "don't know what they're striking about." Clements accused "left wing" unionists from West Virginia of "trying to destroy the union." The miners in Alabama returned to work on 3 September, but only after the West Virginians had begun to end their protest.[82]

Out-of-state pickets provoked Alabama miners to walk out again during the following summer. This strike, which idled more than ten thousand Alabama miners, also grew out of a West Virginia dispute that spread to surrounding coalfields. At the height of the strike, ninety thousand of the nation's miners walked out to protest what they believed was federal judges' unfair use of court injunctions against the union. District 20 leaders tried to convince miners to return to work at a meeting at the Birmingham Municipal Auditorium, but union members remained openly defiant. "We're not going back to work," some shouted. "When West Virginia gets their jobs back we'll go back," others cried out. A day later, the West Virginia miners began to return to work, followed by the Alabamians.[83]

A combination of factors provoked a walkout by Alabama miners in the summer of 1977. A divisive national union election and cutbacks to UMWA Welfare and Retirement Fund benefits caused West Virginia miners to strike. When out-of-state pickets appeared at many operations in Alabama, miners in that state also refused to work. Baker attacked the picketers as members of "subversive" groups. "We are doing everything we possibly can to discourage picketing because we do not have a labor dispute here," Baker said. "At the present time we have stranger pickets from West Virginia visiting our mine sites, but we are confident our people are going to work if there are no pickets at their mine site." But when the West Virginia miners left, Alabama miners stayed out. Baker attacked the protesting miners as "a group of people who just don't want to work." Clements joined in the attacks, calling the strikers dupes of "radical fringe" groups. The miners began to return to their jobs only after leaders convened a districtwide meeting at the Walker County Vocational School at which the miners voted to end the walkout.[84]

A few months later, Baker found himself in a difficult reelection fight against Charles Fuller, a longtime UMWA activist with strong backing from the rank and file. In February 1975, Alabama miners had elected Baker to finish out the remainder of Littlefield's term as District 20 president. Baker's victory, however, was not a vote of confidence in his leadership. Instead, the UMWA bureaucrat, who had never worked as a miner, benefited from a split within the miners' ranks. Fuller and African American district representative Earl Brown also sought the District 20 presidency, and they divided Baker's opponents.[85]

No such divisions existed in 1977. Fuller, a former Boyle supporter, also had strong ties with reformers, having run on their ticket in the 1973 elections against Littlefield. Fuller easily defeated Baker in the 1977 election, receiving 5,099 votes to Baker's 1,932.[86] The ascension of Charles Fuller, a moderate who had risen through the ranks, in many ways represented the crest of the democratic reforms of the 1970s in District 20.

Miners needed Fuller's evenhanded leadership. The national strike that began in December 1977 and lasted until the spring of 1978 was among the longest in the union's history. The UMWA confronted operators who were unified in their demands to roll back union militancy and force health care concessions. The strike provoked a number of violent clashes between unionists and state police as miners fanned out across the state in an attempt to shut down nonunion strip mines. Governor Wallace, in the last year of a term and unable to succeed himself, broke with the UMWA and sided with Alabama's nonunion coal operators. He ordered the state troopers to keep the mines open—particularly those located in northeast Alabama, along the Plateau Field—placing the police in direct conflict with union miners who were determined to shut down these operations and strengthen the national UMWA's bargaining position.[87]

The walkout began when the UMWA's national contract expired. Most of Alabama's nonunion coal operations shut down rather than face UMWA protests, but a few remained open in the northeastern part of the state. The clashes with state police began after a roving picket of eight hundred miners left Birmingham in an attempt to shut down several strip mines. When nonunion miners and managers refused to stop work, violence broke out. UMWA members set fire to tires and fought with nonunion miners at a Sand Mountain Minerals mine in Pisgah, then slashed tires and broke vehicle windshields at the Fabius operation nearby. In the wake of these incidents, state troopers warned nonunion miners to stay away from work.[88]

Alabama's nonunion operators, angered by these events, met with Wallace and state police representatives. The governor, in a surprising reversal of his earlier support for the UMWA, ordered the police to keep the mines open. The state troopers assembled four elite platoons of officers and helicopters to comply with the governor's wishes. Officers began surveilling militant unionists and their leaders. Believing they had the governor's support, the nonunion coal operators in northeastern Alabama announced plans to reopen their operations in early January.[89]

When a large roving picket of hundreds of miners left Walker County at the end of the month, the state police were waiting for them. Alerted by an undercover agent, officials followed the procession with a helicopter. As the miners wound their way toward Mentone, a platoon of heavily armed police met them. Clashes erupted when the miners refused to disperse. Troopers pulled some of the miners from their vehicles, damaged their automobiles, ordered others around at gunpoint, and shot tear gas at them. State police arrested between thirty and fifty miners and confiscated firearms and knives. The miners failed to shut down any mines in the area.[90]

The incident angered the UMWA's leaders. Fuller and other District 20 officials met with the governor in Montgomery and complained about the police tactics, accusing Wallace of "declaring war" on the miners' union. Wallace told the miners that he had received information that the nonunion operators had placed land mines along roads leading to their operations and had stationed snipers in the woods. The state police had the best interests of the miners in mind when they stopped the caravan, the governor explained to District 20 officials. Fuller remembered that Wallace told union leaders "that he didn't want to see anybody in his shape—and he pointed, you know, as to him paralyzed, sitting in the wheelchair—that he didn't want to see anybody in that shape, and that was the purpose of the highway patrolmen, to keep from having such as that to happen."[91]

The meeting calmed the atmosphere for a few days. But miners and troopers clashed again outside a Drummond Coal mine in the Winston County community of Natural Bridge. The incident began when miners stopped a convoy of trucks carrying coal for Madison County schools. The miners forced the trucks to dump their cargoes on the road outside the mine's entrance. About two hundred UMWA miners eventually gathered at the mine. When a platoon of fifty state troopers arrived, they met a barrage of rocks and fire from pellet guns. A few troopers received minor injuries, and miners damaged several patrol cars.[92]

Miners and troopers engaged in their largest confrontation during the night and early morning hours of 2–3 February outside Oakman Mining's strip mine in Walker County. Miners suspected that company owner Claude Prater planned to resume mining coal, and after an altercation between nonunion miners and UMWA members, unionists surrounded the operation and refused to let those inside leave. Troopers and miners clashed as officers attempted to escort Prater and his men out of the mine. Both sides fired shots, and troopers believed that at least two sticks of dynamite were thrown at them. The troopers eventually moved the miners out of the way, and the strip miners were evacuated.[93]

Though direct confrontations between miners and state troopers declined after the Oakman skirmish, the strike continued until the end of March. The operators ultimately gained major concessions from the contract that miners had ratified in 1978. The companies retained the ability to discipline miners who engaged in wildcat strikes and won the right to cover working miners under company medical plans, leaving only retired miners covered by the UMWA fund.[94]

While the 1977–78 coal strike marked the end of rank-and-file activism among men in the Alabama coalfields, women were still in the early stages of their fight to claim mining jobs both in the Birmingham District and nationwide. Throughout the decade, women challenged the male monopoly on mining jobs, drawing on both rank-and-file activism and legislation that grew out of the civil rights movement to push for a chance at the pay and benefits that coal mining employment offered. They also confronted a male-dominated world in the mines and in the UMWA. Women developed tactics for dealing with the harassment they experienced as they struggled to keep their jobs.

Though coal mining had traditionally been a male-oriented industry, women always worked in limited roles. Male miners developed a blend of superstitions, customs, and legal restrictions, however, to keep women from widespread employment in the mines. Despite brief gains made during labor shortages during World War I, many states had laws preventing women from working underground. Female miners also historically faced strong opposition from the UMWA, which sought to make mining a male-only occupation. In Alabama, for example, the miners' union played an important role in the effort to prevent women from working in the mines. Mining reform legislation passed in 1935, during the administration of Governor Bibb Graves, included provisions forbidding women "of any age" from working "in or about any coal mine in this State." District 20 President William Mitch cabled his strong approval of the reform package to the prolabor Graves, urging the governor to "recommend in your message to the legislature the passage of this needed coal mining legislation."[95]

Despite the prohibitions against employing women underground, periodic labor shortages in Alabama and elsewhere allowed a few women to work in the industry. Many women evaded restrictions against working underground by taking jobs on the surface, mostly at small family-run operations that sprang up at the end of the 1930s and into the 1940s. These women typically worked alongside their husbands, brothers, and fathers. In 1930, only 9 women worked in the Birmingham District's coal mines; a decade later, that number had grown to 93, and by 1950, officials estimated that 164 women worked in the industry. Female miners' small gains subsequently were erased as the coalfield depression eliminated thousands of jobs.[96]

The surge in demand for coal and the resurgence of the industry in the early 1970s ushered in new opportunities for women. Federal discrimination cases filed by black workers against the country's major steel producers resulted in a series of consent decrees in which the steel companies agreed to hire greater numbers of minorities as well as women. Because many of these steel producers owned coal subsidiaries, women began finding jobs as miners in coalfields by the end of 1973.

Coal companies nevertheless employed few women. By 1977, women made up only about 3 percent of the new miners hired. That year, Tennessee activists formed the Coal Employment Project (CEP). In 1978, the organization filed a massive sexual discrimination complaint against the country's largest coal operators with the Office of Federal Contract Compliance Programs. Within six months of the CEP's legal action, major coal producers began to settle. They paid thousands of dollars in back wages to women they had failed to hire and agreed to increase female employment levels until women made up 30 percent of the coal workforce. By 1979 almost three thousand women worked in the nation's mines.[97]

Alabama's women began to find jobs in the mines in 1975, when Alabama By-Products hired six women to work at its huge SEGCO No. 1 mine in Parrish. Among the first to cross the portal was Betty Jones. Jones, whose father had worked in the mines, told a journalist that she took the job "because I have three children to feed, didn't have a job because the plant where I worked cut back on its work force, and because the money in mining is good." Many of the men resented her presence underground. "Some of them wouldn't talk to us, then some of them did," she remembered more than two decades later. "Some of them were real rude and said ugly things, but you just have to ignore it."[98]

Like Jones, Mary Ellis had other miners in her family. She was working as a division manager at Sears when she drove her cousin to apply for a job at a U.S. Steel mine in 1976. "The place was just full of men—naturally no women—and some of them started bugging me to put in my application," she remembered. Ellis eventually worked at the same mine that had employed her father, and she enjoyed support from miners who remembered him. She paired up with another woman, Martha Foster, who "helped me more than I can say. She wasn't afraid to talk back. Before long, nobody saw one of us without the other."[99]

Men commonly threatened women as they went underground for the first time. Sadie Jones, a single mother with five children, claimed that male miners threatened her with both guns and knives. Soon after she took her job in the mid-1970s, she began carrying a knife with her when her shift began, and she made sure that the men she worked with knew about it. "I said, 'When you start cutting on me, I'll start cutting on you. I don't play—I came down here to work. I know I'm invading a man's world. But I came here to work.' "[100]

Coal mining was heavily mechanized by the mid-1970s, but much of the routine work required a great deal of physical exertion, from shoveling spilled coal and pulling long cables to lifting heavy bags of rock dust and hanging large curtains. Managers initially hired women who had experience in manufacturing industries, like Jones, and were used to the heavy labor. Elizabeth Laird, hired in 1976 when she was fifty-four years old, found work underground easier than her job as a spinner in a textile mill. Mill work "was the hardest work I've ever done," said Laird, who had worked in mills since 1941. "Face ventilation is the easiest job I ever done, and it's the hardest work in the mines."[101]

Laird initially took a mining job to support her three children, one of whom had been paralyzed in an automobile accident. Her marriage had broken up in the early 1970s, and her husband's child support payments were not enough for the family to make ends meet, forcing her to work two jobs. "The mines was the only place where I could work one job and have time with my youngest son, and make him a living and send him to school," she recalled.[102]

The operators tried to limit the number of women who worked in their mines. Two years after the first women found jobs underground at SEGCO, as employment in the coal industry soared, officials estimated that only forty women were among the more than nine thousand workers in Alabama's coal mines.[103]

Birmingham District women concerned about the lack of access to these good-paying jobs joined together and formed the Association of Women in Industry (AWI) in the spring of 1978 after they completed coal mining training classes but could not find jobs. The AWI focused on helping women find jobs in Birmingham's heavy industries—coal mines, steel mills, and foundries. To help build an organization, the group held regular meetings and began to circulate a newsletter. "We try to give support and encouragement to each other through social activities and mutual assistance," an early edition of the AWI newsletter proclaimed. "Together we can fight job discrimination, for equal rights on the job and for better conditions for everyone, both men and women."[104]

The AWI used direct action to achieve its goals. Activists carried carloads of women to mines to apply for jobs, then returned later to check on the status of their applications. LaMarse Moore encountered the women outside a mine office where she had applied for a job. Impressed with their strategy, Moore joined the organization and accompanied the women on the trips to the mines. "We pushed. We fought. We didn't back down. We really fought for it, to get into the mine," she remembered. "We didn't just go and fill out applications to get in the mines. We really fought for it."[105]

In many ways, Moore typified the women who sought work in the mines. She had recently returned to the state to help take care of ailing relatives after living for more than twenty years in Chicago. Moore held a series of low-paying jobs in an attempt to support her two children. "It was so funny," she remembered years later. "I worked in a restaurant about a month. I couldn't deal with it. That wasn't me. And I sold Avon as a means of support." Moore hoped for a job that offered her status, independence, and decent pay. In Chicago, she had worked as a radio dispatcher for a cab company, as a machine operator in a factory, and at a laundry. Shortly before deciding to return to Edgewater, the coal mining community outside Birmingham where she had grown up, Moore had hoped to begin a career as a truck driver. So when Moore heard about coal companies hiring female miners, she quickly applied for work underground. "The benefits— the money in that day, you know in 1978, for a black person—especially a black woman . . . that was good money," she recalled. "And then you think about the benefits, because I had kids, you know."[106]

Moore and other African American women played an important role in the AWI. The group's leaders worked hard to bring black and white women together, and the organization in many ways faced challenges similar to those that Alabama's coalfield activists had faced in attempting to bring back the UMWA during the 1930s. At a fall 1978 meeting with AWI members, national activists noted both the organization's interracial composition and the fact that the black and white women seemed unaccustomed to working together. "It seemed that occasionally I could sense some tension between the black and white women—but I think this was due more to unfamiliarity than to hostility," commented CEP activist Connie White. "For black women and white women to show up at the same mine, applying for jobs together is really a great thing." Despite the difficulty of crossing the color line, CEP staff estimated that the AWI's membership, like the UMWA several generations earlier, was evenly divided between black and white women.[107]

Early in its existence, the AWI took a strong stand for racial equality, sending letters in August 1978 to the Birmingham City Council, Mayor David Vann, and the *Birmingham News* criticizing city officials for allowing the Ku Klux Klan to use the local civic center for a rally. Klan members, AWI officials wrote, "oppose equal rights for women, and try to keep blacks and whites divided. The Klan's attitudes and activities hold all of us back, as many of us can see by the actions of the Klansmen in our workplaces."[108]

Alabama activists pushed the CEP to call a national conference in 1979 to highlight the challenges that women faced in the mines and to forge alliances between women in mining and other heavy industries. AWI members linked their challenges to the civil rights struggles of the 1960s, noting that the potential opportunities women had in the mines were a part "of the broad movement toward equal rights for all citizens." Here as well, racial concerns remained central, with AWI activists pushing to address the "absolute necessity" of building alliances between white and black women in the mines.[109]

AWI members also drew on another legacy of the black freedom movement when they used civil rights laws to take legal action against Alabama coal operators when the trips to mine sites failed to garner many jobs. The women sought relief through the Equal Employment Opportunity Commission and the Office of Federal Contract Compliance Programs. In her complaint, Jennifer Gunn, one of the AWI's founders, stated her belief that since she had applied at U.S. Steel's Concord Mine in the spring of 1978, the company had hired twenty-three "inexperienced" men. When Gunn called to inquire about the status of her application, she was told "that applications are only good for three months and that I would have to submit a new application the next time they were taken." In late January 1979, U.S. Steel finally agreed to hire Gunn as a general inside laborer.[110]

In February 1979, the AWI filed sex discrimination complaints against U.S. Steel, Alabama By-Products, Mead, and Jim Walter Resources. The AWI charged that all of the companies, which had federal contracts, had records of "blatant discrimination against women in their hiring practices for jobs in coal mines." Most Alabama operators eliminated women from their applicant pools by relying on word of mouth to fill mine vacancies. The AWI activists hoped to force the companies to end such discriminatory hiring practices, requiring the operators to advertise their entry-level openings. They hoped to compel the companies to establish goals and timetables for employing women "that will guarantee that there be full equality for women in all employment practices." They also wanted back pay for women who had not been hired.[111]

The legal strategy worked, and most of the coal producers agreed to settle and begin hiring women and advertising their openings. The companies agreed to use "good faith" to increase the number of women in their operations. Attorney David Gespass, who represented the AWI activists, was particularly enthusiastic about settlements the organization obtained from Mead and Jim Walter, which emphasized the "class-wide nature of the discrimination" against the women. The publicity and the concessions from the companies, he hoped, would increase the "applicant flow from women at those mines." By the end of 1980, federal census records indicated that 815 of Alabama's 12,790 coal miners were women, including 108 African American women.[112]

The jobs underground provided women with wages and benefits that made a profound difference in their lives. Pearlie Gray, a hospital worker who made two hundred dollars a week and lived in public housing, found a job as an inside laborer at a Jim Walter Resources mine in 1979. She saw her pay triple and moved her family into a Birmingham subdivision. "No more government projects. No more food stamps," she said. "When I got the job in the mine, I was able to afford things that I only dreamed of before." Lula Peterson of Bessemer earned even less from her jobs at a laundry and a cleaning service before she found work at a coal mine in 1979. Peterson went to work in the mines for her children: "I wanted them to go to college and stuff. I was thinking about that."[113]

Life underground proved dangerous for women in different ways than it was for men. Incidents in the summer and fall of 1979 provided women miners in Alabama with a dramatic illustration of the potential for violence as they crossed into a male-dominated world. Several women at Jim Walter Resources' No. 4 mine in Tuscaloosa County reported a series of attempts by company officials and male miners to intimidate and harass the women after they distributed copies of a socialist newspaper at the mine site. The newspaper, *The Militant*, contained a report about alleged safety violations at the mine. In response, male miners set the women's automobiles on fire, stole their purses, and "made threats" on their lives. The miners, Sara Jean Johnston, Geraldine Lattimore, and Ellen Bobroff, found themselves assigned to work in "isolated" parts of the mine. On 31 August, a group of about fifteen male miners attempted to prevent the women from leaving the mine. The women subsequently refused to return to work and filed charges against the company with the National Labor Relations Board. "We want to return to our jobs, but we will go back only if they guarantee our safety," Johnston said.[114]

Women miners more commonly endured harassment in the form of lewd language, jokes, and pranks. Patricia Brown reported numerous incidents of verbal and physical intimidation. At one point, a miner on another shift began to draw obscene pictures of Brown for her and other members of her shift to find when they arrived at work. "The first time I saw it, I felt terrible," Brown said. "I cried all night about it. I cried and cried."[115]

Like African American miners facing job losses decades earlier, Brown and other women developed ways of dealing with such harassment. Brown put on an "act" when she went to work. "One thing about coal mining. You can't go into coal mining and just be yourself," Brown said. "You have to always put on an act. Like for me, it's this tough act. . . . If someone punches me, I punch them back." Brown made sure her coworkers knew they could not physically harass her. "Whatever you start with them, you're going to have to continue for all your coal mining time," she said. "So they know down there not to touch. . . . I don't want them feeling on me."[116]

Moore also confronted managers and coworkers who tried to harass her. Once, while riding the elevator to the surface after her shift, she overheard a male miner challenge another man to place his hands on her. Moore turned to the two men and said, "If you do, you are through for this world, because I will cut your neck off and tap dance on your liver." The assertiveness had its intended effect. By the time the miners reached the surface, Moore found herself alone in the front of the elevator. "For about two weeks after that, when we would get on the elevator," she recalled, "they would just leave me by myself and they would all go to the back."[117]

Women nevertheless remained vulnerable in the male-dominated underground world. In the spring of 1981, the CEP released a study in which more than half the women miners surveyed reported that managers had propositioned them, while 76 percent of the respondents reported that male miners had harassed them. More than a third of the women said they received more difficult and dangerous work assignments than male miners. Most shockingly, 17 percent of the women surveyed said that they had been physically assaulted at work.[118]

For black women, racism also remained a tremendous problem. Many African American women believed that they received more difficult work assignments than white women or white men and suspected that the Ku Klux Klan had a presence among white workers and managers. Brown worked with one alleged member of the organization. "He's friendly toward me. We get along fine on the section. He don't seem to show any prejudice," she said. "I told him one night, 'I hope you don't sic your boys on me, because half a dozen of them would be killed.' I'd put my .357 on them. I do have a gun. I carry a gun with me all the time." African American women were not the only miners who believed the Klan had a presence underground. White miner Charlene Griggs told an interviewer that a fellow miner once asked her to join the organization, an offer she refused. "The KKK is still around here, but they're quiet," she said. "It's no telling how many we've got at the mines. They're not really open about it."[119]

The UMWA's record with women miners proved mixed. Though many female miners came from the coal communities of the Birmingham District and had relatives who were union supporters and members, the UMWA earned a general reputation for not supporting its women members in Alabama. When Moore filed a grievance against Jim Walter Resources, for example, she suspected that her union representative collaborated with the company. "In front of them it was one thing, and behind your back it was another thing," she said. Brown rarely filed grievances with her local if she felt mistreated at work because she worried that she might be branded a troublemaker by both the union and the company.[120]

An illustration of the miners' union's lackluster response to its new members came when representatives from the CEP traveled to meet with women activists in Alabama in the fall of 1978. The national group had scheduled a meeting with Clements, Alabama's representative on the union's IEB. Clements, one of District 20's most active reformers only a few years earlier, missed the meeting. Other union officers, including Dwight Cagle, vice president of a UMWA local, were more supportive. Though Cagle admitted that adjusting to women in the mines was "a little rough at first," he believed that women had the right to work in coal mines.[121]

Griggs's situation illustrated the type of difficulty women faced in dealing with UMWA members, some of whom were her own family members. After she started working in the mines, an uncle who was a miner made his objections to her chosen career known at a family reunion. "He walked by me and he said, 'Charlie, you could make yourself a living without getting a job like that. You were doing just fine as you was,'" Griggs remembered. But her father and other members of her family, many of them union activists, supported her. Griggs's father "has always been proud" of her mining career, she told an interviewer, and early on he "would give me advice, tell me to take it easy, and not to push it."[122]

Women made impressive gains in the mines despite the opposition they encountered and the UMWA's lackluster support for their cause. The most serious crisis they faced, however, came when the employment boom that underpinned their efforts began to fade. In the early 1980s, the coal industry entered a steep employment depression from which it has not recovered. Most women hired in the 1970s lost their jobs in the ensuing decade as demand for coal began to drop. The number of miners plummeted dramatically during the early part of the 1980s, from more than 13,000 at the start of the decade to 7,628 in 1983. By the end of the 1980s, Alabama had only 6,304 miners.[123] The global environment became an even greater threat during the 1990s, as imports began to flood into the Birmingham District from mines in the western United States and Colombia.

Alabama miners confronted challenges on many different fronts in the 1960s and 1970s. African Americans continued to suffer from the legacy of discrimination as the region's industrial economy limped along. Despite an increase in mining employment, coal communities featured shocking poverty and declining populations, in many ways mirroring the problems that Birmingham faced. The growth of strip mining made conditions worse for the small coal towns, sometimes pitting miners and the UMWA against these struggling communities. However, successes also occurred. Women, a new force in the Birmingham District, drew on old traditions of rank-and-file activism, combined with new legal avenues that grew out of the civil rights movement, to enter the mines in large numbers for the first time.

Though Alabama coal miners enjoyed an increase in employment during the 1970s, the growth of the export business had hidden costs, as the case of Southern Company's imports from South Africa illustrated. The failure to stop the imports represented a turning point for the UMWA in Alabama. The costs of global markets would grow as coal imports began to flood into the Birmingham District. Coal production would begin to decline and unemployment again became part of everyday life for Alabama miners.

CHAPTER SEVEN

The Era of Global Competition, 1980–2003

Hard times had returned to the Alabama coalfields at the twentieth century's close. In the 1980s and 1990s, most Alabama miners lost their jobs or retired as demand slackened and coal poured in from outside the state. In the 1990s, the stream of imports turned into a flood, as millions of tons of coal flowed into the region from mines in western states and other countries. State figures told the depressing story. Only 3,043 miners worked in the Alabama coalfields in 2001, down from around 13,000 two decades earlier. Production dropped from a high of more than twenty-eight million tons in 1990 to just over nineteen million tons a decade later.[1] The failure to stop imports from South Africa in the early 1970s loomed large over the Birmingham District's coalfields as the new millennium dawned.

Much of the decline in Alabama's production and the rise in foreign imports could be traced to Drummond Coal, which had become the Birmingham District's largest and most influential coal producer during the 1970s. In the late 1980s, Drummond began to invest overseas, opening a huge surface mine in Colombia the following decade. By the late 1990s, the Pribbenow mine produced millions of tons of coal per year, and it began to flood the southeastern United States, capturing markets that had previously been supplied by Birmingham District coal. At the same time,

Drummond had closed most of Alabama operations, laying off more than fifteen hundred miners. Only the company's high-tech Shoal Creek mine, on the border of Jefferson and Tuscaloosa Counties, which produced 3.9 million tons of coal per year and employed about 650 people, remained active. By contrast, the company's massive Colombian operation produced an estimated 16 million tons of coal a year and employed more than 1,000 miners. In 2003, Drummond announced that it had purchased additional coal reserves in Colombia and hoped to double its production.[2]

Few Birmingham District miners expected the Alabama industry's downward trend to reverse in their lifetimes. When they lost jobs as mines shut down, many miners realized that their mining careers were over and either retired or looked for other employment. "You don't have to be no damn Birmingham psychologist to know that the Alabama coal miner is dying," miner Bill Rutherford proclaimed.[3]

The decline of the state's coal industry also had profound ramifications for safety. Alabama's underground mines, which contained high levels of explosive methane gas, were among the country's most dangerous operations. The national United Mine Workers of America (UMWA), local safety committees, and federal officials warned about the potential for disaster for years. In the mid-1990s, for example, the federal Mine Safety and Health Administration (MSHA) listed seven Alabama mines among the ten most dangerous in the country. Four were operated by Jim Walter Resources, two belonged to Drummond, and one was run by U.S. Steel. Many of these warnings went unheeded, with tragic results. In the fall of 2001, a pair of explosions at Jim Walter Resources' Blue Creek No. 5 mine in Brookwood—one of the mines consistently cited by federal regulators and the UMWA as unsafe—killed thirteen miners.[4]

Miners at the close of the twentieth century found themselves caught up in a system of capital mobility that allowed coal companies and consumers to look outside the region and country to satisfy their demands. The coal industry had transcended the boundaries of geology and geography that it had begun to test with the South African and Australian imports in the early 1970s. Drummond's Colombian adventures represented a new phase in the increasingly globalized world of coal production. Such capital mobility is not new, as the work of historian Jefferson Cowie has demonstrated, but it has accelerated as national economies have become increasingly integrated.[5] The declines in production and employment that resulted from the globalization of the Alabama coal industry in the 1980s and 1990s took a toll on working conditions and most importantly on safety standards. The explosions that tore through the No. 5 mine in many ways reflected the pressures generated from another era of economic decline in the Alabama coalfields.

(((

Mining employment in Alabama continued to grow until 1980, then began to drop dramatically. Initially, most of the job losses came at the state's strip mines, where employment dropped by almost half—from 5,451 miners in 1980 to 2,604 in 1985. Strip mining production declined from 16.8 million tons in 1980 to 13 million in 1985. But by the middle of the decade, the job losses had hit the underground mines as well. Between 1980 and 1985 the number of miners working underground in Alabama dropped from 7,284 to 6,100. Though employment in underground mines declined, production increased from 9.2 million tons in 1980 to 13.6 million tons five years later.[6]

Small strip miners traced their problems to a host of different sources. Some blamed their decline on new environmental regulations. Laws passed in the 1970s required strip miners to partially reclaim the land they disturbed. The additional costs and a dramatic rise in interest rates made it harder for many small mining companies to stay in business. Smaller mines also found themselves competing with larger operations owned by companies such as Drummond. These mines featured huge draglines and produced massive amounts of coal. The price tag for these machines approached forty million dollars each, well beyond the means of small operators, but using such equipment allowed the large companies to mine coal more cheaply than their smaller competitors.[7]

International and national economic trends also played a role. Strip miners blamed many of their woes on a drop in international oil prices in the early 1980s, which made coal a less attractive source of energy. The national recession during these years added to the problems.[8]

Even without a general economic slowdown, Alabama's small coal companies would have faced hard times. The coal-purchasing policies of Alabama Power, which alone consumed more than half of the state's coal, favored bigger operators. In the 1970s, the utility entered into numerous long-term purchasing agreements with large Alabama operators, including Drummond. By the late 1980s, these contracts provided more than 90 percent of Alabama Power's needs, removing an important market for small operators' coal.[9]

In underground mines, companies such as Jim Walter Resources and Drummond began introducing long-wall mining machines into their operations in the 1980s. These machines held up the mine roof and sliced coal out with a steel plow or a rotating cutting machine. They eliminated many miners' jobs and dramatically increased production levels.[10]

The state's overall coal production continued to rise during the 1980s, going from twenty-six million tons in 1980 to more than twenty-eight million in 1990. Mechanization of underground mines and the numerous problems strip mines faced, however, cut the number of miners from 12,735 to 6,304.[11]

Alabama's problems with coal production were not isolated. By 1983, the UMWA reported that more than one-third of its members nationally—almost sixty-two thousand miners—had lost their jobs during the downturn in coal employment. The decline in membership and the industry's difficulties forced the UMWA to take a more conciliatory posture toward the companies. In Alabama, this approach took root after a ten-week spring 1981 strike. When the UMWA's national contract with major coal operators expired in 1984, Alabama union officials and the state's largest coal companies reached an agreement that avoided a strike. District 20 President Tom Youngblood proclaimed the no-strike deal with Drummond, Jim Walter Resources, and other major producers "a historic agreement representing a new era of management and union relations." The first such contract in the nation's coalfields, the deal allowed Alabama's companies to operate even during a national strike as long as they agreed to sign the national contract that negotiators for the union and Bituminous Coal Operators' Association reached. The UMWA and Drummond officials continued the agreement three years later. The UMWA's national president, Richard Trumka, singled out Drummond executives for their "enlightened corporate leadership." For his part, Gary Drummond, the firm's chief executive, warned his company's miners that their high wages "can be paid only if there is continued cooperation between labor and management so the company can remain competitive in selling its product on the world coal market."[12]

New problems for Alabama miners emerged in the 1990s. Large surface mines in the western United States produced huge amounts of coal that began to find markets in Alabama. The amount of coal that these operations produced dwarfed that of even the most productive Alabama mines. A single operation in Wyoming, ARCO Coal's Black Thunder mine, produced thirty-one million tons of coal in 1991, more than all of Alabama's mines combined. The state's power companies began to import low-cost coal from the West.[13]

In addition, Drummond began its overseas adventures during the 1980s. Reports of massive Colombian investments by the Birmingham District's largest coal producer sent shock waves through the coalfields. Journalists noted that the company had spent four hundred million dollars by 1987 to develop its mine in La Loma. Drummond officials hoped that the mine would eventually yield six million tons of coal a year, more than any single operation in Alabama could hope to produce. Unionized Alabama miners, who earned about thirty-two thousand dollars a year at the end of the 1980s, worried they would find themselves competing against Colombian miners who earned only twelve hundred to eighteen hundred dollars a year. Miners and even other operators feared that regional industries and power companies could import coal from the Colombian operation through the state-of-the-art McDuffie coal terminal in Mobile, the same facility that had helped to revive the Alabama coalfields a generation earlier. Many Birmingham District producers, including Jim Walter Resources, had seen some of their Japanese exports decline as a recession swept that country's steel industry. Some overseas consumers of Alabama coal who faced dismal economic conditions could not honor their long-term agreements.[14]

Production at the surface mine at La Loma, eventually named the Pribbenow mine, surpassed Drummond's early predictions. Miners at the operation produced seven million tons of coal a year by the late 1990s. Gary Drummond boldly predicted the demise of the Alabama industry in a speech before Birmingham business leaders at the end of the decade. Imports from Colombia and mines in western states would cause what remained of Birmingham District production to drop by half in coming years, Drummond said. "We're people of the world operating in a world economy," he told the business leaders. "We can't make apologies for that."[15]

Nor, for that matter, did Drummond atone for his company's involvement in Colombia's bloody politics. Colombian miners earned less than their Alabama counterparts, but mining in that country carried other costs. Not since Charles DeBardeleben had turned Alabama Fuel and Iron's mining camps into armed fortresses to fight off UMWA organizers during the New Deal had an Alabama coal producer adopted such militaristic measures. Between four hundred and six hundred armed guards, complete with a company-furnished barracks and training facility, protected the Pribbenow mine from guerrilla attacks. Colombia's unstable political situation forced Drummond officials to fly in and out of the country on private airplanes to avoid being kidnapped.[16]

Leftist guerrillas affiliated with the Revolutionary Armed Forces of Colombia (FARC) active in the region demanded a 10 percent tax on coal coming from the mine. When Drummond officials refused to pay, the rail line that carried coal between La Loma and the coast was bombed several times. FARC also reportedly kidnapped several Drummond employees and held them for ransom. When the company refused to pay, the rebels released the employees. The security problems prompted Gary Drummond to meet and share his concerns with Colombian political leaders.[17]

The company seemed less interested in the security of the men who represented the workers at the Pribbenow mine. The Colombian miners had a union at the facility, but its leaders soon became targets in the conflicts among the FARC, government forces, and the rightist paramilitaries allied with the government. In the spring of 2001, two of the union's leaders, Valmore Locarno and Victor Orcasita, were assassinated as they left the La Loma operation. That fall, the new union president, Gustavo Soler, met the same fate. Witnesses attributed the killings to right-wing paramilitaries, which typically believed that union leaders sympathized with the FARC. Such events occurred regularly in Colombia. More than 120 unionists died in the year that preceded the murders outside La Loma, and almost 3,800 union officials had been murdered since the mid-1980s.[18]

But many activists believed that Drummond benefited directly from the murders of the union leaders at its Colombian mine. The United Steelworkers of America and the International Labor Rights Fund, along with Colombian unions and family members, eventually filed federal lawsuits in Birmingham that accused Drummond of "encouraging" the assassinations of the three union leaders. "We have evidence that the paramilitaries who killed the three union leaders were in fact working for Drummond," said fund president Terry Collingsworth. The company denied the accusations. "We're not involved with the paramilitaries in these types of activities," said Mike Tracy, a Drummond spokesman. "We really feel for these victims. Our sympathy goes out to their families." In the Birmingham media, the company used harsher language, calling the charges a "grossly unfair attack on our integrity and reputation."[19]

A year later, the company announced a major expansion of the Pribbenow mine with the purchase of additional coal reserves. If brought into production, the mine at La Loma could yield up to thirty-two million tons a year. The miners at La Loma "aren't represented by a labor union," the *Birmingham News* claimed in its reporting of the Drummond announcement.[20]

Whatever the outcome of the lawsuits, the expansion of the Pribbenow mine was bad news for the Birmingham District's miners. In a little over twenty years, almost ten thousand of them had lost their jobs. Production also had dropped from more than twenty-eight million tons in 1990 to less than twenty million in 2001. In 1996, Alabama mines had produced thirteen million tons for export markets. Four years later, however, the state's companies exported only three million tons, while an estimated five million tons of coal came from Colombia through Mobile. For its part, Drummond had closed all of its Alabama operations with the exception of Shoal Creek. In Walker County, once the heart of Alabama's union country, only one minor underground mine and a scattering of small strip operations remained. The UMWA, its membership decimated by layoffs, could do little but complain. "Drummond failed to honor its verbal statement to the UMWA never to ship Colombian coal to Alabama," said District 20 President

John Stewart. "It was bad enough to take away our jobs after making money off our backs, but to send us coal mined with slave labor is really disgraceful."[21]

By the 1980s, the downturn that descended on the Alabama coal industry had enveloped Jim Walter Resources. After entering the coal industry in the 1970s, the Tampa-based company had invested an estimated seven hundred million dollars to develop deep underground mines in Tuscaloosa and Jefferson Counties on the Blue Creek coal seam. The operations were expensive, and geologic conditions forced the company to develop among the deepest mines in the country, some of them more than two thousand feet underground. The prospect of lucrative contracts with major Japanese steel producers encouraged the company to overlook both the expense and danger. During the following decade, Jim Walter became a leader in incorporating long-wall technology, introducing the machines in its underground operations and boosting production to record levels. Company officials, however, did not expect a recession to sweep the Japanese steel industry in the 1980s. By the end of the decade, many of these companies were unable to honor their contracts for Alabama coal, and Jim Walter Resources began to lay off miners.[22]

The company's troubles continued into the 1990s. By the end of the decade, its mining division had begun to lose large amounts of money—$37 million in 1999 and $182 million the following year. Production at its Alabama mines dropped from 6.5 million tons to 5.9 million during the same period, while the selling price of a ton of Blue Creek coal declined from almost $42 a ton to about $35 a ton. Faced with such a bleak outlook, the company tried to sell its coal division in 1999 but failed to find an interested buyer.[23]

In the mid-1990s, when the MSHA survey listed four Jim Walter Resources mines among the country's most dangerous based on the number of "significant and substantial" safety violations, company spokesperson Dennis Hall reacted angrily. "There are lies, damn lies and statistics," he said. "You can twist anything to make someone look bad, but if you look closely at the number of hours that inspectors spent at Jim Walter Number 7 and Number 4, you'll see they spent three to four times as long at our mines as they did at mines on the bottom of the list."[24]

Hall did not publicly speculate about what might have attracted federal investigators' attention. But federal regulators were not the only people expressing concerns with safety at his company. A *United Mine Workers Journal* article on conditions at Jim Walter Resources' No. 4 mine by journalist Marat Moore warned in the mid-1980s "that the potential is there for one of the worst mine disasters in nearly a century." Moore cited a potentially deadly mix of high levels of explosive methane gas, frequent ignitions, violations of safety laws, and the company's poor attitude toward safety. UMWA international health and safety representative David Lawson and others singled out the company's confrontational management style as a major impediment to mine safety. "We have tried everything with the company. We've tried to sit down and reason with them. We've held safety blitzes," Lawson said. "If company officials don't change their attitude, a lot of people are going to get killed."[25]

Conditions at the No. 5 mine in Brookwood had worsened by the end of the 1990s. Miners claimed that managers, worried about keeping production levels high, harassed workers if they turned off mining machinery when dangerous levels of methane gas were present. The mine led Alabama in safety citations in 2000, compiling 525 violations and $77,078.18 in fines. Local union officials complained regularly to federal officials, but they took little action. In 2000 and 2001, for example, the mine's local safety committee members reported 2,300 "conditions requiring correction." A regular inspection of the mine in September 2001 found numerous violations, 10 of them "significant and substantial." The same month, federal investigators found dangerously high methane concentrations and discovered problems with the company's ventilation system. They also recorded high levels of coal dust and noted that the mine had "unsupported roof areas." Mike Boyd, whose job was to pump methane and other gases out of the mine, warned managers that the situation underground was dangerous. "I raised total hell with all of Jim Walter's management," he said. "I let them know what was going to happen. I told management they were going to blow some damn people up. It's like it fell on deaf ears."[26]

On the evening of 23 September 2001, a pair of explosions tore through the No. 5 mine, killing thirteen miners. The first explosion occurred at about 5:15 p.m. after a roof collapsed and a spark from a damaged battery ignited methane gas, damaging the mine's ventilation system. As methane levels rose, a second blast erupted about fifty minutes later. Most of the miners died in the second explosion as they attempted to rescue a trapped coworker. One survived the blasts but later died of his injuries. Those killed included Gaston Adams, Ray Ashworth, Nelson Banks, Dave Blevins, Clarence Boyd, Wendell Johnson, John Knox, Dennis Mobley, Charles Nail, Joe Riggs, Charles Smith, Joseph Sorah, and Terry Stewart.[27]

The investigations that followed blamed the explosions on a host of different causes. Federal investigators cited Jim Walter Resources for seven instances of "high negligence" in connection with the explosions. UMWA safety officials compiled a report that laid much of the blame on federal regulators, who failed to force the company to correct dangerous conditions that contributed to the miners' deaths. "The Mine Safety and Health Administration allowed many violations to languish well after the required abatement dates had passed and kept fines low," said Joe Main, the UMWA's safety administrator. "Since the mid-1990s, numerous complaints have been filed by miners and the union about lax enforcement."[28]

Shortly after the union issued its report on the disaster, MSHA admitted that some of its investigators had failed to enforce regulations that required the company to inspect mines for hazards before and during shifts. The investigators also did not enforce provisions that required coal companies to conduct regular fire drills. The Birmingham MSHA office, known as District 11, also cited the No. 5 mine for fewer "significant and substantial" violations than other underground coal mines. Nationally, about 40 percent of the citations that MSHA inspectors issued were of a "significant and substantial" nature, twice the level found at the No. 5 mine.[29]

Union investigators and federal officials found examples of conflicts of interest in the District 11 office. The agency's Alabama office had employed an inspector who had worked for Jim Walter less than two years before he was hired, a violation of MSHA policy. The agency also admitted that regional MSHA officials had not maintained adequate oversight and guidance, and the heads of the Alabama office were transferred to the bureau's headquarters in Virginia. The federal report also noted that samples taken from the section of the mine where the explosions occurred revealed that the coal dust was too combustible to comply with federal requirements. The samples were taken a few days before the disaster, but the laboratory analysis of them was not available until 28 September. Federal authorities found that high levels of coal dust had contributed to the explosions.[30]

The tragic deaths of the thirteen miners were overshadowed by national and international events. The explosions at the No. 5 mine, the worst mining disaster in two decades, occurred less than two weeks after the 11 September terrorist attacks on the World Trade Center, the Pentagon, and in the skies over Pennsylvania. Though politicians and bureaucrats hailed the dead miners as heroes and even held a memorial for them a few days after the disaster, fighting terrorism grabbed more headlines than any crusade for a renewed commitment to mine safety could ever hope for. A year later, the dramatic rescue of nine miners from a flooded mine in Pennsylvania only a few miles from where one of the hijacked passenger jets had crashed made national news and swept away the memory of the Brookwood tragedy outside of Alabama. The Pennsylvania miners met with President George W. Bush and had their story made into a television movie.[31]

Jim Walter officials began the process of reopening the No. 5 mine in December 2001. As employment levels grew, the work provided much-needed employment to the hundreds of miners who had been laid off since the fatal explosions. But the return was short lived. In December 2003, Walter officials announced plans to close the operation. The families of the victims continued to suffer. In the winter of 2002, a few months after their husbands were killed, several of the widows protested in front of the No. 5 mine, demanding that Jim Walter officials distribute the $840,000 the company had raised and placed in a trust on their behalf. The women needed the money and strongly disagreed with the regulations that restricted their access to the trust. "We want [Jim Walter officials] to let go of it," said Ann Stewart. "The money is rightfully ours." The widows also claimed that they felt humiliated by the forms they had to fill out to access the trust. "I feel like they were trying to be helpful but they haven't been successful in it," said Teresa Boyd, who was raising three children. "It's almost like they are not listening. It makes us feel like we don't know how to handle our own money." Janice Nail was even more blunt: "I'm not going to beg for it. I'll do without."[32]

Many of the families of the victims, who now faced life without their primary breadwinners, turned to the courts as a last option. By the fall of 2002, ten of the thirteen families had filed wrongful death lawsuits against Jim Walter Resources, charging the company with contributing to "conditions that were extremely dangerous and hazardous, creating risks of death and serious injury."[33]

On the first anniversary of the disaster, miners dedicated a black granite memorial to the victims at the West Brookwood Church. Miners and managers planted thirteen juniper trees next to the monument. Like coal miners and coal communities, juniper trees are known for their ability to survive in challenging environments.[34]

CONCLUSION

As the new century dawned, the way of life that had sustained gener-ations of Birmingham District miners lived on. After several periods of rebirth and decline, coal mining had become a relatively high-paying, mechanized job, but one that required a much smaller workforce. Among the continuities tended to be potential for danger, the cyclical nature of the business, and the presence of the United Mine Workers of America (UMWA).

In many ways, the UMWA and its members could point to tremendous material advances they had brought to the coalfields since the early 1930s. With benefits figured in, miners earned about thirty-two dollars an hour in 2002, a testament to how the miners' union had brought positive change to the Birmingham District.[1] In the area of race relations, however, the UMWA's legacy was mixed.

❨ ❨ ❨

As this study has showed, the UMWA sometimes confronted the color line in bold ways when the union reemerged in Alabama during the New Deal Era. African American miners responded to the union's promises with action, and they flocked to the union fold. Indeed, black miners in the 1930s were often the union's most enthusiastic supporters, comprising a majority of the UMWA's membership in Alabama during its first years. In return, the UMWA generally supported their rights in the workplace, and union officials John L. Lewis and William Mitch sometimes strongly spoke up on behalf of black miners' rights away from the mines as well. By the end of the 1930s, however, the UMWA in Alabama had moved away from its deal with its black members.

When it returned to the Alabama coalfields, the UMWA had made important compromises on race relations. The union did not completely breach the color line that served as the foundation for social relations in the Birmingham District and in key ways left the props of white supremacy in place within its bureaucratic structure. The union remained under white control, and although African Americans served in secondary leadership roles, their advancement within the union was limited. By the end of the 1930s, the racial policies of the UMWA and the industrial union movement it spawned in Alabama became the focus of intense debate. The miners' union was shaped by the racial tensions that swept through the Birmingham District early in World War II. The UMWA's racially charged efforts to raid the locals of the International Union of Mine, Mill, and Smelter Workers illustrated how the reaction against the biracialism of the industrial union movement had led the miners' union to move away from its progressive vision. The results of this drift would prove disastrous for African American coal miners in the decades that followed.

The person at the center of this storm was William Mitch, whose vision shaped the way that the UMWA and the rest of the industrial union movement dealt with the issue of race in Alabama. Mitch at times proved a forceful speaker on behalf of African American rights, even when the miners' union seemed to be moving away from its commitments. Elements of the miners' union colluded with white secessionists within Mine Mill in the early 1940s, yet the District 20 president earned grudging praise from opponents for his ability to both rally support among African American unionists and serve as an advocate for them in the industrial union movement. Mitch's views on race therefore were complex. In many ways, they mirrored the organization he headed.

Likewise, Mitch's relations with the Alabama rank and file also were puzzling. While miners rallied to the UMWA banner by the thousands in the early 1930s, Mitch also worked to contain their militancy. In the UMWA's first decade in Alabama, the District 20 president fought dissident movements that were often led by leftists. During World War II, he struggled to maintain control over the coalfields at a time when rank-and-file miners attempted to force the Birmingham District's coal producers to live up to their agreements. Mitch and the UMWA seemed to support the rank-and-file miners' actions on some occasions yet on others clearly opposed the workers. District 20 leaders, particularly Mitch, seemed most concerned when dissident movements operated outside their control. In these instances, Mitch tried to rein the miners in. Again, as with race, Mitch's relationship with the rank and file was full of contradictions.

In the end, on both the issues of race and rank and file militancy, Mitch placed the UMWA as an institution above the concerns of Alabama miners generally and African Americans in particular. The UMWA's initial caution on race relations could be attributed at least in part to the perception on the part of Mitch and other union leaders that to push too far would provoke a reaction that might destroy the organization in Alabama. Mitch and the rest of the state UMWA leaders consequently turned their backs on African Americans when it seemed politically necessary to do so or even when such actions were perceived as serving the union cause.

Institutional concerns proved paramount in Mitch's relationship with the rank and file as well. Mitch fought the communist-led movements of the 1930s, especially when he believed that they pushed for confrontations with the Alabama operators at times of organizational weakness. During the World War II walkouts, Mitch followed Lewis's lead, occasionally encouraging rank-and-file miners' militancy. When organized movements openly operated outside of the union's control, however, Mitch and other UMWA leaders worked hard to contain them. The wartime emergency undoubtedly caused the District 20 leadership to fear the public and federal government reaction the strikes might provoke. On the issue of local wildcat strikes, Mitch and the District 20 leadership typically placed institutional concerns first, siding with the companies.

Why Mitch chose this course remains unclear. One plausible explanation might lie in the miners' union's Alabama history. For almost half a century before 1933, the coal operators and state officials had enjoyed a great deal of success in defeating, time and again, the union's efforts to establish a permanent coalfield presence. Mitch was no doubt aware of this history, and the open hostility with which elites greeted the UMWA's reemergence in Alabama made a strong impression. The Great Depression had weakened the industrial and political elites that had previously defeated the union. The New Deal and the expansion of the federal government helped miners rebuild their old movement and led to the union's permanent establishment in Alabama. But the old elites found a home in the conservative wing of the Democratic Party, remaining a potent force, as illustrated by the success enjoyed by Frank Dixon, Chauncey Sparks, and the Dixiecrat movement. This fact led the District 20 leadership, including Mitch, to proceed with caution.

Another plausible explanation for Mitch's actions in regard to African Americans and the rank and file in Alabama can be found in his early career in the

UMWA. In Indiana, as secretary-treasurer of District 11 from 1915 to 1931, Mitch had held leftist views. He ran for Congress in 1920 as a member of the socialist-leaning Labor Party of Indiana. In 1921, Lewis appointed Mitch to the union's Nationalization Research Committee, where he served with John Brophy, president of UMWA District 2, and Christ Golden, leader of District 9. The committee explored the controversial issue of government ownership of the nation's coal industry, which Mitch generally supported. Lewis, however, opposed this idea and worked to undermine the committee and its most prominent members. Mitch survived this crisis by distancing himself from these leftists after Lewis's opposition caused the nationalization effort to collapse.

Mitch enjoyed enough support to retain his position as secretary-treasurer in Indiana throughout the turbulent 1920s, when miners in District 11 routinely turned out their state leaders. Mitch's strong support for the national UMWA president eventually became a liability, however, and in 1931 he went down to defeat at the hands of an anti-Lewis candidate. This event plunged Mitch, then roughly fifty years old, into a crisis. After sixteen years as a union officer, he found himself with only limited options for employment in an industry ravaged by the depression and declining union membership. Lewis eventually appointed Mitch as a "special representative" with the UMWA and then sent him to Alabama.[2] By 1933, then, Mitch's future was directly connected to the fates of both John L. Lewis and the institution he headed.

Events in Indiana also affected Mitch's position on the issue of race. Early in the 1920s, District 11 found itself in a state of crisis as the Ku Klux Klan made major inroads among rank-and-file coal miners. In 1923, District 11 President John Hessler estimated that 75 percent of UMWA members "eligible" to join the Indiana Klan had done so. The rise of the Klan placed the UMWA in a difficult position, since the organization's constitution banned Klan membership. Hessler, who claimed he was neither a member of the Klan nor "eligible for membership," urged Lewis and the union's International Executive Board to allow the UMWA in Indiana to avoid expelling miners who violated the union's constitution and joined the Klan. The UMWA president agreed with Hessler and advised Indiana leaders to "use their influence" and prevent Klan membership from becoming an issue, encouraging District 11 leaders to stop cases on the matter from being brought up.[3]

The UMWA's international convention took up the issue of Klan membership in 1924. Van Bittner, whom Lewis had sent to lead a strike in Alabama a few years earlier, Hessler, and several other leaders asked convention delegates to approve a measure that would remove the ban on Klan membership from the UMWA constitution, arguing that the ban could not be enforced. But the delegates disagreed,

and the measure was overwhelmingly rejected. The ban on Klan membership remained part of the union's constitution.[4]

Mitch's role in this controversy in Indiana remains obscure. As secretary-
treasurer during this time, he had to deal with Klan members and probably
accepted their votes. However, his close associate, UMWA attorney H. A. Henderson, broke with Hessler on the issue of the Klan. Henderson had initially
warned that the UMWA faced potential lawsuits if it expelled Klan members. He
apparently modified his position on the matter and opposed Hessler's efforts to
have the ban lifted. As a result, Hessler attempted to have Henderson removed
as a District 11 lawyer. Henderson later wrote to Mitch that the Klan "was the
arch enemy fundamentally of everything that was near and dear to the principles
that you and I hold to be just." For his part, Mitch replied that Hessler's actions
were the result of "his ignorance, and I felt that was about it when he became
so wrapped up in the Klan and wanted to put you out because you opposed the
Klan."[5]

Trying to read Mitch's actions in this debate is difficult, but it seems clear
that although he opposed the Klan's ideology, Mitch largely remained outside
the fray. In this respect, he essentially followed the lead of Lewis, who encouraged local leaders to avoid the issue. The incident foreshadowed Mitch's later
actions. Both during the 1930s and 1940s, when the UMWA's racial policies came
under attack in Alabama, and after World War II, when the Klan made inroads
among the Birmingham District's white miners, Mitch and the rest of the state
UMWA leaders backed away from the union's commitment to its black members
and refused to take a strong stand against racism. In the case of race relations,
as with rank-and-file activism, institutional concerns remained paramount for
Mitch, even when they came at the expense of some UMWA members.

The ramifications of the UMWA's racial policies became evident during the
coalfield depression that followed World War II. Most of Alabama's miners lost
their jobs during this era. When new, highly mechanized mines later opened and
the industry became more reliant on strip mining, the coal operators whitened
their workforce, and by the end of the 1960s, African Americans had virtually
been eliminated from the coal industry. In the chaos of this era, the miners' union
did little to help African Americans.

The coal operators decided whom they hired at their operations, so they bear
primary responsibility for the demise of black miners. But the UMWA, Mitch,
and the rest of the Alabama leadership also played an important role because they
were slow to embrace the cause of black miners, a legacy of the failure directly
to confront racial issues in the 1930s and early 1940s. African American miners,
left largely to their own devices, struggled mightily and impressively, and some

managed to enjoy the benefits and wages for which generations had fought so hard. In the end, however, their numbers were relatively small.

In later decades, the ramifications of the shift in the composition and character of District 20 became apparent. When the coalfield economy rebounded in the 1970s, the UMWA and its new leadership could not meet the challenges posed by globalization. The coalitions that the miners' union formed with activists and liberals during the South African coal boycott of the mid-1970s were circumscribed by the union's narrow focus on job protection and could not confront the unified power of the Southern Company and the federal government. Mobile's black longshoremen, in particular, were reluctant partners in the UMWA's protectionist boycott. The actions of white District 20 leaders, who attempted to bully the dockworkers' leaders into supporting the protest, merely confirmed these reservations.

The allies that the UMWA sought out in Alabama in the 1960s and 1970s offered little help in the long run. George Wallace, for example, remained out of the violent strike in 1966, thereby benefiting the UMWA. However, he also declined to intervene in the miners' efforts to prevent the South African coal imports, implicitly siding with the Southern Company, and then openly broke with the UMWA during the 1977–78 strike and used the state's power to keep the nonunion mines working.

In the case of women miners, furthermore, the UMWA in Alabama repeated many of its earlier mistakes. Women, like African Americans, received little support from the union but remained extremely loyal to it. Women's struggles in the 1970s and 1980s in many ways embodied both the older traditions of coalfield solidarity and newer forms of civil rights activism. Like black miners from another era, women were largely left to develop their own strategies for finding and keeping jobs in the mines.

Institutionally speaking, the UMWA survived these failings but did so at a high cost. At the start of the new millennium, the miners' union still maintained a small office building in Birmingham, though it was dwarfed by its ever-expanding neighbor, the University of Alabama–Birmingham. The coal industry employed just a few thousand miners, most of them at operations in remote parts of the Birmingham District. Miners at these operations worried about the health of the coal industry and their future in it, while the union focused on preserving the jobs that remained.

NOTES

Abbreviations

ACOA/AMI Records	Alabama Coal Operators' Association/Alabama Mining Institute Records, 1908–84, Department of Archives and Manuscripts, Birmingham Public Library, Birmingham, Ala.
ADIR	Alabama Department of Industrial Relations
AFICO Records	Alabama Fuel and Iron Company Records, 1917–63, W. S. Hoole Special Collections Library, University of Alabama, Tuscaloosa
BAH	*Birmingham Age-Herald*
BN	*Birmingham News*
BP	*Birmingham Post*
BPH	*Birmingham Post-Herald*
CEP Collection	Coal Employment Project Collection, Archives of Appalachia, East Tennessee State University, Johnson City
FDR Library	Franklin D. Roosevelt Presidential Library, Hyde Park, N.Y.
FEPC Collection	Fair Employment Practices Commission, 1941–46, Microfilm Collection, Archives and Special Collections, Robert Woodruff Library, Atlanta University Center, Atlanta
Fund Archives	United Mine Workers of America Health and Retirement Fund Archives, West Virginia University, West Virginia and Regional History Collection, Morgantown
JLL	John L. Lewis
NYT	*New York Times*
PDC	President-District Correspondence, United Mine Workers of America Archive, Historical Collections and Labor Archives, Paterno Library, Pennsylvania State University, State College
Samford OHC	Oral History Collection, Special Collection Department, Samford University, Birmingham, Ala.
TCSH	Clipping Files, Tutwiler Collection of Southern History, Birmingham Public Library, Birmingham, Ala.
TN	*Tuscaloosa News*
UMWA WRF	United Mine Workers of America Welfare and Retirement Fund, United Mine Workers of America Archive, Historical Collections and Labor Archives, Paterno Library, Pennsylvania State University, State College
UMWJ	*United Mine Workers Journal*
UN	*Union News*
WLOHP	Working Lives Oral History Project, W. S. Hoole Special Collections Library, University of Alabama, Tuscaloosa
WM	William Mitch

Preface

1. "Victim Said He 'Wanted Out' of Family Vocation," *TN*, 26 September 2001.

Introduction

1. Ernest Walker, interview by author, tape recording, Jasper, Ala., 29 June 2001.
2. Ibid.
3. Ibid.
4. U.S. Department of Commerce, Bureau of the Census, *Fifteenth Census*, 118; and U.S. Department of Commerce, Bureau of the Census, *1990 Census*, 86. On African American membership in the UMWA in Alabama, see Clayton and Mitchell, *Black Workers*, 323.
5. Northrup, *Organized Labor*, 154; Stein, "Southern Workers in National Unions," 188; Norrell, "Caste in Steel," 672–73, 686; Honey, *Southern Labor*, 7. Historian Ronald Lewis examines the decline of black miners in *Black Coal Miners in America*, 167–90.
6. See Hill, "Myth-Making as Labor History," 133; Hill, "Problem of Race," 189. This debate, as historian Eric Arnesen noted almost a decade ago in "Up from Exclusion," does not break down easily into two distinct groups.
7. Nelson, *Divided We Stand*, xxxiii, xl; Nelson, "Class, Race, and Democracy," 351–74; Nelson, "Organized Labor." See also Minchin, *Color of Work*, esp. 25–28. David Roediger is the best-known "whiteness" scholar; see his *Wages of Whiteness*, 8–12; *Towards the Abolition of Whiteness*; and "Race and the Working Class Past." Other important recent works in this area include Foley, *White Scourge*; Brattain, *Politics of Whiteness*. Sociologist and historian W. E. B. Du Bois first developed the idea of white workers and the "public and psychological wage" in his expansive overview of the Reconstruction Era (*Black Reconstruction in America*, 700). For critical assessments of studies of whiteness, see Arnesen, "Whiteness"; Kolchin, "Whiteness Studies."
8. Korstad, *Civil Rights Unionism*, 5; Honey, *Southern Labor*.
9. Draper, "New Southern Labor History," 90.
10. McKiven, *Iron and Steel*; Norrell, "Caste in Steel." Norrell's article cited here appeared earlier than Hill's but has been used by scholars (Hill among them) as evidence for Hill's point of view. In a similar vein, Draper found that leaders of state labor councils, particularly in Alabama, faced outright rebellions from their white rank-and-file members over liberal civil rights policies in the years after the 1954 *Brown* decision (*Conflict of Interests*, esp. 107–21).
11. See McKiven, *Iron and Steel*.
12. Norrell, "Labor at the Ballot Box," 202; Norrell, "Caste in Steel," esp. 670, 679.
13. Kelley, *Hammer and Hoe*, 151; Stein, "Southern Workers in National Unions," 183; Stein, *Running Steel, Running America*.
14. Montgomery, "Introduction: Union Activists in Industry and in the Community," in *Black Workers' Struggle*, ed. Huntley and Montgomery, 1–31, esp. 17–24; Huntley, "Iron Ore Miners"; Huntley, "Red Scare," 129–45; Huntley, "Rise and Fall," 197–208.
15. Letwin, *Challenge of Interracial Unionism*, 192. See also Worthman, "Black Workers."
16. Kelly, *Race, Class, and Power*, 12–14.

17. Alexander, "Rising from the Ashes," 62–83.

18. Scholars have debated how strongly industrial unions should have embraced the wider social vision articulated by Left-led unions like the FTA. On one side are historians such as Honey and Korstad, who argue that unions that supported the struggle for black economic, social, and political rights had the most success at making headway in the South. This is particularly illustrated in the limited organizing victories such unions enjoyed during the CIO's Operation Dixie, which began in the spring of 1946 and ended (though not officially) a short time later. See Korstad, *Civil Rights Unionism*, esp. 289–300; Honey, *Southern Labor*, 225–44. While not excusing the tendency of many CIO unions to marginalize black workers and women, other observers have suggested that the reaction against leftists in general and unions in particular that followed World War II made embracing such a bold agenda difficult. See, for example, Zieger, *CIO*, 240. For a general overview of the issue of race during Operation Dixie, see Griffith, *Crisis of American Labor*, 62–87. Labor journalist Art Preis praised the CIO's integrationist agenda but acknowledged that industrial unions generally did not succeed in breaking the existing patterns of hiring and upgrading of African American workers. The failure of Operation Dixie and of the CIO to expand its influence in the South, he argued, left the region in the control of "white supremacists and labor-haters" (*Labor's Giant Step*, 375–77).

19. U.S. Department of Commerce, Bureau of the Census, *Sixteenth Census*, 52–54.

20. Stein, *Running Steel, Running America*, 38. I am not the first person to make this argument. See Kelley, "Birmingham's Untouchables: The Black Poor in the Age of Civil Rights," in *Race Rebels*, 77–100. See also Eskew, *But for Birmingham*; McWhorter, *Carry Me Home*. For an overview of the era of World War II through the early 1970s in the Alabama coalfields, see Glenn Feldman, "Alabama Coal Miners," 84–110. For employment levels, see U.S. Department of Commerce, Bureau of the Census, *Census of Population: 1950*, 2–228; ADIR, *Annual Statistical Report, Fiscal Year 1969–1970*, Folder 3.26, ACOA/AMI Records. The employment levels for 1970 are tricky. I have chosen to use state figures here because they are generally conservative when compared with federal numbers, both in terms of production and employment. The 1970 census did not separate coal mining from other forms of mining, so the total number of miners was much higher, at almost 8,500. See U.S. Department of Commerce, Bureau of the Census, *1970 Census*, 164. Ronald Lewis listed the number of coal miners in Alabama as 4,515, which is close to the state estimates (*Black Coal Miners in America*, 192–93). For overviews of the Sunbelt phenomenon, see Mohl, *Searching for the Sunbelt*; Wright, *Old South, New South*; Cobb, *Selling of the South*; Schulman, *From Cotton Belt to Sunbelt*; Bartley, *New South*.

21. Sugrue, *Origins of the Urban Crisis*, 6, 8–11. See also Katz, *"Underclass" Debate*.

22. Ronald Lewis, *Black Coal Miners in America*, 171, 177–80; Northrup, *Organized Labor*, 166–71; Barnum, *Negro*, 34–36.

23. Kelly, *Race, Class, and Power*, 9.

24. For examples, see Cowie, *Capital Moves*; Flamming, *Creating the Modern South*; Nelson Lichtenstein, *State of the Union*; Stein, *Running Steel, Running America*. On the effect of this process on the South, see Cobb, *Selling of the South*.

25. Cowie, *Capital Moves*, 183; ADIR, *Annual Report, Statistical Supplement, Fiscal Year 2001*.

ONE. Race, Class, Gender, and Community before 1941

1. Jobie Thomas, interview by Brenda McCallum, unidentified, and Cliff Kuhn, transcript, Bessemer, Ala., 25 April 1983, WLOHP.

2. For a discussion of how memory changes over time, see Portelli, *Death of Luigi Trastulli*, 26. On the incomplete nature of segregation, see Hale, *Making Whiteness*, 8; Gilmore, *Gender and Jim Crow*, 73–74.

3. Alexander, "Rising from the Ashes," 67–68. For statistics, see U.S. Department of Commerce, Bureau of the Census, *Fifteenth Census*, 118; U.S. Department of Commerce, Bureau of the Census, *Sixteenth Census*, 54; Letwin, *Challenge of Interracial Unionism*, 23; Ronald Lewis, *Black Coal Miners in America*, 191–92.

4. Bobby Wilson, *America's Johannesburg*, 161; McKiven, *Iron and Steel*, 56–60; Brownell, "Birmingham, Alabama"; Harris, *Political Power in Birmingham*; Alexander, "Rising from the Ashes," 64; Kelly, *Race, Class, and Power*, 153.

5. Brattain, *Politics of Whiteness*, 6; Hall et al., *Like a Family*; Flamming, *Creating the Modern South*; Bryant Simon, *Fabric of Defeat*; Fink, *Fulton Bag*; Flynt, *Poor but Proud*, 107; Gilmore, *Gender and Jim Crow*, 22–25; Hunter, *To Joy My Freedom*, 114–20. For other heavy industries in Alabama, see McKiven, *Iron and Steel*, 2.

6. U.S. Department of Commerce, Bureau of the Census, *Fifteenth Census*, 114; U.S. Department of Commerce, Bureau of the Census, *Sixteenth Census*, 52; Savage, "Re-gendering Coal," 234; Marat Moore, *Women in the Mines*, xxxii; Letwin, "Interracial Unionism," 543–46. On laws that excluded African Americans from work in textile mills, see Gilmore, *Gender and Jim Crow*, 23; Hall et al., *Like a Family*, 66–67. On African Americans in the coal industry in Alabama, see Letwin, *Challenge of Interracial Unionism*, 23; Ronald Lewis, *Black Coal Miners in America*, 191–92. For statistics, see U.S. Department of Commerce, Bureau of the Census, *Fifteenth Census*, 118; U.S. Department of Commerce, Bureau of the Census, *Sixteenth Census*, 54.

7. Kelly, *Race, Class, and Power*, 194–96; Letwin, *Challenge of Interracial Unionism*, 185–88.

8. Korson, *Coal Dust on the Fiddle*, 29, 35; Archie Green, *Only a Miner*, esp. 3–31.

9. Letwin, *Challenge of Interracial Unionism*, 10, 14–17, 23; Chapman et al., *Iron and Steel Industries*, 54–56; White, *Birmingham District*, 33; Taft, *Organizing Dixie*, 19; McKiven, *Iron and Steel*, 9–10, 12; Alabama Mining Institute, *Coal Mining in Alabama*, Folder 3.39, ACOA/AMI Records.

10. Rogers et al., *Alabama*, 446–47; Brownell, "Birmingham, Alabama," 33–44.

11. Alexander, "Rising from the Ashes," 63; Board of Mediation, "Alabama's Coal Mining Industry in Relation to the Current Inactivity of the State's Coal Mines," Folder 11, Box SG12258, Frank Dixon Papers, Alabama Department of Archives and History, Montgomery, Ala.; "Coal Mining in Alabama: Utilization and Distribution of Coal," in Alabama Mining Institute, *Coal Mining in Alabama*.

12. Letwin, *Challenge of Interracial Unionism*, 18–20; Wright, *Old South, New South*, 168; Woodward, *Origins of the New South*, 302; Rogers et al., *Alabama*, 446–47; Brownell, "Birmingham, Alabama," 33–44; McKiven, *Iron and Steel*, 91–93; "Coal Mining in Alabama: Utilization and Distribution of Coal," in Alabama Mining Institute, *Coal Mining in Alabama*; Alexander, "Rising from the Ashes," 63; Board of Mediation, "Alabama's Coal Mining Industry in Relation to the Current Inactivity of the State's Coal Mines."

13. "Coal Mining in Alabama: Preparation of Coal," and "Coal Mining in Alabama," in Alabama Mining Institute, *Coal Mining in Alabama*; Chapman et al., *Iron and Steel Industries*, 176–79; Cloyd M. Smith and Ball, *Mech Annual*, 144.

14. "Coal Mining in Alabama: Preparation of Coal," in Alabama Mining Institute, *Coal Mining in Alabama*.

15. "Coal Mining in Alabama: Faults," "Coal Mining in Alabama: Preparation of Coal," and "Coal Mining in Alabama," in Alabama Mining Institute, *Coal Mining in Alabama*; Chapman et al., *Iron and Steel Industries*, 176–79; Cloyd M. Smith and Ball, *Mech Annual*, 144.

16. "Coal Mining in Alabama: Cutting, Shooting, and Loading the Coal," in Alabama Mining Institute, *Coal Mining in Alabama*; Cloyd M. Smith and Ball, *Mech Annual*, 43; Chapman et al., *Iron and Steel Industries*, 178; Ronald Lewis, *Black Coal Miners in America*, 168–69.

17. Ronald Lewis, *Black Coal Miners in America*, 169; "Coal Mining in Alabama: Cutting, Shooting, and Loading the Coal," in Alabama Mining Institute, *Coal Mining in Alabama*; Cloyd M. Smith and Ball, *Mech Annual*, 43, 58, 115.

18. Northrup, *Organized Labor*, 169–70; Cloyd M. Smith and Ball, *Mech Annual*, 43, 58, 115; Ronald Lewis, *Black Coal Miners in America*, 166–69; "Coal Mining in Alabama: Cutting, Shooting, and Loading the Coal," in Alabama Mining Institute, *Coal Mining in Alabama*; Chapman et al., *Iron and Steel Industries*, 178; U.S. Department of Commerce, Bureau of the Census, *Fifteenth Census*, 118; U.S. Department of Commerce, Bureau of the Census, *Sixteenth Census*, 52, 54.

19. "Coal Mining in Alabama: Cutting, Shooting, and Loading the Coal," "Coal Mining in Alabama: Development and Mining Methods," and "Coal Mining in Alabama: Ventilation," in Alabama Mining Institute, *Coal Mining in Alabama*; Flynt, *Poor but Proud*, 127–28; Cloyd M. Smith and Ball, *Mech Annual*, 57–58; Shifflett, *Coal Towns*, 87–88; Dix, *What's a Coal Miner to Do?* 2–5, 38; Letwin, *Challenge of Interracial Unionism*, 21; James Custred, interview by author, tape recording, Goodsprings, Ala., 13 July 2001; Claude A. Crane, interview by Jim Nogalski, transcript, Warrior, Ala., 20 March 1979, Samford OHC.

20. Ed Stover, interview by author, tape recording, Goodsprings, Ala., 13 July 2001; Leon Alexander, interview by Peggy Hamrick, transcript, Birmingham, Ala., 8, 17 July 1984, WLOHP.

21. Shifflett, *Coal Towns*, 103–4; Earl Brown, interview by Cliff Kuhn, transcript, Birmingham, Ala., 29 June 1984, WLOHP; Walker, interview; "Coal Mining in Alabama: Development and Mining Methods," in Alabama Mining Institute, *Coal Mining in Alabama*; Letwin, *Challenge of Interracial Unionism*, 21.

22. Flynt, *Poor but Proud*, 132; Kelly, *Race, Class, and Power*, 66; *Third Annual Report of the Department of Industrial Relations to the Governor of Alabama, Fiscal Year Ending September 30, 1941*, Folder 2.41, ACOA/AMI Records.

23. Flynt, *Poor but Proud*, 129.

24. Walker, interview; Alexander, interview.

25. Dix, *What's a Coal Miner to Do?* 84, 93.

26. Letwin, *Challenge of Interracial Unionism*, 23; Ronald Lewis, *Black Coal Miners in America*, 191–92; U.S. Department of Commerce, Bureau of the Census, *Sixteenth Census*, 52, 54.

27. Letwin, *Challenge of Interracial Unionism*, 23–24, 26.

28. Alex Lichtenstein, *Twice the Work*, 3, 73–104; Kelly, *Race, Class, and Power*, 90–94; Letwin, *Challenge of Interracial Unionism*, 28–30; Rogers et al., *Alabama*, 423.

29. Alexander, "Rising from the Ashes," 64.

30. Chafe, Gavins, and Korstad, *Remembering Jim Crow*, 229; Herndon, *Let Me Live*, 59–60.

31. Northrup, *Organized Labor*, 160; Ronald Lewis, *Black Coal Miners in America*, 170; Archie "Dropo" Young, interview by author, tape recording, Birmingham, Ala., 7 July 2001; Earl Brown, interview.

32. Chafe, Gavins, and Korstad, *Remembering Jim Crow*, 229; Louise and Cleatus Burns, interview by Cliff Kuhn, transcript, Jasper, Ala., 12 June 1984, WLOHP.

33. Northrup, *Organized Labor*, 159–60.

34. Harry Burgess, interview by author, tape recording, Carbon Hill, Ala., 13 July 2001; Walker, interview; Alexander, "Rising from the Ashes," 66; Ronald Lewis, *Black Coal Miners in America*, 69.

35. Harris, *Political Power in Birmingham*, 186–87; Eskew, *But for Birmingham*, 54.

36. Harris, *Political Power in Birmingham*, 190, 195–96.

37. Brownell, "Birmingham, Alabama," 28–29; Bobby Wilson, "Black Housing Opportunities," 51–52; Bobby Wilson, *America's Johannesburg*, 157 (table), 161.

38. Harris, *Political Power in Birmingham*, 34, 56, 58, 200–201; Brownell, "Birmingham, Alabama," 28–29; Rogers et al., *Alabama*, 343–54.

39. "Coal Mining in Alabama: Mine Villages and Health," in Alabama Mining Institute, *Coal Mining in Alabama*.

40. "Annual Report of President, 1934," Folder 2, Box 4643, AFICO Records; "The Debardeleben [*sic*] Oasis—Unionism's Last Frontier," *Alabama*, 29 March 1937, 11, "Coal Mining Companies—DeBardeleben Coal" File, TCSH; "From Despondency to Happiness, from Idle Land and Idle Hours," *Alabama*, 24 January 1938, "Coal Mining Companies—Alabama Fuel and Iron" File, TCSH; White, *Birmingham District*, 191–92; "Resolution of Alabama Mining Institute," 15 January 1942, Folder 1.18, ACOA/AMI Records.

41. "From Despondency to Happiness"; F. R. Bell, General Manager, "To the President and Board of Directors: Annual Report on Operations, 1934," Folder 2, Box 4643, AFICO Records; "Model Communities Developed at Mine," *BN*, 1 July 1936, "Coal Mining Companies—Alabama Fuel and Iron" File, TCSH.

42. Earl Brown, interview; Walker, interview; William E. Mitch Jr., interview by Cliff Kuhn, transcript, Birmingham, Ala., 27 June 1984, WLOHP; Kelly, *Race, Class, and Power*, 85; "Debardeleben [*sic*] Oasis."

43. Earl Brown, interview; "Debardeleben [*sic*] Oasis."

44. "From Despondency to Happiness."

45. "Bodies of Nine Taken from Acmar Mine after Blast," *BN*, 11 July 1941; Flynt, *Poor but Proud*, 131–32; "From Despondency to Happiness"; "Annual Report of President, 1934," AFICO Records.

46. "From Despondency to Happiness."

47. "Annual Report of President, 1934," AFICO Records; "Debardeleben [*sic*] Oasis."

48. Tindall, *Emergence of the New South*, 330; Rikard, "Experiment in Welfare Capitalism," 92–93; Bond, *Negro Education in Alabama*, 241, 243.

49. Rickard, "An Experiment in Welfare Capitalism," 131–32, 140, 143.

50. See generally ibid., esp. 164–65; Tindall, *Emergence of the New South*, 330.

51. Ollie Lee Cale, interview by Gary Sherrer, transcript, Docena, Ala., 12 March 1979, Samford OHC; Margaret Glasgow Dorsett, interview by Lonette Lamb, transcript, Edgewood, Ala., 26 February 1979, Samford OHC; Ronald Lewis, *Black Coal Miners in America*, 69; Rikard, "Experiment in Welfare Capitalism," 243.

52. LaMarse Moore, interview by author, tape recording, 17 May 1999, 25 June 2001, Edgewater, Ala.; Dorsett, interview; "History of Edgewater from 1911," Folder SC3069, Samford University Special Collection Department, Historical Manuscripts, Birmingham, Ala.

53. Mary Parsons Gray, interview by Dana Norman, transcript, Atlanta, n.d., Samford OHC.

54. Christine Cochran, interview by Jerry Tapley, transcript, Docena, Ala., 15 March 1979, Samford OHC; Rikard, "Experiment in Welfare Capitalism," 245–46; Lowell, "Housing," 248–49.

55. Herndon, *Let Me Live*, 58; Cochran, interview.

56. C. K. Maxwell to S. R. Benedict, 31 July 1923, Folder 3.1.1.43.2, Alabama Power Company Corporate Archives, Birmingham, Ala.

57. Ibid.

58. A. B. Aldridge to E. A. Yates, 10 November 1924, Samuel Benedict to E. A. Yates, 4 November 1924, both in Folder 3.1.1.43.2, Alabama Power Company Corporate Archives.

59. Alexander, "Rising from the Ashes," 64; Louise and Cleatus Burns, interview; Earl Brown, interview.

60. Gene McDaniel, interview by author, tape recording, Nauvoo, Ala., 21 July 2001; Charles Fuller, interview by author, tape recording, Jasper, Ala., 24 January 1997; Flynt, *Poor but Proud*, 115, 117.

61. Walker, interview; Fred Bass Sr., interview by author, tape recording, Brookside, Ala., 1 August 2001.

62. Earl Brown, interview.

63. Thomas, interview; Rikard, "Experiment in Welfare Capitalism," 60–61; Kelly, *Race, Class, and Power*, 135, 143–47.

64. Dix, *What's a Coal Miner to Do?* 12.

65. Solon Roberts, interview by Carl Elliott, Jasper, Ala., 12 June 1978, Carl Elliott Papers, W. S. Hoole Special Collections Library, University of Alabama, Tuscaloosa.

66. James "Bentley" White, interview by author, tape recording, Bucksville, Ala., 1 August 2001.

67. William W. Collins, interview by author, tape recording, Woodstock, Ala., 16 June 1997.

68. Louise and Cleatus Burns, interview; Melba Wilbanks Kizzire, interview by Joy Richardson, Docena, Ala., 12 March 1979, Samford OHC.

69. C. D. Patterson, interview by Curtis W. Jones, transcript, Parish, Ala., 28 April 1975, Samford OHC; Thomas, interview.

70. "History of Edgewater from 1911"; Dorsett, interview.

71. Flynt, *Poor but Proud*, 119; Brown and Davis, introduction to *It Is Union and Liberty*, 1–2.

72. "Annual Report of President, 1934," AFICO Records.

73. Luther V. Smith, interview by Benny Hendrix, transcript, Quinton, Ala., 27 November 1974, Samford OHC; Collins, interview.

74. Dorsett, interview.

75. Isaac Pritchet, interview by author, tape recording, Edgewater, Ala., 25 June 2001; Rikard, "Experiment in Welfare Capitalism," 228–29.

76. Collins, interview; Walker, *Struggle and the Joy*, 137.

77. Curtis McAdory, interview by Peggy Hamrick, Irondale, Ala., 23 August 1984, WLOHP; Shifflett, *Coal Towns*, 191–92; Kelly, *Race, Class, and Power*, 105–6.

78. Mitch, interview by Kuhn; Shifflett, *Coal Towns*, 195; Herbert South, interview by Carl Elliott, Jasper, Ala., 16 August 1974, Elliott Papers.

79. LaMarse Moore, interview; E. L. McFee, interview by Jim Nogalski, transcript, Birmingham, Ala., 9 March 1979, Samford OHC; "History of Edgewater from 1911."

80. Louise and Cleatus Burns, interview; McCallum, "Gospel of Black Unionism," 108–33; Kelley, *Hammer and Hoe*, 149.

81. Cochran, interview; McAdory, interview; Brownell, "Birmingham, Alabama," 36.

82. Annie Latenosky Patchen, interview by Peggy Hamrick, transcript, Brookside, Ala., 20 June 1982, Folder 809.3.1.2.32, Papers and Related Materials, Birmingfind Project, Department of Archives and Manuscripts, Birmingham Public Library, Birmingham, Ala.; Adams, *Blocton*, 54–55, 61; Flynt, *Poor but Proud*, 120; Harris, *Political Power in Birmingham*, 36.

83. Rosengarten, "Reading the Hops," 69–70.

84. Young, interview.

85. Louise and Cleatus Burns, interview.

86. "History of Edgewater from 1911"; Thomas, interview.

87. McAdory, interview; Adams, *Blocton*, 48; Rikard, "Experiment in Welfare Capitalism," 251; Beito, *From Mutual Aid to the Welfare State*, 2–3.

88. Lois Bonds, interview by Ben Cleary, transcript, Docena, Ala., 27 February 1979, Samford OHC; Rikard, "Experiment in Welfare Capitalism," 252.

89. Flynt, *Poor but Proud*, 120; Dix, *What's a Coal Miner to Do?* 87.

90. Collins, interview; Flynt, *Poor but Proud*, 120

91. Burgess, interview; LaMarse Moore, interview.

92. Nancy Letitia Inman, interview by Barry Anderson, transcript, Pleasant Grove, Ala., 3 March 1979, Samford OHC; Thomas, interview; Flynt, *Poor but Proud*, 120; Kelly, *Race, Class, and Power*, 74–75.

93. "History of Edgewater from 1911."

94. Inman, interview; Patchen, interview; Louise and Cleatus Burns, interview; Thomas, interview.

95. A. J. Snead, interview by Kenneth Smith, transcript, Sandusky, Ala., 4 March 1979, Samford OHC; Ila Hendrix, interview by Ben Hendrix, transcript, Sumiton, Ala., 1 May 1976, Samford OHC; Louise and Cleatus Burns, interview; Cale, interview.

96. Hendrix, interview; Louise and Cleatus Burns, interview.

97. Hendrix, interview; LaMarse Moore, interview.

98. LaMonte, *Politics and Welfare in Birmingham*, 92; Tuten, "Regulating the Poor in Alabama," 49; Cochran, interview.

99. Rogers et al., *Alabama*, 465, 476; LaMonte, *Politics and Welfare in Birmingham*, 90.

100. LaMonte, *Politics and Welfare in Birmingham*, 110, 115, 119.

101. Ibid., 110, 114, 115, 119; Rogers et al., *Alabama*, 465; Flynt, *Poor but Proud*, 284.

102. U.S. Department of Commerce, Bureau of the Census, *Fifteenth Census*, 109; Board of Mediation, "Alabama's Coal Mining Industry in Relation to the Current Inactivity of the State's Coal Mines"; Alexander, "Rising from the Ashes," 63; "Coal Mining in Alabama: Utilization and Distribution of Coal," in Alabama Mining Institute, *Coal Mining in Alabama*.

103. Board of Mediation, "Alabama's Coal Mining Industry in Relation to the Current Inactivity of the State's Coal Mines"; "History of Coal: Number Two," in Alabama Mining Institute, *Coal Mining in Alabama*.

104. Adams, *Blocton*, 197–98.

105. "Annual Report of the President, 1934," AFICO Records.

106. Rikard, "Experiment in Welfare Capitalism," 275–76, 290; Rogers et al., *Alabama*, 466.

107. Elmer Burton, interview by Sybil Burton, 3 December 1974, Samford OHC.

108. Louise and Cleatus Burns, interview.

109. Burgess, interview.

110. Rogers et al., *Alabama*, 490–91; Flynt, *Poor but Proud*, 288; LaMonte, *Politics and Welfare in Birmingham*, 123.

111. Tindall, *Emergence of the New South*, 494–95; Flynt, *Poor but Proud*, 288; LaMonte, *Politics and Welfare in Birmingham*, 123; Rogers et al., *Alabama*, 490–91.

112. Louise and Cleatus Burns, interview; Woodie Roberts, interview by Carl Elliott, Jasper, Ala., 23 May 1978, Elliott Papers.

TWO. The UMWA and the Color Line in Alabama, 1933–1942

1. Alexander, "Rising from the Ashes," 71; Kelly, *Race, Class, and Power*, 126–27; Clayton and Mitchell, *Black Workers*, 323.

2. JLL to Walter Jones, 9 October 1933, Walter Jones to JLL, 5 October 1933, both in PDC, Folder 33, Box 95; Alexander, "Rising from the Ashes," 72; Taft, *Organizing Dixie*, 87–88. Important overviews of Jones are found in Constance Price, interview by Cliff Kuhn, transcript, Birmingham, Ala., 18 July 1984, WLOHP; F. C. Jones, interview by Cliff Kuhn, transcript, 26 June 1984, WLOHP; Marshall, *Labor in the South*; Kelley, *Hammer and Hoe*. On Jones's organizing ability, see Earl Brown, interview; Mitch, interview by Kuhn.

3. Walter Jones to JLL, 15 November 1933, Folder 33, Box 95, PDC; Thornton, *Dividing Lines*, 143.

4. Walter Jones to JLL, 15 November 1933, Folder 33, Box 95, PDC; Alexander, "Rising from the Ashes," 71; Thornton, *Dividing Lines*, 143.

5. WM to JLL, 27 November 1933, Folder 33, Box 95, PDC. Mitch denied that he had planned to hire Harrison and claimed only to have hoped to get him appointed to the Divisional Coal Labor Board.

6. William Raney to JLL, 27 November 1933, Folder 44, Box 95, PDC; JLL to WM, 15 December 1933, Folder 34, Box 95, PDC; Walter Jones to JLL, 15 November 1933, Folder 33, Box 95, PDC. For protests over the transfer, see Herman Byers to JLL, 5 January 1934, J. H. Chapman, J. A. Cooper, and Kyle Seale to JLL, 8 January 1934, Herbert Weaver to JLL, 9 January 1934, all in Folder 40, Box 95, PDC. On the problems with Dalrymple, see WM to JLL, 23 October 1933, Folder 32, Box 95, PDC. Mitch's concerns appear in WM to JLL, 27 November 1933, Folder 33, Box 95, PDC.

7. Walter Jones to JLL, 29 November 1933, Folder 33, Box 95, PDC; Alexander, "Rising from the Ashes," 71; "Memorandum to the Secretary-Treasurer," 27 August 1937, Folder 26, Box 96, PDC.

8. The organizing efforts among Birmingham coal miners before the New Deal era have been well chronicled. The most important recent works include Kelly, *Race, Class, and Power*; Letwin, *Challenge of Interracial Unionism*. The literature on the establishment of the union under the auspices of the New Deal is less developed. The most comprehensive accounts appear in Taft, *Organizing Dixie*; Alexander, "Rising from the Ashes"; Marshall, *Labor in the South*; Flynt, *Poor but Proud*.

9. Rogers et al., *Alabama*, 481; Alexander, "Rising from the Ashes," 62.

10. Taft, *Organizing Dixie*, 83–84; Board of Mediation, "Alabama's Coal Mining Industry in Relation to the Current Inactivity of the State's Coal Mines."

11. Taft, *Organizing Dixie*, 82–84; Alexander, "Rising from the Ashes," 68–69, 73.

12. Kelley, *Hammer and Hoe*, 139–40; Alexander, "Rising from the Ashes," 76–77; Taft, *Organizing Dixie*, 120–23; "Vales Wins District 11 Union Race," *Terre Haute (Ind.) Post*, 15 January 1931, Folder 16, Box 1, William Mitch Papers, Historical Collections and Labor Archives, Paterno Library, Pennsylvania State University, State College. An overview of Mitch's career in Indiana can be found in Folders 1–16, Box 1, Mitch Papers.

13. Carl McKeever, interview by author, tape recording, Nauvoo, Ala., 19 July 2001; Burgess, interview; Taft, *Organizing Dixie*, 84; Alexander, "Rising from the Ashes," 70–71.

14. Taft, *Organizing Dixie*, 85–86.

15. Alexander, "Rising from the Ashes," 76; Taft, *Organizing Dixie*, 85–86, 92.

16. Earl Brown, interview; Mitch, interview by Kuhn; McAdory, interview; Clayton and Mitchell, *Black Workers*, 347.

17. Alexander, interview; Clayton and Mitchell, *Black Workers*, 323.

18. McWhorter, *Carry Me Home*, 55; Ronald Lewis, *Black Coal Miners in America*, 176; Dubofsky and Van Tine, *John L. Lewis*, 347–50.

19. Henry Mayfield to JLL, 5 June 1941, Folder 55, Box 96, PDC; W. L. Bush to JLL, 8 April 1941, Folder 53, Box 96, PDC.

20. John Hagood to JLL, 7 December 1934, Folder 44, Box 95, PDC; John Doyce and H. A. Doss to JLL, Folder 42, Box 95, PDC.

21. Taft, *Organizing Dixie*, 88; Alexander, "Rising from the Ashes," 73.

22. Taft, *Organizing Dixie*, 88; Alexander, "Rising from the Ashes," 73–74; Walker, *Struggle and the Joy*, 29–34.

23. Taft, *Organizing Dixie*, 89; Alexander, "Rising from the Ashes," 74–75.

24. Alexander, "Rising from the Ashes," 75. Alexander cites a 19 April 1934 letter from W. Carson Adams to Miller.

25. Taft, *Organizing Dixie*, 90–91.

26. WM to A. D. "Denny" Lewis, 2 December 1938, Box 96, Folder 36, PDC; Burgess, interview; Marshall, *Labor in the South*, 151. See also Clayton and Mitchell, *Black Workers*, 346; Alexander, interview; Kelley, *Hammer and Hoe*, 64; McWhorter, *Carry Me Home*, 47.

27. Clayton and Mitchell, *Black Workers*, 345–46; WM to JLL, 16 June 1933, Folder 37, Box 95, PDC.

28. Northrup, *Organized Labor*, 167.

29. Alexander, interview.

30. Northrup, *Organized Labor*, 168.

31. Ibid., 167–70; "Mine Agreement Covering Operations at the Mines of DeBardeleben Coal Corporation, 1934," Folder 46, Box 95, PDC; "Agreement Covering Operations at Wylam No. 8 (Edgewater-Docena-Hamilton) Mine of the Tennessee Coal, Iron and Railroad Company, 1934," Folder 47, Box 95, PDC; "Mine Agreement, 1935," Folder 8, Box 96, PDC; "Wage Agreement between Alabama Coal Mine Operators and District 20, United Mine Workers of America, April 1, 1937, to April 1, 1939," and "Agreement between Tennessee Coal, Iron and Railroad Company, United Mine Workers of America District No. 20, 1942," Folder 3, Box 2, Mitch Papers; WM, "Testimony before the Committee on Fair Employment Practice, Birmingham, Ala., 18 June 1942," Headquarters Records, Reel 17, 93, FEPC Collection.

32. Board of Mediation, "Alabama's Coal Mining Industry in Relation to the Current Inactivity of the State's Coal Mines."

33. Northrup, *Organized Labor*, 170–71; Ronald Lewis, *Black Coal Miners in America*, 173; "Coal Mining in Alabama: Competitive Market Situation," in Alabama Mining Institute, *Coal Mining in Alabama*.

34. Taft, *Organizing Dixie*, 92–93; Alexander, "Rising from the Ashes," 75–77.

35. "Alabama Miners Call Strike to Force Hand of Stalling Operators," *UMWJ*, 15 September 1941; "11,000 Idle as Strikes Here Grow," *BAH*, 4 September 1941; "All Mines but Two in Operation," *BAH*, 9 September 1941.

36. See Collins, interview; White, interview.

37. "Annual Report of President Charles F. DeBardeleben, March 1934, Margaret, Alabama," Folder 6, Box 4641, AFICO Records.

38. "Debardeleben [*sic*] Oasis."

39. Taft, *Organizing Dixie*, 91–92; McWhorter, *Carry Me Home*, 52. See also "Despondency to Happiness, from Idle Land and Idle Hours," *Alabama*, 24 January 1938, "Coal Mining Companies—Alabama Fuel and Iron" File, TCSH.

40. "Annual Report of President, 1934," Folder 2, Box 4643, AFICO Records; WM to JLL, 20 December 1934, Folder 48, Box 95, PDC.

41. Marshall, *Labor in the South*, 145–46.

42. George V. Hutchings, statement, n.d., W. L. Clayton, Houston Mize, Horace Gomer, and J. D. Burnham, statement, 20 October 1934, "Statement by Overton Miners," 20 October 1934, all in Folder 48, Box 95, PDC.

43. "Woman Charges Superintendent Fired on Miners," *BP*, 30 October 1935, Folder 7, Box 96, PDC.

44. "Union Warns Mine Owners," *BP*, 4 November 1935, "Woman Charges Superintendent Fired on Miners," *BP*, 30 October 1935, both in Folder 7, Box 96, PDC.

45. WM to Sidney Hillman, 16 January 1941, Folder 23, Box 96, PDC; Taft, *Organizing Dixie*, 92–93; Alexander, "Rising from the Ashes," 77; McWhorter, *Carry Me Home*, 52.

46. WM to JLL, 30 March 1942, Folder 7, Box 97, PDC; WM to Frank Dixon, 9 January 1942, WM to Earl Houck and Kelly Hopkins, 22 July 1942, both in Folder 9, Box 97, PDC; "Ala. Fuel and Iron Co. Agrees to Disestablish Co. Union—14 Miners Reinstated—with Pay," *UMWJ*, 15 August 1942; Prince DeBardeleben, "To the Stockholders and Directors of Alabama Fuel and Iron Co., 1942," Folder 2, Box 4642, AFICO Records.

47. This situation is treated in Alexander, "Rising from the Ashes," 79.

48. "Decision and Direction of Election, Tennessee Coal, Iron and Railroad Company and United Mine Workers of America, District 20, C.I.O.," Folder 55, Box 96, PDC.

49. WM to JLL and Philip Murray, 8 February 1941, Folder 23, Box 96, PDC; Taft, *Organizing Dixie*, 94.

50. W. B. Turner, interview by Don Sullivan, transcript, Docena, Ala., 3 March 1979, Samford OHC; WM to JLL, 6 April 1936, Folder 19, Box 96, PDC.

51. J. F. Vance to WM, 12 October 1938, WM to Philip Murray, 4 October 1938, both in Folder 36, Box 96, PDC; Alexander, interview.

52. WM to Philip Murray, 4 October 1938, Folder 36, Box 96, PDC.

53. Stein, "Southern Workers in National Unions," 191; Kelley, *Hammer and Hoe*, 139–40; Alexander, "Rising from the Ashes," 76–77; Taft, *Organizing Dixie*, 120–23. On craft unions, see WM to JLL, 2 May 1936, 30 April 1936, both in Folder 16, Box 96, PDC. For accounts of the Florence meeting, see Kelley, *Hammer and Hoe*, 139; Taft, *Organizing Dixie*, 120–21; Alexander, "Rising from the Ashes," 76–77.

54. "Have Communists Obtained a Fast Hold on Alabama?" and "Mitch of Indiana," both in Folder 17, Box 96, PDC; Kelley, *Hammer and Hoe*, 141; Norrell, "Labor at the Ballot Box," 213–14; Thornton, *Dividing Lines*, 151.

55. "Have Communists Obtained a Fast Hold on Alabama?" "Mitch of Indiana," and "Birds of a Feather," all in Folder 17, Box 96, PDC.

56. Marshall, *Labor in the South*, 152; "Our Answer to John Altman's Statement," Folder 17, Box 96, PDC.

57. "Decision and Direction of Election"; WM to JLL and Philip Murray, 8 February 1941, Folder 53, Box 96, PDC; WM to JLL, 21 March 1939, Folder 45, Box 96, PDC.

58. WM to JLL, 1 March 1941, Folder 54, Box 96, PDC; WM to JLL, 21 March 1939, Folder 45, Box 96, PDC.

59. "Proceedings, Board of Mediation, Statement Submitted by the AFL," Folder 12, Box SG12258, Dixon Papers; "Coal Mine Reopening Requested by Dixon Pending New Contract," *BN*, 23 April 1941; Dubofsky and Van Tine, *John L. Lewis*, 390.

60. WM to JLL, 1 July 1941, Folder 1, Box 97, PDC; "Vote Ordered in TCI Mines to Name Agent," *UMWJ*, 1 July 1941; "Decision and Direction of Election." See also "United Mine Workers Voted as Bargaining Agency for Four Mines," *BN*, 1 July 1941; "UMWA Wins Easily in Alabama Contest," *UMWJ*, 15 July 1941; Taft, *Organizing Dixie*, 94; Alexander, "Rising from the Ashes," 79.

61. Mitch, interview by Kuhn; Alexander, interview.

62. Turner, interview; Mitch, interview by Kuhn; Alexander, interview.

63. "Statement of William A. Mitch," Folder 30, Box SG12278, Dixon Papers. A ver-

sion of Mitch's statement also appears in "Statement of William A. Mitch, Birmingham, Alabama, Subject: Senate Bill 1280," Folder 6, Box 97, PDC.

64. Bunche, *Political Status*, 175.

65. Ibid., 253–55.

66. Ibid., 270; Norrell, "Labor at the Ballot Box," 204.

67. Bunche, *Political Status*, 274.

68. Ibid., 265, 267.

69. Sullivan, *Days of Hope*, 64–67, 69–70, 99–101; Kelley, *Hammer and Hoe*, 185; Norrell, "Labor at the Ballot Box," 206.

70. "Starnes Will Address Group," *BP*, 1 December 1938, Folder 36, Box 96, PDC.

71. WM to A. D. Lewis, 2 December 1938, Folder 36, Box 96, PDC. For an example of an account that places Mitch at the center of the SCHW in Birmingham, see McWhorter, *Carry Me Home*, 47.

72. "Statement of Yelverton Cowherd" and "Statement of William A. Mitch," Folder 30, Box SG12278, Dixon Papers.

73. "Mitch Is Defended by Alabama Senators," *BN*, 7 April 1941.

74. William Barnard, "Old Order Changes," 417; Flynt, "Bibb Graves," 173–80; Glenn Feldman, "Frank M. Dixon," 185–89; W. David Lewis, *Sloss Furnaces*, 426; Rogers et al., *Alabama*, 495, 501.

75. William Barnard, *Dixiecrats and Democrats*, 3; Rogers et al., *Alabama*, 501.

76. WM to JLL, 2 May 1941, Folder 54, Box 96, PDC; "Coal Mine Reopening Requested by Dixon," *BN*, 10 April 1941; "Dixon Moves to End Coal Dispute, Names Conciliation Board," *BN*, 12 April 1941.

77. "Alabama's Coal Mining Industry in Relation to the Current Inactivity of the State's Coal Mines" and "Coal Producers, Miners of Dixie Arrive at Pact," *BN*, 30 April 1941.

78. "Coal Strike May Be Ended Today with Mines to Reopen Monday," *BN*, 8 May 1941; "Operators and Miners Negotiate Peace Terms," *BN*, 10 May 1941; "Benefits Held Up," *BN*, 4 May 1941; "Department of Industrial Relations, Release No. 17," 3 May 1941, Folder 1, Box SG12258, Dixon Papers.

79. Taft, *Organizing Dixie*, 108–10.

80. Kelley, *Hammer and Hoe*, 143; Taft, *Organizing Dixie*, 109.

81. Taft, *Organizing Dixie*, 110.

82. "Steel Plant at Ensley Closes with Picketing," *BAH*, 27 September 1941; "TCI Forces to Resume Work," *BAH*, 29 September 1941.

83. See untitled statements by Dixon, Folder 9, Box SG12268, Dixon Papers; "Steel Plant at Ensley Closes with Picketing," *BAH*, 27 September 1941; "TCI Forces to Resume Work," *BAH*, 29 September 1941.

84. "TCI Forces to Resume Work," *BAH*, 29 September 1941. See also Stein, "Southern Workers in National Unions," 192.

85. Prince DeBardeleben to Frank Dixon, 29 September 1941, Folder 9, Box SG12268, Dixon Papers.

86. Sitkoff, "Racial Militancy," 661–63; Daniel, "Going among Strangers," 886–911.

87. Sitkoff, "Racial Militancy," 666; Tindall, *Emergence of the New South*, 713–14; Goodwin, *No Ordinary Time*, 167–70, 246–52.

88. Reed, *Seedtime*, 66, 68.

89. "Editorial," *Alabama*, 12 June 1942, Folder 30, Box SG12267, Dixon Papers.

90. Mark Ethridge to Stephen Early, 22 June 1942, "Fairness Based on Reason, Not Emotion, Is Racial Problem's Need," *Louisville (Ky.) Courier-Journal*, 21 June 1942, both in "Committee on Fair Employment Practice, January–July 1942" Folder, Box 3, Official File 4245, Office of Production Management, C–F, g1941–April 1943, FDR Library.

91. "Elemental Fairness," *BN*, 18 June 1942, "Press Clippings Digest," 6 July 1942, "Committee on Fair Employment Practice" Folder, Box 3, Official File 4245, Office of Production Management, C–F, g1941–April 1943, FDR Library.

92. "FDR Group Wins Negro Job Pact in Alabama," *Daily Worker*, 19 June 1942; "Will Stop Anti-Negro Policy, Alabama Shipyard Head Pledges," *Daily Worker*, 20 June 1942; "F.D.R. Hearings Crack Jim Crow Wall in Deep South," *Daily Worker*, 22 June 1942; "Editorial," *Alabama*, 12 June 1942, Folder 30, Box SG12267, Dixon Papers; Stein, "Southern Workers in National Unions," 193; Frederickson, *Dixiecrat Revolt*, 32–34; Sullivan, *Days of Hope*, 157–58; Norrell, "Labor at the Ballot Box," 225–26; Norrell, "Caste in Steel," 680.

93. WM, testimony before the Committee on Fair Employment Practice, 93, FEPC Collection.

94. Reed, *Seedtime*, 72, 75.

95. Odum, *Race and Rumors of Race*, 36.

96. Bryant Simon, "Fearing Eleanor," 86.

97. Odum, *Race and Rumors of Race*, 54–55, 73–89; Bryant Simon, "Fearing Eleanor," 89.

98. These reports are located in "Observational Reports on Black/White Relations (1943) 1 of 5" Folder, Box 58, Howard Odum Papers, MSS 3164, Additions after 1990, Manuscript Department, Wilson Library, University of North Carolina at Chapel Hill. I am grateful to Michelle Brattain for helping me locate these documents.

99. "Attack on Race Principles Laid to U.S. by Dixon," *BN*, 24 July 1942; Reed, *Seedtime*, 73.

100. William Barnard, *Dixiecrats and Democrats*, 3; Tindall, *Emergence of the New South*, 724; Reed, *Seedtime*, 90–91.

101. I. W. Rouzer to Joe Starnes, 29 July 1942, Folder 30, Box SG12277, Dixon Papers.

102. Glenn Feldman, *Politics, Society, and the Klan*, 288; Norrell, "Labor at the Ballot Box," 211–13, 227; "Unionists Fight Jim Crow—Beaten," *Daily Worker*, 5 August 1942; "Terror in South Brought before White House," *Daily Worker*, 7 August 1942.

103. Thomas H. Vaden, "Report of Liaison Officer SOS on Racial Relations in Alabama," 5 August 1942, Folder 27, Box SG12277, Dixon Papers.

104. Ibid.

105. "Statement by Commissioner Eugene 'Bull' Connor," Folder 31, Box SG12277, Dixon Papers.

106. "Statement by Cooper Green," Folder 31, Box SG12277, Dixon Papers; Kelley, *Race Rebels*, 55–75.

107. "Statement by Holt McDowell," Folder 31, Box SG12277, Dixon Papers.

108. "Statement by W. R. Sims," Folder 31, Box SG12277, Dixon Papers.

109. Oliver T. McDuff, "Synopsis," 8 September 1942, Folder 31, Box SG12277, Dixon Papers.

110. On the break between the UMWA and the CIO, see Zieger, *CIO*, 136–39; Dubofsky and Van Tine, *John L. Lewis*, 407–13; Taft, *Organizing Dixie*, 123.

111. See "Report of William Mitch, President of District No. 20, United Mine Workers of America, Convention, May 8–9–10, 1942, Birmingham, Ala.," Folder 8, Box 97, PDC.

112. "Report of the Alabama CIO Convention, May 16–17, 1942, Birmingham, Alabama," Folder 7, Box 7, M. H. Ross Papers, 1930–86, Georgia State University, William Russell Pullen Library, Southern Labor Archives, Atlanta.

113. "Report of the Alabama CIO Convention"; "Beddow Chosen as President of Union Council," *BAH*, 18 May 1942.

114. "Report of the Alabama CIO Convention"; "Beddow Chosen as President of Union Council," *BAH*, 18 May 1942; "State CIO Convention Expected to Put Okeh on John L. Lewis," *BAH*, 17 May 1942.

115. "Beddow Chosen as President of Union Council," *BAH*, 18 May 1942.

116. "State CIO Convention Expected to Put Okeh on John L. Lewis," *BAH*, 17 May 1942; "Report of the Alabama CIO Convention."

117. "Memorandum on Southern Conspiracy against War Effort, July 28, 1942," Folder 7, Box 7, Ross Papers; "Lewis Linked to 'White Supremacy Plot,'" *Daily Worker*, 17 August 1942.

118. "Memorandum on Southern Conspiracy."

119. For accounts of this campaign, see Huntley, "Rise and Fall," 197–208; Huntley, "Iron Ore Miners," 123–74. Some former Mine Mill unionists joined District 50 in the early 1950s. See "New Local Gets UMW Charter," *BN*, 19 October 1953, "Labor Unions— Alabama Scrapbooks, Volumes 1–3," Microfilm, Department of Archives and Manuscripts, Birmingham Public Library, Birmingham, Ala.

THREE. The World War II Strikes, 1941–1945

1. "To Locals of the United Mine Workers of America, District No. 20" [circular], 18 February 1942, Folder 6, Box 10, District 36, Birmingham, Alabama Series, United Steelworkers of America Archive and Oral History Collection, Historical Collections and Labor Archives, Paterno Library, Pennsylvania State University, State College.

2. Annual report of H. E. Mills, 19 January 1945, Folder 1.21, ACOA/AMI Records.

3. Zieger, *CIO*, 150; Nelson Lichtenstein, *Labor's War at Home*, 121; Preis, *Labor's Giant Step*, 196; Cronenberg, *Forth to the Mighty Conflict*, ix; Feldman, "Alabama Coal Miners," 84–110.

4. Lipsitz, *Rainbow at Midnight*, 63, 75, 88; Nelson Lichtenstein, *Labor's War at Home*, 121, 125, 154–55.

5. Tindall, *Emergence of the New South*, 694–700.

6. Nelson, "Organized Labor," 956; Cronenberg, *Forth to the Mighty Conflict*, 49, 51, 74.

7. Cronenberg, *Forth to the Mighty Conflict*, 49, 51, 74. This influx of military and defense-related spending is described in Tindall, *Emergence of the New South*; Bartley, *New South*; Wright, *Old South, New South*; Cobb, *Selling of the South*; Schulman, *From Cotton Belt to Sunbelt*.

8. Rogers et al., *Alabama*, 511; Cronenberg, *Forth to the Mighty Conflict*, 48, 51.

9. *Second Annual Report of the Department of Industrial Relations to the Governor of Alabama, Fiscal Year Ending September 30, 1940*, Folder 2.40, ACOA/AMI Records; *Fourth Annual Report of the Department of Industrial Relations to the Governor of Alabama, Fiscal Year Ending September 30, 1942*, 126–27, Folder 2.43, ACOA/AMI Records; ADIR, *Annual Statistical Report, Fiscal Year 1944–1945*, Folder 3.2, ACOA/AMI Records.

10. Minutes of Annual Meeting of Board of Governors of the Alabama Mining Institute, 14 July 1942, Folder 1.18, ACOA/AMI Records.

11. "Testimony of William Mitch before the Labor Supply Committee," Montgomery, Ala., 27 July 1943, Folder 15, Box SG12498, Chauncey Sparks Papers, Alabama Department of Archives and History, Montgomery.

12. I. W. Rouzer to Frank B. Broadway, 28 July 1943, Folder 15, Box SG12498, Sparks Papers.

13. "Report of Committee," 28 July 1943, Folder 15, Box SG12498, Sparks Papers.

14. Ibid.; Preis, *Labor's Giant Step*, 177.

15. Lon F. Thompson to JLL, 24 March 1942, Folder 7, Box 97, PDC.

16. Preis, *Labor's Giant Step*, 175, 179; Dubofsky and Van Tine, *John L. Lewis*, 417–18; Zieger, *CIO*, 168–69; Dubofsky, *State and Labor*, 188; Brattain, *Politics of Whiteness*, 114–15.

17. I. W. Rouzer to Chauncey Sparks, 5 July 1943, Folder 17, Box SG12409, Sparks Papers; Brattain, *Politics of Whiteness*, 114; Nelson, "Organized Labor," 961; Cronenberg, *Forth to the Mighty Conflict*, 90.

18. Zieger, *CIO*, 143; Dubofsky and Van Tine, *John L. Lewis*, 415; Nelson Lichtenstein, *Labor's War at Home*, 71.

19. Alexander, "Rising from the Ashes," 73; Kelley, *Hammer and Hoe*, 64.

20. WM to JLL, 26 October 1933, William Stone to Charles Knight, 19 October 1933, both in Folder 32, Box 95, PDC.

21. WM to JLL, 11 December 1933, Folder 32, Box 95, PDC.

22. Kelley, *Hammer and Hoe*, 65; Alexander, "Rising from the Ashes," 74–77.

23. G. L. Johnson, circular, 27 February 1935, Box 1, Folder 11, Mitch Papers; Kelley, *Hammer and Hoe*, 65, 138; Alexander, "Rising from the Ashes," 74–77.

24. For examples, see JLL to L. W. Murty, 19 March 1935, L. W. Murty to JLL, 13 March 1935, both in Folder 53, Box 95, PDC. On the situation in Coal Valley, see WM to JLL, 21 September 1934, Folder 43, Box 95, PDC.

25. Alexander, "Rising from the Ashes," 77–78.

26. WM to JLL, 23 October 1933, Folder 32, Box 95, PDC.

27. WM to Philip Murray, 8 June 1934, Folder 51, Box 95, PDC; WM to JLL, 23 October 1933, Folder 32, Box 95, PDC; Walter Jones to JLL, 29 November 1933, Folder 33, Box 95, PDC; WM to Noel Beddow and Yelverton Cowherd, 13 July 1938, Folder 6, Box 10, District 36, Birmingham, Ala., Series, United Steelworkers of America Archive and Oral History Collection.

28. WM to JLL, 27 November 1933, Folder 33, Box 95, PDC.

29. WM to JLL, 23 October 1933, Folder 32, Box 95, PDC.

30. A. N. Barrentine to JLL, 28 October 1933, Folder 36, Box 95, PDC.

31. J. H. Chapman, J. A. Cooper, and Kyle Seale to JLL, 8 January 1934, Herbert Weaver to JLL, 9 January 1934, both in Folder 40, Box 95, PDC. Information on Dalrymple's trans-

fer appears in JLL to WM, 15 December 1933, Folder 34, Box 95, PDC. Both Mitch and Dalrymple had requested transfers from Alabama.

32. JLL to WM, 15 November 1934, WM, W. H. Raney, John Parsons, J. W. Heathcock, W. H. Huey, and Walter Jones to JLL, 10 November 1934, both in Folder 44, Box 95, PDC.

33. "Alabama Miners Call Strike to Force Hand of Stalling Operators," *UMWJ*, 15 September 1941; "Arms Unit Asks Mines to Reopen," *BAH*, 5 September 1941; "11,000 Idle as Strikes Here Grow," *BAH*, 4 September 1941; Dubofsky and Van Tine, *John L. Lewis*, 398, 401–2, 404.

34. "Mine Case Reopened by Board," *BAH*, 20 September 1941; "Miners Ordered Back to Work," *BAH*, 6 September 1941; "All Mines but Two in Operation," *BAH*, 9 September 1941; WM to JLL, 6 September 1941, Folder 2, Box 97, PDC; "National Defense Mediation Board, in the Matter of Alabama Coal Operators and United Mine Workers of America," case 20-C, 20–21 October 1941, Folder 3, Box 97, PDC.

35. "Miners of Area Vote for Work," *BAH*, 22 September 1941.

36. For descriptions of this dispute, see WM to John O'Leary, 14 August 1945, Folder 27, Box 97, PDC.

37. WM to John O'Leary, 14 August 1945, WM to Arthur Short, 7 August 1945, both in Folder 27, Box 97, PDC.

38. Arthur Short to JLL, 6 August 1945, WM to Arthur Short, 7 August 1945, WM to John O'Leary, 14 August 1945, all in Folder 27, Box 97, PDC.

39. WM to JLL, 25 October 1944, Folder 24, Box 97, PDC.

40. WM to JLL, 10 February 1944, Folder 23, Box 97, PDC; JLL to WM, 6 April 1944, WM to JLL, 5 May 1943, both in Folder 24, Box 97, PDC.

41. WM to JLL, 25 October 1944, Folder 24, Box 97, PDC.

42. Preis, *Labor's Giant Step*, 177.

43. "10 Killed in Blast at Praco Mine," *BN*, 11 May 1943.

44. JLL et al. to W. M. Perryman, 12 May 1943, Folder 13, Box 97, PDC.

45. WM to JLL, 3 July 1941, WM to Huey Sewell, 3 July 1941, both in Folder 1, Box 97, PDC.

46. Howard Nail and R. H. Walker to JLL, 17 March 1942, Folder 7, Box 97, PDC.

47. "United States Department of the Interior, Bureau of Mines, Coal Mine Inspection Report, Sayreton No. 2 Mine, Republic Steel Corporation, Sayretown [*sic*], Jefferson County, Alabama," 4–10 February 1943, Folder 16, Box 97, PDC.

48. "Failure to Observe Safety Laws Brought Death to 25 Sayreton Miners—19 Injured," *UMWJ*, 15 September 1943; "Report, John E. Jones and Harrison Combs to T. J. Thomas, Director, Health and Safety Division, Coal Mines Administration," 4 September 1943, "Report, Harrison Combs to John L. Lewis," 7 September 1943, both in Folder 16, Box 97, PDC.

49. "Failure to Observe Safety Laws Brought Death to 25 Sayreton Miners—19 Injured," *UMWJ*, 15 September 1943; "Report, John E. Jones and Harrison Combs to T. J. Thomas, Director, Health and Safety Division, Coal Mines Administration," 4 September 1943, "Report, Harrison Combs to John L. Lewis," 7 September 1943, both in Folder 16, Box 97, PDC.

50. "Report, Harrison Combs to John L. Lewis," 7 September 1943, Folder 16, Box 97, PDC.

51. "Report, Harrison Combs to John L. Lewis," 7 September 1943, Folder 16, Box 97, PDC; "Failure to Observe Safety Laws Brought Death to 25 Sayreton Miners—19 Injured," *UMWJ*, 15 September 1943. Combs's report was composed from several investigations conducted after the blast. See "Report, John E. Jones and Harrison Combs to T. J. Thomas, Director, Health and Safety Division, Coal Mines Administration," 4 September 1943, Folder 16, Box 97, PDC.

52. WM to JLL, 10 February 1944, 18 January 1944, JLL to Arthur Atchley, 19 January 1944, 24 January 1944, Cliff Black and Fred Darvis Otis to JLL, 25 January 1944, all in Folder 23, Box 97, PDC.

53. WM to JLL, 25 October 1944, Folder 23, Box 97, PDC.

54. Ibid.

55. WM to JLL, 19 May 1943, Folder 16, Box 97, PDC.

56. WM to H. M. Smith, 27 June 1944, Folder 24, Box 97, PDC.

57. Ibid.

58. "Strikes Occurring over Racial Issues during Period July 1943 to December 1944," Reports on Strikes Folder, Office Files of Joy Davis, Headquarters Records, Reel 72, FEPC Collection.

59. Ibid.

60. M. B. Calvin to JLL, 10 October 1944, Folder 21, Box 97, PDC.

61. Dubofsky and Van Tine, *John L. Lewis*, 420–21; Taft, *Organizing Dixie*, 144.

62. Henry Dickerson to JLL, 25 April 1943, Folder 13, Box 97, PDC; WM to T. J. Thomas, 1 March 1943, Folder 12, Box 97, PDC; WM to JLL, 17 April 1943, Folder 13, Box 97, PDC.

63. Minutes of Annual Meeting of Members of the Alabama Mining Institute, 15 December 1942, Folder 1.18, ACOA/AMI Records.

64. WM to JLL, 27 March 1943, Folder 11, Box 97, PDC.

65. "T.C.I. Coal Miners Fail to Go to Work," *BN*, 24 April 1943; "State's Union Miners, Operators to Consult over Temporary Pact," *BN*, 26 April 1943; WM to JLL, 17 April 1943, JLL to Members of Local Union 6255, 15 April 1943, both in Folder 13, Box 97, PDC.

66. "Alabama Coal Mines to Be Open Saturday for Any Who Return," *BN*, 30 April 1943; "Miners Quitting in Many Districts," *BN*, 27 April 1943; "Work Shutdown Threat Increases in Alabama Mines," *BN*, 28 April 1943; I. W. Rouzer to Chauncey Sparks, 30 April 1943, 1 May 1943, 3 May 1943, all in Folder 13, Box SG12409, Sparks Papers; Dubofsky and Van Tine, *John L. Lewis*, 427.

67. "Leaders Expect to Get Pits Open Soon as Possible," *BN*, 3 May 1943; "Alabama Mines Are Preparing for U.S. Control," *BN*, 1 May 1943; "Alabama Mines Action on Coal Order Awaited," *BN*, 2 May 1943; Taft, *Organizing Dixie*, 144.

68. "All State Mines to Adopt Longer Work Week Plan," *BN*, 6 May 1943; "State's Captive Mines Ordered to Instigate Six-Day Work Week," *BN*, 7 May 1943; "Leaders Expect to Get Pits Open Soon as Possible," *BN*, 3 May 1943.

69. "The People v. John Lewis," *BN*, 18 May 1943; "The President Acts," *BN*, 2 May 1943.

70. "State Coal Miners Join in Nationwide Stoppage of Work," *BN*, 1 June 1943; "Independence Day Sees Miners Back at Work," *BN*, 5 July 1943; Dubofsky and Van Tine, *John L. Lewis*, 430–34; Taft, *Organizing Dixie*, 144–45.

71. Charlie Langford and Leman Session to Chauncey Sparks, 9 June 1943, WM to Chauncey Sparks, 7 June 1943, Chauncey Sparks to WM, 4 June 1943, all in Folder 17, Box SG12409, Sparks Papers; "Governor Asks Mitch to Call Miners to Jobs," *BN*, 4 June 1943.

72. "Coal Confusion," *BAH*, 26 June 1943; "UMW Head's Acts Held Treasonable by Alabama Group," *BN*, 3 June 1943.

73. "Their Country or John L. Lewis: The Miners Must Choose" [advertisement], *BN*, 2 June 1943, "Strikes, Alabama Coal Miners, 1941–1950" File, TCSH.

74. Nelson Lichtenstein, *Labor's War at Home*, 167–68; Dubofsky, *State and Labor*, 190.

75. "The Bradford Act, Creating the Department of Labor," Folder 9, Box SG12417, Sparks Papers, 8; Taft, *Organizing Dixie*, 155.

76. H. E. Mills, Annual Report, Exhibit C, 8 February 1944, Folder 1.20, ACOA/AMI Records.

77. Minutes of Meeting of Board of Governors, 2 July 1943, 30 June 1943, 29 June 1943, 1 July 1943, Harold McDermott to I. W. Rouzer, 20 July 1943, all in Folder 1.19, ACOA/AMI Records.

78. "Miners Walkout Cuts Coal Output to Mere Dribble," *BN*, 21 June 1943; "State Mines Stoppage Checks Production of Steel for War Use," *BN*, 21 June 1943; "Miners in Alabama Stand by for Orders to Return to Work," *BN*, 23 June 1943; "District's Output of Iron Touches Three-Year Low," *BN*, 27 June 1943.

79. "Governor Asks Mitch to Call Miners Back to Jobs," *BN*, 4 June 1943.

80. "Coal Industry Here Virtually Dormant Despite Work Order," *BN*, 25 June 1943; "Mitch Asks Men to Produce Coal in Strong Rebuke," *BN*, 28 June 1943.

81. "Coal Industry Here Virtually Dormant Despite Work Order," *BN*, 25 June 1943; "State's Miners Adopting 'What's the Use' Attitude," *BN*, 30 June 1943.

82. "Independence Day Sees Miners Back at Work," *BN*, 5 July 1943; "State's Miners Adopting 'What's the Use' Attitude," *BN*, 30 June 1943.

83. "Coal Industry Here Virtually Dormant Despite Work Order," *BN*, 25 June 1943.

84. "Lewis Tells Miners to Return to Work," *BN*, 16 October 1943; "Nearly 7,000 Miners Are Idle as Stoppage Spreads in Alabama," *BN*, 14 October 1943.

85. "Unheated Offices, No Gas for Homes, T.C.I. Shutdown Confronting City Monday," *BN*, 29 October 1943; "Alabama Miners' Work Stop Hangs on Persistently," *BN*, 26 October 1943; "Miners in State Arrive at Crossroads of Strike," *BN*, 17 October 1943; Dubofsky and Van Tine, *John L. Lewis*, 437–38.

86. "3,200 State Miners Begin Back-to-Jobs Move after Pleas," *BN*, 18 October 1943; "Serious Industrial and Domestic Gas Dearth Faces City," *BN*, 19 October 1943.

87. "Ultimatum in Coal Strike Given by F.D.R. as Walkout Spreads," *BN*, 30 October 1943.

88. "Mr. Lewis and the Miners," *NYT*, 18 October 1943; "Alabama Miners—Still Out," *BAH*, 23 October 1943.

89. William H. Davis to Franklin Roosevelt, 29 October 1943, "Coal Strikes, July 1943 to February 1944" Folder, Box 13, Official File 407b, Labor, FDR Library; "Union Chiefs

Wire Miners to Return as Seizure Nears," *NYT*, 24 October 1943; "Board Calls Mine Leaders in Failure to Halt Strikes; Soft Coal Shortage Acute," *NYT*, 23 October 1943.

90. "Unheated Offices, No Gas for Homes, T.C.I. Shutdown Confronting City Monday," *BN*, 29 October 1943.

91. "Ultimatum in Coal Strike Given by F.D.R. as Walkout Spreads," *BN*, 30 October 1943; "Unheated Offices, No Gas for Homes, T.C.I. Shutdown Confronting City Monday," *BN*, 29 October 1943.

92. Chauncey Sparks to WM, 27 October 1943, Folder 10, Box SG12417, Sparks Papers.

93. "It Must Be Ended!" *BN*, 21 October 1943; "Intolerable!" *BN*, 20 October 1943.

94. "To Hinder Production Is to Hinder the Winning of the War," *Birmingham Labor Advocate*, November 1943.

95. "Miners Summoned Back to Jobs Following Agreement on Wages," *BN*, 4 November 1943; "U.S. Seizes Mines; Showdown Nears on Order to Work," *BN*, 2 November 1943; Dubofsky and Van Tine, *John L. Lewis*, 439.

96. Dubofsky and Van Tine, *John L. Lewis*, 439–40.

97. WM to Local Unions 5795, 6256, 6257, 6273, and 8032, 21 March 1944, Folder 23, Box 97, PDC.

98. JLL to Local Unions 5840, 7918, 5988, 6173, 6255, 5831, and 8022, 6 June 1944, WM to JLL, 6 June 1944, Felman Huey and Harry S. Blackwell to JLL, 9 June 1944, all in Folder 24, Box 97, PDC.

99. Felman Huey and Harry S. Blackwell to JLL, 9 June 1944, Folder 24, Box 97, PDC.

100. "Alabama Miners Vote Better Than 13 to 1 to Authorize Striking," *BN*, 29 March 1945; Dubofsky and Van Tine, *John L. Lewis*, 454.

101. Dubofsky and Van Tine, *John L. Lewis*, 454–55.

102. "Back to Work Move Is Gaining Impetus in State Coal Mines," *BN*, 5 April 1945.

103. "Intimidation Blamed in Coal Mine Tieup," *BN*, 19 April 1945; "Undercurrents in State Coal Mine Walkout," *BN*, 20 April 1945; W. Emmett Brooks to Herbert E. Smith, 23 April 1945, Folder 13, Box SG12498, Sparks Papers; JLL to Alabama Locals, 19 April 1945, Folder 25, Box 97, PDC.

104. "Strange and Deplorable," *BN*, 20 April 1945; "Gov. Sparks Wires Ickes for Prompt Action in Coal Strike," *BN*, 20 April 1945; Abe Fortas to Chauncey Sparks, 23 April 1945, Folder 13, Box SG12498, Sparks Papers.

105. "Undercurrents in State Coal Mine Walkout," *BN*, 20 April 1945.

106. "Miners in Alabama Returning to Their Jobs in Rapid Order," *BN*, 23 April 1945; "Most of State Miners Are Expected Back on Job by Monday," *BN*, 22 April 1945; "Miners Are Admonished to Return to Their Jobs," *BN*, 21 April 1945.

107. Dubofsky and Van Tine, *John L. Lewis*, 456; "Coal Mine Strike Still Darkest Industrial Cloud," *BN*, 9 October 1945; "Lewis Orders End to Soft Coal Strike Effective Monday," *BN*, 17 October 1945; I. W. Rouzer to Chauncey Sparks, 23 April 1945, Folder 13, Box SG12498, Sparks Papers.

108. H. E. Mills, Annual Report, 19 January 1945, Folder 1.21, ACOA/AMI Records.

109. Board of Mediation, "Alabama's Coal Mining Industry in Relation to the Current Inactivity of the State's Coal Mines."

110. Burgess, interview.

111. Ibid.

112. Northrup, *Organized Labor*, 171.

FOUR. Race, Economic Decline, and the Fight for the Welfare and Retirement Fund, 1946–1950

1. B. L. Allen, W. L. Allen, C. E. Benton, and C. S. Sanderson, "Ku Klux Klan Activities Jefferson County Alabama," 25 June 1949, 1, Folder 5, Box SG12644, James E. Folsom Papers, Alabama Department of Archives and History, Montgomery, Alabama; Fred Bass Sr., interview.

2. Allen et al., "Ku Klux Klan Activities"; Fred Bass Sr., interview; Flynt, *Poor but Proud*, 119, 123; Patchen, interview.

3. Allen et al., "Ku Klux Klan Activities"; Fred Bass Sr., interview.

4. Ibid.

5. "Klan Head Here Denies Unit Was Involved in Raid," *BN*, 24 June 1948, Ku Klux Klan Scrapbooks, Microfilm, Department of Archives and Manuscripts, Birmingham Public Library, Birmingham, Ala.; Glenn Feldman, *Politics, Society, and the Klan*, 285, 298.

6. Stetson Kennedy, "Klan Prepares to Take over Unions," *The Worker*, 19 December 1948, Anti-Negro Groups Clipping File, Hollis Burke Frissell Library, Tuskegee University, Tuskegee, Ala.; Glenn Feldman, *Politics, Society, and the Klan*, 10; Eskew, *But for Birmingham*, 53.

7. Grafton and Permaloff, *Big Mules and Branchheads*, 73; Rogers et al., *Alabama*, 529.

8. Rogers et al., *Alabama*, 524.

9. Ronald Lewis, *Black Coal Miners in America*, 180, 192–93; Barnum, *Negro*, 4–5.

10. For Alabama production numbers, see ADIR, *Annual Statistical Report, Fiscal Year, 1944–1945*, Folder 3.2, ACOA/AMI Records; ADIR, *Annual Report, Statistical Supplement, 1960*, Folder 3.17, ACOA/AMI Records; Barnum, *Negro*, 67.

11. "Coal Mining in Alabama: Utilization and Distribution of Coal," in Alabama Mining Institute, *Coal Mining in Alabama*; "A. W. Vogtle Speaks to Rotary Club on Walker County Coal," *UN*, 30 June 1949; Seltzer, *Fire in the Hole*, 55.

12. I. W. Rouzer to Ben Moreell, 6 September 1946, Folder 126, Box 4, Elliott Papers; Shotts, *Some Significant Recent Changes*, 70.

13. "Okay to Start on Natural Gas," *UN*, 23 June 1949; "Mine Operators Gloomy on Walker Coal Future," *UN*, 1 September 1949.

14. Shotts, *Some Significant Recent Changes*, 70; Seltzer, *Fire in the Hole*, 55.

15. See ADIR, *Annual Statistical Report, Fiscal Year 1944–1945*, Folder 3.2, ACOA/AMI Records; ADIR, *Annual Statistical Report, Fiscal Year 1949–1950*, Folder 3.7, ACOA/AMI Records; ADIR, *Annual Statistical Report, Fiscal Year 1960*, Folder 3.17, ACOA/AMI Records; Shotts, *Some Significant Recent Changes*, 70.

16. I. W. Rouzer to members of the Alabama Mining Institute, 7 October 1949, Folder 338, Box 14, Elliott Papers.

17. D. A. Thomas to C. F. Davis, 2 October 1950, Folder 53, Box 97, PDC.

18. Carl Elliott to Cyrus Ching, 20 October 1949, Folder 338, Box 14, Elliott Papers.

19. John O'Leary to James Terry, 13 July 1945, 19 July 1945, Folder 29, Box 97, PDC; "Resolution of Board of Directors," 18 September 1941, Folder 3, Box 4643, AFICO

Records; Alabama Mining Institute, "Resolution," 15 January 1942, Folder 1.18, ACOA/AMI Records.

20. Earl Houck to JLL, John O'Leary, and Thomas Kennedy, 8 March 1946, Folder 29, Box 97, PDC.

21. James Terry to John O'Leary, 30 July 1945, Folder 29, Box 97, PDC.

22. Minutes, Board of Directors Meeting, 17 June 1949, 9 September 1949, 17 September 1948, Folder 4, Box 4643, AFICO Records.

23. Minutes, Board of Directors Meeting, 15 December 1950, 16 August 1950, 15 September 1950, 16 June 1950, Folder 4, Box 4643, AFICO Records.

24. William Mitch Jr., interview by author, tape recording, Birmingham, Ala., 30 July 2001; "Alabama Fuel and Iron Co. Looks Down That Long, Long Road toward Oblivion," *BN*, 5 December 1950, "Coal Mines and Mining—Alabama" File, TCSH.

25. "Alabama Fuel and Iron Co. Looks Down That Long, Long Road toward Oblivion," *BN*, 5 December 1950, "Coal Mines and Mining—Alabama" File, TCSH.

26. Lester F. Lawrence, "Organize," *UN*, 24 February 1949.

27. U.S. Department of Labor, Bureau of Employment Security, "Classification of Labor Market Areas According to Relative Labor Supply," Folder 901, Box 36, Elliott Papers; "A. W. Vogtle Speaks to Rotary Club on Walker County Coal," *UN*, 30 June 1949.

28. Carl Elliott to Oscar Chapman, n.d., Folder 1428, Box 43, Elliott Papers; Statement by Carl Elliott, n.d., Folder 847, Box 35, Elliott Papers; Carl Elliott to Lister Hill and John Sparkman, 9 June 1950, Folder 828, Box 34, Elliott Papers.

29. Grafton and Permaloff, *Big Mules and Branchheads*, 59–60, 74–75.

30. Ibid., 62.

31. Ibid.

32. Alabama Department of Archives and History, *Alabama Official and Statistical Register, 1947*, 481–83; Grafton and Permaloff, *Big Mules and Branchheads*, 59–60, 62, 70, 74–76; Rogers et al., *Alabama*, 529.

33. Alabama Department of Archives and History, *Alabama Official and Statistical Register, 1947*, 490–91; Grafton and Permaloff, *Big Mules and Branchheads*, 71, 74; William Barnard, *Dixiecrats and Democrats*, 30, 41.

34. Elliott and D'Orso, *Cost of Courage*, 86.

35. Ibid., 86, 89, 91.

36. Lester Lawrence to JLL, 26 March 1948, Folder 42, Box 97, PDC; Elliott and D'Orso, *Cost of Courage*, 91.

37. William Barnard, *Dixiecrats and Democrats*; Frederickson, *Dixiecrat Revolt*; Rogers et al., *Alabama*, 534.

38. Grafton and Permaloff, *Big Mules and Branchheads*, 80.

39. Key, *Southern Politics in State and Nation*, 633–35; Rogers et al., *Alabama*, 533; William Barnard, *Dixiecrats and Democrats*, 61–62, 171 n.52; Grafton and Permaloff, *Big Mules and Branchheads*, 80–81.

40. William Barnard, *Dixiecrats and Democrats*, 95–124.

41. Glenn Feldman, *Politics, Society, and the Klan*, 290, 295; "Klan Files Incorporation Papers in County Court," *BP*, 20 July 1946, "County's Law Officers Ponder Cross Burning Demonstrations Here," *BN*, 28 March 1946, both in Klan Scrapbooks.

42. "Alabama Ku Klux Weighing Merge with Georgians after Pep Show Here," *BN*, 25

April 1949, "Klan Has Meeting at Courthouse Here," *BN*, 18 April 1947, both in Klan Scrapbooks.

43. "Alabama Ku Klux Weighing Merge with Georgians after Pep Show Here," *BN*, 25 April 1949, "Klan Files Incorporation Papers in County Court," *BP*, 20 July 1946, both in Klan Scrapbooks.

44. Glenn Feldman, *Politics, Society, and the Klan*, 9–10, 299–301.

45. "Union Leaders Urged to Condemn Upsurge of Klanism," *Atlanta Daily World*, 3 July 1948; "Morris Probe Is Denounced as Klan Denies Camp Raid," *BP*, 23 June 1948, Anti-Negro Groups Clipping File; Glenn Feldman, *Politics, Society, and the Klan*, 298; Thornton, *Dividing Lines*, 160–61.

46. Stetson Kennedy, "Klan Prepares to Take over Unions," *The Worker*, 19 December 1948, Anti-Negro Groups Clipping File.

47. Huntley, "Iron Ore Miners," 123, 162, 168; Huntley, "Red Scare," 129–45; Norrell, "Caste in Steel," 673, 684; Zieger, *CIO*, 281–82; Glenn Feldman, *Politics, Society, and the Klan*, 300.

48. For another account of the night riding described in this chapter, see Glenn Feldman, *Politics, Society, and the Klan*, 283–324.

49. Allen et al., "Ku Klux Klan Activities."

50. Ibid.

51. Ibid.; "Hooded Men Slug Woman, Burn Crosses," *BAH*, 12 June 1949, Klan Scrapbooks.

52. Allen et al., "Ku Klux Klan Activities"; Glenn Feldman, *Politics, Society and the Klan*, 301.

53. Allen et al., "Ku Klux Klan Activities"; "Jurors Are Out Only 66 Minutes Deciding Verdict," *BN*, 30 October 1949, Anti-Negro Groups Clipping File.

54. Allen et al., "Ku Klux Klan Activities."

55. "New Hotbed of Terrorism Is Uncovered," *BAH*, 2 July 1949, "Report Tells of Violence near Praco as Grand Jury Keeps Up Quiz," *BN*, 6 July 1949, Klan Scrapbooks; Mary Alice (Henderson) Kilgore, interview by Special Agents Thomas B. Landess and August J. Baumgartner, Chicago, 8 March 1966, Folder 1308.2.4, Sixteenth Street Baptist Church Bombing Investigation Files, U.S. Federal Bureau of Investigation, Microfilm, Department of Archives and Manuscripts, Birmingham Public Library, Birmingham, Ala.

56. "New Hotbed of Terrorism Is Uncovered," *BAH*, 2 July 1949, "Report Tells of Violence near Praco as Grand Jury Keeps Up Quiz," *BN*, 6 July 1949, both in Klan Scrapbooks.

57. "New Hotbed of Terrorism Is Uncovered," *BAH*, 2 July 1949, Klan Scrapbooks; Jack Alexander, interview by Special Agent John Kresek, Jasper, Ala., 14 February 1966, Folder 1308.2.4, Sixteenth Street Baptist Church Bombing Investigation Files; "Report Tells of Violence near Praco as Grand Jury Keeps Up Quiz," *BN*, 6 July 1949, Klan Scrapbooks.

58. Allen et al., "Ku Klux Klan Activities"; "Brookside Councilmen in 'Red Hot' Dispute," *BP*, 10 October 1949, "Brookside, Alabama" File, TCSH.

59. "14 Face Arrest Today after Flog Probe," *BAH*, 11 July 1949, Klan Scrapbooks; Allen et al., "Ku Klux Klan Activities"; "Brookside Councilmen in 'Red Hot' Dispute," *BP*, 10 October 1949, "Brookside, Alabama" File, TCSH. Elmer Brock and his brother, Jack, a former Alabama State Federation of Labor president, went on to become some of the

more notorious people in the Alabama labor movement. See Norrell, "Labor Trouble," 250–72.

60. "Brookside Councilmen in 'Red Hot' Dispute," *BP*, 10 October 1949, "Brookside, Alabama" File, TCSH.

61. "Folsom Hits at Hooded Mobsters," *BP*, 27 June 1949, "Crackdown Ordered against Robed Bands," *BAH*, 14 May 1949, both in Klan Scrapbooks.

62. "Act. No. 139," and "Alabama Tears Mask from Klan and Others," *BAH*, 29 June 1949, Klan Scrapbooks.

63. "Trawick Asks House Committee to Let Us Solve Own Problems," *UN*, 30 June 1949; "A Reply to a 'Friend,'" *UN*, 23 June 1949.

64. "Non-partisans Denounce KKK," *UN*, 17 July 1949.

65. Dewey Salter and Jerald Hanson to WM, 7 November 1949, Folder 50, Box 97, PDC; "Alabama: It Sure Was Pretty," *Newsweek*, 7 November 1949, Anti-Negro Groups Clipping File; Allen et al., "Ku Klux Klan Activities."

66. WM to Jerald Hanson, 15 November 1949, Folder 50, Box 97, PDC.

67. "Alabama: It Sure Was Pretty," *Newsweek*, 7 November 1949; "Jurors Are Out Only 66 Minutes Deciding Verdict," *BN*, 30 October 1949, Anti-Negro Groups Clipping File; Allen et al., "Ku Klux Klan Activities"; "State Police Get Names, Numbers after Hoods Spotted in Adamsville," *BN*, 18 June 1949, Klan Scrapbooks. Lollar was likely not the only person affiliated with Holt McDowell's department who had Klan connections. Glenn Feldman notes that after the 1948 incident at the Girl Scout camp, "deputies publicly endorsed the raid" (*Politics, Society, and the Klan*, 298).

68. "Committee of 15 Is to Fight Mobism," *BP*, 23 June 1949; "Prohibits Masks," *BN*, 24 June 1949; "Morris Home Burglary Report Adds Confusion in Flog Probe," *BAH*, 22 July 1949, Klan Scrapbooks.

69. "14 Face Arrest Today after Flogging Probe," *BAH*, 11 July 1949; "State Loses Again in Flogging Trials," *BN*, 29 March 1950; "Not Guilty Verdict Causes State to Drop 41 Flog Cases," *BN*, 7 June 1951. Chambliss later became the best-known Klan terrorist in Birmingham. In 1977 he was convicted of murder for his role in the infamous September 1963 Sixteenth Street Baptist Church bombing that killed four young African American girls. His career is described in detail in McWhorter, *Carry Me Home*.

70. Mulcahy, *Social Contract*, 3–4; Seltzer, *Fire in the Hole*, 57; Dubofsky and Van Tine, *John L. Lewis*, 454–55.

71. "Why Miners Strike" [letter to the editor], *BN*, n.d., Folder 29, Box 97, PDC; U.S. Department of Commerce, Bureau of the Census, *Census of Population: 1950*, 2–230; Seltzer, *Fire in the Hole*, 57; Dubofsky and Van Tine, *John L. Lewis*, 459.

72. Mulcahy, *Social Contract*, 7–8; Dubofsky and Van Tine, *John L. Lewis*, 458–59; Seltzer, *Fire in the Hole*, 57.

73. "No Trouble Seen Here and Pickets Are Not Being Used," *BN*, 2 April 1946; "22,000 Out in Alabama," *BP*, 2 April 1946, Folder 29, Box 97, PDC.

74. "Most of Alabama Mines Closed Despite Seizure," *BN*, 22 May 1946; Mulcahy, *Social Contract*, 7–8; Seltzer, *Fire in the Hole*, 58; Dubofsky and Van Tine, *John L. Lewis*, 461.

75. "Fuel-Starved Mills Stir Lazily as All Pits Resume Work," *BN*, 3 June 1946.

76. Dubofsky and Van Tine, *John L. Lewis*, 462–63, 466–67, 470–71; Dubofsky, *State and Labor*, 194–95.

77. "State Will Go Along with Lewis' Order, Says William Mitch," *BN*, 30 March 1947; Dubofsky and Van Tine, *John L. Lewis*, 470; "Rock-Dust Laxity Revealed by U.S. Bureau of Mines," *BN*, 31 March 1947; "List of Mines Closed in State," *BN*, 3 April 1947.

78. WM, statement, 4 April 1947, WM to James E. Folsom, 4 April 1947, both in Folder 16(a), Box SG13415, Folsom Papers.

79. WM to James E. Folsom, 4 April 1947, Folder 16(a), Box SG13415, Folsom Papers; Lee Grant Cleveland to JLL, 6 November 1946, Folder 32, Box 97, PDC. The loss of the job left Cleveland, who had a family of five, destitute. In the fall of 1946 he wrote a letter to Lewis asking for a $100 donation "to put my kids thrue school and . . . . buy some food for my family." The union denied the request but did attempt to help Cleveland get his job back (Lee Grant Cleveland to JLL, 28 September 1946, John O'Leary to Lee Grant Cleveland, 4 October 1946, both in Folder 32, Box 97, PDC).

80. WM to James E. Folsom, 4 April 1947, Folder 16(a), Box SG13415, Folsom Papers.

81. "Improved Conditions Urged at Memorial in Jasper," *BN*, 4 April 1947; "Seek Aid of Governor for Safe Mines—Mitch," *BN*, 2 April 1947.

82. Alabama Mining Institute, "Press Release," 9 April 1947, Minutes, "Called Meeting, Board of Governors," 8 April 1947, both in Folder 1.22, ACOA/AMI Records.

83. "Mine Operators Rush Corrections in State Slopes," *BN*, 4 April 1947.

84. WM to James E. Folsom, 20 July 1949, Folder 5, Box SG13453, Folsom Papers; James E. Folsom to WM, 18 July 1949, Folder 4, Box SC13453, Folsom Papers; Press Release, n.d., Folder 116(b), Box SG13415, Folsom Papers; Minutes, Board of Governors Meeting, 12 April 1947, Folder 1.22, ACOA/AMI Records. As if to dramatize the problems miners faced in Alabama, TCI's huge Edgewater mine exploded in July 1948, killing eleven people. Three of those who died were with a construction crew that was sinking a shaft into the mine. Six miners and two supervisors perished underground, and at least three other miners were severely injured in the blast (WM to John Owens, 6 August 1948, JLL, Thomas Kennedy, and John Owens to Troy C. Hosmer, 31 July 1948, both in Folder 43, Box 97, PDC).

85. Minutes, "Special Meeting of Members of the Alabama Mining Institute for the Purpose of Considering the Proposed Wage Agreement," 9 July 1947, Folder 1.22, ACOA/AMI Records; Dubofsky and Van Tine, *John L. Lewis*, 472–73; "Only One Slope Is Open in State, Survey Shows," *BN*, 24 June 1947.

86. "Many of Captive Diggings Halted over Alabama," *BN*, 15 March 1948; "Alabama Strike Will Continue, Leaders Declare," *BN*, 3 April 1948; Dubofsky and Van Tine, *John L. Lewis*, 477.

87. Dubofsky and Van Tine, *John L. Lewis*, 481–83.

88. "Alabama Lags behind Rest of Nation in Miners' Return," *BN*, 12 April 1948; "State's Mining Operations Gain," *BN*, 14 April 1948; "Local Coal Union Chieftain Urges Men to Return," *BN*, 12 April 1948; Dubofsky and Van Tine, *John L. Lewis*, 480–83.

89. Dubofsky and Van Tine, *John L. Lewis*, 484–85.

90. "State Coal Area Seen as 'Worst' Problem," *BN*, 16 September 1949; Dubofsky and Van Tine, *John L. Lewis*, 484–85.

91. Luther Barrett to JLL, 24 October 1949, Folder 50, Box 97, PDC.

92. James H. Lackey to JLL, 15 October 1949, Folder 50, Box 97, PDC.

93. James Harbin to JLL, 24 October 1949, Searcy Sullivan to JLL, 18 October 1949, both in Folder 50, Box 97, PDC.

94. Guston Ambrose and F. L. Turner to JLL, 17 October 1949, Folder 50, Box 97, PDC.

95. JLL to John Owens, 1 November 1949, Folder 50, Box 97, PDC.

96. Mrs. Louis D. Hill to JLL, October 1949, Folder 50, Box 97, PDC.

97. M. Sullivan, Clyde Hardin, and W. W. Carter to JLL, 24 October 1949, Guston Ambrose and F. L. Turner to JLL, 17 October 1949, Folder 50, Box 97, PDC.

98. "One Arrested; Damage Heavy; No Motive Given," *BN*, 14 November 1949; "Operator Testifies He Recognized Two of Men Who Raided Mine on June 13," *BAH*, 26 July 1949; "Defendants in Coal Mine Raid to Testify in Kirkpatrick Trial," *BAH*, 27 July 1949, Klan Scrapbooks.

99. Juanita Milam to Jim Folsom, 30 September 1949, Folder 4, Box SG13454, Folsom Papers; Earl Houck to JLL, 6 December 1949, Folder 50, Box 97, PDC; "Wounded UMW Man near Death; Pit Shuts Down," *BN*, 29 September 1949; "Walker Miner Shot in Gun Battle over Non-Union Mine Working," *UN*, 29 September 1949; "Miners Mass at Funeral as Women Plead for Law," *UN*, 13 October 1949.

100. "Coal-Laden Truck Blasted by Rifles in Battle near Sargossa Strip Mine," *UN*, 10 November 1949; "Shots Are Fired at Coal-Laden Truck on Jasper-Cullman Highway Tuesday," *UN*, 27 October 1949; "Dynamiting of Truck in Carbon Hill Brings State Aid in Fighting Probe," *UN*, 20 October 1949.

101. Dubofsky and Van Tine, *John L. Lewis*, 486; "Back to Work District Gets Shot in Arm," *BN*, 10 November 1949.

102. "Strike Nearing Full Scale Here," *BN*, 6 February 1950; "State Mines Are All Down," *BN*, 7 February 1950; "Mitch Urges Idle Miners' Return," *BN*, 11 November 1950; Dubofsky and Van Tine, *John L. Lewis*, 486–88.

103. "Funds Spent, Miners Face Food Crisis," *BN*, 8 February 1950.

104. Clancy Lake, "But They Can't Eat Learning," *BN*, 8 February 1950.

105. Ibid.

106. WM to Thomas Kennedy, 10 March 1952, Folder 5, Box 98, PDC; WM to John Mates, 9 November 1951, Folder 3, Box 98, PDC.

107. Dubofsky and Van Tine, *John L. Lewis*, 488–89; Mulcahy, *Social Contract*, 31–32.

108. Seltzer, *Fire in the Hole*, 63, 66, 70; Dubofsky and Van Tine, *John L. Lewis*, 488–89; Mulcahy, *Social Contract*, 31–32.

FIVE. Industrial Transformation and the Struggle over Health Care, 1950–1961

1. "Officers Called to Area Firm," *TN*, 13 January 1961; "Abston Firm Files Suit against Union," *TN*, 17 January 1961; untitled clipping, *BPH*, 18 January 1961, Folder 28, Box 98, PDC.

2. Val Mitch to Josephine Roche, 12 September 1961, Folder 6, Box 2 of 4, Legal Counsel General Correspondence, Series II, Office of Director Records, Fund Archives; WM to Thomas Kennedy, 12 December 1960, Folder 28, Box 98, PDC.

3. Willard P. Owens to Thomas Kennedy, W. A. Boyle, John Owens, and Earl E. Houck, 21 July 1961, Folder 29, Box 98, PDC; WM to Thomas Kennedy, 12 December 1960, 12 January 1961, Folder 28, Box 98, PDC; Val Mitch to Josephine Roche, 12 September 1961,

Folder 6, Box 2 of 4, Legal Counsel General Correspondence, Series II, Office of Director Records, Fund Archives.

4. Barnum, *Negro*, 8, 43–44, 62, 67; Ronald Lewis, *Black Coal Miners in America*, 170; U.S. Department of Commerce, Bureau of the Census, *Fifteenth Census*, 118; U.S. Department of Commerce, Bureau of the Census, *Census of Population: 1950*, 2–234.

5. Schulman, *From Cotton Belt to Sunbelt*, 157–59, 175–79, 191–92; Tindall, *Emergence of the New South*, 694–97, 700–701, 731; Cobb, *Selling of the South*.

6. Bartley, *New South*, 119; Rogers et al., *Alabama*, 583.

7. Bobby Wilson, *Race and Place in Birmingham*, 109.

8. Ibid.; Stein, *Running Steel, Running America*, 90; White, *Birmingham District*, 96.

9. Kelley, *Race Rebels*, 79–82, 84; Eskew, *But for Birmingham*, 53–83; Bobby Wilson, *Race and Place in Birmingham*, 109; Rogers et al., *Alabama*, 545; Stein, *Running Steel, Running America*.

10. Sugrue, "Structures of Urban Poverty," 88.

11. I. W. Rouzer to Hugh Morrow and Claude Lawson, 6 May 1954, Folder 2.5, ACOA/ AMI Records; Milton Fies, "The Future of Coal and How One Group of Southern Electric Utility Companies Is Planning to Meet It," 8 June 1953, "Coal Mines and Mining— Alabama" File, TCSH.

12. Charles S. Johnson and Clifton R. Jones, "Memorandum on Negro Internal Migration, 1940–1943," Fisk University, 16 August 1943, "Committee on Fair Employment Practices, August–September 1943" Folder, Box 4, Official File 4245g, Office of Production Management, May 1943–44, FDR Library.

13. U.S. Department of Commerce, Bureau of the Census, *Census of Population, 1960: Subject Reports*, 53, 59; U.S. Department of Commerce, Bureau of the Census, *Census of Population, 1950: Special Reports*, 4B-41; Wright, *Old South, New South*, 255–56.

14. U.S. Department of Commerce, Bureau of the Census, *Census of Population, 1960: Subject Reports*, 29, 35; U.S. Department of Commerce, Bureau of the Census, *Census of Population, 1950: Special Reports*, 4B-37.

15. "Analysis of Labor Force—Jasper, Alabama, Labor Market Area, May 1949 and March 1956," Folder 3663, Box 76, Elliott Papers.

16. Cecil Morgan to JLL, n.d., Folder 52, Box 97, PDC.

17. Ibid.

18. McDaniel, interview.

19. Custred, interview.

20. Rikard, "Experiment in Welfare Capitalism," 323, 325–27.

21. Melba Wilbanks Kizzire, " 'Beneath these Hills': Docena, the People, Yesterday, Today, and Tomorrow," Folder SC2549, Special Collection Department, Samford University, Birmingham, Ala.; Rikard, "Experiment in Welfare Capitalism," 327.

22. Barnum, *Negro*, 43.

23. "A Cornfield Now—below Lies a Fortune in Coal," *BP*, 17 December 1945, "Coal Mines and Mining—Alabama" File, TCSH; "Radical Coal Mine Machine Starts Experiment at TCI," unidentified source, 7 January 1949, "New Machine, Coal Mining," *BPH*, 27 July 1950, both in "Coal Industry and Trade, Alabama, 1934–1958," Microfiche, Birmingham Public Library, Birmingham, Ala.

24. Shotts, *Some Significant Recent Changes*, 78–79; Fies, "Future of Coal."

25. "Maxine, Dream of Two Industries Here, Is Mechanical, Engineering Wonder," *BN*, 26 September 1954, "Coal Mines and Mining—Alabama" File, TCSH; Shotts, *Some Significant Recent Changes*, 79. Another of Fies's ideas was an attempt to burn coal underground, creating gases that might have industrial uses. This "coal gasification project" began at seams near Alabama Power's Gorgas mine in the late 1940s. The project, a cooperative effort between Alabama Power and the federal government, was scrapped in the 1950s when it failed to live up to expectations. See " 'Gasification' of Mine Begins," *BN*, 21 January 1947, "Coal Industry and Trade—Alabama 1934–58" File, Microfiche, Birmingham Public Library; "Coal Gasification Funds Refused," *BPH*, 29 April 1953, "Coal Industry and Trade" File, TCSH.

26. Fies, "Future of Coal," 3–4; Shotts, *Some Significant Recent Changes*, 70; untitled clipping, *BN*, 2 August 1953, Folder 13, Box 98, PDC.

27. These figures appear in A. W. Vogtle, "Coal by Wire," *Public Utilities Fortnightly*, 26 March 1959, Folder 4830, Box 102, Elliott Papers.

28. "Progress Pulls Props on Miners," *BN*, 13 November 1960, "Coal Mines and Mining—Alabama" File, TCSH; "Strip Coal Mining Gain for Alabama Is Sharp," *BAH*, 14 August 1944, "Coal Industry and Trade—Alabama, 1934–58" File, Microfiche, Birmingham Public Library. On surface mining, see Barnum, *Negro*, 31; Shotts, *Some Significant Recent Changes*, 75.

29. U.S. Department of the Interior, Bureau of the Mines, *This Is Mining*, 12–13.

30. "Biggest Mouth in Alabama Shakes Out Black Coal by Truckload," *BN*, 5 January 1958, "Coal Mining Companies—DeBardeleben Coal" File, TCSH. See also "DeBardeleben's Waterside Mine Put in Operation," *BN*, 21 September 1956, "Coal Mines and Mining—Alabama" File, TCSH; "DeBardeleben Christens Huge New Dragline," *BPH*, 8 January 1953, "Growing Alabama Industry Brings Big Expansion at Our Waterside Mine," *BN*, 5 January 1956, both in "Coal Mining Companies—DeBardeleben Coal" File, TCSH.

31. "Agreement between Tennessee Coal, Iron, and Railroad Company and United Mine Workers of America (District No. 20), Covering Coal Mining Operations at Wylam, Hamilton, Edgewater, and Docena Mines," Folder 3, Box 2, Series F, Agreements, Mitch Papers; "William Mitch, Testimony before the Committee on Fair Employment Practice, Birmingham, Ala., 18 June 1942," Headquarters Records, Reel 17, FEPC Collection, 93.

32. Barnum, *Negro*, 29, 44; Ronald Lewis, *Black Coal Miners in America*, 170; Hawley, "Negro Employment," 278.

33. Young, interview.

34. Barnum, *Negro*, 31–32, 44. Barnum noted that blacks who worked at strip operations typically found jobs at smaller mines where the workforce reflected the traditional racial makeup of mines in the area.

35. WM to William B. Young, 13 July 1946, W. B. Young to JLL, 14 August 1946, both in Folder 32, Box 97, PDC.

36. Thomas N. Crawford to Thomas Kennedy, 12 November 1953, Folder 10, Box 98, PDC.

37. Hawley, "Negro Employment," 238–39; Ronald Lewis, *Black Coal Miners in America*, 171.

38. Barnum, *Negro*, 43–44; Hawley, "Negro Employment," 285.

39. Walker, interview.

40. Ibid.

41. Earl Brown, interview.

42. Ibid.; Chafe, Gavins, and Korstad, *Remembering Jim Crow*, 239–41.

43. Ibid.

44. Young, interview; Chafe, Gavins, and Korstad, *Remembering Jim Crow*, 242.

45. Chafe, Gavins, and Korstad, *Remembering Jim Crow*, 243; Young, interview.

46. Fred Bass Sr., interview.

47. See U.S. Department of Commerce, Bureau of the Census, *1970 Census*, 164; Barnum, *Negro*, 65. The census listed the number at 1,868 black miners, or about 22 percent of the total. But the census in 1970 did not differentiate between coal mining and other types of mining. Historian Ronald Lewis placed the number of black miners lower, at 806, or about 18 percent of the mining workforce (*Black Coal Miners in America*, 193).

48. "City Will Get UMW Welfare Area Office," *BAH*, 31 December 1948, Labor Union Scrapbooks, Microfilm, Department of Archives and Manuscripts, Birmingham Public Library, Birmingham, Ala.

49. Scribner, *Renewing Birmingham*, 41–46; Jefferson County Coordinating Council, *Jefferson County Survey*, 3, 7–8.

50. Lorin E. Kerr and Paul Streit, "Review of Hospitalization in the Birmingham Medical Area," 30 April–4 May 1956, Folder 18, Box 4 of 11, Series II, Office of the Director, UMWA Correspondence, 1946–72, Fund Archives.

51. Ibid.

52. Ibid.; Rikard, "Experiment in Welfare Capitalism," 332–33.

53. "Protest Alabama Hospital Bias" [press release], 19 April 1951, Microfilm, National Association for the Advancement of Colored People, Birmingham File, 1951–55, Department of Archives and Manuscripts, Birmingham Public Library, Birmingham, Ala.; "Where Will UMW Place Its J-H Hospital Patients?" *BPH*, 18 March 1953; "UMW Welfare Fund Ends J-H Connection," *BN*, 10 July 1953, Labor Union Scrapbooks. In 1951, the Birmingham chapter of the National Association for the Advancement of Colored People had strongly protested the death of an African American woman who was refused admission to the hospital. "Such an incident should have never occurred nor should be allowed to happen again," officials with the organization argued.

54. A. L. Pickens to JLL, 2 November 1948, Folder 45, Box 97, PDC; Mulcahy, *Social Contract*, 18.

55. W. T. McDonald to JLL, 11 March 1948, Folder 15, Box 6, UMWA WRF; Seltzer, *Fire in the Hole*, 90; Dubofsky and Van Tine, *John L. Lewis*, 511.

56. Henry Allai and John Kmetz to JLL, 25 May 1955, WM to JLL, 1 June 1955, both in Folder 16, Box 98, PDC.

57. Viola Hill, "Cross Reference Sheet," 28 April 1954, Folder 17, Box 16, UMWA WRF. On cutbacks, see Dubofsky and Van Tine, *John L. Lewis*, 512; Seltzer, *Fire in the Hole*, 90.

58. John Morrison to Josephine Roche, 11 August 1954, Folder 18, Box 4 of 11, UMWA Correspondence, 1946–72, Series II, Office of the Director, Fund Archives.

59. Alfred Brown, Dave Brown, Troy Hosmer, and J. B. Benson to JLL, 18 August 1949, Folder 49, Box 97, PDC.

60. J. B. Benson, "Cross Reference Sheet," 15 February 1952, H. B. Odom, "Cross Reference Sheet," 26 February 1952, both in Folder 14, Box 16, UMWA WRF.

61. Lou Mutry and Glenn Terry, "Cross Reference Sheet," 14 February 1952, H. B. Odom, "Cross Reference Sheet," 26 February 1952, J. B. Benson, "Cross Reference Sheet," 15 February 1952, Lou Mutry, "Cross Reference Sheet," 14 February 1952, all in Folder 14, Box 16, UMWA WRF.

62. George D. Glover to JLL, 21 July 1954, H. V. Higgins and J. B. Benson to JLL, 27 May 1954, both in Folder 18, Box 4 of 11, UMWA Correspondence, 1946–72, Series II, Office of the Director, Fund Archives.

63. "Verbatim Listing of All Written Complaints Received by Area Medical Office during November 1955," Folder 18, Box 4 of 11, UMWA Correspondence, 1946–72, Series II, Office of the Director, Fund Archives.

64. Derickson, *Black Lung*, 1–21.

65. Mrs. Joseph Phillips to JLL, 12 January 1955, Folder 15, Box 98, PDC; Seltzer, *Fire in the Hole*, 96; McAteer, *Miner's Manual*, 110–11.

66. Derickson, *Black Lung*, 122–23; "Gains Honor," unidentified publication, 21 July 1946, "Surname Vertical File, Freear–Frings," Microfilm Collection, Birmingham Public Library, Birmingham, Ala.; WM to Josephine Roche and Warren Draper, 2 November 1951, Folder 3, Box 98, PDC.

67. WM to Josephine Roche and Warren Draper, 2 November 1951, Folder 3, Box 98, PDC; Derickson, *Black Lung*, 123.

68. WM to Josephine Roche and Warren Draper, 2 November 1951, Folder 3, Box 98, PDC; "Proceedings: 13th Constitutional Convention of the Alabama State Industrial Union Council, CIO," Mobile, 17–19 April 1952, AFL-CIO Records, Alabama AFL-CIO Office, Montgomery, Ala.; Derickson, *Black Lung*, 124; *Journal of the House of Representatives, 1951*, 278, 508, 608–9, 890–92.

69. Grafton and Permaloff, *Big Mules and Branchheads*, 146.

70. "Dr. Friedman's Name Dropped from Docks List," *BN*, 7 January 1956; "There Is a Doctor in the House Named Louis Friedman," *Montgomery Advertiser*, 17 August 1955; "Friedman Named to ABC Board," *BN*, 10 November 1956; "McRae, Friedman Get New State Jobs," *BN*, 30 December 1958, "Surname Vertical File, Freear–Frings," Microfilm Collection, Birmingham Public Library.

71. J. B. Benson, "Cross Reference Sheet," 23 February 1956, Glenn Terry and Frank FitzPatrick, "Cross Reference Sheet," 25 February 1956, both in Folder 18, Box 16, UMWA WRF.

72. Warren Draper to JLL, 20 July 1954, Folder 8, Box 4 of 11, UMWA Correspondence, 1946–72, Series II, Office of the Director, Fund Archives.

73. J. B. Benson, "Cross Reference Sheet," 23 February 1956, Folder 18, Box 16, UMWA WRF; Warren Draper to Allen Koplin, 21 November 1955, Folder 8, Box 4 of 11, UMWA Correspondence, 1946–72, Series II, Office of the Director, Fund Archives.

74. Warren Draper to Josephine Roche, 23 November 1955, Box 4 of 11, UMWA Correspondence, 1946–72, Series II, Office of the Director, Fund Archives.

75. Ibid.

76. Ibid.

77. Ibid.

78. WM to Josephine Roche, 28 December 1955, Josephine Roche to WM, 19 December 1955, both in Box 4 of 11, UMWA Correspondence, 1946–1972, Series II, Office of the Director, Fund Archives.

79. Allen Koplin to Warren Draper, 9 February 1956, Box 4 of 11, UMWA Correspondence, 1946–72, Series II, Office of the Director, Fund Archives.

80. Kerr and Streit, "Review of Hospitalization."

81. Ibid.

82. Seltzer, *Fire in the Hole,* 73.

83. "Report of William Mitch, President, District 20, UMWA," Seventh Biennial Convention, United Mine Workers of America, Birmingham, Ala., 1–2 August 1947, Folder 38, Box 97, PDC; WM to John O'Leary, 3 September 1946, Folder 31, Box 97, PDC.

84. "Report of William Mitch, President, District 20, UMWA."

85. WM to JLL, 6 February 1953, Folder 8, Box 98, PDC.

86. Thomas Crawford, n.d., Folder 12, Box 98, PDC.

87. WM to Thomas Kennedy, 23 April 1954, Folder 12, Box 98, PDC.

88. WM to JLL, 14 January 1959, "Mine Owner Sues UMW over Pay Pact," *Knoxville (Tenn.) News-Sentinel,* 15 January 1959, both in Folder 24, Box 98, PDC. In 1971, the U.S. Supreme Court ruled that the protection clauses violated the Sherman Antitrust Act. The case, brought by Tennessee Consolidated Coal, targeted the protective wage agreement between Pittsburgh's Consolidation Coal and the UMWA. See Seltzer, *Fire in the Hole,* 77–79.

89. WM to Thomas Kennedy, 26 August 1960, Folder 27, Box 98, PDC. The lawsuits are listed in Folder 3 and Folder 4, Box 2 of 4, Legal Council General Correspondence, Series II, Office of Director Records, Fund Archives.

90. Dubofsky and Van Tine, *John L. Lewis,* 518.

91. James T. Hatcher to Thomas Kennedy, 23 May 1960, Folder 26, Box 98, PDC; WM to Thomas Kennedy, 5 May 1960, Folder 29, Box 98, PDC.

92. Berry Tatum and Charles Fuller to Thomas Kennedy, 18 August 1960, Folder 27, Box 98, PDC.

93. WM to Thomas Kennedy, 26 August 1960, Folder 27, Box 98, PDC.

94. "Officers Called to Area Firm," *TN,* 13 January 1961.

95. Oscar Hill to JLL, 15 December 1947, Folder 16, Box 6, UMWA WRF.

96. See list of lawsuits, Folder 3, Box 2 of 4, Legal Council General Correspondence, Series II, Office of Director Records, Fund Archives.

97. Val Mitch to Josephine Roche, 12 September 1961, Folder 6, Box 2 of 4, Legal Counsel General Correspondence, Series II, Office of Director Records, Fund Archives; WM to Thomas Kennedy, 12 December 1960, Folder 28, Box 98, PDC.

98. WM to Thomas Kennedy, 12 January 1961, Thomas Kennedy to WM, both in Folder 28, Box 98, PDC; list of lawsuits, Folder 3, Box 2 of 4, Legal Council General Correspondence, Series II, Office of Director Records, Fund Archives.

99. Val Mitch to Josephine Roche, 12 September 1961, Folder 6, Box 2 of 4, Legal Counsel General Correspondence, Series II, Office of Director Records, Fund Archives; Willard P. Owens to Thomas Kennedy, W. A. Boyle, John Owens, and Earl E. Houck, 21

July 1961, Folder 29, Folder 28, Box 98, PDC; "Officers Called to Area Firm," *TN*, 13 January 1961; "Abston Firm Files Suit against Union," *TN*, 17 January 1961; National Labor Relations Board Complaint, 13 January 1961, District 20 Correspondence, 1961, Folder 28, Box 98, PDC.

SIX. Globalization, Race, and Gender, 1961–1980

1. "500 Miners Greet Southern Co. Board in Birmingham," *Great Speckled Bird*, 3 June 1974.

2. "Hundreds Protest Southern Co. Action," *BPH*, 23 May 1974; "500 Miners Greet Southern Co. Board in Birmingham," *Great Speckled Bird*, 3 June 1974.

3. "500 Miners Greet Southern Co. Board in Birmingham," *Great Speckled Bird*, 3 June 1974; "Hundreds Protest Southern Co. Action," *BPH*, 23 May 1974; "UMWA Launches Battle to Stop South African Coal Imports," *UMWJ*, 1–15 June 1974; "Miners Oppose Imports of Coal," *NYT*, 27 May 1974.

4. Other examples of union workers facing such challenges are numerous. For important recent accounts, see Cowie, *Capital Moves*; Juravich and Bronfenbrenner, *Ravenswood*.

5. "Jim Walter Mines Victim of Boom Turned Sour," *BN*, 20 May 1987. On Drummond, see "Drummond Legacy Lives On," *BN*, 18 May 1987.

6. Seltzer, *Fire in the Hole*, 128.

7. U.S. Department of Commerce, Bureau of the Census, *1980 Census*, 497; U.S. Department of Commerce, Bureau of the Census, *1970 Census*, 164; ADIR, *Annual Statistical Report, Fiscal Year 1969–1970*, Folder 3.26, ACOA/AMI Records; Ronald Lewis, *Black Coal Miners in America*, 192–93.

8. Marat Moore, *Women in the Mines*, xxv, xxxvi.

9. McWhorter, *Carry Me Home*, 15.

10. Ibid., 95–99.

11. Important overviews of this era in Birmingham are found in Eskew, *But for Birmingham*, 20–23, 106–7, 121–51, 153–57, 310–12; Thornton, *Dividing Lines*, 239–53; Carter, *Politics of Rage*, 82–87; Grafton and Permaloff, *Big Mules and Branchheads*, 186–90, 192–202, 204–11; McWhorter, *Carry Me Home*.

12. Rogers et al., *Alabama*, 569; Norrell, "Labor Trouble," 257–58.

13. For an overview of Wallace's political activities in the 1960s, see Carter, *Politics of Rage*.

14. Draper, *Conflict of Interests*, 108–13.

15. Minutes, Unemployment Compensation Committee Meeting, 9 December 1964, George Wallace to Thomas Crawford, 2 December 1964, both in "Labor Department 13 October 1964 to 27 September 1965" Folder, Box SG22365, George Wallace Papers, Alabama Department of Archives and History, Montgomery; Thomas Crawford to George Wallace, 26 September 1963, "Industrial Relations, 7 January 1963 to 26 September 1963" Folder, Box SG22365, Wallace Papers. When I examined the first term of the Wallace administration for my master's thesis in the spring of 1997, I documented the folder titles in a different manner than I used in later visits to the state archives.

16. For examples of UMWA leaders' early efforts to combat the SLU's entrance into the Birmingham District, see UMWA, Minutes of International Executive Board Meeting, 12–

14 June 1963, Folder 70-5, Box 70, Miners for Democracy Collection, Archives of Labor and Urban Affairs, Walter P. Reuther Library, Wayne State University, Detroit; Gaventa, *Power and Powerlessness*, 172; "Alabama Coal Miners Still Out," *BPH*, 12 April 1966; "State Mineworkers Start Return to Work," *BN*, 13 April 1966; "Most State Miners Still Not Working," *BN*, 20 April 1966; Seltzer, *Fire in the Hole*, 88.

17. See K and S employees to Wallace, 5 May 1966, 6 May 1966, Donald Peters to George Wallace, 2 May 1966, all in "Labor Department, 10 May 1966 to 30 September 1966" Folder, Box SG22804, Wallace Papers.

18. "Delegation Calls: Governor Vows Aid in Strike," *Jasper (Ala.) Daily Mountain Eagle*, 13 May 1966, "Labor Department, 10 May 1966 to 30 September 1966" Folder, Box SG22804, Wallace Papers; C. W. Russell to Cecil C. Jackson Jr., 9 May 1966, "Labor Department, 1 October 1964 to 9 May 1966" Folder, Box SG22804, Wallace Papers; Arlis Fant to Donald Peters, 10 May 1966, "Labor Department, 10 May 1966 to 30 September 1966" Folder, Box SG22804, Wallace Papers.

19. See Woodrum, "Reforming Dixie," 72–82. Mitch died on 12 July 1974.

20. Address by Thomas Crawford to the Alabama Mining Institute, 2 May 1963, Folder 1.25, ACOA/AMI Records. Black miner Leon Alexander remembered Crawford differently. He and Beane directly confronted a Jefferson County registrar who would not let Alexander register to vote. See Chafe, Gavins, and Korstad, *Remembering Jim Crow*, 277. At the national level, the UMWA strongly opposed Wallace, particularly in his 1968 independent presidential bid. See "Which Side Are You On?" *UMWJ*, 1 October 1968. Two weeks later, the journal ran an editorial under the headline, "George Wallace and Hitler" (*UMWJ*, 15 October 1968).

21. U.S. Department of Labor, *Industry Wage Survey: Bituminous Coal Mining*, 11–2, 44, Folder 40, Box 15, Series VII: Black Employment, Various Industries, Wharton School Industrial Research Unit Papers, University Archives and Records Center, University of Pennsylvania, Philadelphia.

22. Rungeling and Ignatin, *Black Employment in Birmingham*, 109–12.

23. Ibid., 81–83, 90, 109–12; Stein, *Running Steel, Running America*, 50; Rogers et al., *Alabama*, 581; Bobby Wilson, "Racial Segregation Trends"; Fly and Reinhart, "Racial Separation during the 1970s," 1255–62.

24. "Rural Life Still Prevails in Community near City," *BN*, 8 February 1973, "Mulga, Alabama" File, TCSH.

25. "Mayor Country Believes Water Would Solve Cardiff's Problems, Make It Grow," *BN*, 17 November 1962, "Cardiff, Alabama" File, TCSH.

26. H. G. "Pete" Harmon to Ben Erdreich, 16 February 1977, Folder 2.4, Ben Erdreich Papers, Department of Archives and Manuscripts, Birmingham Public Library, Birmingham, Ala.; "Minutes of the Public Hearing," 2 March 1976, Minor High School, Folder 1.27, Erdreich Papers.

27. "Minutes of the Public Hearing."

28. "Home Owners near Strip Mines Hopping Mad about Blasting," *BN*, 3 March 1976, "Problems from Strip Mine Worsen at Beltona," *BPH*, 2 September 1974, both in "Coal Mines and Mining—Strip" File, TCSH. Drummond was not the only coal company that had these sorts of problems with residents.

29. ADIR, *Annual Statistical Report, Fiscal Year 1974–1975*, Folder 3.31, ACOA/AMI

Records; ADIR, *Annual Statistical Report, Fiscal Year 1969–1970*, Folder 3.26, ACOA/AMI Records; ADIR, *Annual Statistical Report, Fiscal Year 1964–1965*, Folder 3.21, ACOA/AMI Records.

30. "Reclaiming Ravaged Land," *Birmingham News Magazine*, 7 April 1968, "Coal Mines and Mining—Strip" File, TCSH; "Progress Pulls Props on Miners," *BN*, 13 November 1960, "Coal Mines and Mining—Alabama" File, TCSH.

31. "Strip Mining Laws Called 'Farce,'" *Columbiana (Ala.) Shelby County Reporter*, 10 February 1977, "Coal Mines and Mining—Strip" File, TCSH; Bailey, *Surface Mining in Alabama*, 4, 7–8, 14, 21–22, "Coal Mines and Mining—Strip" File, TCSH.

32. "Strip Mining Flaw," *BN*, 8 February 1977, "Coal Mines and Mining—Strip" File, TCSH; "Strip Mining Laws Called 'Farce,'" *Columbiana (Ala.) Shelby County Reporter*, 10 February 1977, "Coal Mines and Mining—Strip" File, TCSH; Bailey, *Surface Mining in Alabama*, 4, 7–8, 14, 21–22, "Coal Mines and Mining—Strip" File, TCSH.

33. "Miner Fears Bill May Destroy Job," *BN*, 17 July 1974, "State UMW Opposes U.S. Strip-Mine Bill," *BPH*, 17 July 1974, both in "Coal Mines and Mining—Strip" File, TCSH. The national UMWA, by contrast, supported the legislation.

34. Sam Littlefield to George Wallace, 15 May 1974, Folder 24, Box SG22695, Wallace Papers.

35. "Jim Walter Mines Victim of Boom Turned Sour," *BN*, 20 May 1987.

36. "Drummond Legacy Lives On," *BN*, 18 May 1987.

37. "Drummond Coal Company: Shaping an Industry's Future," *AmSouth* 1, no. 3 (1984), "Coal Industry and Trade—Alabama" File, TCSH; "Drummond Legacy Lives On," *BN*, 18 May 1987.

38. "Drummond Legacy Lives On," *BN*, 18 May 1987; "Drummond Coal: A Growing (and Very Quiet) State Firm Gets National Ranking," *Huntsville Times*, 30 May 1982, "Coal Mining Companies—Alabama" File, TCSH; "Drummond Coal Company: Shaping an Industry's Future," *AmSouth* 1, no. 3 (1984), "Coal Industry and Trade—Alabama" File, TCSH; "State Feels Cut of Mine in Soil, Life," *BN*, 24 June 1977, "Coal Mines and Mining—Alabama" File, TCSH.

39. "Takeover of ABC Was Swift," *BPH*, 9 April 1979, "Alabama By-Products Corp." File, TCSH.

40. "Praco Residents Get a 6-Month Reprieve from Company," *BPH*, 10 December 1981; "Company Town Closes Its Doors, Evicts Residents," *BPH*, 7 December 1981; "Takeover of ABC Was Swift," *BPH*, 9 April 1979, "Alabama By-Products Corp." File, TCSH.

41. "Drummond Legacy Lives On," *BN*, 18 May 1987.

42. "U.S. Pipe's Parent Firm Signs Coal Pacts with Japanese," *BPH*, 28 March 1975, "Coal Mines and Mining—Alabama" File, TCSH; "Walter Mines Victim of Boom Turned Sour," *BN*, 20 May 1987.

43. "Coal Strip Mining Operation Would Get Boost from Canal," *BN*, 21 November 1965, "Coal Mines and Mining—Strip" File, TCSH; Milton H. Fies, "Report Relating to Recent Exploration for Coal in a Limited Area of Jackson County, Alabama, in the Plateau Field," 2 February 1962, Folder 6205, Box 140, Elliott Papers; "Drummond Coal: A Growing (and Very Quiet) State Firm Gets National Ranking," *Huntsville Times*, 30 May 1982, "Coal Mining Companies—Alabama" File, TCSH.

44. "Consolidated Coal Bidding for Mulga?" *BN*, 19 September 1978, "Coal Mining Companies—Alabama" File, TCSH.

45. "Alabama Coal Reserves Go Deep into Next Century," *BN*, 2 April 1972, "Underground Coal Mining Experiencing Resurgence," *TN*, 18 August 1974, both in "Coal Mines and Mining—Alabama" File, TCSH.

46. *Alabama Coal Data,* 105, table 50 (including import and export data from 1970 to 1990); "Mines Deal Out Half Million for Facility," *BN*, 9 March 1972, "Coal Mines and Mining—Alabama" File, TCSH.

47. "Japanese Air Pollution Boosts State Mining," *BN*, 20 June 1971, "State Feels Cut of Mine in Soil, Life," *BN*, 24 June 1977, "Coal Mines and Mining—Alabama" File, TCSH; "Drummond Coal Company: Shaping an Industry's Future," *AmSouth* 1, no. 3 (1984), "Coal Industry and Trade—Alabama" File, TCSH.

48. Stein, *Running Steel, Running America*, 207.

49. Seltzer, *Fire in the Hole*, 126–27.

50. ADIR, *Annual Statistical Report, Fiscal Year 1969–1970*, Folder 3.26, ACOA/AMI Records; ADIR, *Annual Statistical Report, Fiscal Year 1980*. These reports from after 1980 are held in the Birmingham Public Library's document collection.

51. Seltzer, *Fire in the Hole*, 112–13. Overviews of this era are found in Clark, *Miners' Fight*; Hopkins, "Miners for Democracy"; Nyden, "Miners for Democracy."

52. Seltzer, *Fire in the Hole*, 112–13, 117–21.

53. "Dora Man to Join Mine Exec. Board," *BN*, 23 December 1972, "UMWA, 1970s" File, TCSH; *UMWJ*, 13 February 1970; "District 20, Alabama," *Miner's Voice*, Winter 1973.

54. Nyden, "Miners for Democracy," 840–41; Woodrum, "Reforming Dixie," 155–58.

55. "UMWA Launches Battle to Stop South African Coal Imports," *UMWJ*, 1–15 June 1974; "UMWA to Fight South African Coal Imports," *UMWJ*, 1–15 May 1974; "Southern Co. Buys S. African Coal," *Great Speckled Bird*, 6 May 1974; "Stop South African Coal: Picket Georgia Power May 21," *Great Speckled Bird*, 20 May 1974; " . . . and Atlantans Protest Ga. Power Involvement There," *Great Speckled Bird*, 3 June 1974.

56. "500 Miners Greet Southern Co. Board in Birmingham," *Great Speckled Bird*, 3 June 1974; "Coal Mining without Blinders," *Atlanta Constitution*, 13 May 1974; "UMWA to Fight South African Coal Imports," *UMWJ*, 1–15 May 1974.

57. "UMWA Launches Battle to Stop South African Coal Imports," *UMWJ*, 1–15 June 1974.

58. Sam Littlefield to Joseph A. Yablonski Jr., 28 May 1974, Folder 24, Box SG22695, Wallace Papers; "UMWA Launches Battle to Stop South African Coal Imports," *UMWJ*, 1–15 June 1974; "Miners Oppose Imports of Coal," *NYT*, 27 May 1974.

59. "UMWA Launches Battle to Stop South African Coal Imports," *UMWJ*, 1–15 June 1974; Joseph A. Yablonski Jr. to William G. Lalor, 6 June 1974, Folder 24, Box SG22695, Wallace Papers.

60. "The Rank and File Speaks: South African Coal Imports," *UMWJ*, 1–15 June 1974.

61. "Statement by Alabama Power Company on Coal Supply for Electric Generation," Folder 24, Box SG22695, Wallace Papers; "Hundreds Protest Southern Co. Action," *BPH*, 23 May 1974; "500 Miners Greet Southern Co. Board in Birmingham," *Great Speckled Bird*, 3 June 1974.

62. "Miners Oppose Imports of Coal," *NYT*, 27 May 1974; "Union Moves to Block

African Coal," *UMWJ*, 16–31 August 1974; Sam Littlefield and Lloyd Baker to "All Local Unions District 20 UMWA," 10 April 1974, "May 1974 Press Releases" Folder, Box SG22491, Wallace Papers.

63. "Alabama Attorney General Asks Ban on Coal from South Africa," *NYT*, 18 August 1974; "Union Moves to Block African Coal," *UMWJ*, 16–31 August 1974.

64. *UMWJ*, 16–31 August 1974.

65. "The Rank and File Speaks," *UMWJ*, 1–15 June 1974.

66. "UMW Shutdown Seen as Prelude to Contract Talks," *BN*, 20 August 1974.

67. "Tight Docks Security Posted," *Mobile Register*, 17 August 1974; "South African Coal Unloaded," *Southern Patriot*, September 1974, Southern Patriot Box, Periodicals Collection, Southern Labor Archives, Special Collections Department, Pullen Library, Georgia State University, Atlanta.

68. "UMW Official Says Labor Will Fight Coal Importing," *Mobile Register*, 22 August 1974.

69. "Mobile Aid Asked in Fight to Turn Back Foreign Coal," *Mobile Register*, 23 August 1974; "UMW Asks Longshoremen Support," *BN*, 23 August 1974; "UMW Official Says Labor Will Fight Coal Importing," *Mobile Register*, 22 August 1974.

70. "South African Coal Unloaded," *Southern Patriot*, September 1974, Southern Patriot Box, Periodicals Collection, Southern Labor Archives; "Non-Union Labor Use Is Forecast," *Mobile Register*, 24 August 1974; Thornton, *Dividing Lines*, 8.

71. "South African Coal Unloaded," *Southern Patriot*, September 1974, Southern Patriot Box, Periodicals Collection, Southern Labor Archives.

72. "UMW Asks Longshoremen Support," *BN*, 23 August 1974; "South African Coal Unloaded," *Southern Patriot*, September 1974, Southern Patriot Box, Periodicals Collection, Southern Labor Archives.

73. "State Docks Work Resumes Except at Handling Plant," *BN*, 27 August 1974; "UMW Removes Docks Pickets," *Mobile Register*, 27 August 1974.

74. "Union Leaders Urge Coal Miners to End Walkout," *BN*, 30 August 1975; "South Africa Coal Unloaded."

75. "Halt Picketing State Docks, Judge Orders," *BPH*, 29 August 1974; "Can't Picket South African Coal, Judge Tells UMW," *BN*, 29 August 1974; Findings of Fact and Conclusions of Law, *Walter C. Phillips, Regional Director of the Tenth Region of the National Labor Relations Board v. International Union, United Mine Workers of America, District 20, United Mine Workers of America, et al.*, U.S. District Court for the Northern District of Alabama, Southern Division, National Archives and Records Administration, East Point, Ga.

76. "UMW Removes Docks Pickets," *Mobile Register*, 27 August 1974; "Unloading of Coal Continues: Longshoremen Return to Jobs at State Docks," *Mobile Register*, 28 August 1974; "Halt Picketing State Docks, Judge Orders," *BPH*, 29 August 1974; Findings of Fact and Conclusions of Law, *Walter C. Phillips, Regional Director of the Tenth Region of the National Labor Relations Board v. International Union, United Mine Workers of America, District 20, United Mine Workers of America, et al.*

77. "Southern Co., U.S. Agree Coal Importing is Stopgap Measure," *BPH*, 28 August 1974; "Customs Refuses Bar on South African Coal," *UMWJ*, 16–28 February 1975.

78. T. W. McDonald to Harry M. Hayes, 12 August 1974, Folder 10–15, "United Mine Workers," Birmingham Police Department Surveillance Files, 1947–80, Birmingham Public Library, Birmingham, Ala.; T. W. McDonald to Harry M. Hayes, 23 May 1974, Folder 10–11(a) "Turning Point Publications," Birmingham Police Department Surveillance Files.

79. "Alabama's UMW Chief Fatally Shot after D.C. Meeting on Coal Strike," *BPH*, 16 November 1974; "Beefed-Up Washington Police Unit Hunts Slayer of State UMW Leader," *BN*, 16 November 1974; "Funeral Set Monday for UMW's Littlefield," *BN*, 17 November 1974, "UMWA, 1970s" File, TCSH; "Littlefield Murderer Gets 20-Year Sentence," *UMWJ*, 16–30 November 1975.

80. "Southern Co. to Buy South African Coal," *UMWJ*, 16–30 November 1976. The new contract was for 7.7 million tons over a ten-year period. For accounts of later protests, see "Southern Co. Foresees No Power Shortages," *Atlanta Journal*, 24 May 1978; "Vogtle: Audit Report Sealed Wallace's Fate," *Atlanta Constitution*, 25 May 1978; "Southern Co. Is Trying to Form Subsidiary," *Atlanta Journal*, 27 May 1981; "Southern Co. to Retain Coal Policy," *Atlanta Journal*, 26 May 1982; "Utility Firm to Continue Plant Vogtle," *Atlanta Journal*, 27 May 1982; "Message to Stockholders," *UMWJ*, July 1985.

81. Walker, interview. For an overview of this period, see Clark, *Miners' Fight*.

82. "Alabama Coal Miners Back on Job," *BPH*, 3 September 1975; "State UMW Officials Predict Coal Miners to Return to Work," *BPH*, 29 August 1975; "5,000 State Coal Miners Due to Return to Work after Strike," *BN*, 2 September 1975; Clark, *Miners' Fight*, 70–73, 171 n.58.

83. "Wildcat Mine Strike Hits Alabama Hard; Thousands Idled," *BN*, 5 August 1976; "End of State Mine Strike May Be Near," *BN*, 12 August 1976; Clark, *Miners' Fight*, 71–73.

84. "Miners Vote to End Strike," *BPH*, 22 August 1977; "Baker Says Pickets Will Be Asked 'Why?'" *BN*, 20 August 1977; "End of State Mine Strike May Be Near," *BN*, 12 August 1976; Clark, *Miners' Fight*, 70–73, 116, 171 n.58.

85. See "District Reports: District 20," *UMWJ*, 1–15 March 1975. Brown would serve as secretary-treasurer of District 20 from 1986 to 1997. See Brown and Davis, *It Is Union and Liberty*, appendix.

86. "District Reports: 20," *UMWJ*, October 1977.

87. Clark, *Miner's Fight*, 114–37; Seltzer, *Fire in the Hole*, 148–66; Woodrum, "Wildcats, Caravans, and Dynamite," 111–29; "District Reports: 20," *UMWJ*, October 1977.

88. "Strikers Close Mines in State, Start Fire, Threaten Officials," *BPH*, 21 December 1977.

89. "State Troopers Mass to Prevent Strikers from Closing Mines," *BPH*, 9 January 1978; "Troopers Prepare for Confrontations in Coal Mine Strike," *BPH*, 10 January 1978. The actions of the UMWA during this strike resulted in a high-profile civil lawsuit that dragged on for years in federal court in Birmingham. See *Oakman Mining Company and Prater Equipment Company v. United Mine Workers of America, Districts 20 and 23, United Mine Workers of America*, Case CV 79-AR-0030-S. The information here came from testimony of James L. Fuqua, 3 October 1984, testimony of James L. Fowler, 3 October 1984, and testimony of Billy R. Wooten, 9 October 1984, *Oakman Mining v. UMWA*.

90. "Wallace and UMW to Seek Strife Halt," *BPH*, 24 January 1978; "Wary Sand Mountain Miners Stay 'Ready' for Roving Pickets," *BN*, 24 January 1978.

91. Testimony of Charles L. Fuller, 3 October 1984, *Oakman Mining v. UMWA*; Fuller, interview; "Wallace and UMW to Seek Strife Halt," *BPH*, 24 January 1978; "Wary Sand Mountain Miners Stay 'Ready' for Roving Pickets," *BN*, 24 January 1978.

92. "Miners Force Coal Dumping, Imperil Schools in Madison," *BPH*, 1 February 1978; "Troopers Hurt Guarding Mine," *BPH*, 2 February 1978.

93. For accounts of the origins of this incident, see Testimony of Alfred Key, 1 October 1984, Deposition of Claude Prater, 5 August 1984, *Oakman Mining v. UMWA*. Newspaper accounts include "Riot-Ready Troopers Face Angry Miners in Walker County," *BPH*, 3 February 1978; "Wallace to Keep Troopers at Mines, Won't Use Guard," *BPH*, 4 February 1978; "Events Leading to Battle: 'Came to Do Some Head-Knocking,'" *BN*, 4 February 1978; "Somber Union Miners Recall Violence; Vow No 'Scab' Coal," *BN*, 4 February 1978; Woodrum, "Wildcats, Caravans, and Dynamite."

94. Seltzer, *Fire in the Hole*, 163–64; Clark, *Miners' Fight*, 129–30.

95. WM to Bibb Graves, 6 May 1935, Folder 14, Box SG12161, Bibb Graves Papers, Alabama Department of Archives and History, Montgomery; *General Laws*, 255.

96. Marat Moore, *Women in the Mines*, xxxv; U.S. Department of Commerce, Bureau of the Census, *Census of the Population: 1950*, 2–228; U.S. Department of Commerce, Bureau of the Census, *Sixteenth Census*, 52; U.S. Department of Commerce, Bureau of the Census, *Fifteenth Census*, 109.

97. Marat Moore, *Women in the Mines*, xxxii–xxxvi, xl–xli; "Fact Sheet: Women in Mining," Betty Jean Hall to CEP Project File, "Meeting with Tom Woodruff," 23 November 1977, Folder 2, Box 1, CEP Collection; Stein, *Running Steel, Running America*, 155–73.

98. Betty Jones, interview by author, tape recording, Jasper, Ala., 6 February 1997; "Coal Mining Not for Women? Six Handle Tough Job at SEGCO No. 1," *BN*, 16 February 1975, "Coal Mines and Mining—Alabama" File, TCSH.

99. "Portrait of a Woman Miner: Mary Ellis of Alabama," *Coal Mining Women's Support Team News!* October–November 1986, Box 82, Folder 36, CEP Collection.

100. "Women Find Acceptance Comes Slowly," *BPH*, 2 October 1986.

101. Elizabeth Laird, interview by Marat Moore, transcript, Cordova, Ala., 4 February 1981, Folder 1, Box 2, Marat Moore Collection, Archives of Appalachia, East Tennessee State University, Johnson City.

102. Ibid.; "A Working Life: Elizabeth Laird," in Marat Moore, *Women in the Mines*, 81–86.

103. Betty Jean Hall to CEP Project File, 23 November 1977, Folder 2, Box 1, CEP Collection; ADIR, *Annual Statistical Report, Fiscal Year 1975*, Folder 3.31, ACOA/AMI Records.

104. "Who We Are—AWI," *Association of Women in Industry Newsletter*, September 1978, Folder 26, Box 50, CEP Collection; "U.S. Steel Settles Complaint by Alabama Women," *Coal Mining Women's Support Team News!* January–February 1979, Folder 28, Box 82, CEP Collection; Betty Jean Hall to CEP Project File, 23 November 1977, Folder 2, Box 1, CEP Collection; ADIR, *Annual Statistical Report, Fiscal Year 1975*, Folder 3.31, ACOA/AMI Records.

105. LaMarse Moore, interview; "Portrait of a Woman Miner: LaMarse Moore," *Coal Mining Women's Support Team News!* January 1982, Folder 31, Box 82, CEP Collection.

106. LaMarse Moore, interview; "Portrait of a Woman Miner: LaMarse Moore," *Coal Mining Women's Support Team News!* January 1982, Folder 31, Box 82, CEP Collection.

107. "Coal Employment Project and Coal Mining Women's Support Team, Progress Report, August 1–November 30, 1978," Folder 6, Box 1, CEP Collection; Connie White to AWI File, 27 November 1978, Folder 26, Box 50, CEP Collection.

108. "AWI Opposes the Klan," *Association of Women in Industry Newsletter*, September 1978, Folder 26, Box 50, CEP Collection.

109. "Minutes of Planning Meeting for a Conference of Women Coal Miners," 27–28 January 1979, Highlander Center, New Market, Tenn., Folder 9, Box 32A, CEP Collection; "AWI Opposes the Klan," *Association of Women in Industry Newsletter*, September 1978, Folder 26, Box 50, CEP Collection.

110. "Settlement Agreement, U.S. Steel and Jennifer Gunn," 24 January 1979, Folder 26, Box 50, CEP Collection; "EEOC Complaint, Jennifer Gunn of Birmingham v. U.S. Steel Concord Mine," 1 November 1978, Folder 26, Box 50, CEP Collection.

111. "Complaint, Office of Federal Contract Compliance Programs, AWI v. Mead Corp., U.S. Steel Corp., Alabama By-Products, and Jim Walters Corp.," "For Immediate Release," Birmingham, Alabama, 25 February 1979, both in Folder 26, Box 50, CEP Collection.

112. U.S. Department of Commerce, Bureau of the Census, *1980 Census*, 497; David Gespass to Betty Jean Hall, 23 April 1979, Folder 26, Box 50, CEP Collection.

113. Lula Peterson, interview by author, tape recording, Bessemer, Ala., 20 July 2001; "Women in the Mines: Going Below to Work Meant Moving Up in the World Financially," *BN*, 22 June 1987, Folder 23, Box 86, CEP Collection.

114. "Autos of Two Female Employees Burned," *BN*, 17 August 1979; "Three Women Claim Threats Made on Jobs," *BN*, 25 August 1979; Tommy Black, "Two Allege Jim Walter Harassment," *BN*, 19 September 1979.

115. Patricia Brown, interview by Marat Moore, transcript, Bessemer, Ala., 25 August 1983, Folder 19, Box 1, Moore Collection; "My Other Life: Patricia Brown," in Marat Moore, *Women in the Mines*, 129–39.

116. Patricia Brown, interview; Marat Moore, *Women in the Mines*, 129.

117. LaMarse Moore, interview.

118. "CEP Releases Sexual Harassment Study Results," *Coal Mining Women's Support Team News!* April 1981, Folder 30, Box 82, CEP Collection.

119. Charlene Griggs, interview by Marat Moore, transcript, Carbon Hill, Ala., 21 August 1983, Folder 20, Box 1, Moore Collection; Patricia Brown, interview.

120. LaMarse Moore, interview; Patricia Brown, interview.

121. "Women Find Acceptance Comes Slowly," *BPH*, 2 October 1986; Connie White to AWI File, 27 November 1978, Folder 26, Box 50, CEP Collection.

122. Griggs, interview.

123. ADIR, *Annual Statistical Report, Fiscal Year 1990*; U.S. Department of Commerce, Bureau of the Census, *1980 Census*, 497; ADIR, *Annual Statistical Report, Fiscal Year 1980*; ADIR, *Annual Statistical Report, Fiscal Year 1983*.

SEVEN. The Era of Global Competition, 1980–2003

1. ADIR, *Annual Statistical Report, Fiscal Year 1980*; ADIR, *Annual Statistical Report, Fiscal Year 1990*; ADIR, *Annual Report, Statistical Supplement, Fiscal Year 2001*; "Mined Out in Alabama," *BN*, 21 May 2000.

2. "Drummond Adds Colombian Coal," *BN*, 12 March 2003; "Drummond: State Coal Nearly Gone," *BN*, 9 September 1999, "Coal Industry and Trade—Alabama" File, TCSH. See also "From Alabama to Colombia—Drummond's 'Trail of Tears,'" *UMWJ*, July–August 2001; "The Colombian Connection," *In These Times*, 23 July 2001.

3. "Depression Dark as a Mine in Coal Industry," *BN*, 17 May 1987; "As Coal Mines Fade Away, Workers Hunt for New Jobs," *NYT*, 2 March 1997.

4. "Mine Rescue Try Fails; 13 Dead," *BN*, 25 September 2001; "Danger Underground," *Atlanta Journal/Atlanta Constitution*, 22 September 1996; "Blue Creek No. 5 Led State in Safety Citations for 2000," *BN*, 2 October 2001; "Ignitions Preceded Alabama Mine Blasts," *Charleston (W.Va.) Sunday Gazette-Mail*, 30 September 2001.

5. See Cowie, *Capital Moves*.

6. ADIR, *Annual Statistical Report, Fiscal Year 1980*; ADIR, *Annual Statistical Report, Fiscal Year 1985*.

7. "Depression Dark as a Mine in Coal Industry," *BN*, 17 May 1987; "Bad Days for Black Rock: Regs Help Put Skids under Many Alabama Coal Firms," *BN*, 11 March 1985.

8. "Depression Dark as a Mine in Coal Industry," *BN*, 17 May 1987; "Bad Days for Black Rock: Regs Help Put Skids under Many Alabama Coal Firms," *BN*, 11 March 1985.

9. "High-Priced Coal Hurts Utility, Small Operators," *BN*, 18 May 1987.

10. "Depression Dark as a Mine in Coal Industry," *BN*, 17 May 1987.

11. ADIR, *Annual Statistical Report, Fiscal Year 1980*; ADIR, *Annual Statistical Report, Fiscal Year 1990*.

12. "No-Strike Contract OK'd by Miners, Drummond Coal," *BPH*, 16 June 1987; "8 Coal Companies, Miners Extend Pact," *BPH*, 4 August 1984; "Miners Approve New Coal Contract," *BN*, 7 June 1981; "35% Unemployment Rate among UMWA Members," *Coal Mining Women's Support Team News!* February 1983, Folder 32, Box 82, CEP Collection.

13. "Drummond: State Coal Nearly Gone," *BN*, 9 September 1999, "Coal Industry and Trade—Alabama" File, TCSH; *Facts about Coal*, 26.

14. "Jim Walter Mines Victim of Boom Turned Sour," *BN*, 20 May 1987; "Colombian Connection Threatens Alabama's Coal Community," *BN*, 18 May 1987; "Drummond Legacy Lives On," *BN*, 18 May 1987.

15. "Drummond: State Coal Nearly Gone," *BN*, 9 September 1999, "Coal Industry and Trade—Alabama" File, TCSH.

16. Ibid.

17. "The Colombian Connection," *In These Times*, 23 July 2001; "Who Killed Locarno and Orcasitas [*sic*]?" *Progressive*, June 2001; "Alabama Coal Giant Is Sued over Three Killings in Colombia," *NYT*, 22 March 2002.

18. "The Colombian Connection," *In These Times*, 23 July 2001; "Who Killed Locarno and Orcasitas [*sic*]?" *Progressive*, June 2001; "Alabama Coal Giant Is Sued over Three Killings in Colombia," *NYT*, 22 March 2002; "Union Leader Killed in Colombia," *BN*, 10 October 2001.

19. "Drummond Says Assassination Suit Effort to Destroy Colombian Jobs," *BN*, 27 March 2002; "Alabama Coal Giant Is Sued over Three Killings in Colombia," *NYT*, 22 March 2002; *Estates of Valmore Lacarno Rodriguez, Victor Hugo Orcasita Amaya, and Gustavo Soler Mora, and SINTRAMIENERGETICA v. Drummond Co., Inc., Drummond Ltd., and Garry* [sic] *N. Drummond*, Case CV-02-N-0665-W, U.S. District Court, Northern District of Alabama, Western Division, Birmingham, Alabama, 14 March 2002, 12, 15. These events are also described in *Juan Aquas Romero v. Drummond Company Inc., Drummond Ltd., Garry* [sic] *N. Drummond, and Augusto Jimenez*, Case CV-03-BE-0575-W, U.S. District Court, Northern District of Alabama, Western Division, Birmingham, Alabama, 13 March 2003.

20. "Drummond Adds Colombian Coal," *BN*, 12 March 2003.

21. "From Alabama to Colombia—Drummond's 'Trail of Tears,'" *UMWJ*, July–August 2001; "The Colombian Connection," *In These Times*, 23 July 2001; ADIR, *Annual Report, Statistical Supplement, Fiscal Year 2001*; ADIR, *Annual Statistical Report, Fiscal Year 1990*; ADIR, *Annual Statistical Report, Fiscal Year 1980*.

22. "Jim Walter Mines Victim of Boom Turned Sour," *BN*, 20 May 1987.

23. "Results Show Coal in Trouble," *BN*, 22 September 2000.

24. "Danger Underground," *Atlanta Journal/Atlanta Constitution*, 22 September 1996.

25. "Stop the Next Farmington," *UMWJ*, May 1984.

26. "Hope Turns to Grief as 9 Rescuers Declared Dead," *TN*, 26 September 2001; "Fire in the Hole," *Mother Jones*, September–October 2002; "Death Underground," *TN*, 29 November 2002; "Union Faults Inspectors for Mine Disaster," *BN*, 23 January 2003; "Blue Creek No. 5 Led State in Safety Citations for 2000," *BN*, 2 October 2001.

27. "32 Lives, 50 Desperate Minutes Underground," *Chicago Tribune*, 23 September 2002; "Mourning Begins for 13 Heroes," *TN*, 26 September 2001; "Mine Rescue Try Fails; 13 Dead," *BN*, 25 September 2001; "Disaster at No. 5 Mine," *Chicago Tribune*, 22 September 2002.

28. "Union Faults Inspectors for Mine Disaster," *BN*, 23 January 2003; "Negligence Cited in Mine, 7 Major Violations Found in Deaths, Regulators Say," *BN*, 12 December 2002.

29. "Mine Deaths, Tests Linked," *BN*, 25 January 2003.

30. Ibid.; "Union Faults Inspectors for Mine Disaster," *BN*, 23 January 2003.

31. For an in-depth account of the rescue of the miners at the Quecreek mine, see "'All Nine Alive,'" *Pittsburgh Post-Gazette*, 4 August 2002.

32. "Miners' Widows Need Money but Company Can't Bust Trust," *BN*, 15 February 2002; "Getting Back to Work in Mine Seen as Tribute," *BN*, 23 September 2002; "Walter to Close No. 5 Mine," *BN*, 2 December 2003.

33. "Fire in the Hole," *Mother Jones*, September–October 2002; "Mine Blast, 13 Deaths Blamed on 'Negligence,'" *Chicago Tribune*, 12 December 2002; "Getting Back to Work in Mine Seen as Tribute," *BN*, 23 September 2002; "Fatal Blast from Below," *TN*, 1 December 2002.

34. "Fatal Blast from Below," *TN*, 1 December 2002; "Getting Back to Work in Mine Seen as Tribute," *BN*, 23 September 2002.

Conclusion

1. "Getting Back to Work in Mine Seen as Tribute," *BN*, 23 September 2002.

2. An overview of Mitch's career in Indiana appears in Folders 1–16, Box 1, Mitch Papers. See also "Labor Leader 50 Years, William A. Mitch Dies," *BN*, 13 July 1974; Dubofsky and Van Tine, *John L. Lewis*, 91–94.

3. John Hessler to JLL, 30 June 1923, JLL to John Hessler, 9 July 1923, both in Folder 17, Box 50, PDC.

4. Fox, *United We Stand*, 260–61.

5. H. A. Henderson to WM, 15 April 1930, WM to H. A. Henderson, 22 April 1930, both in Folder 11, Box 1, Mitch Papers; H. A. Henderson and John A. Riddle to John Hessler, 29 August 1923, Folder 17, Box 50, PDC.

Birmingham Public Library, Periodical Collections, Microfiche Clipping Files
    Coal Industry and Trade, Alabama, 1934–58
    Coal Industry and Trade, Alabama, 1958–74
Birmingham Public Library, Tutwiler Collection of Southern History and Literature,
    Clipping Files
    Alabama By-Products Corporation
    Brookside, Alabama
    Cardiff, Alabama
    Coal Industry and Trade, Alabama
    Coal Mines, Accidents
    Coal Mines and Mining, Alabama
    Coal Mines and Mining, Strip
    Coal Mining Companies, Alabama
    Coal Mining Companies, Alabama Fuel and Iron
    Coal Mining Companies, Brilliant Coal
    Coal Mining Companies, DeBardeleben Coal
    Iron Industry, Birmingham District
    Mulga, Alabama
    Strikes, Alabama, Coal Miners
    TCI, Labor Unions
    United Mine Workers, Alabama
    U.S. Pipe and Foundry
Samford University, Special Collection Department, Historical Manuscripts
    Docena Baptist Church Records
    Docena, Alabama (TCI) Materials
    Historical Material, Scrapbooks, Jefferson County Alabama, Edgewater, Alabama
    "History of Edgewater from 1911 to 1984"
    Kizzire, Melba Wilbanks, " 'Beneath These Hills': Docena, the People, Yesterday,
        Today, and Tomorrow"

Chapel Hill, N.C.

University of North Carolina, Wilson Library, Manuscripts Department
    Howard Odum Papers

Detroit, Mich.

Wayne State University, Archives of Labor, Urban Affairs and University Archives
    Miners for Democracy Collection

Hyde Park, N.Y.

Franklin D. Roosevelt Presidential Library
    President's Official File

Johnson City, Tenn.

East Tennessee State University, Archives of Appalachia
    Coal Employment Project Collection
    Marat Moore Collection

Montgomery, Ala.

Alabama Department of Archives and History
    Alabama Governors' Speeches, Microfilm Collection
    Albert Brewer Papers
    Frank Dixon Papers
    James Folsom Papers
    Bibb Graves Papers
    Guy Hunt Papers
    Forrest "Fob" James Papers
    John Patterson Papers
    Gordon Persons Papers
    Chauncey Sparks Papers
    George Wallace Papers
    Lurleen Wallace Papers
Alabama AFL-CIO Office
    Miscellaneous Records

Morgantown, W.Va.

West Virginia University, West Virginia and Regional History Collection
    United Mine Workers of America Health and Retirement Fund Collection

Philadelphia, Pa.

University Archives and Records Center, University of Pennsylvania
    Wharton School Industrial Research Unit Papers

State College, Pa.

Pennsylvania State University, Paterno Library, Historical Collections and Labor
        Archives
    William Mitch Papers
    United Mine Workers of America Archive
    United Steelworkers of America Archive and Oral History Collection

Tuscaloosa, Ala.

University of Alabama, W. S. Hoole Special Collections Library
    Alabama Fuel and Iron Collection
    Carl Elliott Papers

OTHER WORKS

Adams, Charles Edward. *Blocton: The History of an Alabama Coal Mining Town.* Brierfield, Ala.: Cahaba Trace Commission, 2001.

Ahmed, Nahfiza. "A City Too Respectable to Hate: Mobile during the Era of Desegregation, 1961–1965." *Gulf South Historical Review* 15, no. 1 (1999): 49–67.

Alabama Mining Institute. *Coal Mining in Alabama: A Series of Information Letters.* Birmingham: Alabama Mining Institute, 1936.

Alexander, Peter. "Rising from the Ashes: Alabama Coal Miners, 1921–1941." In *It Is Union and Liberty: Alabama Coal Miners and the UMW,* ed. Edwin L. Brown and Colin J. Davis. Tuscaloosa: University of Alabama Press, 1999.

Armbrister, Trevor. *Act of Vengeance: The Yablonski Murders and Their Solution.* New York: Saturday Review Press, 1975.

Arnesen, Eric. " 'Like Banquo's Ghost, It Will Not Down': The Race Question and the American Railroad Brotherhoods, 1880–1920." *American Historical Review* 99, no. 5 (1994): 1601–33.

———. "Up from Exclusion: Black and White Workers, Race, and the State of Labor History." *Reviews in American History* 26, no. 1 (1998): 146–74.

———. *Waterfront Workers of New Orleans: Race, Class, and Politics, 1863–1923.* Oxford: Oxford University Press, 1991.

———. "Whiteness and the Historians' Imagination." *International Labor and Working Class History* 60 (Fall 2001): 3–32.

Arrighi, Giovanni. "The Social and Political Economy of Global Turbulence." *New Left Review* 20 (March–April 2003): 5–71.

Bailey, Earl. *Surface Mining in Alabama: The Environmental Impact.* N.p.: Alabama Environmental Quality Association, 1975.

Bamberger, Bill, and Cathy N. Davidson. *Closing: The Life and Death of an American Factory.* New York: Center for Documentary Studies, 1998.

Barlett, Donald L., and James B. Steele. *America: What Went Wrong?* Kansas City: Andrews and McMeel, 1992.

Barnard, Thomas, and Brenda Clark. "Clementine in the 1980s (EEO and the Woman Miner)." *West Virginia Law Review* 82 (Summer 1980): 899–936.

Barnard, William. *Dixiecrats and Democrats: Alabama Politics, 1942–1950.* Tuscaloosa: University of Alabama Press, 1974.

———. "The Old Order Changes: Graves, Sparks, Folsom, and the Gubernatorial Election of 1942." In *From Civil War to Civil Rights—Alabama, 1860–1960: An Anthology from the "Alabama Review,"* ed. Sarah Woolfolk Wiggins. Tuscaloosa: University of Alabama Press, 1987.

Barnum, Darold T. *The Negro in the Bituminous Coal Mining Industry.* Philadelphia: University of Pennsylvania Press, 1970.

Bartley, Numan V. *The New South, 1945–1980: The Story of the South's Modernization.* Baton Rouge: Louisiana State University Press, 1995.

Beito, David. *From Mutual Aid to the Welfare State: Fraternal Societies and Social Services, 1890–1967.* Chapel Hill: University of North Carolina Press, 2000.

Bond, Horace Mann. *Negro Education in Alabama: A Study in Cotton and Steel.* 1939; New York: Octagon Books, 1969.

Boydston, Jeanne. *Home and Work: Housework, Wages, and the Ideology of Labor in the Early Republic.* New York: Oxford University Press, 1990.

Boyer, Richard O., and Herbert M. Morais. *Labor's Untold Story: The Adventure Story of the Battles, Betrayals, and Victories of American Working Men and Women.* Pittsburgh: United Electrical, Radio and Machine Workers of America, 1955.

Boyle, Kevin. "'There Are No Union Sorrows That the Union Can't Heal': The Struggle for Racial Equality in the United Automobile Workers, 1940–1960." *Labor History* 36, no. 1 (1995): 5–23.

Branch, Taylor. *Parting the Waters: America in the King Years, 1954–1963.* New York: Touchstone, 1988.

———. *Pillar of Fire: America in the King Years, 1963–1965.* New York: Simon and Schuster, 1998.

Brattain, Michelle. "Making Friends and Enemies: Textile Workers and Political Action in Post–World War II Georgia." *Journal of Southern History* 63, no. 1 (1997): 91–138.

———. "The Politics of Whiteness: Race, Workers, and Culture in the Modern South." Ph.D. diss., Rutgers University, 1997.

———. *The Politics of Whiteness: Race, Workers, and Culture in the Modern South.* Princeton: Princeton University Press, 2001.

———. "The Pursuits of Postexceptionalism: Race, Gender, Class, and Politics in the New Southern Labor History." In *Labor in the Modern South*, ed. Glenn T. Eskew. Athens: University of Georgia Press, 2001.

———. "'So-Called Fair Employment': The Maintenance of Georgia's White Textile Workforce during World War II." Unpublished paper, n.d.

———. "'A Town as Small as That': Tallapoosa, Georgia, and Operation Dixie, 1945–1950." *Georgia Historical Quarterly* 81, no. 2 (1997): 395–425.

Braverman, Harry. *Labor and Monopoly Capital: The Degradation of Work in the Twentieth Century (25th Anniversary Edition).* New York: Monthly Review Press, 1998.

Brenner, Robert. *The Boom and the Bubble: The U.S. in the World Economy.* London: Verso, 2002.

Brett, Jeanne M., and Goldberg, Stephen B. "Wildcat Strikes in Bituminous Coal Mining." *Industrial and Labor Relations Review* 32 (July 1979): 465–83.

Brody, David. *Workers in Industrial America: Essays on the Twentieth Century Struggle.* 2d ed. New York: Oxford University Press, 1993.

Brophy, John. *A Miner's Life.* Madison: University of Wisconsin Press, 1964.

Brown, Edwin, and Colin Davis, eds. *It Is Union and Liberty: Alabama Coal Miners and the UMW.* Tuscaloosa: University of Alabama Press, 1999.

Brownell, Blaine A. "Birmingham, Alabama: New South City in the 1920s." *Journal of Southern History* 38, no. 1 (1972): 21–48.

Brunstetter, Maude Phillips. "The Desperate Enterprise: A Case Study of the Democratization of the United Mine Workers in the 1970s." Ph.D. diss., Columbia University, 1981.

Bunche, Ralph J. *The Political Status of the Negro in the Age of FDR.* Ed. Dewey W. Grantham. Chicago: University of Chicago Press, 1973.

Carlton, David. *Mill and Town in South Carolina, 1880–1920.* Baton Rouge: Louisiana State University Press, 1982.

Farber, David, ed. *The Sixties: From Memory to History*. Chapel Hill: University of North Carolina Press, 1994.

Fehn, Bruce. " 'Chickens Come Home to Roost': Industrial Reorganization, Seniority, and Gender Conflict in the United Packinghouse Workers of America, 1956–1966," *Labor History* 34, nos. 2–3 (1993): 324–41.

Feldman, Glenn. "Alabama Coal Miners in War and Peace, 1942–1975." In *It Is Union and Liberty: Alabama Coal Miners and the UMW*, ed. Edwin L. Brown and Colin J. Davis. Tuscaloosa: University of Alabama Press, 1999.

———. *The Disfranchisement Myth: Poor Whites and Suffrage Restriction in Alabama*. Athens: University of Georgia Press, 2004.

———. "Frank M. Dixon, 1939–1943." In *Alabama Governors: A Political History of the State*, ed. Samuel Webb and Margaret E. Armbrester. Tuscaloosa: University of Alabama Press, 2001.

———. *Politics, Society, and the Klan in Alabama, 1915–1949*. Tuscaloosa: University of Alabama Press, 1998.

Feldman, Lynne B. *A Sense of Place: Birmingham's Black Middle-Class Community, 1890–1930*. Tuscaloosa: University of Alabama Press, 2000.

Filippelli, Ronald L. *Labor in the USA: A History*. New York: Knopf, 1984.

Fink, Gary M. "Efficiency and Control: Labor Espionage in Southern Textiles." In *Organized Labor in the Twentieth-Century South*, ed. Robert H. Zieger. Knoxville: University of Tennessee Press, 1991.

———. *The Fulton Bag and Cotton Mills Strike of 1914–1915: Espionage, Labor Conflict, and New South Industrial Relations*. Ithaca: ILR Press, 1993.

Fink, Gary M., and Merl E. Reed, eds. *Essays in Southern Labor History: Selected Papers, Southern Labor History Conference, 1976*. Westport, Conn.: Greenwood Press, 1977.

———, eds. *Race, Class, and Community in Southern Labor History*. Tuscaloosa: University of Alabama Press, 1994.

Finley, Joseph E. *The Corrupt Kingdom: The Rise and Fall of the United Mine Workers*. New York: Simon and Schuster, 1972.

Fisher, Stephen L., ed. *Fighting Back in Appalachia: Traditions of Resistance and Change*. Philadelphia: Temple University Press, 1993.

Flamming, Douglas. *Creating the Modern South: Millhands and Managers in Dalton, Georgia, 1884–1984*. Chapel Hill: University of North Carolina Press, 1992.

Fly, Jerry W., and George R. Reinhart, "Racial Separation during the 1970s: The Case of Birmingham." *Social Forces* 58, no. 4 (1980): 1255–62.

Flynt, Wayne. *Alabama in the Twentieth Century*. Tuscaloosa: University of Alabama Press, 2004.

———. "Bibb Graves, 1927–1931, 1935–1939." In *Alabama Governors: A Political History of the State*, ed. Samuel Webb and Margaret E. Armbrester. Tuscaloosa: University of Alabama Press, 2001.

———. *Poor but Proud: Alabama's Poor Whites*. Tuscaloosa: University of Alabama Press, 1989.

Foley, Neil. *The White Scourge: Mexicans, Blacks, and Poor Whites in Texas*. Berkeley: University of California Press, 1998.

Foner, Eric. *A Short History of Reconstruction, 1863–1877*. New York: Harper and Row, 1990.

————. *The Story of American Freedom*. New York: Norton, 1998.

Fox, Maier B. *United We Stand: The United Mine Workers of America, 1890–1990*. Washington, D.C.: United Mine Workers of America, 1990.

Franklin, Jimmie. *Back to Birmingham: Richard Arrington, Jr., and His Times*. Tuscaloosa: University of Alabama Press, 1989.

Fraser, Steven, and Gary Gerstle, eds. *The Rise and Fall of the New Deal Order, 1930–1980*. Princeton: Princeton University Press, 1989.

Frederickson, Kari. *The Dixiecrat Revolt and the End of the Solid South, 1932–1968*. Chapel Hill: University of North Carolina Press, 2001.

Gabin, Nancy. *Feminism in the Labor Movement: Women and the United Auto Workers, 1935–1975*. Ithaca: Cornell University Press, 1990.

————. "Time out of Mind: The UAW's Response to Female Labor Laws and Mandatory Overtime in the 1960s." In *Work Engendered: Toward a New History of American Labor*, ed. Ava Baron. Ithaca: Cornell University Press, 1991.

Gaventa, John. *Power and Powerlessness: Quiescence and Rebellion in an Appalachian Valley*. Urbana: University of Illinois Press, 1980.

Gilmore, Glenda Elizabeth. *Gender and Jim Crow: Women and the Politics of White Supremacy in North Carolina, 1896–1920*. Chapel Hill: University of North Carolina Press, 1996.

Goldfield, Michael. *The Decline of Organized Labor in the United States*. Chicago: University of Chicago Press, 1987.

————. "The Failure of Operation Dixie: A Critical Turning Point in American Political Development?" In *Race, Class, and Community in Southern Labor History*, ed. Gary M. Fink and Merl E. Reed. Tuscaloosa: University of Alabama Press, 1994.

Goldstein, George S. "The Rise and Decline of the UMWA Health and Retirement Funds Program, 1946–1995." In *The United Mine Workers of America: A Model of Industrial Solidarity?* ed. John H. M. Laslett. University Park: Pennsylvania State University Press, 1996.

Goodman, Walter. "The Sad Legacy of John L. Lewis." *Dissent* 19 (Winter 1972): 99–106.

Goodwin, Doris Kearns. *No Ordinary Time: Franklin and Eleanor Roosevelt: The Home Front in World War II*. New York: Simon and Schuster, 1994.

Goodwyn, Lawrence. *Democratic Promise: The Populist Moment in America*. Oxford: Oxford University Press, 1976.

Grafton, Carl, and Anne Permaloff. *Big Mules and Branchheads: James E. Folsom and Political Power in Alabama*. Athens: University of Georgia Press, 1985.

Grantham, Dewey W. *The South in Modern America: A Region at Odds*. New York: Harper-Collins, 1994.

Green, Archie. *Only a Miner: Studies in Recorded Coal-Mining Songs*. Urbana: University of Illinois Press, 1972.

Green, Jim. "Holding the Line: Miners' Militancy and the Strike of 1978." *Radical America* 12, no. 3 (1978): 2–27.

Greider, William. *One World, Ready or Not: The Manic Logic of Global Capitalism*. New York: Touchstone, 1997.

Griffith, Barbara S. *The Crisis of American Labor: Operation Dixie and the Defeat of the CIO*. Philadelphia: Temple University Press, 1988.

Gutman, Herbert G. "Black Coal Miners and the Greenback-Labor Party in Redeemer,

————. *Hammer and Hoe: Alabama Communists during the Great Depression.* Chapel Hill: University of North Carolina Press, 1990.

————. *Race Rebels: Culture, Politics, and the Black Working Class.* New York: Free Press, 1994.

————. " 'We Are Not What We Seem': Rethinking Black Working-Class Opposition in the Jim Crow South." *Journal of American History* 80, no. 1 (1993): 75–112.

Kelly, Brian. "Policing the 'Negro Eden': Racial Paternalism in the Alabama Coalfields, 1908–1921, Part One." *Alabama Review* 51, no. 3 (1998): 163–83.

————. "Policing the 'Negro Eden': Racial Paternalism in the Alabama Coalfields, 1908–1921, Part Two." *Alabama Review* 51, no. 4 (1998): 243–65.

————. *Race, Class, and Power in the Alabama Coalfields, 1908–1921.* Urbana: University of Illinois Press, 2001.

Kessler-Harris, Alice. *Out to Work: A History of Wage-Earning Women in the United States.* New York: Oxford University Press, 1982.

Key, V. O. *Southern Politics in State and Nation.* New York: Vintage Books, 1949.

Kolchin, Peter. "Whiteness Studies: The New History of Race in America." *Journal of American History* 89, no. 1 (2002): 154–73.

Korson, George. *Coal Dust on the Fiddle: Songs and Stories of the Bituminous Industry.* Hatboro, Pa.: Folklore Associates, 1965.

Korstad, Robert. *Civil Rights Unionism: Tobacco Workers and the Struggle for Democracy in the Mid-Twentieth-Century South.* Chapel Hill: University of North Carolina Press, 2003.

Korstad, Robert, and Nelson Lichtenstein. "Opportunities Found and Lost: Labor Radicals and the Early Civil Rights Movement." *Journal of American History* 75, no. 3 (1988): 786–811.

Kuhn, Clifford M. *Contesting the New South Order: The 1914–1915 Strike at Atlanta's Fulton Mills.* Chapel Hill: University of North Carolina Press, 2001.

Kuhn, Clifford M., Harlon E. Joye, and E. Bernard West. *Living Atlanta: An Oral History of the City, 1914–1948.* Athens: University of Georgia Press, 1990.

LaMonte, Edward Shannon. *Politics and Welfare in Birmingham, 1900–1975.* Tuscaloosa: University of Alabama Press, 1995.

Laslett, John H. M., ed. *The United Mine Workers of America: A Model of Industrial Solidarity?* University Park: Pennsylvania State University Press, 1996.

Laurie, Bruce. *Artisans into Workers: Labor in Nineteenth-Century America.* New York: Hill and Wang, 1989.

Lawson, Steven F. *Black Ballots: Voting Rights in the South, 1944–1969.* New York: Columbia University Press, 1976.

Letwin, Daniel. *The Challenge of Interracial Unionism: Alabama Coal Miners, 1878–1921.* Chapel Hill: University of North Carolina Press, 1998.

————. "Interracial Unionism, Gender, and 'Social Equality' in the Alabama Coalfields, 1878–1908." *Journal of Southern History* 51, no. 3 (1995): 519–54.

Levenstein, Harvey. *Communism, Anticommunism, and the CIO.* Westport, Conn.: Greenwood Press, 1981.

Levy, Peter B. *The New Left and Labor in the 1960s.* Urbana: University of Illinois Press, 1994.

Lewis, Earl. *In Their Own Interests: Race, Class, and Power in Twentieth-Century Norfolk, Virginia.* Berkeley: University of California Press, 1991.

Lewis, Ronald. *Black Coal Miners in America: Race, Class, and Community Conflict, 1780–1980.* Lexington: University Press of Kentucky, 1987.

Lewis, W. David. *Sloss Furnaces and the Rise of the Birmingham District: An Industrial Epic.* Tuscaloosa: University of Alabama Press, 1994.

Lichtenstein, Alex. "Racial Conflict and Racial Solidarity in the Alabama Coal Strike of 1894: New Evidence for the Gutman-Hill Debate." *Labor History* 36, no. 1 (1995): 63–76.

———. *Twice the Work of Free Labor: The Political Economy of Convict Labor in the New South.* London: Verso, 1996.

Lichtenstein, Nelson. *Labor's War at Home: The CIO in World War II.* Cambridge: Cambridge University Press, 1982.

———. *The Most Dangerous Man in Detroit: Walter Reuther and the Fate of American Labor.* New York: Basic Books, 1995.

———. *State of the Union: A Century of American Labor.* Princeton: Princeton University Press, 2002.

Lipsitz, George. *The Possessive Investment in Whiteness: How White People Profit from Identity Politics.* Philadelphia: Temple University Press, 1998.

———. *Rainbow at Midnight: Labor and Culture in the 1940s.* Urbana: University of Illinois Press, 1994.

Lowell, Esther. "Housing for Negro Employes, United States Steel Corporation." *Opportunity: Journal of Negro Life* 7 (August 1929): 247–49.

Manis, Andrew M. *A Fire You Can't Put Out: The Civil Rights Life of Birmingham's Reverend Fred Shuttlesworth.* Tuscaloosa: University of Alabama Press, 1999.

Marschall, Daniel. "The Miners and the UMW: Crisis in the Reform Process." *Socialist Review* 8, nos. 4–5 (1978): 65–115.

Marshall, F. Ray. *Labor in the South.* Cambridge: Harvard University Press, 1967.

Marx, Karl. *The Economic and Philosophic Manuscripts of 1844.* New York: International Publishers, 1964.

Matthews, John Michael. "The Georgia 'Race Strike' of 1909." *Journal of Southern History* 40, no. 4 (1974): 613–30.

McAteer, J. Davitt. *Miner's Manual: A Complete Guide to Health and Safety Protection Underground.* Ed. Thomas N. Bethell. Washington, D.C.: Occupational Safety and Health Law Center, 1985.

McCallum, Brenda. "The Gospel of Black Unionism." In *Songs about Work: Essays in Occupational Culture for Richard A. Reuss,* ed. Archie Green. Bloomington: Indiana University Press, 1993.

McKiven, Henry. *Iron and Steel: Class, Race, and Community in Birmingham, Alabama, 1875–1920.* Chapel Hill: University of North Carolina Press, 1995.

McMillen, Neil R., ed. *Remaking Dixie: The Impact of World War II on the American South.* Jackson: University Press of Mississippi, 1997.

McWhorter, Diane. *Carry Me Home: Birmingham, Alabama, the Climactic Battle of the Civil Rights Revolution.* New York: Touchstone, 2002.

Milkman, Ruth. *Gender at Work: The Dynamics of Job Segregation by Sex during World War II.* Urbana: University of Illinois Press, 1987.

Minchin, Timothy. "'Color Means Something': Black Pioneers, White Resistance, and

Rogers, William Warren, Robert David Ward, Leah Rawls Atkins, and Wayne Flynt. *Alabama: The History of a Deep South State.* Tuscaloosa: University of Alabama Press, 1994.

Rosengarten, Theodore. "Reading the Hops: Recollections of Lorenzo Piper Davis and the Negro Baseball League." *Southern Exposure* 5 (1977): 62–79.

Salmond, John. *Gastonia, 1929: The Story of the Loray Mill Strike.* Chapel Hill: University of North Carolina Press, 1995.

————. *Miss Lucy of the CIO: The Life and Times of Lucy Randolph Mason, 1882–1959.* Athens: University of Georgia Press, 1989.

Savage, Carletta. "Re-gendering Coal: Female Miners and Male Supervisors." *Appalachian Journal* 27, no. 3 (2000): 232–48.

Schulman, Bruce J. *From Cotton Belt to Sunbelt: Federal Policy, Economic Development, and the Transformation of the South, 1938–1980.* Oxford: Oxford University Press, 1991.

Scott, James C. *Domination and the Arts of Resistance: Hidden Transcripts.* New Haven: Yale University Press, 1990.

Scribner, Christopher MacGregor. "The Quiet Revolution: Federal Funding and Change in Birmingham, Alabama, 1933–1965." Ph.D. diss., Vanderbilt University, 1996.

————. *Renewing Birmingham: Federal Funding and the Promise of Change, 1929–1979.* Athens: University of Georgia Press, 2002.

Scruggs, Frank P. *Coal in Alabama.* Montgomery: Alabama Energy Management Board, 1974.

Seltzer, Curtis. *Fire in the Hole: Miners and Managers in the American Coal Industry.* Lexington: University of Kentucky Press, 1985.

Shifflett, Crandall A. *Coal Towns: Life, Work, and Culture in Company Towns of Southern Appalachia, 1880–1960.* Knoxville: University of Tennessee Press, 1991.

Simon, Bryant. *A Fabric of Defeat: The Politics of South Carolina Millhands, 1910–1948.* Chapel Hill: University of North Carolina Press, 1998.

————. "Fearing Eleanor: Racial Anxieties and Wartime Rumors in the American South, 1940–1945." In *Labor in the Modern South,* ed. Glenn Eskew. Athens: University of Georgia Press, 2001.

————. "Rethinking Why There Are So Few Unions in the South." *Georgia Historical Quarterly* 81, no. 2 (1997): 465–84.

Simon, Richard P. "Hard Times for Organized Labor in Appalachia." *Review of Radical Political Economics* 15, no. 3 (1983): 21–34.

Singal, Daniel Joseph. *The War Within: From Victorian to Modernist Thought in the South, 1919–1945.* Chapel Hill: University of North Carolina Press, 1982.

Sitkoff, Harvard. "Racial Militancy and Interracial Violence in the Second World War." *Journal of American History* 58, no. 3 (1971): 661–81.

Sloss Furnace Association. *Spirit of Steel: Music of the Mines, Railroads, and Mills of the Birmingham District.* Birmingham: Crane Hill, 1999.

Smith, Barbara Ellen. *Digging Our Own Graves: Coal Miners and the Struggle over Black Lung Disease.* Philadelphia: Temple University Press, 1987.

Smith, Cloyd M., and Clayton G. Ball, eds. *Mech Annual.* Washington, D.C.: Mechanization Incorporated, 1940.

Stein, Judith. *Running Steel, Running America: Race, Economic Policy, and the Decline of Liberalism.* Chapel Hill: University of North Carolina Press, 1998.

———. "Southern Workers in National Unions: Birmingham Steelworkers, 1936–1951." In *Organized Labor in the Twentieth-Century South*, ed. Robert H. Zieger. Knoxville: University of Tennessee Press.

Straw, Richard. "The Collapse of Biracial Unionism: The Alabama Coal Strike of 1908." *Alabama Historical Quarterly* 37, no. 2 (1975): 92–114.

———. "The United Mine Workers of America and the 1920 Coal Strike in Alabama." *Alabama Review* 28, no. 2 (1975): 104–28.

Sugrue, Thomas. *The Origins of the Urban Crisis: Race and Inequality in Postwar Detroit.* Princeton: Princeton University Press, 1996.

———. "The Structures of Urban Poverty: The Reorganization of Space and Work in Three Periods of American History." In *The "Underclass" Debate: Views from History*, ed. Michael B. Katz. Princeton: Princeton University Press, 1993.

Sullivan, Patricia. *Days of Hope: Race and Democracy in the New Deal Era.* Chapel Hill: University of North Carolina Press, 1996.

Taft, Philip. *Organizing Dixie: Alabama Workers in the Industrial Era.* Ed. Gary M. Fink. Westport, Conn.: Greenwood Press, 1981.

Tallichet, Suzanne E. "Gendered Relations in the Mines and the Division of Labor Underground." *Gender and Society* 9, no. 6 (1995): 697–711.

———. "Moving Up Down in the Mine: The Preservation of Male Privilege Underground." In *More Than Class: Studying Power in U.S. Workplaces*, ed. Ann E. Kingsolver. Albany: State University of New York Press, 1998.

Tarrow, Sidney. *Power in Movement: Social Movements and Contentious Politics.* 2d ed. Cambridge: Cambridge University Press, 1998.

Thompson, E. P. *The Making of the English Working Class.* New York: Vintage Books, 1963.

Thornton, J. Mills, III. *Dividing Lines: Municipal Politics and the Struggle for Civil Rights in Montgomery, Birmingham, and Selma.* Tuscaloosa: University of Alabama Press, 2002.

Tindall, George B. *The Emergence of the New South, 1913–1945.* Baton Rouge: Louisiana State University Press, 1967.

Trotter, Joe. *Black Milwaukee: The Making of an Industrial Proletariat, 1915–1945.* Urbana: University of Illinois Press, 1985.

———. *Coal, Class, and Color: Blacks in Southern West Virginia, 1915–1932.* Urbana: University of Illinois Press, 1990.

Tuten, James H. "Regulating the Poor in Alabama: The Jefferson County Poor Farm, 1885–1945." In *Before the New Deal: Social Welfare in the South, 1830–1930*, ed. Elna C. Green. Athens: University of Georgia Press, 1999.

Walker, James H. *The Struggle and the Joy: An American Coal Town, Piper, Alabama.* McCalla, Ala.: Instant Heirloom Books, 1994.

Webb, Samuel, and Margaret Armbrester, eds. *Alabama Governors: A Political History of the State.* Tuscaloosa: University of Alabama Press, 2001.

Wheeler, Hoyt N. *The Future of the America Labor Movement.* Cambridge: Cambridge University Press, 2002.

coal gasification, 258n25

coal industry: accidents in, 19–20; and blasting, 19; and continuous mining machines, 1–2, 6, 155–56; early history of, in Alabama, 14–16; economic difficulties of, 56, 117–23 passim, 141–48, 153–54, 214–20 passim; expansion of, in 1960s and 1970s, 192; and exports, 8, 188–89, 190–91; and geology of Alabama, 16–17, 18; and imports, 214–15, 217–18; 219–20; and loading coal, 18–19; and long wall mining, 18, 216; mechanization of, 17–18, 155–56; methods of, 18–19; room-and-pillar method, 19; and segregation, 12, 13, 17–18, 20, 21–23; and truck mines, 16; and washing coal, 16–17; during World War II, 85–86. *See also* strip mining

Coalition to Stop South African Coal, 199

coal miners: convicts as, 20–21; elderly, 39; fathers and sons as, 32; job losses of, after World War II, 117, 119; origins of white, 20; World War II difficulties of, 86–87. *See also* African American miners; coal industry; coal towns; United Mine Workers of America

coal operators: and agreement of 1946, 136; Centralia disaster reaction of, 138–39; and National Industrial Recovery Act, 49; racial policies of, 5, 7, 17–18; and Welfare and Retirement Fund, 137, 139. *See also* Alabama Mining Institute; coal industry; coal towns

coal towns: and AFICO, 24–26; and company guards, 28, 32–33; and company stores, 33; economic conditions of, in 1960s and 1970s, 185–88; and fraternal organizations, 37; and health care, 33–34; payday in, 37–38; post–World War II changes in, 154–55; religious life in, 34–36; segregation in, 11–12, 24, 26–29 passim, 33; and shack rousters, 70; welfare programs in, 25, 28, 33–34, 37; women in, 39

coal workers' pneumoconiosis, 20, 166–67, 192

Cochran, Christine, 28, 35, 39

coke production, 15

Collingsworth, Terry, 219

Collins, Addie Mae, 180

Collins, William, 32, 33, 34, 38

Colombian coal. *See* Drummond Coal Company: and Colombia

Combs, Harrison, 97

commercial rail–connected coal companies, 16

Committee to Stop South African Coal, 194

Communist Party, 4, 78, 83–84; and UMWA, 88–90

Community Chest, 40

Congress of Industrial Organizations (CIO): and Alabama, 47, 50; break of, with AFL, 61–62; break of, with UMWA, 48; opposition of, to poll tax, 65, 68; racial policies of, 2, 4, 47; racial policies of, and elections, 66–67, 124; segregation violations of, during World War II, 76, 77–78; and Southern Conference for Human Welfare, 67; and World War II, 82. *See also* United Mine Workers of America

Connor, Bull, 77

continuous mining machines, 1–2, 6, 155–56

Cooper, Jerome "Buddy," 167

Coosa coalfield, 14

Coosa River Ordnance Plant, 85

Country, Charlie, 186

Cowherd Yelverton, 68, 80

Cowie, Jefferson, 8

Crawford, George Gordon, 27

Crawford, Thomas, 139, 159, 172, 263n20; as District 20 president, 184; and George Wallace, 182

Cruce, Joe, 195

Cunningham, Bob, 106

Custred, James, 155

Jim Walter Homes, 178, 190
Jim Walter Resources, 209; early history of, in Alabama, 190; economic difficulties of, 218, 220; and Number 4 mine, 210, 220–21; and Number 5 mine disaster, 215, 221–23; and safety, 215, 220–21
Johnson, G. L., 89–90
Johnson, Lyndon, 180
Johnson, Wendell, 221
Johnston, Sara Jean, 210
Jones, Betty, 206
Jones, Sadie, 207
Jones, Walter, 44, 63, 81, 91; and District 20, 45–47; and John Altman, 62; and John L. Lewis, 45; and William Mitch, 45, 46–47, 62–63

Kahler Plaza Hotel, 176–77
K and S Coal and Clay Mining, 183
Kelley, Claude, 172
Kelley, Robin D. G., 4
Kelly, Brian, 5, 7
Kennedy, Thomas, 173, 192
Kerr, Lorin, 167, 170
Killingsworth, Boyd, 134
Kimbrough, J. Thurman, 131
Kincey, Robert, 112
King, Andy, 97
Kizzire, Melba Wilbanks, 32, 155
KKK. See Ku Klux Klan
Knights of Labor, 5
Knox, John, 221
Koplin, Allen, 162, 168, 169; and African American miners, 169; and cutbacks to Welfare and Retirement Fund, 165, 166; and miner protests, 170. See also Welfare and Retirement Fund
Korson, George, 14
Korstad, Robert, 3, 233n18
Krug, Julius, 136
Ku Klux Klan (KKK), 7–8, 12, 28, 52, 181; coal miner involvement in, 116–17; and gender, 127; in Indiana, 227–28; labor movement opposition to, 133; and Mine Mill, 128–29; and "morality," 127–28;

in 1970s, 208–9, 211; post–World War II night riding of, 115–16, 126–35; rebirth of, in Birmingham, 126–27; and UMWA efforts to raid Mine Mill, 81; working-class support for, 128–29. See also Mitch, William; United Mine Workers of America

labor agents, 31
Labor's Non-Partisan League, 133
Lacarno, Valmore, 219
Lackey, James, 141–42
Laird, Elizabeth, 207
Lattimore, Geraldine, 210
Lawrence, Alton, 79
Lawrence, Lester, 122, 125
Lawson, David, 221
Lawyers' Committee for Civil Rights under Law, 196
League to Maintain White Supremacy, 76
Letwin, Daniel, 5
Lewis, A. D. "Denny," 54
Lewis, John L., 78, 120; and AFICO violence, 59; and African Americans, 51–52; and mine disasters, 95–96, 98; retirement of, 173; and strike of 1944, 110; and Walter Jones, 45; and Welfare and Retirement Fund, 135–36, 139, 140–41, 145, 146–47; and William Dalrymple, 46, 48–49, 91–92
Lewis, Ronald, 7
Lewisburg mine, 22, 51, 154
Lichtenstein, Alex, 21
Lipsitz, George, 83
Littlefield, Sam: and anticommunism, 199; death of, 200; as District 20 president, 193; and South African coal imports, 194, 197–98, 199; and strip mining, 188
Little Steel Formula. See under National War Labor Board
Lloyd Noland Hospital, 163
Lollar, C. A. "Brownie," 134–35
Louisville and Nashville Railroad, 175
Lucy, Autherine, 180

Stover, Ed, 48
Streit, Paul, 170
strip mining, 29, 156–71, 179, 186–88, 216
Sugrue, Thomas, 7
Sullivan, Searcy, 142
Sumiton, Ala., 198–99
Sunbelt economy, 26, 150–52, 184–85
surface mining. See coal industry; strip
  mining
Swanger, H. A., 148
SWOC (Steel Workers Organizing
  Committee), 70–71. See also United
  Steelworkers of America

Taft-Harley Act, 140
Tarrant, Lewis, 80–81
Tatum, Berry, 173
TCI. See Tennessee Coal, Iron, and
  Railroad Company
Tedford, Howard, 195
Tennessee Coal, Iron, and Railroad
  Company (TCI), 3, 15, 21, 24, 106, 177;
  changes to, after World War II, 151–52,
  155; growth of, 15; and segregation, 28–
  29; and seniority, 157–59 passim; and
  steelworker organizing efforts, 70–71;
  and UMWA organizing efforts, 56, 60–
  61, 63–65; welfare programs of, 27–28
Tennessee-Tombigbee Waterway, 191
Tennessee Valley Authority, 191
Terry, Glenn, 165
Terry, James, 107
textile industry: and race relations, 12–13;
  and World War II wages, 87
Thomas, D. A., 120
Thomas, Jobie, 11, 37, 38
Thomas, Virgil, 59
Thompson, Lon, 86–87
Thurmond, Strom, 126
Tindall, George, 150
Tracey, Mike, 219
Trawick, Paul, 133
Truman, Harry, 126, 137, 139
Trumka, Richard, 217
Turner, W. B., 60, 65

Union Supply Company, 155
United Mine Workers of America
  (UMWA), 43; and AFICO, 26, 56, 57–60;
  African American support for, 52; and
  break with CIO, 48; and Centralia mine
  disaster, 137–40; communist influence
  in, 88–90; conciliatory posture of, in
  the 1980s, 217; dissident movements in,
  88–93, 105–6, 111–12; District 50 of, and
  Mine Mill, 80–81, 129; early organizing
  victories of, 56; and George Wallace,
  182–83, 188, 204–5; and International
  Longshoremen's Association, 197–
  200; interracial cooperation of, in
  early organizing, 52–53; and Klan,
  52, 81, 128, 133–34, 135, 227–28; and
  mechanization, 55–56; and reform
  movement of the 1960s and 1970s,
  192–93; and representation election at
  TCI, 64; and safety after World War II,
  137–39; and safety during World War II,
  95–98; and seniority, 157–59; and South
  African coal boycott, 176–77, 193–201,
  229; and Southern Conference for
  Human Welfare, 67–68; and Southern
  Labor Union, 182–83, 184; split of,
  with Alabama State Industrial Union
  Council, 79–80; split of, with CIO,
  78–80; and unemployed miners, 89–90;
  and women, 89–90, 205, 211–12, 229.
  See also Mitch, William; Welfare and
  Retirement Fund
—racial policies, 1, 2, 5–6, 7, 9, 13; and
  congressional race of 1936, 62–63; and
  efforts to register African Americans,
  66; and "gradualism," 53–54; and
  gubernatorial race of 1946, 124; legacy
  of, 224–29; during New Deal era,
  47–48, 51–52; post–World War II,
  160–62; and segregation, 54–55, 72; and
  "UMW formula," 53; and white miners,
  52
—strikes: 1920–21, 13, 48; 1941, 64, 69–70,
  92–93; 1943, 100–109; 1944, 109–10;
  1945, 110–14; 1948, 140; 1949–50, 140–